MAD SCHOLARS

Critical Perspectives on Disability
Beth A. Ferri, Arlene S. Kanter, Eunjung Kim, *and* Michael Gill, *Series Editors*

Other Titles in Critical Perspectives on Disability

Acts of Conscience: World War II, Mental
Institutions, and Religious Objectors
Steven J. Taylor

Disability and Mothering: Liminal Spaces of Embodied Knowledge
Cynthia Lewiecki-Wilson and Jen Cellio-Miller, eds.

Disability Rhetoric
Jay Timothy Dolmage

Picturing Disability: Beggar, Freak, Citizen,
and Other Photographic Rhetoric
Robert Bogdan with Martin Elks and James Knoll

Righting Educational Wrongs: Disability Studies in Law and Education
Arlene S. Kanter and Beth A. Ferri, eds.

MAD SCHOLARS

Reclaiming and Reimagining the Neurodiverse Academy

Edited by
Melanie Jones & Shayda Kafai

Syracuse University Press

This book will be made open access within three years of publication thanks to Path to Open, a program developed in partnership between JSTOR, the American Council of Learned Societies (ACLS), University of Michigan Press, and The University of North Carolina Press to bring about equitable access and impact for the entire scholarly community, including authors, researchers, libraries, and university presses around the world. Learn more at https://about.jstor.org/path-to-open/

Copyright © 2024 by Syracuse University Press
Syracuse, New York 13244-5290

All Rights Reserved

First Edition 2024

24 25 26 27 28 29   6 5 4 3 2 1

∞ The paper used in this publication meets the minimum requirements of the American National Standard for Information Sciences—Permanence of Paper for Printed Library Materials, ANSI Z39.48-1992.

For a listing of books published and distributed by Syracuse University Press, visit https://press.syr.edu.

ISBN: 9780815638476 (hardcover)
9780815638469 (paperback)
9780815657149 (e-book)

Library of Congress Cataloging-in-Publication Data

Names: Jones, Melanie (Melanie Veronica), editor. | Kafai, Shayda, editor.
Title: Mad scholars : reclaiming and reimagining the neurodiverse academy / edited by Melanie Jones and Shayda Kafai.
Description: First edition. | Syracuse, New York : Syracuse University Press, 2024. |
Series: Critical perspectives on disability, | Includes bibliographical references and index. |
Summary: "Through a collection of essays, this volume explores the lived experiences of neurodivergent academics"— Provided by publisher.
Identifiers: LCCN 2024010940 (print) | LCCN 2024010941 (ebook) |
ISBN 9780815638469 (paperback) | ISBN 9780815638476 (hardback) |
ISBN 9780815657149 (ebook)
Subjects: LCSH: People with disabilities in higher education—United States. |
People with disabilities in higher education—Canada. | People with mental disabilities—Education (Higher)—United States. | People with mental disabilities—Education (Higher)—Canada | Neurodivergent people—Education (Higher)—United States. | Neurodivergent people—Education (Higher)—Canada | Graduate students—Mental health—United States. |
Graduate students—Mental health—Canada. | Education, Higher—United States—Psychological aspects. | Education, Higher—Canada—Psychological aspects.
Classification: LCC LC4818.38 .M34 2024 (print) | LCC LC4818.38 (ebook) |
DDC 378.0087—dc23/eng/20240429
LC record available at https://lccn.loc.gov/2024010940
LC ebook record available at https://lccn.loc.gov/2024010941

Manufactured in the United States of America

Contents

Introduction
Naming Ourselves Mad
Melanie Jones and Shayda Kafai   *1*

Part One
Mad Pathways, Mad Exits   *21*

1. Don't Call It "Mental Health"
A Discussion on Disability Euphemisms and Disability Community
Sav Schlauderaff   *29*

2. My PhD Drove Me Crazy (but I Was Already Mad)
Shawna Guenther   *45*

3. Complaint as a Maddening Practice
Moving through the University as a Mad Grad Student
Rebecca-Eli M. Long   *64*

4. Rest as Feminist Disability Praxis, or How to Write
While Flaring, Depressed, and Totally Burned Out
Jess L. Wilcox Cowing   *75*

5. Diary of a Mad Black Woman in the Academy
Sydney F. Lewis   *87*

Part Two
Researching the Self   *101*

6. I'm Too Crazy for a Job
Thoroughbreds, Fuckups, and Autistic, Mad, Disabled,
Femme Grassroots Intellectual-Freedom Portals
Leah Lakshmi Piepzna-Samarsinha   *107*

vi   Contents

7. Embrace the Lie
Seeking Truths through Reading, Madly
Melanie Jones   126

8. The Madmotherscholar in Academia and Beyond
Caché Owens   145

9. In-Cite
The Mad Possibility of Interethnography
Sarah Cavar   164

10. The Subject Is Mad
Rua Williams   175

Part Three
Disclosure and Disruptive Pedagogies   191

11. Mad Lyrics
Toward an Embodied, Community-Responsive
Pedagogy of Care in Academia
Kelan L. Koning   197

12. Mad Pedagogy in Disabling Academia
Liz Miller   209

13. Teaching for Mad Liberation
Crip Dreaming toward a Transformative Pedagogy of Madness
Samuel Z. Shelton   221

14. Learning and Teaching Bad as Resistance
Queer Crip Pilipinx Bad Pedagogy
Pau Abustan   236

15. "The Deadly Space Between"
Toward a Mad Pedagogy and Mad Methodology
A-M McManaman   252

16. Crazy Femme Pedagogies
Toward an Archive
Jesse Rice-Evans and Andréa Stella   265

Part Four
Mad Imaginaries
From Kinship to Community 285

17. Mad Resilience, Mad Kinship
Alternative Responses to Student Mental Health Crises
Sarah Smith and Grace Wedlake 289

18. Anchoring in Mad Solidarity
Sarah Arvey Tov 302

19. Mad Laughter
*On Finding and Forming Graduate
Communities through Memes*
Kim Fernandes 319

20. On Mad Advantage, Redux
Covering, Passing, Negotiating (in) Higher Education
Diane R. Wiener 331

21. Landing without Falling
The Fucking Blue Dots
Holly Pearson 346

22. Orienting toward Togetherness
A Mad Phenomenology
Shayda Kafai 357

Glossary 373

Contributor Biographies 379

Index 387

MAD SCHOLARS

Introduction

Naming Ourselves Mad

Melanie Jones and Shayda Kafai

> We are sitting beside you. No, we are you.
> —Brenda Jo Brueggemann et al., "Becoming
> Visible: Lessons in Disability" (2001)

This collection explores how our Mad selfhood is understood, articulated, and engaged through our capacity as scholars.[1] It wonders where we might go if we embraced that overlap instead of shunning it: if we probed its depths and exploded its boundaries. From the start, *Mad Scholars* has emerged from a place of hopeful, desperate imagining. What does—and what could—it look like to be Mad in academia? What does—and what could—it mean to claim such an identity openly as a researcher, an educator, and a member of a broader intellectual community?

These are not idle questions. In *Mad at School* in 2011, Margaret Price called on faculty and administrators to interrogate "the stories that

---

1. Within Mad studies, the terms *Mad* and *Madness* often serve as a helpful umbrella for a multitude of identitarian positions and social-political stances. As a field, Mad studies brings "together terms that in some ways are diametrically opposed" and pushes up against "the limits of protocols of academic practice." The contributors to this collection embrace how the "slippery and unruly" aspect of the field and its chosen terms aids in both resisting theoretical ossification and encouraging political alliances across communities (Aho, Ben-Moshe, and Hilton 2017, 294). Nonetheless, readers from outside disability studies and related fields will find many terms in this book unfamiliar. To facilitate understanding without interrupting or overloading our chapters, we have provided a glossary that defines and contextualizes key words, phrases, and movements.

are told about mental disability in U.S. higher education" and to consider "what it means to have a disabled (unsound, ill, irrational, crazy) mind in the educational realm, a realm expressly dedicated to the life of the mind" (2). Since this book's publication, crucial texts have detailed the manifold ways in which ableism and sanism pervade North American colleges and universities.[2] A growing number of monographs and essay collections have been dedicated to exploring the theoretical implications of disabled scholarship and to unpacking specific barriers to equity, accessibility, and care.[3]

Mad Scholars takes a different approach: imagining concrete paths to Mad education and liberation, framed in languages that have been too long denied. Twenty-four voices from the United States and Canada, spanning almost a dozen disciplines and covering every stage of academic scholarship, join here to assert our divergent bodyminds in defiance. We reject the suffocating rigidity of academic sanism, whose forces pathologize us and treat us as problems to be excised or contained. We refuse the implicit mandate that educators must feign nonconformity and pay lip service to diversity while ignoring those voices desperate for concrete change. We assert the unspoken secret of academic life: that Mad Scholars have been here all along. We—the neurodivergent, the neuroqueer, the disabled, the disordered, the crip—are part of the backbone of academic life and remain a major force in its innovation.

What can we discover when we don't just acknowledge sanism but also interrogate the ways we push back against it? What can we imagine

---

2. Jay T. Dolmage's *Academic Ableism: Disability and Higher Education* (2017) rigorously details the ways in which disability "has been constructed as the inverse or opposite of higher education" (3). Nicole Brown's *Lived Experiences of Ableism in Academia: Strategies for Inclusion in Higher Education* (2021), in turn, documents how institutions often systematically bar the disabled, chronically ill, and neurodivergent from job security and advancement.

3. On the implications of disabled scholarship, see, for example, *Disability Rhetoric* (Dolmage 2014) and *Ableism in Academia: Theorising Experiences of Disabilities and Chronic Illnesses in Higher Education* (Leigh and Brown 2020). Recent examinations include *Negotiating Disability: Disclosure and Higher Education* (Kerschbaum, Eisenman, and Jones 2017) and *Mental Health among Higher Education Faculty, Administrators, and Graduate Students: A Critical Perspective* (Housel 2021).

Introduction   3

if Mad scholars were no longer exoticized or pathologized but were treasured as resources, recognized as assets, and embraced as potential change makers? Such questions cannot be answered by a single voice, nor should they be read through the lens of one monolithic perspective.[4] As the following section elaborates, our contributors interpret the label *Mad scholar* through many lenses and incorporate myriad definitions and identities under the umbrella term *Mad*. What this collection is not, then, is any attempt to essentialize what a Mad scholar is or to present Mad identity as a homogenous collective. We call for recognition and for honest engagement, but this call is not raised under a banner of transcendent revelation. The multifaceted, varied experiences of Mad scholarship can encompass disorientation, pain, and struggle as much as it can empathy, creativity, or challenges to the status quo. We are not ignorant of the incredible privilege we hold in claiming the identity of a Mad scholar. Nor are we unaware that this (re)claiming, if embraced too unquestioningly, may further alienate and silence those whose experiences cannot be rehabilitated into a generative subject position.

We gather instead to further move our culture's broader understanding of disability from "textual abstractions" to "tangible bod[ies]." We similarly aim to shift conversations in and about academia specifically to center the "potency of disability as an experience of social or political dimensions" (Mitchell 2002, 16). These twenty-two chapters position Mad scholars as a community whose knowledge and skills are not only acceptable but also crucial to reorienting and reimagining higher education. The still controversial assertion that someone can "both be mentally ill and lead a rich and satisfying life" (Saks 2007, 333) is not the close of our arguments but their beginning. What binds our contributors, amid their diverse backgrounds and perspectives, is their commitment to recenter Mad scholarship as an abundant yet undervalued resource. We are not here to say we

4. One of the most toxic manifestations of sanism is the assumption that cognitive-emotional difference, grouped under the label *Madness*, is uniform in appearance and easily distinct from saneness (Foucault 1972). Such attitudes, even when approached as something transcendent, still position madness as intrinsically opposed to the "work of the mind" embraced by higher education (Wolframe 2013; Dolmage 2017).

can do the work of scholarship, too. We are here to affirm that we have been doing it in different and potentially far better ways than the current system would ever permit or know and that we seek intersectional, interdisciplinary alliances to revolutionize that system further.

Mad Scholars invites those outside our community to witness and learn from this meaning making. More than this, however, it provides a place for *us*, one of vulnerability, connectivity, and kinship. This collection, ultimately, is for you: the crip undergraduate struggling to finish her thesis; the neurodiverse researcher failing to get funding for his fieldwork; the Mad educator fighting for the classroom they envision; all Mad scholars who have spent decades patching together spaces of communion and hope. The lived knowledge you carry is our lifeblood. The synthesizing and complicating and invigorating of these knowledges are the first steps we take to reimagining a space worthy of the identity we claim.

> People with schizophrenia—people like me—read the papers and watch the evening news. We see how the illness is portrayed and how a friend-in-the-making is likely to perceive us, once they hear the truth. We move forward with great caution because we must. We'd have to be . . . well, crazy to do otherwise.
> —Elyn Saks, *The Center Cannot Hold* (2007)

We all have seen them: the panicked headlines, the frantic book titles, the sobering statistics. Across North America, researchers have documented alarming spikes in depression, anxiety, self-harm, and suicidal ideation on college campuses.[5] There is a mental health crisis, we are told, sweeping through undergraduate populations, infecting graduate students and early-stage faculty, and threatening the very future of North American academia. According to this neoliberal model of "mental health," to be Mad means only to suffer—and to do it in the wrong way. As Mad scholars, we can only be read as symptoms of a problem that must be eradicated—one

---

5. See, for example, "Evidence for a Mental Health Crisis in Graduate Education" (Evans et al. 2018), "Increased Rates of Mental Health Service Utilization by U.S. College Students" (Lipson, Lattie, and Eisenberg 2018), "The Prevalence and Predictors of Mental Health Diagnoses and Suicide among U.S. College Students" (Liu et al. 2018).

Introduction 5

flimsy accommodation, feel-good pep talk, and underpaid therapist at a time.

That colleges and universities have woefully inadequate responses to the mental and emotional needs of their students is clear enough.[6] Underlying the resultant slogans of helping and healing, however, is the assumption that any divergence from "mental health," as defined by neoliberal models of capitalist achievement, has no place within higher education as it is meant to be. Undergraduates and younger scholars may have crises—all, we are assured, the result of recent, external phenomena—but the ivory tower must remain a realm of compulsory able-bodiedness and able-mindedness. By extension, its faculty must adhere to a version of the normate that is dedicated to hierarchization of knowledge and an effacement of cognitive and emotional differences—even as these differences are enhanced and various sufferings exacerbated by the academy's very structure.[7] At all levels, members of the ivory tower must embody and replicate "disciplines of normalization" that seem to emanate from everywhere and nowhere (Wendell 1996, 88).[8]

To be Mad in the academy, then, is to carry "a personal deficit that must be 'heroically' and 'secretly' borne" (Price 2011, 104). It is implicitly and at times explicitly to reject the very notion of the Mad scholar as an

---

6. One particularly bleak study found "eighty-six percent of students with psychiatric disabilities withdraw from college before completing their degrees" (Price 2011, 23).

7. The normate, as Rosemarie Garland-Thomson elaborates in *Extraordinary Bodies: Figuring Physical Disability in American Culture and Literature* (1997), is a composite identity position that is idealized (thus impossible for a subject to truly embody) and presented as average (thus casting the subject as abnormal when they inevitably fall short). The normate, seemingly defined by absolute independence, rationality, and physical prowess, often acts instead as a blank space of supposed neutrality, subsequently casting the disabled and divergent—and, in turn, the female, the trans, the nonwhite, and the poor—as lacking or wrong.

8. This process, even as it rests on the assertion of an unquestioned neutral position, is one of perpetual imbalance and turmoil. Therí A. Pickens asserts that anxieties surrounding how to conceptualize ability "lurk[] as an undercurrent within the academy, sometimes creating a riptide between the turbulent waters of superior thinking and the threat of madness" (2019, 243).

identity we can ever claim. The normative "discourse of academic rationality and neutrality," a discourse "heavily dependent on patriarchal and colonialist discourses of both gender and racial otherness," still structures our institutions at every level (Wolframe 2013, par. 31). The concept of a moral and mental neutral from which we deviate—a Mad excess that is nonetheless read as an absence, a negation, a lack (Foucault 1972)—meanwhile infuses every aspect of how we discuss academic work and how we evaluate its actors.

Resisting the dominant narrative means shifting our rhetorical position to dangerous, uncertain ground. The assumption that an academic is "reasonable, trustworthy, safe to be around, and capable of taking care of and making decisions for [themselves]" is often abruptly withheld following the revelation of a psychiatric diagnosis or even the suspicion of cognitive difference (Wolframe 2013, par. 6). In the end, although *disability justice* may be a more frequent buzzword on campus, even activist scholars often "silently believ[e] they'd rather die than be us . . . and are still running shit the exact same way that makes or forces most of us to stay home" (Piepzna-Samarasinha 2018, 123). To be physically, mentally, or emotionally disabled is to be immediately cast as incapacitated and unproductive. Our differences are at best a state to overcome and more likely a burden to be pitied. When we are not mute victims or perfect martyrs, we are cast as liabilities—or even ticking time bombs. Higher education is just as susceptible as other institutions to the lure of effacing structural violence by making mental illness into a boogeyman, as responses to school shootings can attest.[9]

---

9. There is a horrific price for the specter of the violent "madman," one paid by the most vulnerable and marginalized populations in the Americas. A report by the Ruderman Family Foundation in 2016 found almost half of the people who die at the hands of police have some kind of disability. Aggregate studies indicate that only 3 to 5 percent of people diagnosed with a mental illness commit violent acts but are two and a half times more likely to be victims of violence than the undiagnosed (Ellis 2016).

After the Virginia Tech shooting in 2007, Administrator Katherine S. Newman of the University of Massachusetts openly bemoaned the protections afforded by the American with Disabilities Act, arguing its expansion of civil rights keep schools from "yield[ing up] clues to an unraveling mind." Such is Newman's sense of alarm in a *Chronicle of Higher*

To expose the sheer number of Mad scholars in academia—to champion the neurodivergent lecturer, embrace the crip professor, value the disordered adjunct, defend the disabled teaching assistant—would be to reject the pervasive myth that "everyone in academe is mentally 'normal' until something 'happens to' us" (Price 2011, 51). This collection rests on precisely that rejection. Stigmatized and silenced as we might be, Mad scholars are an integral and growing part of higher education. One of the most ironic aspects of academic sanism, in fact, may lie in how many contributors to this collection and how many of our colleagues were drawn to academic life by the promise that our different ways of thinking, our unique approaches to problems, and our resistance to the status quo would be valued and championed. This assumption, in the humanities and social sciences at least, is often furthered by the theoretical embrace of fundamental questions surrounding truth, reality, testimony, and witnessing and by the growth of programs dedicated to disability studies, the nascent field of Mad studies, and the broader medical and health humanities.[10] We enter higher education eager to access collaborative knowledge and form an intellectual community that we assume is possible only within its hallowed walls—only to find some of the most toxic manifestations of sanism replicated at every stage of our careers.

Education article that she openly calls for police forces and educational institutions to work together to track and imprison "people with mental problems" who appear suspicious, including those who "have committed no illegal acts" (Newman 2007, 20). She is far from alone in her response, as made clear in studies such as *Mad at School* by Margaret Price and *Gun Violence and Mental Illness* (2016) edited by Liza Gold and Robert Simon.

10. Although the foci of scholars in disability studies, Mad studies, and medical humanities often intersect, these fields' ideological positions, assumptions regarding ability, capacity, and voicing, and favored methodologies can be starkly at odds. Diane Price Herndl positions disability studies and medical humanities especially as almost antithetical, from their respective origins in civil rights movements and medical schools to their attitude toward disability in general. "The definition of disability used in disability studies," she points out, "focuses not on the body but on the social; disability is not something that a person possesses but something one encounters when dealing with other people or with physical spaces that are inaccessible." By contrast, "disease . . . is almost always understood as located in the body itself" (2005, 593).

8   Jones and Kafai

For too long our stories have been spoken for us, admitting only fractions of a rich and wide narrative. That narrative has been restricted and dominated by administrators, deans, outside funders, and fellow faculty who cannot understand "why we would want to bring mad perspectives into the classroom" or the town hall or the hiring committee (Wolframe 2013, par. 31). We are sick of being driven out of fields we long to transform; we are maddened by the condescension, effacement, and at times brutal violence amassed against us. We challenge the false neutrality upon which our fields continue to rest and advocate for the "anti-normalization" (McWade, Milton, and Beresford 2015, 306) that many colleges embrace in theory and hardly ever enact in practice. Building on decades of work by activists within and without the ivory tower, we raise our voices and expose our throats. We claim the danger, the uncertainty, and the promise of the title *Mad scholar* so that we can do justice to the multitudes it contains.

> No term in the history of madness is neutral: not mental illness, madness, or any other term.
> —Geoffrey Reaume, "Mad People's History" (2006)

But what do we mean when we say the word *Mad?*[11] The contributors to this collection position themselves at the intersection of various identities, often in tension with one another. The labels they take up alongside this umbrella term include *neurodiverse, neuroqueer, crip, mentally ill,* and *disabled* as well as *psychiatric consumer/survivor.*[12] Although all reject the biomedical essentialism that underpins Western conceptions of Madness, many take up psychiatric diagnoses as tools to help anchor their

---

11. As Price reminds us, "the problem of naming" for disability studies scholars "acquires a particular urgency when considered in the context of disabilities of the mind, for often the very terms used to name persons with mental disabilities have explicitly foreclosed our status as persons" (2011, 9).

12. The employment of *Mad* as an umbrella term encompassing multiple identities demonstrates one of several ways in which Mad Pride is indebted to similar movements within the LGBTQ+ community, including many members' recent embrace of the umbrella term *queer.* For more on the parallels between these movements, see *Crip Theory: Cultural Signs of Queerness and Disability* (McRuer 2006).

Introduction 9

cognitive-emotional map, even as others flatly reject the medical model in favor of sociological stances.[13]

When we take up the label *Mad*, we do so to encompass a vast "constellation of behaviors, experiences, feelings and issues" that have been rejected and denigrated within Western settler-colonial institutions as deviant, debilitating, excessive, and wrong (Beresford 2020, 1339). We signify a commitment to "scholarship, theory, and activism" that centers "the lived experiences, history, cultures, and policies" of those who identify openly and at times proudly as cognitively or emotionally divergent from the normate model of the stable, the rational, and the sane (Mark Anthony Castrodale, qtd. in Beresford 2020, 1337). Acknowledging the long history of "positive and person-centered discourses" that have arisen from claiming this umbrella term as well as recognizing the advantages of its "broad historical sweep" (Price 2011, 10), we also take up *Mad* as a word that forces us to grapple immediately with the fear, the distrust, and the provocation it evokes.[14]

Within this toxic morass, we claim the rights of the feared, the distrusted, and the provoking: "that we should not push meekly for minor concessions, but instead change the world into a fit place for us to live in" (Curtis et al. 2011, 8). Drawing on disability justice frameworks, where "all bodies are unique and essential" and "have strengths and needs that must be met," we assert our value "not despite the complexities of our bodies"—of our minds, our moods, our souls—"but because of them" (Piepzna-Samarasinha 2018, 21). We orient ourselves, through the lens of

13. The sociological model emerged during the antipsychiatric movements of the 1960s and 1970s and focuses on environmental and social triggers to explain mental illness. In this model, factors such as structural traumas, cultural differences, and social stigmas produce an overwhelming distress, which is then falsely attributed to an individual medical pathology. For more on the sociological and biomedical models and their influence, see *Models of Mental Health* (Davidson et al. 2015).

14. The denigration of the disabled, disordered, and divergent, after all, "is in our drinking water. Written into works of fiction, religious texts, newspapers, art, drama, film, the annals of history, and, yes, into the academic curriculum . . . [b]eliefs about disabled people, our worth and potential, are inscribed in these texts" (Linton 2006, 137).

each part and the voice of each chapter in this book, toward radical forms of recognition and reevaluation.

We do not, we cannot, speak for the Mad community as a whole, nor do we claim that this collection encompasses all that a Mad scholar might be. It is no coincidence that the fields represented in this collection are predominantly associated with the humanities and the social sciences, with those few contributors who work in science, technology, engineering, and math either incorporating humanities perspectives into their research or having come previously from humanities backgrounds. Although disciplines in the humanities and social sciences may often exoticize Madness, within many departments there are nonetheless conversations around the fluidity of the label *Mad* and its potential attachment to the title *scholar*. The same cannot be said for most of the programs within the sciences. This may be particularly true for psychiatry and medicine, where these interventions are most needed.[15]

As fraught as our experiences have been within the ivory tower, leading several of us to be driven out of it, we were still initially granted entry. That is more than can be said for the innumerable thinkers whose diagnoses strip them of choices, who are denied access to care and then subjected to punitive medicine,[16] or whose unwillingness or inability to "pass" exposes them to other forms of ableism, up to and including

15. In the days that followed our initial call for papers, we received two emails from medical students and one Facebook message from a PhD candidate working at the intersection of history and the physical sciences. The messages were almost identical in content and tone. The writers longed to submit a chapter for the collection but were terrified that sharing their experiences would irreparably damage their futures. *Mad Scholars* is as much for these writers and the thousands like them as it is for those able to openly claim space in this growing constellation.

16. Romantic conceptions of schizophrenia, for instance, are rampant in theoretical discussions. Schizophrenia has been taken up for decades as a metaphor for everything from capitalism to postmodernism. Yet the speech of actual people diagnosed with schizophrenia is still overwhelmingly "treated as an index of sanity or insanity, with referentiality only to diagnostic criteria, and without referentiality to the civic world" (Prendergast 2008, 60). The same is true for psychosis and often for bipolar disorder.

horrific acts of violence.[17] This violence increases exponentially when factoring in the intersections of race, gender, sexual identity, and class. While some scholars can safely disclose within their particular institution, most are able to do so "only within networks of support that [nevertheless] regularly exclude people of color, LGBTQ individuals, women, and physically disabled individuals" (Stefan 2018, par. 2), exclusions that often expose the pervasive link between compulsory able-bodiedness and white-supremacist thinking.[18]

We reject the false binary between the "extraordinary mad person" tolerated by the academy—the one who never discloses, never needs accommodation, and never affects mass change—and the "bad mad" still viscerally feared and attacked. Some of us speaking to you now—as PhD students, as tenure-track faculty, as lecturers, as independent scholars— have been the "homeless person muttering on a bus" or the "figure lying restrained on a hospital gurney" (Price 2011, 1–2), those figures so often

---

17. Cynthia Lewiecki-Wilson has emphasized how violence against those perceived to be mentally ill or disabled is fed by Western conceptions of "the liberal humanist subject[,] . . . defined by their ability to engage in verbal rhetoric." Those whose speech diverges too sharply or who do not communicate in ways recognized and comprehended via social norms are excluded "not only from rhetoricity but also from full citizenship" and in the most extreme cases from being considered human or even alive (2003, 158). In the latter case, governments around the world have targeted Mad communities with police violence, mass sterilization, and even state-authorized genocide (Sfera 2013), particularly within multiply marginalized communities, such as impoverished Black and Indigenous people and people of color (Salas 2020).

18. Ethan Watters' *Crazy Like Us* (2010) argues that the "endlessly complex and unique forms" of emotional-cognitive expression that exist around the world are being rapidly "bulldozed by disease categories and treatments" outsourced by the United States (2–3), while DSM-recognized mental illnesses "found only in other cultures"—unlike those in Western culture, which are supposedly universal—"are often treated like carnival sideshows" (5). Yet responses to this psychiatric bulldozing can be just as susceptible to the normative underpinnings of white supremacy. Critics have criticized Mad studies in the past for "failing to engage with Black people[,] [for] its Eurocentrism and narrow origins in the Northern hemisphere [sic], and for not involving/including the South or even necessarily being relevant to it" (Beresford 2020, 1340).

employed to justify dehumanizing violence against the Mad. Many more of us have not. We often operate in spaces of incredible privilege—even as those spaces can abruptly swing into arenas of appalling abuse.

As these chapters were compiled, patterns emerged that underscored the disproportionate toll of this violence on nonwhite bodyminds.[19] It is no coincidence that the ten chapters by contributors who are Black folx, Indigenous folx, and people of color (BIPOC) detail institutional barriers, toxic microaggressions, and overt acts of aggression whose reach and extent exceed those recounted in other chapters.[20] Nor is it a coincidence that so many of these contributors are now either independent scholars, pursuing "alt-ac" (alternative academic) careers, or are preparing to leave the academy.[21] The systemic barriers already before them and the virulent biases against which they already contend have been exacerbated by the intersection of multiply marginalized identities and then compounded by inequalities laid bare during the COVID pandemic.[22]

19. As Peggy McIntosh lays out, "Whites [*sic*] are taught to think of their lives as morally neutral . . . average, and also ideal, so that when we work to benefit others, this is seen as work which will allow 'them' to be more like 'us'" (2019, 30). As a result, assumptions regarding what is (not) an illness, what is (not) rhetoric, and what is (not) a path to healing often unconsciously replicate many of the exclusionary, harmful tactics of the medical-industrial complex against which these advocates are fighting.

20. The threat of constituting "the mad subject . . . as the white subject at the horizon of whiteness" (Rachel Gorman, qtd. in Pickens 2019, 6), beyond its obvious straight-jacketing of cognitive-emotional diversity, is that it allows "the mad white subject" to be reabsorbed into universalist discourses, with attendant assumptions regarding the inferiority, animalism, or nonhumanity of the nonwhite Mad subject.

21. In *Inside Higher Ed*, Chavella T. Pittmann details how "higher education institutions sabotage their retention of BIPOC women" in particular "by assigning heavy teaching loads, allowing students and colleagues to resist the often-transformative teaching of those academics, and establishing tenure practices that amplify gendered and raced oppression" (2021). In the same publication, Therí A. Pickens also argues that "because of structural oppression, Jim Crow, redlining, all of those things, there's a higher prevalence of disabilities and chronic illnesses among Black folks in the United States" (qtd. in Burke 2021).

22. The pandemic's devastating effects—discussed in several of this volume's chapters—have in some ways been only a more exacerbated version of the financial instability, emotional alienation, and fear of retaliation that many of our contributors face every

Introduction 13

At the same time, a different and intriguing pattern has also emerged over the course of this project. Although a significant number of cisgender women are represented, almost as many writers are transgender, agender, bigender, or nonbinary. More than half of us identify as LGBTQ+. No contributor identifies as a cisgender man. The sheer difference in scale between these statistics and worldwide averages encourages further examination. Recent studies, for instance, suggest strong correlations between the taking up of a queer identity—with its myriad variations in gender and sexuality—and the taking up of a Mad one—with its similarly vast encompassing of categories such as mentally ill, neurodivergent, neuroqueer, and crip (Moagi et al. 2021). Such research tends to emphasize the "poor mental health" of LGBTQ+ communities due to social stigma, citing very real issues regarding higher rates of self-harm and suicidal ideation in these groups (Bentley 2021; Medina-Martínez et al. 2021).[23] Another explanation, however, based on direct feedback from the writers in this collection, suggests that in a world where openly claiming a noncis, nonheterosexual, and nonmale identity already exposes one to hostility, contributors feel less inclined to hide a Mad identity as well and are more prepared to embrace diversity and fluidity as positive traits.

> What transformation would need to occur before those who pursue academic discourse can be "heard" (which I take to mean "respected"), not in spite of our mental disabilities but with and through them?
> —Margaret Price, *Mad at School* (2011)

This book is another step in a series of movements laid down by members of the Mad community and its allies. We owe an immense debt to the

---

day. The process of negotiating deadlines, reassessing our capacities at various stages, and recognizing the growing weight of COVID-19 on our bodyminds has suffused every aspect of this project.

23. In 2023, the American Psychiatric Association found that "LGBTQ+ individuals are more than twice as likely as heterosexual men and women to have a mental health disorder in their lifetime. They are 2.5 times more likely to experience depression, anxiety, and substance misuse compared with heterosexual individuals" (American Psychiatric Association 2023).

scholars before us who fought for the academy to recognize Mad worth. We owe just as much to the countless activists who have called for our community more broadly to be embraced and for us to recognize what we give the world. Reclaiming and reimagining higher education are just two small aspects of an ongoing, variegated fight against the sanism and ableism that pervade and corrode our society today.

By using twenty-two lenses to examine and imagine what "our current articulations of disability are saying in the here and now" (Titchkosky 2001, 138), we contribute to that work by exploring the infinite richness of our lived experiences. *Mad Scholars* is a rallying cry against the stereotype of Mad people as incapable of "rational" communication and intellectual innovation (Prendergast 2008). It refuses to accept the rigid, narrow boundaries by which higher education still defines the rational, the rhetorical, and the meaningful, even for those it grants some measure of power. In that spirit, we reject the recuperation of the Mad scholar into neoliberal subjecthood (Houghton 2019). The goal of this collection is not to sell ourselves as underappreciated assets in academia. It is to express how wasted potential and systemic harm are integral aspects of the current system and to explore how Mad scholars work at the borders of—and at times explicitly against—that system to promote innovation and seek liberation.

Each part in this volume occupies one of the myriad interlocking spaces within academia: the suffocating minutiae of administrative offices and career development; the fraught yet fueling fields of research; the dangers and opportunities of the kairotic classroom; the unraveling and restitching of academic communities. All the contributors elaborate on the indebtedness of ableism to white supremacy and settler colonialism, to misogyny and heterosexism, and to class stratification and oppression. We urge readers to be prepared to grapple with those intersections as they explore these chapters. Specific iterations of structural violence—such as police brutality, forced institutionalization, and intimate partner violence—are marked by content warnings at the beginning of each chapter, as are discussions of self-harm or suicide. Part one, "Mad Pathways, Mad Exits," exposes the degree to which programs and policies supposedly meant to foster intellectual difference and protect neurodivergent scholars only further traumatize and disenfranchise them and explores how Mad scholars navigate these treacherous waters. Part two, "Researching the Self," reflects on working in academia as a Mad Researcher, considering to what degree our intellectual paths and senses of self are allowed or encouraged to overlap. Part three, "Disclosure and Disruptive Pedagogies," explores how teaching informs our understanding of Mad liberation, in particular the ways in which our innovations there are indebted to embracing diversities of care. Part four, "Mad Imaginaries: From Kinship to Community," ends the volume by asking how Mad scholars might form bonds that transform the academy within and beyond its walls, examining both institutional reforms and radical gestures of support.

Each contributor to this volume builds on a practice of critical community self-study.[24] Most of our chapters explicitly privilege autoethnographic research. They meld the personal and political with the aim of "attend[ing] to the complexities arising from social structures, language use and meaning making, and the formation of identities through interlocking privileges and forms of oppression" (Schnellert et al. 2019, par. 13). Many of our chapters embrace critical-creative forms, and all draw on diverse methodologies of evidence and expression. As important as it is that we tell you these secrets, expose these truths, what matters equally is *how* we tell them—the unchecked emotions, the sharp edges, the questions voiced and left to linger.

We hope that these chapters create fractals, multidirectional patterns we all can follow to unlearn old lessons and arrive someplace new. You are invited here into a culture that reconfigures the meanings and applications of pedagogy, collegiality, scholarly inquiry, and liberatory education. It is time to move past the systemic oppressions that have built academia and have broken apart its promise. It is time to begin creating something better. May we be open, proud, and made known to one another. Here, together, may we truly begin to render academia Mad.

24. This entails "considering how our experiences, roles, and identities are shaped by our own diversities" (Schnellert et al. 2019, par. 13) and elaborating on these personal insights through recourse to disability studies, queer theory, feminist theory, and critical race theory, among other schools of thought.

Works Cited

Aho, Tanja, Liat Ben-Moshe, and Leon J. Hilton. 2017. "Introduction: Mad Futures: Affect/Theory/Violence." In *Mad Futures: Affect/Theory/Violence*, edited by Tanja Aho, Liat Ben-Moshe, and Leon J. Hilton. Special Issue, *American Quarterly* 69, no. 2: 291–303. https://www.jstor.org/stable/26360849.

American Psychiatric Association. 2023. "Diversity & Health Equity Education." At https://www.psychiatry.org/psychiatrists/diversity/education/lgbtq-patients.

Bentley, Leann. 2021. "Why Does the LGBTQIA+ Community Suffer from Poor Mental Health at Higher Rates?" University of Utah Health, July. At https://healthcare.utah.edu/healthfeed/2021/07/why-does-lgbtqia-community-suffer-poor-mental-health-higher-rates.

Beresford, Peter. 2020. "'Mad,' Mad Studies and Advancing Inclusive Resistance." *Disability & Society* 35, no. 8 (2020): 1337–42. At https://doi.org/10.1080/09687599.2019.1692168.

Brown, Nicole. 2021. *Lived Experiences of Ableism in Academia: Strategies for Inclusion in Higher Education*. Bristol, UK: Policy Press.

Brueggemann, Brenda Jo, Linda Feldmeier White, Patricia A. Dunn, Barbara A. Heifferon, and Johnson Cheu. 2001. "Becoming Visible: Lessons in Disability." *College Composition and Communication* 52, no. 3: 368–98. At https://www.jstor.org/stable/358624.

Burke, Lilah. 2021. "A Difficult Pathway." *Inside Higher Ed*, May 12. At https://www.insidehighered.com/news/2021/05/12/faculty-disabilities-say-academe-can-present-barriers.

Curtis, Ted, Robert Dellar, Esther Leslie, and Ben Watson. 2011. Introduction to *Mad Pride: A Celebration of Mad Culture*, edited by Ted Curtis, Robert Dellar, Esther Leslie, and Ben Watson, 7–8. Brentwood, UK: Chipmunka.

Davidson, Gavin, Jim Campbell, Ciaran Shannon, and Ciaran Mulholland, eds. 2015. *Models of Mental Health*. London: Palgrave Macmillan.

Dolmage, Jay Timothy. 2014. *Disability Rhetoric*. Syracuse, NY: Syracuse Univ. Press.

———. 2017. *Academic Ableism: Disability and Higher Education*. Ann Arbor: Univ. of Michigan Press.

Ellis, Justin. 2016. "Media Missing the Story: Half of All Recent High Profile Police-Related Killings Are People with Disabilities." Ruderman Family Foundation. At https://rudermanfoundation.org/media-missing-the-story-half-of-all-recent-high-profile-police-related-killings-are-people-with-disabilities.

Evans, Teresa M., Lindsay Bira, Jazmin Beltran Gastelum, L. Todd Weiss, and Nathan L. Vanderford. 2018. "Evidence for a Mental Health Crisis in Graduate Education." *Nature Biotechnology* 36:282–84. At https://doi.org/10.1038/nbt.4089.

Foucault, Michel. 1972. *Histoire de la folie à l'âge classique*. Paris: Gallimard.

Garland-Thomson, Rosemarie. 1997. *Extraordinary Bodies: Figuring Physical Disability in American Culture and Literature*. New York: Columbia Univ. Press.

Gold, Liza H., and Robert I. Simon, eds. 2016. *Gun Violence and Mental Illness*. Arlington, VA: American Psychiatric Association.

Herndl, Diane Price. 2005. "Disease versus Disability: The Medical Humanities and Disability Studies." *PMLA* 120, no. 2: 593–98. At https://doi.org/10.1632/S0030812900167951.

Houghton, Elizabeth. 2019. "Becoming a Neoliberal Subject." *Ephemera: Theory and Politics in Organization* 19, no. 3: 615–26. At https://ephemerajournal.org/sites/default/files/pdfs/contribution/19-3houghton_0.pdf.

Housel, Teresa Heinz, ed. 2021. *Mental Health among Higher Education Faculty, Administrators, and Graduate Students: A Critical Perspective*. Washington, DC: Lexington.

Kerschbaum, Stephanie L., Laura T. Eisenman, and James M. Jones. 2017. *Negotiating Disability: Disclosure and Higher Education*. Ann Arbor: Univ. of Michigan Press.

Leigh, Jennifer, and Nicole Brown, eds. 2020. *Ableism in Academia: Theorising Experiences of Disabilities and Chronic Illnesses in Higher Education*. London: UCL Press.

Lewiecki-Wilson, Cynthia. 2003. "Rethinking Rhetoric through Mental Disabilities." *Rhetoric Review* 22, no. 2: 156–67. At https://www.jstor.org/stable/3093036.

Linton, Simi. 2006. *My Body Politic: A Memoir*. Ann Arbor: Univ. of Michigan Press.

Lipson, Sarah Ketchen, Emily G. Lattie, and Daniel Eisenberg. 2018. "Increased Rates of Mental Health Service Utilization by U.S. College Students: 10-Year Population-Level Trends (2007–2017)." *Psychiatric Services*, online publication Nov. 5. At https://doi.org/10.1176/appi.ps.201800332.

Liu, Cindy H., Courtney Stevens, Sylvia H. M. Wong, Miwa Yasui, and Justin A. Chen. 2018. "The Prevalence and Predictors of Mental Health Diagnoses and Suicide among U.S. College Students: Implications for Addressing

Disparities in Service Use." *Depression and Anxiety* 36, no. 1: 8–17. At https://doi.org/10.1002/da.22830.

McIntosh, Peggy. 2019. "White Privilege: Unpacking the Invisible Knapsack." In *On Privilege, Fraudulence, and Teaching as Learning*, edited by Peggy McIntosh, 29–34. New York: Routledge.

McRuer, Robert. 2006. *Crip Theory: Cultural Signs of Queerness and Disability*. New York: New York Univ. Press.

McWade, Brigit, Damian Milton, and Peter Beresford. 2015. "Mad Studies and Neurodiversity: A Dialogue." *Disability & Society* 30, no. 2: 305–9. At https://doi.org/10.1080/09687599.2014.1000512.

Medina-Martínez, J., Carlos Saus-Ortega, María Montserrat Sánchez-Lorente, Eva María Sosa-Palanca, Pedro García-Martínez, and María Isabel Mármol-López. 2021. "Health Inequities in LGBT People and Nursing Interventions to Reduce Them: A Systematic Review." *International Journal of Environmental Responsibility and Public Health* 18, no. 22. https://doi.org/10.3390/ijerph182211801.

Mitchell, David T. 2002. "Narrative Prosthesis and the Materiality of Metaphor." In *Disability Studies: Enabling the Humanities*, edited by Sharon L. Snyder, Brenda Jo Brueggemann, and Rosemarie Garland-Thomson, 15–30. New York: Modern Language Association of America.

Moagi, Miriam M., Anne E. van der Wath, Priscilla M. Jiyane, and Richard S. Rikhotso. 2021. "Mental Health Challenges of Lesbian, Gay, Bisexual and Transgender People: An Integrated Literature Review." *Health SA Gesondheid: Journal of Interdisciplinary Health Sciences* 26, no. 1487. At https://doi.org/10.4102/hsag.v26i0.1487.

Newman, Katherine S. 2007. "Before the Rampage: What Can Be Done?" *Chronicle of Higher Education* 53, no. 35. At https://www.chronicle.com/article/before-the-rampage-what-can-be-done.

Pickens, Therí Alyce. 2019. *Black Madness :: Mad Blackness*. Durham, NC: Duke Univ. Press.

Piepzna-Samarasinha, Leah Lakshmi. 2018. *Care Work: Dreaming Disability Justice*. Vancouver: Arsenal Pulp Press.

Pittmann, Chavella T. 2021. "Colleges Must Change to Retain BIPOC Women Faculty (Opinion)." *Inside Higher Education*, Apr. 30. At https://www.insidehighered.com/advice/2021/04/30/retain-bipoc-women-faculty-colleges-must-remove-obstacles-they-face-opinion.

Prendergast, Catherine. 2008. "The Unexceptional Schizophrenic: A Post-postmodern Introduction." *Journal of Literary Disability* 2, no. 1: 55–62. At https://go.gale.com//ps/i.do?p=AONE&u=anon~3a418e21&id=GALE|A243 528216&v=2.1&it=r&sid=googleScholar&asid=e5cb9555.

Price, Margaret. 2011. *Mad at School: Rhetorics of Mental Disability and Academic Life.* Ann Arbor: Univ. of Michigan Press.

Reaume, Geoffrey. 2006. "Mad People's History." *Radical History Review* 94:170–82.

Saks, Elyn R. 2007. *The Center Cannot Hold.* New York: Hyperion.

Salas, Gabriela. 2020. "A Brief History of Sterilization Abuse in the U.S. and Its Connection to ICE Mass Hysterectomies in Georgia." National Women's Health Network. At https://nwhn.org/a-brief-history-of-sterilization-abuse-in -the-u-s-and-its-connection-to-ice-mass-hysterectomies-in-georgia/.

Schnellert, Leyton, Pamela Richardson, Earllene Roberts, Sara McDonald, Carolyn MacHardy, Assunta Rosal, Jewelles Smith, et al. 2019. "Enacting Equity in Higher Education through Critical Disability Studies: A Critical Community Self-Study." *Disability Studies Quarterly* 39, no. 2. At https:// dsq-sds.org/article/view/6150/5252.

Sfera, Adonis. 2013. "Can Psychiatry Be Misused Again? (Opinion)." *Frontiers in Psychiatry* 4. At https://www.frontiersin.org/articles/10.3389/fpsyt.2013.00101 /full.

Stefan, Hayley A. 2018. "A (Head) Case for a Mad Humanities: *Sula*'s Shadrack and Black Madness." *Disability Studies Quarterly* 38, no. 4. At https://dsq -sds.org/article/view/6378/5123.

Titchkosky, Tanya. 2001. "Disability: A Rose by Any Other Name? 'People-First' Language in Canadian Society." *Canadian Review of Sociology and Anthropology* 38, no. 2: 125–40. At https://doi.org/10.1111/j.1755-618X.2001.tb0 0967.x.

Watters, Ethan. 2010. *Crazy Like Us: The Globalization of the American Psyche.* New York: Free Press.

Wendell, Susan. 1996. *The Rejected Body: Feminist Philosophical Reflections on Disability.* New York: Routledge.

Wolframe, PhebeAnn M. 2013. "The Madwoman in the Academy, or, Revealing the Invisible Straightjacket: Theorizing and Teaching Saneism and Sane Privilege." *Disability Studies Quarterly* 33, no. 1. At https://dsq-sds.org/article /view/3425/3200.

Part One

Mad Pathways, Mad Exits

Many in our Mad, neurodiverse community are drawn to academia because of its claims of refuge and its avowed commitment to nonconformity and freedom (Sassower 1994; Lewis 2008; Tilak 2008; Luongo 2021). We enter with ample spoons to manifest supportive, co-created networks of reciprocal learning.[1] We enter higher education with expectations and hopes of an innovative, inclusive culture, but we instead often find ourselves in places that are rigid, prohibitive, and often deeply antagonistic to our neurodivergence (Price 2011; Kerschbaum, Eisenman, and Jones 2017; Wolframe 2013; Brown 2020). When we realize this, we are counseled by the somatic and visceral, by the resolve in our guts. We often feel the institutional limits and distortions in embodied/enminded ways,[2] and it is in these ways that we seek renewal and resistance. Rather than being shamed and limited by our Madness,

1. The spoon metaphor and spoon theory come from the work of Christine Miserandino (2017). As a person with a chronic illness, Miserandino defines a spoon as a metaphoric tangible unit of energy. She identifies spoons as finite, particularly for disabled and chronically ill communities; one might, for example, have fewer spoons depending on the day and whether one's symptoms are flaring up or not.

2. Disability and performance artist-scholar Petra Kuppers crafted the term *enminded* as a way to describe how we come to "have a mind"; just as we are learning and moving in embodied ways, so too do we move in enminded ways (2014, 44).

we Mad scholars desire to be led by it; we know that so much is lost when the only response to Madness is eradication and erasure. The Mad scholars in part one resist the institutional narrative that our minds "must run like steely machinery, always reliable, always stable" (Samuels 2017, 19). By pressing against academia's "disciplines of normality" (Wendell 1996, 88), these writers illuminate the failures and gaps within the institution.

Beyond pathology and stigma, Madness here becomes a threshold, a place of invigoration where we are encouraged to unsettle the normative expectations that so often regulate and constrain our bodyminds. When our neurodiversity informs us as educators and learners, we can begin to maneuver through what Shawna Guenther (she/her) names the "Mad making" of academia, its sanist demands of coherence and rigor, its mandates of togetherness. It is Mad making to work in an "academic ecosystem" that encourages and even forces us to "normalise and homogenise ways of working and being a scholar" (Brown 2020, 5). It is Mad making to enter an ecosystem that does not frame us as knowledge producers (Mitchell and Snyder 2001; Milton 2014; Russo and Beresford 2015). And yet we know that there is power in revealing these systems of Mad making. As Mad scholars, we uncover Mad articulation; we offer Mad testimony.

For Jess L. Wilcox Cowing (she/they), Mad making occurs when we are forced to contend with academia's capitalist demands of productivity and burnout culture.[3] For Sydney F. Lewis (she/her), it is misogynoir and anti-Black

3. Although scholars have explored the burnout culture of academia (Fowler 2015; Sabagh, Hall, and Saroyan 2018; Johnson and Lester 2021), and although conversations about burnout abound on #AcademicTwitter threads, Wilcox Cowing's chapter in this volume uniquely incorporates Mad studies and a politic of rest (Hersey 2022).

racism, what she identifies as academia's "logics of abuse," that gaslight and pathologize Mad Black women.[4] Fueled by our Mad knowledge (Russo and Beresford 2015), this chapter foregrounds Mad "microrebellions" (Price 2011, 7) against a structure that seeks to make us palatable, sanitized, and concealed. We Mad scholars refuse this constructed, forced agreeability. We seek more.

In naming these recurrent patterns of sanism and its intersections, in affirming the gaps, we are also empowered to gather ways to push back. To lead with Madness emboldens us to persist in asking questions despite academia's restrictive parameters. It encourages us, for example, to untangle what health truly means in the neoliberal university,[5] as Sav Schlauderaff (they/them) writes: "Whom does the centering of 'health' serve, and whom does it erase?" Mad questioning is not a passive act. It is something that Mad, neurodiverse academics do at great risk. It requires so much of us, and yet it is something that our own experiences have magnetized us toward. From the place of Mad questioning, when our capacity allows,

---

4. Recent examinations of racialization, carcerality, and Madness include *The Protest Psychosis: How Schizophrenia Became a Black Disease* (Metzl 2010), *Disability Incarcerated: Imprisonment and Disability in the United States and Canada* (Ben-Moshe, Chapman, and Carey 2014), *Black Madness :: Mad Blackness* (Pickens 2019), and *How to Go Mad without Losing Your Mind: Madness and Black Radical Creativity* (Bruce 2021).

5. Health is not neutral territory. Disability studies scholars such as Lennard Davis (2014), Susan Wendell (1996), and Simi Linton (1998) have written extensively about "health" as a normative extension of ableism and the biomedical model of disability. Specifically, Paul Longmore (2003) and Eli Clare (2017) have explored the narrative of cure—the mandate that if one is sick or disabled, one must return to health and "get well" in order to arrive at full personhood (Murphy 1990, 20).

we push back with the intention of creating an accessible, communally supportive space. Rebecca-Eli M. Long (she/her) refers to this process as a "reconceptualization" of academia, a communal invitation that offers us ways to reenvision the often retraumatizing experience of making an institutional complaint while one is Mad.[6]

With its inquiry, part one also serves as a threshold, a portal collectively designed out of necessity. Our Mad need as scholars grows out of exhaustion, out of witnessing sanism's extraction and coercion (Kerschbaum 2013; Price et al. 2017; Brown and Leigh 2018). This work situates itself in the "critical activism" of Mad studies, in the "continuation [of the discipline rather] than an entirely new trajectory of inquiry and practice" (Menzies, LeFrançois, and Reaume 2013, 12). As an invitation, as a calling-in, our Mad needs encourage us to begin here, in the place of naming not just ourselves or the institutions that oppress us but also how structures allegedly meant to "help" us end up replicating or exacerbating harm.

Works Cited

Ahmed, Sara. 2017. "Complaint as Diversity Work." *Feminist Killjoys* (blog), Nov. 10. At https://feministkilljoys.com/2017/11/10/complaint-as-diversity-work/.

———. 2018. "The Time of Complaint." *Feminist Killjoys* (blog), May 30. At https://feministkilljoys.com/2018/05/30/the-time-of-complaint/.

———. 2021. *Complaint!* Durham, NC: Duke Univ. Press.

Ben-Moshe, Liat, Chris Chapman, and Allison C. Carey, eds. 2014. *Disability Incarcerated: Imprisonment and Disability in the United States and Canada*. London: Palgrave Macmillan.

6. See "Complaint Is Diversity Work" (Ahmed 2017), "The Time of Complaint" (Ahmed 2018), and *Complaint!* (Ahmed 2021).

Brown, Nicole. 2020. "Introduction: Theorising Ableism in Academia." In *Ableism in Academia: Theorising Experiences of Disabilities and Chronic Illnesses in Higher Education*, edited by Nicole Brown and Jennifer Leigh, 1–10. London: UCL Press.

Brown, Nicole, and Jennifer Leigh. 2018. "Ableism in Academia: Where Are the Disabled and Ill Academics?" *Disability & Society* 33, no. 6: 985–89.

Bruce, La Marr Jurelle. 2021. *How to Go Mad without Losing Your Mind: Madness and Black Radical Creativity*. Durham, NC: Duke Univ. Press.

Clare, Eli. 2017. *Brilliant Imperfection: Grappling with Cure*. Durham, NC: Duke Univ. Press.

Davis, Lennard J. 2014. *Enforcing Normalcy: Disability, Deafness, and the Body*. London: Verso.

Fowler, Sean. 2015. "Burnout and Depression in Academia: A Look at the Discourse of the University." *Empedocles: European Journal for the Philosophy of Communication* 6, no. 2: 155–67. At https://doi.org/10.1386/ejpc.6.2.155_1.

Hersey, Tricia. 2022. *Rest as Resistance: A Manifesto*. Boston: Little Brown Spark.

Johnson, Adam P., and Rebecca J. Lester. 2021. "Mental Health in Academia: Hacks for Cultivating and Sustaining Well-being." *American Journal of Human Biology* 34, no. 1. At https://onlinelibrary.wiley.com/doi/10.1002/ajhb.23664.

Kerschbaum, Stephanie L. 2013. "On Rhetorical Agency and Disclosing Disability in Academic Writing." *Rhetoric Review* 33, no. 1: 55–71. https://doi.org/10.1080/07350198.2014.856730.

Kerschbaum, Stephanie L., Laura T. Eisenman, and James M. Jones, eds. 2017. *Negotiating Disability: Disclosure in Higher Education*. Ann Arbor: Univ. of Michigan Press.

Kuppers, Petra. 2014. *Studying Disability Arts and Culture: An Introduction*. London: Bloomsbury Academic.

Lewis, Magda. 2008. "Public Good or Private Value: A Critique of the Commodification of Knowledge in Higher Education—a Canadian Perspective." In *Structure and*

Agency in the Neoliberal University, edited by Joyce E. Canaan and Wesley Shumar, 65–86. London: Routledge.

Linton, Simi. 1998. *Claiming Disability: Knowledge and Identity*. New York: New York Univ. Press.

Longmore, Paul. 2003. *Why I Burned My Book and Other Writings on Disability*. Philadelphia: Temple Univ. Press.

Luongo, Nicole Marie. 2021. "Your Diagnosis Will Not Protect You (and Neither Will Academia): Reckoning with Education and Dis-ease." *International Journal of Drug Policy* 98, no. 1. At https://doi.org/10.1016/j.drugpo.2021.103450.

Menzies, Robert, Brenda A. LeFrançois, and Geoffrey Reaume. 2013. "Introducing Mad Studies." In *Mad Matters: A Critical Reader in Canadian Mad Studies*, edited by Brenda A. LeFrançois, Robert Menzies, and Geoffrey Reaume, 1–22. Toronto: Canadian Scholars' Press.

Metzl, Jonathan. 2010. *The Protest Psychosis: How Schizophrenia Became a Black Disease*. Boston: Beacon Press.

Milton, Damian E. M. 2014. "Autistic Expertise: A Critical Reflection on the Production of Knowledge in Autism Studies." *National Autistic Society* 18, no. 7. At https://doi.org/10.1177/1362361314525281.

Miserandino, Christine. 2017. "The Spoon Theory." In *Beginning with Disability: A Primer*, edited by Lennard J. Davis, 174–78. London: Routledge.

Mitchell, David T., and Sharon L. Snyder. 2001. *Narrative Prosthesis: Disability and Dependencies of Disclosure*. Ann Arbor: Univ. of Michigan Press.

Murphy, Robert F. 1990. *Body Silent: The Different World of the Disabled*. New York: Norton.

Pickens, Therí Alyce. 2019. *Black Madness :: Mad Blackness*. Durham, NC: Duke Univ. Press.

Price, Margaret. 2011. *Mad at School: Rhetorics of Mental Disability and Academic Life*. Ann Arbor: Univ. of Michigan Press.

Price, Margaret, Mark S. Salzer, Amber O'Shea, and Stephanie L. Kerschbaum. 2017. "Disclosure of Mental Disability by College and University Faculty: The Negotiation of Accommodations, Supports, and Barriers." *Disability Studies Quarterly* 37, no. 2. At https://dsq-sds.org/article/view/5487/4653.

Russo, Jasna, and Peter Beresford. 2015. "Between Exclusion and Colonisation: Seeking a Place for Mad People's Knowledge in Academia." *Disability & Society* 30, no. 1: 153–57. At https://doi.org/10.1080/09687599.2014.957925.

Sabagh, Zaynab, Nathan C. Hall, and Alenoush Saroyan. 2018. "Antecedents, Correlates and Consequences of Faculty Burnout." *Educational Research* 60, no. 2: 131–56. At https://doi.org/10.1080/00131881.2018.1461573.

Samuels, Ellen. 2017. "Passing, Coming Out, and Other Magical Acts." In *Negotiating Disability: Disclosure and Higher Education*, edited by Stephanie L. Kerschbaum, Laura T. Eisenman, and James M. Jones, 15–24. Ann Arbor: Univ. of Michigan Press.

Sassower, Raphael. 1994. "On Madness in the Academy." *Journal of Higher Education* 65, no. 4: 473–85. At https://doi.org/10.1080/00221546.1993.11778511.

Tilak, Jandhyala B. G. 2008. "Higher Education: A Public Good or a Commodity for Trade?" *Prospects* 38, no. 4: 449–66. At https://doi.org/10.1007/s11125-009-9093-2.

Wendell, Susan. 1996. *The Rejected Body: Feminist Philosophical Reflections on Disability*. London: Routledge.

Wolframe, PhebeAnn M. 2013. "The Madwoman in the Academy, or, Revealing the Invisible Straightjacket: Theorizing and Teaching Saneism and Sane Privilege." *Disability Studies Quarterly* 33, no. 1. At https://dsq-sds.org/article/view/3425/3200.

1

Don't Call It "Mental Health"

A Discussion on Disability Euphemisms and Disability Community

Sav Schlauderaff

There is a duality to what survival means in academia:
that it is success and living.
Death is always already in the room, in our pasts, in our present
realities. Academia is haunted by the continuous past/present/future
of suicide—
but will it help us now?
I don't even have the answers for myself here.
I am just sick and sad and lonely and unwell and in pain.
The only thing I do know is that I am not alone.
Perhaps I have found consolation in that?
We are collectively sick together, have been sick, and been made sick.
And what can we do with that?

> —Sav Schlauderaff, "graduate school has made
> me sick" (2018)

Content notes: suicide, suicidality, anti-Blackness,
eugenics, colonialism, institutionalization

The Desire for "Health"

How are we taught to understand and view health? The World Health Organization (WHO) defines *health* as "a state of complete physical, mental and social well-being and not merely the absence of disease or infirmity" (WHO n.d.a). In *Brilliant Imperfection* (2017), by contrast, in pointing

29

out how "the American Heritage Dictionary [likewise] defines cure as the 'restoration of health,'" Eli Clare argues, "Those three words seem simple enough, *but actually health is a mire*" (2017, 14, italics added). Jonathan Metzl expands on this assertion in his introduction to the anthology *Against Health* (2010): "Health is a desired state, but it is also a prescribed state and an ideological position. . . . [H]ealth is a concept, a norm, and a set of bodily practices whose ideological work is often rendered invisible by the assumption that it is a monolithic, universal good" (2, 9).

The inclusion of these various perspectives is how I started a course I have taught in gender and women's studies, "Feminist Interpretations of Health," as a way to highlight how these societal definitions of health are constructed around an ideal that is imposed on us as an innate "good" that we are expected to aim for. People are constantly in the process of striving for health: through gym memberships, the consumption of never-ending diet products, and the surveillance of our "health" through wearable trackers and wellness apps. The constant pressure to fit a monolithic definition of *healthy* is not only due to the commodified nature of health and its ties to social status but also because being ill, being disabled, being Mad, is defined as undesirable. The repetitive messaging we receive is that *surely, no one would want to be unwell, sick, or ill,* but for people like me, being constantly, chronically ill is my reality. I exist within the overlaps and under the umbrellas of disability, chronic illness, Madness, mental illness, mental disability, and psychiatric diagnoses—and proudly identify as such.[1] And yet I still feel the need to showcase all the ways I am "working on" my physical and mental health, to prove my desirability and worth.

This work of becoming desirable through health comes into play especially in the workplace. The WHO defines *mental health* "as a state of well-being in which every individual realizes his or her own potential, can cope with the normal stresses of life, can *work productively and fruitfully,* and is *able to make a contribution to her or his community*" (WHO

---

1. In this chapter, I use the terms *Mad, mentally ill, mentally disabled, chronically ill,* and *psychiatric diagnoses*. I do not always list out all of these terms together or may select to use only one of them. A plethora of terms is used within disability studies and Mad studies. To read more, see Price 2011 and Kafai 2012.

n.d.b, italics added). This pivot to focus on productivity directly aligns with Talila "TL" Lewis's collaborative working definition of *ableism* as "a system of assigning value to people's bodies and minds based on societally constructed ideas of normalcy, productivity, desirability, intelligence, excellence, and fitness" (2022, par. 1). Worth and value are therefore directly tied to one's proximity to a particular definition of health, which several scholars, including Lewis, have shown is rooted in anti-Blackness, eugenics, colonialism, and capitalism. This connection is particularly harmful to Mad and mentally ill/mentally disabled individuals because many diagnoses are chronic. As the medical anthropologist Arthur Kleinman explains, "Acute diseases are a success, *chronic illnesses are a failure*," and so practitioners "find chronic illness messy and threatening. . . . Predictably, *the chronically ill become problem patients* in care, and they reciprocally experience their care as a problem in the health care system" (1988, 6, 17, italics added). Even when chronically ill people try to work within the structures meant to provide care for us to heal our bodyminds, we are continuously shut out, reprimanded, and labeled as a problem.[2] Further, we are likewise shut out of and distanced from the "healthy" disabled community (Wendell 2001). How then are we meant to talk about our Madness through the lens and language of "mental health"? How will we ever get to discuss the impact of our illnesses on our daily lives if we continue to be engulfed in euphemisms?

Mental health and wellness have become large public-health and social justice issues on university and college campuses. The language of "mental health" has become some of the only language available to Mad and mentally ill individuals to navigate the university, acquire work extensions from professors or supervisors without full disclosure, or find community. Even with this influx of mental health initiatives and programs, disability, illness, sickness, and ableism are frequently left out of such programs. Students, staff, and faculty are instead met with resources focused on self-care, "healthy" eating, exercise, and decreasing stress. Moreover,

---

2. It is important to note that the mistreatment and harm that chronically ill people experience within health care is heightened for those who are multiply marginalized.

these mental health initiatives, programs, and events are often only providing resources for how to better *our individual* mental health rather than focusing on the systemic and institutional forces that create mental health concerns at universities. As I write in my poem "graduate school has made me sick," "we are forced to / taught to desire and strive for actions that make ourselves sicker" through this focus on hyperproductivity (Schlauderaff and Schlauderaff 2018). The structure and essence of academia do not offer a place for our bodyminds to thrive. This is to say that addressing mental health at universities is important, but not if "health" is just a euphemism for "be fit," "be productive," "be happy," "conform." This constrictive understanding of mental health in academia and of what the mentally healthy student and university employee is does not leave enough space for the variety of ways Madness, mental illness, and psychiatric diagnoses are experienced. In these discussions about "mental health," Mad and mentally ill people's experiences need to be centered both in the ways that we engage with our own sense of well-being and in the ways the directive to strive for mental health is imposed upon us.

This chapter aims to engage with questions around the uptake of "mental health" by universities and calls for a questioning of the function of "health" when we are aiming to discuss illness. Whom does the centering of "health" serve, and whom does it erase? Can we push back against the university's focus on individualizing mental health? What are the impacts of resources going to health and wellness programming instead of to tangible resources and policy changes? What are the connections between the use of the term *mental health* and disclosure? And what can we learn from the community building that is happening on and off campuses?

The Mental Health Landscape at Universities and the Rise of Wellness Programs

On average, 1,100 US college students die by suicide every year (Wilcox et al. 2010, 289), and suicide is the second leading cause of death among college students and adolescents globally (Patel et al. 2018; National Institute of Mental Health 2019). In the most recent National College Health Assessment III report for undergraduate and graduate students by the American College Health Association (ACHA) in the fall of 2019, around one-third of students in both populations were diagnosed with one or more "ongoing or chronic conditions" categorized under "mental health."[3]

However, most students with mental illnesses, mental disabilities, or mental health concerns do not seek out campus resources such as counseling or support groups. A study by the WHO World Mental Health International College Student project in 2018 reported that only 16.4 percent of college students diagnosed with disorders identified in the Composite International Diagnostic Interview of the *Diagnostic and Statistical Manual of Mental Disorders* (DSM) IV will seek counseling services (Harvard Medical School n.d.). In addition to concerns around stigma or lack of knowledge of services, there is the problem of sheer numbers; according to the Association for University and College Counseling Center Directors' annual survey of counseling centers in eight countries in 2019, the overall mean ratio for students to counseling staff was 1,318 to 1, with a maximum ratio of 6,348 to 1 (LeViness et al. 2019, 36). Thus, many universities, especially larger institutions, do not meet the International Accreditation of Counseling Services (IACS) (n.d.) recommendation of one counselor for every 1,000 to 1,500 students.[4] Therefore, while effective treatment is needed, the number of students at risk and in need of

---

3. The "ongoing or chronic conditions" listed are attention deficit disorder (ADD) and attention deficit hyperactivity disorder (ADHD); alcohol or other drug-related abuse or addiction; anxiety; autism spectrum disorder; bipolar disorder or related conditions (for example, bipolar I and II, hypomanic episode); borderline personality disorder (BPD); avoidant personality or dependent personality disorder; or another personality disorder (ACHA 2019a, 14, and 2019b, 14).

4. For example, my current university, the University of Arizona, is a large institution. There are twenty-nine Counseling and Psychological Services (CAPS) staff (Campus Health n.d.) for the 45,918 students (University Analytics and Institutional Research n.d.), giving a student-to-staff ratio of around 1,583 to 1, which also does not meet the IACS recommended ratio (IACS n.d.). According to a report issued in 2017, 3,600 students on campus were served, indicating that CAPS reaches about 8.25 percent of the campus at the University of Arizona (University Analytics and Institutional Research n.d.). With only a fraction of the campus being reached, students have long wait times, often up to six weeks, to see someone through CAPS (Uhlorn 2019).

treatment overwhelmingly exceeds the capacity of counseling services at universities (Auerbach et al. 2018, 633, 635).

This huge gap has led campuses to engage in alternative measures to address mental health and stress concerns on campus through a "wellness" lens. Yet although the embrace of "wellness" initiatives and "mental health" programming and support may appear to be a net benefit to students, we need to understand the motives and the surveillance tools utilized within these programs and initiatives on campus. These programs align with the imagined and enforced individual responsibility of the biocitizen,[5] wherein students, staff, and faculty are told to "Eat better. Exercise more. Sleep well," and they often stop at simply "raising awareness." As Jay Timothy Dolmage outlines in *Academic Ableism* (2017), "The euphemism 'wellness' also works rhetorically to demand that we do not discuss disability, especially mental illness/mental disability/madness" (56–57). It is important to highlight that these wellness campaigns are not just polite encouragements. University employees' health insurance is often directly tied to their "wellness" through tracking and surveillance of their health (58). Put plainly, "Wellness programs, then, might be defined as contemporary 'opportunity structures' for forms of eugenic thinking" (56–57). The reinforcement of health on campus comes with the cost of pushing out Mad, disabled, and mentally ill students, staff, and faculty, discouraging us from seeking out and accessing care or forcing us to hide our diagnoses for fear of retaliation (Brown and Leigh 2018, 987).

These realities are not perpetuated solely by wellness programs and campus health centers. Higher education as a whole "encourages students and teachers alike to accentuate ability, valorize perfection, and stigmatize anything that hints at intellectual (or physical) weakness" (Dolmage 2017, 3). Students with "invisible" disabilities are doubly stigmatized, both for the diagnoses they may have and because they are constantly labeled as faking their disabilities, exaggerating their accommodations, or otherwise taking advantage of the system and their instructors (Dolmage 2017, 10; Kafai 2021, 185–86). There are the additional fears not only of incompetency

---

5. For more on the biocitizen, see Roberts 2011, 220–21.

around mental disability but also of violence, instability, and irrationality from us (Price 2011; Wolframe 2012; Kafai 2021). This pressure also affects faculty members with mental illnesses/mental disabilities, as outlined in the recent research by Margaret Price, Mark Salzer, Amber O'Shea, and Stephanie Kerschbaum (2017). Most faculty with mental disabilities are not familiar with accommodations for themselves and tend not to request them; Price and her colleagues found that although the majority did disclose to at least one person on campus, they rarely look to colleagues (29 percent) and supervisors (25 percent) for support (2017, par. 1). Kerschbaum succinctly states, "The reality is that disability to many still signals *disqualification*" (2014, 69, italics added), and Price adds that "persons with mental disabilities are *presumed not to be competent, nor understandable, nor valuable, nor whole*" (2011, 26, italics added). Thus, there is a need to perform "wellness" and "saneness" not only to be successful but also to be seen as deserving and human within academia.

These pressures make decisions to disclose diagnoses both difficult and potentially harmful within academia. Moreover, the decision to disclose isn't a singular or fixed decision—it is messy and complicated and shifting. What I disclose and how I disclose continuously vary due to the unpredictability of my pain, fatigue, flashbacks, dissociation, intrusive thoughts, and (lack of) ability to stay grounded in "reality" as well as the reminder that my suicidality is always waiting on the horizon and can become all-encompassing in an instant. Disclosure of disability is complex because my disabilities are complex, and my "less visible" disabilities exist on the border between Mad and sane,[6] between a desirable and undesirable bodymind in academia.

The danger of the wellness model and disclosure is perhaps most clearly understood by looking at the treatment of students who have sought out psychiatric treatment, especially those who have attempted suicide, have reported (or have been reported for) suicidal ideation, or have more stigmatized mental illnesses. As Esmé Weijun Wang relates

---

6. "As a third positionality, the mad border body is an alternative to the sane/mad construction in that it advocates for a disruption of binary logic all together" (Kafai 2012, abstract).

in her memoir *The Collected Schizophrenias* (2019), being hospitalized twice at the Yale Psychiatric Institute was deemed a "breach of etiquette"; she was asked to leave Yale immediately and was not allowed to reenter campus. "Rather than receiving help," Wang writes, "mentally ill students are frequently, as I was, pressured into leaving—or ordered to leave—by the schools that once welcomed them. *The underlying expectation is that a student must be mentally healthy to return to school,* which is difficult and unlikely to happen to the degree the administration would like. This is saying, essentially, that *students should not have severe mental illness*" (73, italics added). Wang's assessment of her experience at Yale speaks to the overwhelming pressure that students face to perform health (and thus to hide mental illness) within a specific timeframe if they want to remain in higher education. It should be reiterated that these policies and others such as mandatory reporting create barriers for students that make accessing care and accommodations a high-risk choice wherein we need to weigh our survival against remaining in higher education. Wang's experience is not uncommon, nor is it unique to Yale.

Across campuses, the trend has been toward increasing wellness programming rather than toward addressing the negative impact of the university and academia on mental illness. There have been vast increases in programs utilizing dogs to "de-stress" (Binfet 2017; Haggerty and Mueller 2017), mindfulness programs, meditation apps, and yoga classes (Lemay, Hoolahan, and Buchanan 2019; Ahmad et al. 2020; Martinez 2020), alongside other mental health and wellness-based initiatives—all of which focus on ways for individuals to reduce their *own* stress levels and to center their *own* mental health. (What does it mean, anyway, to be offered a dog to pet when "stress" isn't the reason you can't get out of bed for class?) Universities jump on these "fun" opportunities, which may provide short-term help but do not get to the source of the *un*wellness of students, staff, and faculty. As Mimi Khúc, a self-described writer, scholar, and teacher of all things unwell, writes in a letter to her daughter in the special issue "Open in Emergency" of the *Asian American Literary Review*,

> I am writing you to tell you the lie of the thing called wellness. My child, the world *makes us sick and then tells us it is our fault.* Sickness

as individual pathology, a lack of ability or will to achieve wellness. *The world tells us what wellness looks like*, and marks it as normal, moral. Like whiteness, wellness is an ideal to strive for, a state of being in constant performance. . . . People are not to be measured by their usefulness, their ability to perform health, their proximity to racialized, gendered ideals. I need you to understand that *we are all differentially unwell.* (2019, n.p., italics added)

Higher education "encourages students and teachers alike to accentuate ability, valorize perfection, and stigmatize anything that hints at intellectual (or physical) weakness" (Dolmage 2017, 3). This problem will not be solved through "mental health" and "wellness" initiatives; we need to address mental illness/mental disabilities, Madness, ableism, and sanism directly.

Euphemistically Speaking: The Potentiality and Harms with/in "Mental Health"

There is a lack of clarity around disability and mental illness terminology. Some terms, such as *depression*, lack clarity because of their dual lay and medical uses (Ong et al. 1995, 910). Others, such as *Madness*,[7] hold an ambiguity due to lack of familiarity but also to their multiple meanings outside of "mental illness" altogether (Bailey and Mobley 2018, 12; Pickens 2019, 4). And still others, such as *trauma* and *triggered*, have entered into mainstream culture but have been mocked and willfully misinterpreted.[8] Disability studies scholars and disability activists have pushed back against the numerous euphemisms for disability—*differently abled, handicapable, special,* and so on—which through their use obscure rather

---

7. "[The term *Mad*] is less recognizable in the United States, which can be used to its advantage, since its infrequency helps detach it from implication in medical and psychiatric industries. . . . [*Mad*] achieves a flexibility that *mental illness* and *cognitive disability* do not" (Price 2011, 10).

8. "Misuses of the words 'trauma' and 'trigger' have led to serious misinterpretations of both the psychosomatic experience of trauma and the embodiment of its corresponding affect. As with other disabilities, the lack of accurate public knowledge and understanding about the lived experiences of trauma has led to yet another ill-conceived conversation about us, without us" (Carter 2015, par. 2).

38   Schlauderaff

than reclaim disability identity. The ambiguity and misinterpretation of these terms have impacts on mentally ill and mentally disabled people because they remove real concerns and access needs and instead mock or trivialize them.

The term *mental health* teeters on this line. Its meaning is vast and changeable: it can be interpreted to refer to stress, self-care, sadness, heartbreak, relationship conflict, a need to set boundaries, intergenerational trauma, the trauma of racism or anti-Blackness, *or* mental illness. All of these interpretations are important conversations I have seen happening through mental health programming and discussions on campus, especially within spaces utilizing healing justice and disability justice frameworks.[9] In my almost twelve years in academia, I have met numerous people with psychiatric diagnoses and chronic illnesses who did not identify as Mad, mentally ill, chronically ill, or disabled but who *did* feel comfortable discussing their experiences when the conversations were framed around mental health.[10] Examples of this choice in practice may look like healing circles; transformative justice being implemented and taught at cultural and resource centers; and mutual aid being offered through crowdsourcing funds and resources both for individuals in the community and for specific organizations.[11] Moreover, the term *mental health* is also used by many organizations and collectives, such as BEAM, Project LETS, the Fireweed Collective, and Depressed While Black.[12] These spaces then

9. To learn more about healing justice, see Kindred Southern Healing Justice Collective n.d. *Disability justice* is a term and framework coined by Patty Berne, Mia Mingus, Stacey Park Milbern, Leroy Moore, Eli Clare, and Sebastian Margaret (Berne 2015).

10. This comfortability with engaging in spaces/conversations about "mental health" rather than about mental illness and Madness may be attributed to the stigma associated with the latter, the more frequent use of the term *mental health*, and the emphasis on "resilience" and "recovery" in mental health care. For more on this issue, see Howell and Voronka 2012; Bossewitch 2016.

11. For more on transformative justice, see Transform Harm n.d. For more on mutual aid, see Big Door Brigade n.d.

12. For more on the use of the term *mental health* by these organizations and collectives, see BEAM n.d.; Depressed While Black n.d.; Fireweed Collective n.d.; and Project LETS n.d.

allow for the *source* of mental health problems to be addressed rather than just the symptoms, as we see with mental health programming created by universities.

The ambiguity of the term *mental health* also may provide space for disclosure in academic spaces without needing to out one's specific diagnosis or symptoms. Using a term within most people's vocabulary that is less stigmatized *does* serve a function. Simply put, emailing or texting "I have been having a hard time with my mental health lately. Could I have an extension?" stands in to provide the access I need when the dangers of disclosing specific psychiatric diagnoses or explaining the real impacts of my mental illnesses are too risky. Therefore, there are benefits to the ambiguity of the term *mental health* beyond its use as a method to avoid potentially harmful disclosures of mental illness. And perhaps most importantly, there are ways to work within the "mental health" and "wellness" frameworks that positively affect Mad and mentally ill people and don't decenter our specific experiences or our needs. However, we must continue to emphasize that "mental health concerns" are not individual problems to be "solved." We need to look at the roots; academia needs to understand its own role in exacerbating mental health concerns and systemically harming our bodyminds.

And we still must ask: What would the university look like if it didn't punish Madness and mental illness? If we were to have accessible resources that don't involve risky disclosure? What would it mean to push against the desire for "health" and "wellness" and against how they have been defined for us? Throughout this chapter, I have touched on and included the works by Mad, mentally ill, crip, and disabled activists, artists, students, and educators.[13] This is to say that this work is already being done inside and outside of academia. And yet we still need to break down punitive policies such as involuntary leave and mandatory reporting that are enforced on campus. We still need to push for tangible resources such as free education, expanded disability services, more counseling employees and unlimited appointments, and the hiring of counselors and healers

---

13. Many disability justice activists have written about "crip wisdom." See, for example, Disability Visibility Project 2016; Piepzna-Samarasinha 2018; and Wong 2018.

specifically for Black and Indigenous people, people of color, LGBTQIA+ people, and disabled people on campus.

This isn't an argument for people to stop organizing or building community around mental health or for people to stop receiving mental health care. It is a call for universities to stop funding only those programs centered around striving for students to be individually "healthy," for universities to stop pretending that Mad, mentally ill, and mentally disabled people do not exist at their institution, and to stop pushing us out of academia. It is a call for vulnerable acts of disclosure not to be the only means for Madness and mental illness to enter into the conversation or the only way for necessary access needs to be met. This is a reminder that we deserve to learn, work, and educate in a space where we feel supported. As Kai Cheng Thom writes in her essay "The Myth of Mental Health," "There is a sickness that hides in the thing we call health. There is wisdom and power, in the thing we call Madness: power to hurt and harm, yes, but also power to help us see ourselves, to help us envision a different world, to bring about transformation and change and death and rebirth" (2019, 10). In other words, we deserve the time–space to determine what healing means to us and what our own relationship to "mental health" looks like.

Works Cited

Ahmad, Farah, Christo El Morr, Paul Ritvo, Nasih Othman, Rahim Moineddin, Iqra Ashfaq, et al. 2020. "An Eight-Week, Web-Based Mindfulness Virtual Community Intervention for Students' Mental Health: Randomized Controlled Trial." *JMIR Mental Health* 7, no. 2: art. E15520.

American College Health Association (AHCA). 2019a. "Graduate/Professional Student Reference Group Executive Summary United States." National College Health Assessment III. At https://www.acha.org/documents /ncha/NCHA-III_Fall_2019_Undergraduate_Reference_Group_Executive _Summary.pdf.

———. 2019b. "Undergraduate Student Reference Group Executive Summary United States." National College Health Assessment III. At https://www .acha.org/documents/ncha/NCHA-III_Fall_2019_Undergraduate_Reference _Group_Executive_Summary.pdf.

Auerbach, Randy P., Philippe Mortier, Ronny Bruffaerts, Jordi Alonso, Corina Benjet, Pim Cuijpers, Koen Demyttenaere, et al. 2018. "WHO World Mental Health Surveys International College Student Project: Prevalence and Distribution of Mental Disorders." *Journal of Abnormal Psychology* 127, no. 7: 623–38. At https://doi.org/10.1037/abn0000362.

Bailey, Moya, and Izetta Autumn Mobley. 2018. "Work in the Intersections: A Black Disability Studies Framework." *Gender & Society* 33, no. 1. At https://doi.org10.1177/0891243218801523.

BEAM. n.d. "About Us." At https://www.beam.community/whatwebelieve.

Berne, Patty. 2015. "Disability Justice—a Working Draft by Patty Berne." Sins Invalid, June 9. At https://www.sinsinvalid.org/blog/disability-justice-a-working-draft-by-patty-berne.

Big Door Brigade. n.d. "What Is Mutual Aid?" At https://bigdoorbrigade.com/what-is-mutual-aid/.

Binfet, John-Taylor. 2017. "The Effects of Group-Administered Canine Therapy on University Students' Wellbeing: A Randomized Controlled Trial." *Anthrozoös: A Multidisciplinary Journal of the Interactions of People and Animals* 30, no. 3: 397–414.

Bossewitch, Jonah S. 2016. "Dangerous Gifts: Towards a New Wave of Mad Resistance." PhD diss., Columbia Univ. At https://doi.org/10.7916/D8RJ4JFB.

Brown, Nicole, and Jennifer Leigh. 2018. "Ableism in Academia: Where Are the Disabled and Ill Academics?" *Disability & Society* 33, no. 6: 985–89. At https://doi.org/10.1080/09687599.2018.1455627.

Campus Health. n.d. "People." Univ. of Arizona. At https://health.arizona.edu/people.

Carter, Angela. 2015. "Teaching with Trauma: Trigger Warnings, Feminism, and Disability Pedagogy." *Disability Studies Quarterly* 2, no. 35. At https://dsq-sds.org/article/view/4652/3935.

Clare, Eli. 2017. *Brilliant Imperfection: Grappling with Cure*. Durham, NC: Duke Univ. Press.

Depressed While Black. n.d. "About." At https://www.depressedwhileblack.com/#about.

Disability Visibility Project. 2016. "#CripWisdom: Interview with the Artists of Sins Invalid." Oct. 10. At https://disabilityvisibilityproject.com/2016/10/10/crip-wisdom-interview-with-the-artists-of-sins-invalid/.

Dolmage, Jay Timothy. 2017. *Academic Ableism: Disability and Higher Education*. Ann Arbor: Univ. of Michigan Press.

Fireweed Collective. n.d. Homepage. At https://fireweedcollective.org/.

Haggerty Julie M., and Megan K. Mueller. 2017. "Animal-Assisted Programs in Higher Education." *Innovative Higher Education* 42:379–89. At https://doi.org/10.1007/s10755-017-9392-0.

Harvard Medical School. n.d. "The WHO World Mental Health International College Student (WMH-ICS) Initiative." At https://www.hcp.med.harvard.edu/wmh/college_student_survey.php.

Howell, Alison, and Jijian Voronka. 2012. "Introduction: The Politics of Resilience and Recovery in Mental Health Care." In "The Politics of Resilience and Recovery in Mental Health Care," edited by Alison Howell and Jijian Voronka. *Studies in Social Justice* 6, no. 1: 1–7. At https://doi.org/10.26522/ssj.v6i1.1065.

International Accreditation of Counseling Services (IACS). n.d. "Staff to Student Ratios." At https://iacsinc.org/staff-to-student-ratios/#:~:text=Since%20the%20standard%20ratio%20of,higher%20ratio%20is%20legally%20vulnerable.

Kafai, Shayda. 2012. "The Mad Border Body: A Political In-Betweeness." *Disability Studies Quarterly* 33, no. 1. At https://doi.org/10.18061/dsq.v33i1.3438.

———. 2021. "The Politics of Mad Femme Disclosure." *Journal of Lesbian Studies* 3, no. 25: 182–94.

Kerschbaum, Stephanie L. 2014. "On Rhetorical Agency and Disclosing Disability in Academic Writing." *Rhetoric Review* 33, no. 1: 55–71.

Khúc, Mimi. 2019. "Guest Editor's Note." In "Open in Emergency," edited by Mimi Khúc. Special issue on Asian American mental health, *Asian American Literary Review* 10, no. 2 (Fall–Winter): no page.

Kindred Southern Healing Justice Collective. n.d. "What Is Healing Justice?" At http://kindredsouthernhjcollective.org/what-is-healing-justice/.

Kleinman, Arthur. 1988. "The Meaning of Symptoms and Disorders." In *The Illness Narratives: Suffering, Healing, and the Human Condition*, 3–30. New York: Basic.

Lemay, Virginia, John Hoolahan, and Ashley Buchanan. 2019. "Impact of a Yoga and Meditation Intervention on Students' Stress and Anxiety Levels." *American Journal of Pharmaceutical Education* 83, no. 5: 747–52.

LeViness, Peter, Kim Gorman, Lynn Braun, Linda Koenig, and Carolyn Bershad. 2019. *The Association for University and College Counseling Center Directors Annual Survey—2019*. Indianapolis, IN: AUCCCD.

Lewis, Talila "TL." 2022. "Working Definition of Ableism—January 2022 Update." *Talila A. Lewis* (blog), Jan. 1. At https://www.talilalewis.com/blog/working-definition-of-ableism-january-2022-update.

Martinez, Gabrielle. 2020. "Opinion: University Mental Health Resources Are Inadequate, Students Need More Than Goat Yoga and Therapy Dogs." *LSU Reveille,* Feb. 22. At https://www.lsureveille.com/opinion/opinion-university-mental-health-resources-are-inadequate-students-need-more-than-goat-yoga-and-therapy/article_eb53bd92-54e4-11ea-b07e-ebee3502a9fe.html.

Metzl, Jonathan M. 2010. "Introduction: Why 'against Health'?" In *Against Health: How Health Became the New Morality,* edited by John M. Metzl and Anna Kirkland, 1–14. New York: New York Univ. Press.

National Institute of Mental Health. 2019. "Suicide." Apr. At https://www.nimh.nih.gov/health/statistics/suicide.shtml.

Ong, Lucille M. L., Johanna C. De Haes, Alaysia M. Hoos, and Fritz B. Lammes. 1995. "Doctor–Patient Communication: A Review of the Literature." *Social Science and Medicine* 40, no. 7: 903–18.

Patel, Vikram, Shekhar Saxena, Crick Lund, Graham Thornicroft, Florence Baingana, Paul Bolton, Dan Chisholm, et al. 2018. "The Lancet Commission on Global Mental Health and Sustainable Development." *The Lancet* (British ed.) 392, no. 10157: 1553–98. At https://doi.org/10.1016/S0140-6736(18)31612-X.

Pickens, Therí Alyce. 2019. *Black Madness :: Mad Blackness.* Durham, NC: Duke Univ. Press.

Piepzna-Samarasinha, Leah Lakshmi. 2018. *Care Work: Dreaming Disability Justice.* Vancouver: Arsenal Pulp Press.

Price, Margaret. 2011. *Mad at School: Rhetorics of Mental Disability and Academic Life.* Ann Arbor: Univ. of Michigan Press.

Price, Margaret, Mark S. Salzer, Amber O'Shea, and Stephanie L. Kerschbaum. 2017. "Disclosure of Mental Disability by College and University Faculty: The Negotiation of Accommodations, Supports, and Barriers." *Disability Studies Quarterly* 37, no. 2. At https://doi.org/10.18061/dsq.v37i2.5487.

Project LETS. n.d. "About." At https://projectlets.org/about.

Roberts, Dorothy. 2011. *Fatal Invention: How Science, Politics, and Big Business Re-create Race in the Twenty-First Century.* New York: New Press.

Schlauderaff, Sav, and Shosh Schlauderaff. 2018. "Visual Poem 'graduate school has made me sick.'" *Sunday Sentiments* (blog), Dec. 12. At https://savschlauderaff.wixsite.com/website/post/visual-poem-graduate-school-has-made-me-sick.

Thom, Kai Cheng. 2019. "The Myth of Mental Health." In "Open in Emergency," edited by Mimi Khúc. Special issue on Asian American health, *Asian American Literary Review* 10, no. 2 (Fall–Winter): 2–10.

Transform Harm. n.d. "Transformative Justice." At https://transformharm.org/transformative-justice/.

Uhlorn, Brittany L. 2019. "Additional Counselors Cut UA Student Appointment Wait Times in Half." *Tucson.com*, last modified Nov. 3. At https://tucson.com/news/local/additional-counselors-cut-ua-student-appointment-wait-times-in-half/article_ea079715-2b57-54da-a8c2-3ac5eee3cbb8.html.

University Analytics and Institutional Research. n.d. "Enrollment." Univ. of Arizona. At https://uair.arizona.edu/content/enrollment.

Wang, Esmé Weijun. 2019. *The Collected Schizophrenias: A Memoir*. Minneapolis, MN: Graywolf Press.

Wendell, Susan. 2001. "Unhealthy Disabled: Treating Chronic Illnesses as Disabilities." *Hypatia* 16:17–33. At https://www.jstor.org/stable/3810781.

Wilcox, Holly C., Amelia M. Arria, Kimberly M. Caldeira, Kathryn B. Vincent, Gillina M. Pinchevsky, and Kevin E. O'Grady. 2010. "Prevalence and Predictors of Persistent Suicide Ideation, Plans, and Attempts during College." *Journal of Affective Disorders* 127, nos. 1–3: 287–94. At https://doi.org/0.1016/j.jad.2010.04.017.

Wolframe, PhebeAnn M. 2012. "The Madwoman in the Academy, or, Revealing the Invisible Straightjacket: Theorizing and Teaching Saneism and Sane Privilege." *Disability Studies Quarterly* 33, no. 1. At https://doi.org/10.18061/dsq.v33i1.

Wong, Alice, ed. 2018. *Resistance and Hope: Essays by Disabled People. Crip Wisdom for the People*. N.p.: Disability Visibility Project.

World Health Organization (WHO). n.d.a. "Constitution." At https://www.who.int/about/who-we-are/constitution.

———. n.d.b. "WHO Urges More Investments, Services for Mental Health." At https://www.who.int/mental_health/who_urges_investment/en.

2

My PhD Drove Me Crazy (but I Was Already Mad)

Shawna Guenther

> ***Content notes***: self-harm, disordered eating,
> mental and emotional abuse

I am the Madwoman in the department, and it shows. My mental illness shows itself in my physicality: I make myself as small as possible and scurry along without meeting anyone's eyes; my voice is quiet and uncertain; my shoulders are hunched; my hands play with bits of paper or pens, betraying my unease; my elbows bleed from scratching.

To associate myself, a mentally ill literary critic, with a seminal text that analyzes Victorian women writers and characters who displayed various psychological abnormalities seems apt (Gilbert and Guber 1979).[1] But I am not tucked away in an attic. I am on campus, in the classroom; I am at academic conferences, at the lectern; I am in person, within the conversations.[2] Unlike those Victorian women, I am in the present and the future, open and ready to be accepted; I demand my real voice—my

---

I owe significant gratitude to Shayda Kafai for her kindness and compassion as well as for her thoughtful suggestions regarding this chapter.

1. I call myself "mentally ill" because I am aware that I suffer from real illness of a psychiatric nature. I am also "disabled" because the effects of my illness—and the medications—are functionally disabling in many ways.

2. In my own academic practice, I consider how and why authors represent mentally ill characters within their literary and cultural contexts.

mentally ill voice—be heard. I refuse to hide, silently, in the attic. I have come to a place where I do not hide my mental illness because it is part of who I am and what I do, personally and professionally.[3] In the past ten years or so, I have made a concerted effort in my academic writing and speaking to engage with and frame mental illness—to remove the silence, shame, and stigma—as a significant concern to the health of universities.

I am open and honest about my mental illness in all aspects of interactions with others for three main reasons. First, I am no longer willing or able to put on the sane disguise. Having lived with mental illness for more than forty years, I am exhausted. Physical exhaustion is often a symptom of mental illness and a side effect of medications. Mental exhaustion exhibits as inability to concentrate, read comprehensively, synthesize ideas, and so on. At one point, I was unable to grade essays until I spent a few days in the hospital recalibrating my brain. As a graduate student and professor, I have hidden my crazy under a calm, stable demeanor that requires significant and draining effort. Some days I have to observe *carpe diem cras*—accept that I will not actively participate in life today, but maybe tomorrow. The speed at which I perform when I can perform is necessary to compensate for days when I cannot function. Sometimes I experience what I call "mental mania," the mess of multiple ideas that overwhelms me, preventing any useful engagement with or concentration on any of them. This mania, however, has its advantages. Some of the ideas are more fruitful than those coming from a level head. Sometimes I can develop them when my mind calms down. Mania (nonclinical) and obsessive-compulsive disorder, or OCD (low level in my case), can be effective when properly channeled.

Second, I know from experience and from academic and governmental studies that mental illness is a global epidemic. The World Health Organization (WHO) estimates that "every 40 seconds, someone loses their life to suicide" (2019, par. 1). Shayda Kafai and Melanie Jones indicated

---

3. In my paper presentation "Renegotiating Utopia: Where Is the New Harmony for the Marginalized?" (Guenther 2018), I listed characteristics of a mentally ill person. Then I announced that I had all of those characteristics, yet I was in the position of authority at that moment, despite—or because of—being mentally ill.

in their call for papers for this volume that there is "an avalanche of news articles about spikes in mental illness on campus" (2020). Although specific information is undisclosed, medical accommodations for university students are increasingly based on mental illnesses. For example, in-class tests, pop quizzes, in-class discussions, oral evaluations, and firm assignment deadlines can induce anxiety. I frequently receive emails explaining students' absenteeism as a direct effect of mental illness—from the inability to leave one's dwelling to the unchangeability of scheduled psychiatric appointments. For those of us who are aware of the myriad symptoms of mental illnesses, clues in students' writing and behavior are becoming more evident.[4] As a professor, I clearly see a need to provide a space for open discussion with students about mental illness. Frank discussions and major policy changes in academia are imperative.

Third, if people with mental illness do not describe their realities or challenge conventional understandings of mental health, change cannot occur (Arsenault 2020).[5] If the very institution that encourages research and scholarship, intellectual creativity and interdisciplinary cooperation, and acknowledgment of and solution to problems does not recognize its own failings in its practices of exclusion and sanism based on mental health, then Mad scholars must provide their own driving force in advocating for worthwhile, successful, and innovative people whose medical conditions allegedly render them inferior in the academic landscape. But herein lies the paradox of academia in general. PhebeAnn Wolframe suggests that academics are assumed to be "sane by default" (2013, par. 6). However, the very qualities that make people able to rise to the acme of academic achievement can be associated with both sanity/ability and insanity/disability. For example, one might consider a doctoral student or

---

4. In its report *Mental Disorders* (2022), WHO estimates that "280 million people suffer from depression" (par. 4).

5. Part of my objective in this chapter is to explain the complexities of living with mental illness to those without such illness. I have found that it is extremely difficult to convince people that mental illness is real, incapacitating, and incurable. Sanist understandings of what mental illness is and what it does to a person need to be reframed to make profound change possible.

professor as being either persistent (sanity/ability) or unable to move into the nonacademic world (insanity/disability); possessing academic attention to detail, depth, and vigor or demonstrating compulsion; accepting the inevitable isolation and dedication required for research or exhibiting asocial behavior; speaking about one's work with confidence or demonstrating narcissism.

Further, as Ellen Samuels demonstrates, the transformation from being perceived as abled to being perceived as disabled "takes place at the intersection of multiple identities, locations, and assumptions" (2017, 16). One criterion that changes the perception of someone's emotion as either sadness or depression is a persistent affect lasting at least six weeks. Thus, does a person suddenly transform from having a "normal" emotional response to having a mental illness at forty-three days? If a person experiences a depressed episode, is that person always to be considered mentally ill? Are only those who have a certain number of such episodes defined as mentally ill? And so on. Extrapolating the conclusions of Jan W. Valle, Santiago Solis, Donna Volpotta, and David J. Conner, we can say that scholars need to "explore how society constructs disabilities" and how people "internalize, appropriate, and/or resist those mainstream definitions" (2004, 4).

Here, I am exposing my own Madness to show how I suffer, cope, and achieve as a person, student, academic, and advocate because my mental illness affects every aspect of my life, and I am never going to be "cured." I can reframe myself within the Mad genius paradigm and show how my mental illness sometimes improves my functioning. As I reveal my experience as a doctoral student, I demonstrate my Mad pathways through some of the systemic discrimination within the academy. Finally, I show some of the forms of resilience and advocacy I employ as a professor and scholar. Within academia, systemic sanist barriers already require Mad scholars to forge new pathways and forms of resilience to survive, but we can employ those same ways and forms to advocate for policy changes about mental health and for protections and equity for those with mental illness.

My Crazy Self as Text

I am Mad. My immediate response upon seeing the call for papers for this anthology on Mad scholarship was one of panic. I felt as if someone had peered into my mind, discovered I was crazy, and was going to out me.[6] That has been my fear for a very long time: people are going to find out that I should not be in academia because I am mentally ill. When I applied to my doctoral program, I was completely shocked that I was accepted as one of only two people admitted that semester. My projected image to others, I have been told, is one of intelligence and competence but also of low self-esteem.[7] So initially I believed I could hide my crazy, but that idea left me in the middle of my first class on the first day of my first semester.[8] The more time I spent at the university, the more convinced I became that I had a massive judgment stamped on my forehead: insane.[9] I thought people would see those stereotypical signs of Madness: difficulty socializing, inappropriate verbal responses, lack of emotion—the person who somehow is not quite "normal." Many people have told me that my particular brand of Madness is a "good crazy." Most people describe me using some derivative of *Mad* rather than *ill*.[10] Nevertheless, despite everything going on in my disturbed mind, I managed to survive and succeed.

But my mental illness did not begin with the university. It began before puberty, but I was not diagnosed with a mood disorder until I was

6. To be clear, my use of the term *crazy* here is tongue-in-cheek. I am not crazy; I *just* have mental illness.

7. Consider how I describe *my* interpretation of my physical presence in the academy earlier in the chapter.

8. In hiding my "crazy" on days when I had to go to the university, I got dressed—something I rarely do if not leaving the house—and I suppressed my emotions. As soon as I returned home, I would collapse on my bed, and the emotions would release themselves as tears or nightmares. That first day, however, the hiding proved exceedingly difficult. This is a narcissistic dilemma—I assumed that people were specifically scrutinizing me, yet just sitting in a classroom would not make me the focus of others, especially others who may have been feeling as uncomfortable as I was.

9. This reminds me of Hester Prynne's red fabric A and the injustice and danger of attaching labels to humans in Nathaniel Hawthorne's *The Scarlet Letter* (1850).

10. For example, a student told me that I was "good crazy," indicating that although I did not speak and act the way so-called normal people do, my antics were amusing and not ill intentioned. In a culture that renders Madness and Blackness "interchangeable" (Pickens 2019, 3), *good crazy* is also a racialized term indicating that one is not dangerous or threatening.

twenty-seven, after the birth of my third child in four years. Although my doctor initially thought I was experiencing postpartum depression, interviews with health professionals showed that I had been suffering from depression for most of my life, beginning with my alienation strategies in kindergarten, gaining strength at menarche, increasing rapidly with a spate of family deaths in a short period during my adolescence, gathering momentum during my undergraduate years, and reaching fever pitch in August 1995. In addition to severe and chronic depression (without psychosis), I have been, bit by bit, diagnosed with seasonal affective disorder, mild OCD, general anxiety disorder, disordered eating, disordered sleeping, complex post-traumatic stress disorder, chronic grief, and possibly borderline personality disorder.[11] As my brother likes to say, I dance not only to the beat of a different drummer but also to the beat of a drummer no one else can hear.[12] However, this endearing sibling insult reiterates the Mad genius dichotomy: perhaps I have a unique creative or intellectual perspective or way of exhibiting such perspectives. Indeed, I find I am able to think in several directions at once and host a catalog of critical and creative ideas in my crazy mind space. In succumbing to what for me are

11. The *Diagnostic and Statistical Manual of Mental Disorders V* (2013) defines borderline personality disorder as "a pattern of instability in personal relationships, intense emotions, poor self-image and impulsivity. A person with borderline personality disorder may go to great lengths to avoid being abandoned, have repeated suicide attempts, display inappropriate intense anger, or have ongoing feelings of emptiness" (943). Perhaps.

12. My mental illness manifests symptomatically on three levels: the mental/emotional, the physical, and the medicinal. Mentally, I have a battle with myself every morning and every night. My brain tells me that I need to die, that I am useless. Physically, I cannot fall asleep, or I cannot awake. I forget to eat. Triggers cause days of crying, self-harming behaviors, and often complete incapacitation. Anxiety leads to asthma attacks as well as shaking and sweating. I experience all these symptoms even while I am taking two different antidepressants. The medications cause weight gain, hyperactivity, and inability to concentrate. These symptoms are just a sample of the effects that the combined illnesses and cocktail of medications cause. If, as some people would have it, I stopped taking the pills, I would require hospitalization. At least the student union medical insurance covers 50 percent of the cost of medications and up to $1,000 per year on psychotherapy (but at $250 per fifty minutes, therapy is still a luxury).

natural impulses, I can read myself as a multiplicitous text, donning various personae to fit into various required modes of thinking or situations.[13] Further, I realize that even a Mad text can produce meaning.[14] Perhaps in Madness there is a gift.

The Mad-Making PhD

Almost every doctoral student/candidate or recent graduate I have asked claims that feelings of failure, insecurity, inability, and depression are a normal part of the academic process.[15] If such claims are as widespread as they appear, then the system is toxic and needs to be completely overhauled. Academic rigor is essential, but emotional and mental abuse, intentional or not, is unacceptable. The mere fact that these scholars— as well as professors, supervisors, committees, and department/graduate chairs—are so willing to label these feelings as normal indicates a dire need to rethink and restructure how we become academics, how these personal reactions form our professional selves and practices, and why we allow the perpetuation of such cruel and unusual punishment. I began a special-case PhD program in English at a Canadian university.[16] Many

13. I do not mean to suggest that I have multiple personality disorder.

14. Because mental illness is of the mind and seemingly not of the body, Margaret Price writes that people with mental illness "share common experiences of disempowerment as rhetors" (2011, 18).

15. My care team must frequently differentiate for me whether my emotional responses and thoughts are "normal" or products of mental illness. I forget that people without mental illness also have negative thoughts and emotions, but the difference between theirs and mine is related to the level or duration of feeling an emotion, the overresponse to an act or statement, or the internal repetition of a thought.

16. Although I had been accepted at another university with a traditional program, because I had children ages eleven, ten, and eight, I was unable to relocate. My university did not have a doctoral program in English, so I was admitted as a "special case." You could say I was in a class of my own (comedy is my most effective self-soothing strategy if I can avoid self-deprecating humor). My program consisted of a second-language proficiency, three two-semester research projects (that is, six semesters in total), each concluding with a fifty-page research paper and an oral exam—based on the McGill University (Montreal, Quebec) model—and a doctoral proposal, dissertation, and defense.

52   Guenther

problems, of course, occurred all the way through it, but I managed to get to the thesis-proposal stage.[17] I experienced the same feelings that my own students described. What I now consider important is that despite the usual and extra problems, difficulties, and emotions of a doctoral program, I, as a mentally ill student, persevered, studied, wrote, presented, and worked as well as any other graduate student. I do not know whether I had to forge a different pathway than most, but a stubborn commitment to complete the program even as I felt I was continually hitting my head against a brick wall might be an effect of mental illness, especially considering that I greatly feared the label *failure*.

Unfortunately, I was forced to withdraw from the program due to a mental collapse precipitated by an adverse drug reaction. This is an example of one of the problems with treating mental illness—the cure being worse than the ailment. Prior to taking the drug injections, the two weeks before every menstrual period I felt as I did without antidepressants, meaning that half of my life was consumed by full-on depression.[18] With injections, my condition was so bad that I walked into my bathroom one day, saw the toothpaste, hand soap, and moisturizer and could not remember which one to put on my toothbrush. My mental capacity had diminished significantly within three months of taking the medication and required two years for recuperation. But two years was apparently too long. When I

17. Whenever I tried to negotiate for myself in that uncharted territory, I was repeatedly told by the department graduate chair that the Faculty of Graduate Studies and Research considered me "a whiny student." I learned later that none of my concerns had reached the faculty. For example, although the department assured me that one of the project supervisors had been replaced—his abuse of me stemming from his own (admitted) mental illness—it had not officially made the change. In response, I demanded that the project be replaced by another. Although I did complete an additional project, the department did not officially delete the incomplete project. Thus, my permanent academic record has a failing grade—officially signed by the professor in question—thus invalidating applications for scholarships and grants in perpetuity.

18. The proposed solution was a hysterectomy, for which there was a year-long waiting list. In the meantime, the doctor provided monthly injections of medication (Lupron Depot) that forced my body to simulate menopause.

applied to return to my program, I was rejected.[19] Regardless of the reason, those in authority in the department strategically used my illness against me, betraying their commitment to me as a student. This was the first time I ever acknowledged that my mental illness stood in the way of my academic life. This is just one specific example among many that highlight my battle with university ableism in terms of mental disability: a student can be ill only for a limited time. I filed a human rights violation complaint with the university's ombudsman and the province's Human Rights Commission, but the ombudsman did not do his job correctly, and despite the commission official's agreement that the university had violated my human rights, the case fell to the side. Neither the ombudsman (strangely enough, a PhD in psychology), whose very raison d'être was to act for the student, nor the civil rights officer performed their functions as controls of discriminatory behaviors by institutions and authorities. Thus, the fight fell on me—the student—but I was too ill to carry through with the case on my own.[20] Clearly, there was no disability justice for me at that time.

19. I initially planned to take sick leave. However, my supervisor stressed that such leave could last only 365 days, after which I had to return as a full-time student, recovered or not. She suggested I withdraw from the program, which would require my reapplication once I was well. She informally assured me that I would be readmitted. Being ill, I believed her. Now I understand her intention was to remove a problem: me. I never received an official explanation of the rejection of my reapplication to the program. I can understand why in some disciplines a two-year absence might require some retraining and/or updating, but in the study of early modern literature two years is insignificant. The department had no academic reason that I should not be readmitted: my program was more than halfway complete, and I had been receiving merit scholarships up until I withdrew. With my application, I included a thesis statement and proposal that one committee member unofficially approved before submission. Maybe the department's graduate committee thought I was "insane," yet the department continued to let me teach. The reason for the rejection might have been entirely unrelated to me: many of the professors in the department were worried that if I succeeded, the Faculty of Graduate Studies and Research would force the department to introduce a permanent PhD program.

20. The model of disability in which the disabled person, rather than society, must change tends to be evident in paradigms that define people through dichotomous opposition.

I began my current doctoral program at a different university—one with an established PhD program—in 2014. Because I am what is medically referred to as "high achieving," I appear on paper in a positive light. My curriculum vitae (CV) does not seem to reflect a student struggling with mental illness: good grades; plenty of conference presentations, book chapters, and journal articles; membership in university, professional society, and community-service organizations. My CV does reflect a student with a mental illness because it is *my* CV, but it does not *betray* a student with mental illness. My academic record demonstrates that mental illness does not preclude satisfactory or even exemplary academic performance. And since I had already gotten to the proposal stage in my previous attempt, I had an impressive bibliography and a clear concept of what I wanted to examine. Thus, my acceptance into the program was not hindered by any obvious barriers other than my own fears and lack of confidence. But, for me, the acceptance was more a personal matter of reclaiming my intellectual standing—and keeping my mental illness secret.

But if chasing a PhD was supposed to bypass—or at least keep hidden—my mental illness, I was soon to learn that it did not. Each aspect of my program offered both positive and negative possibilities. Taking courses, I thought, would be easy—it was just coursework. After going to the first class, meeting the other doctoral students, and seeing the syllabus, I immediately felt the familiar fear that I was not up to the challenge. All of the students were younger than I—fresh, eager, excited, perhaps not even jaded yet. I had already lived a lot of my life, and I felt alienated, not because they intentionally alienated me but because we had nothing in common other than the courses. I also felt that they were so much closer to the material. Because I had been teaching first-year English for ten years and been immersed in early modern medical literature for my doctorate while mothering young children, I was unfamiliar with contemporary texts, newer genres such as graphic novels and anime, and new technological modes of creativity and criticism. I did my best playing catch-up, but my knowledge distance translated into my feelings of collegial distance and inadequacy.

I realized that my fears had overtaken me when I began panicking on every class day, hoping snow or something else would close the university;

I was fidgety and nervous, avoiding eye contact with the professor, and terrified that I would be called upon to answer; I was nauseated and made my rash patches bleed.[21] At forty-seven, I felt like a child. And when my first graded paper was returned to me, I realized that my fears were being translated into a stiffness in style, formulaic argumentation, and over-punctuation. However, there was a benefit to my mental illness. At one point, I asked my course mates how long they took to write term papers. On average, they spent two and a half weeks. I spent three days: one each for research, writing, and editing.

Despite my nagging self-doubt and insecurity, I made it to the stage of studying for my comprehensive exams. The comprehensive-exam phase of a doctoral degree in most literature departments in Canada is an ar-chaic form of torture that places a student in an artificial situation of try-ing to become familiar with a massive number of texts over a period of twelve months and responding to examiner's questions in three consecu-tive nightmares: three-hour written examinations on two consecutive days and on the third day a two-hour oral exam in front of four professors, with every text read for the entire year as fair game for questioning.[22] The pur-pose of this phase is to ensure the student's wide-reaching knowledge of the period's literature. However, the testing method is incompatible with any circumstance that one would encounter as an academic. I am baf-fled, for example, at the ridiculous expectation for a person to remember a specific line from a poem read once. During the year, I had occasional meetings with my supervisor. She would say, "Tell me about what you have read since we last met," and I would do so. At first, I felt like a bab-bling idiot, but near the end of the year I was fully able to demonstrate my familiarity with the texts of the period. At that time, I also met with each

21. I always have at least one stress rash somewhere on my body. The most obvious are those on my two elbows, so regardless of the temperature I wear long-sleeved clothing. When I was teaching in Canada, I often had these rashes on my eyelids and below my eyes or on my neck, so I sometimes began my lectures with, "Don't be afraid . . . I know I look horrible. And, no, it's not contagious."

22. I have advocated for a break of a day or two between the written and oral exams, but so far I have been unsuccessful. I would like to have the entire process overhauled.

of the examiners and spoke with them in a similar fashion. Given that I could fluently converse with these experts in my field, the conversations—particularly if I had had more with the examiners—would have proven my "worth" without the insanity of the exams. Even if each had asked me to write essays on a particular subject within the scope of the reading list, my knowledge would have been evident. There is absolutely no reason why universities cannot reconsider the methodology of comprehensive exams.

Beyond my fear of the exercise itself, the reading period was one of almost entire isolation: reading fourteen hours a day nearly every day for a year, I barely finished a reading list that included early modern English prose, drama, and poetry.[23] I almost completely removed myself from society, feeling that I needed every second to get through the materials—the task was all-consuming. I did not cook, shop, clean, bathe, or even get dressed except on the days I had to meet with professors. My cat took it upon herself to be both taskmaster and therapist, as animals tend to do. She would tell me when it was time to take a break, but she would also remind me when the break was over. She was the only one who shared my hours of work.[24] However, by the end of the studying period, I was at the point of being afraid to resocialize.

At the oral exam, I was so terrified that when the examiners asked me to read one of my written answers and suggest what I might change, I was unable to read. I was exhausted. I was sweating. If I had not been sitting, I would have fallen down. Three out of the four examiners judged me satisfactory, which meant I failed.[25] I was not surprised. During the exam,

23. I proudly mentioned to another doctoral student that I had just finished reading all the texts on my comps list. He laughed and suggested that most students do not read all the material.

24. Because I was the only student in the Department of English studying the early modern period at that time, I had no one with whom I could study. Similarly, a person studying, say, medieval literature would likely be a singleton.

25. From my perspective, some discrepancy exists in the rule about passing. Before my exam, the department indicated that to pass a student had to be given a satisfactory judgment by all four examiners. I was told later that a student needed only three of four, evidently a long-standing standard. So if, as I was told immediately after my oral examination, three examiners found me satisfactory, I should have passed—yet I did not. The

I could almost feel my mind turning on and off, like having an electrical short circuit. I was extremely calm when my supervisor told me I had to redo the oral exam in six months. I did not feel anything that day—I was too numb. The impact soon came with deep feelings of failure, self-loathing, and embarrassment. Then I was mad: not crazy but angry. I had worked harder on that preparation than on anything I had ever done before. I had shown my supervisor and two other experts that I knew my material. I was even working in my field already: teaching, publishing, and presenting conference papers, but on this *one* day. . . . All at once I realized that I was not the problem. The process was an institutional barrier based not on ability or knowledge but on unrealistic memory retention and retrieval, one of the most significantly affected abilities for people with mental illness.[26]

My preparation for the second oral was limited. I re-read a few texts. I organized the notes I had made. More than studying, I had to consider how I could ensure success.[27] The retrospective view of my failed oral actually empowered me. The examiner who had failed me was replaced owing to an unrelated circumstance, so I had not yet embarrassed myself in front of the fourth. Further, the second oral would not be preceded by two days of written exams, so I would not be as tired. But I had to find a way around the memory issue, a part of mental illness that I cannot hide. I realized I needed a medical accommodation. I questioned whether this was fair or a form of cheating, but knowing it was the only solution, I demanded one. My supervisor also felt as if she should have foreseen my anxiety—which I had been exhibiting since the start of this process—and not let me take the exams without the accommodation. Fortunately, the university, the faculty, and the department accepted my request to receive

---

department and my first supervisor—whom I had replaced—have silently deemed my reading of the situation a failure of my memory.

26. Mental illnesses and the medications prescribed for them cause a range of memory problems. Further, memory blockage is one of the body's most effective coping mechanisms, whether convenient or not, whether beneficial or not. In my case, I also have memory disruption from a head injury sustained in 2012.

27. Failure on the second exam meant expulsion from the program.

the exam questions twenty-four hours in advance.[28] The second go-round, I felt like an entirely different person—which one of the examiners noticed and mentioned. I was confident, assured, and intelligent, and I passed. I was not only able to answer the questions (I had not prepared answers in advance), but I could negotiate ensuing questions. Several years later, I asked some other students what they thought about my accommodation—I had been too embarrassed at the time. One stated that having been in classes with me, she did not realize I was ill and needed an accommodation. Perhaps my self-perception distorted my interpretation of others' perceptions of me. I also realized that perhaps my crazy was not showing as much as I thought.[29]

However, what ultimately allowed me to accept my need for a medical accommodation was my experience with students—and I cannot stress strongly enough how often this direction of education occurs and the extent of its necessity. Accommodations that I and the school made for them did not negatively affect my perception of them because I knew the legitimacy of the disabilities and the necessary adjustments. If the department and the university agreed that they needed the accommodation, then clearly the academy recognized, to some degree at least, that medical accommodations are necessary for some students. In retrospect, I ask: If a student requires a medical accommodation at the undergraduate level (or in grade school), why do we expect a student to "educate out of" this need in graduate school? Mental illness does not go away as one ages or learns, although it often changes. Surely, navigating higher degrees with personal challenges illustrates a student's adaptability, resilience, tenacity, skill, and ingenuity.

The dissertation research and writing provided another set of obstacles. Here I thought I had an edge because I had completed a great deal of research before I withdrew from my previous program. Unfortunately, I

---

28. By the time of my thesis defense, I realized that I was more deeply internalized, alienated, depressed, and out of control than ever before. However, I received a medical accommodation and successfully defended my dissertation in December 2022.

29. Being mentally ill, I am never sure whether I am acting "normally" or being paranoid.

found that relying on those materials was a mistake. Because of my deteriorating mental health at that time, the inaccuracy of those materials made them unusable. Again, I isolated myself with my computer and diligently researched more than four hundred early modern medical texts. Most of my communications with my supervisor were through email. The pattern of desocialization was beginning again. And that was when my mental illnesses began to take over. My isolation and growing paranoia made me want to refuse all teaching and research assistantships offered to me. Fortunately, sometimes I was in a "good" mood when the offer was made, and I accepted. For several months, I was completely convinced that my supervisor *hated* me—despite her constant willingness to recommend me for scholarships and support me in every venture. And for several months, I did no academic work at all until a colleague explained why I apparently did not want to finish my degree: I have a fear of success. I realize how ridiculous this sounds, but it made sense to me. If I finished my thesis, defended it, and graduated, what would I do then? Not only would I have to make changes to my life, but I would lose the security of my isolated world. Indeed, as I contemplated obtaining a medical accommodation for my thesis defense, I realized that I was more deeply internalized, alienated, depressed, and out of control than ever before. I am still struggling with these aspects of my illness.

Working Like Crazy

Perhaps those of us in literature departments have a different perspective on the Mad scholar discussion because we often analyze texts that confront human experience and characters who are mentally ill to varying degrees—consider love sickness in Juliet and her Romeo or the mad scientist Victor Frankenstein or the paranoid delusions of Tyler Durdon in *Fight Club*—and we tend to spend our professional lives working in fictive realms. And just as in the works we examine, we recognize a creative bent that softens the borders of crazy and thins the line between Madness and genius. Nevertheless, to confess to being mentally ill—like a stripping off of the academic regalia that makes one fit for peer review—is risky because academia, even as it contributes to disabled thought and action, is intellectually ableist.

I have been a practicing academic for a long time—I began teaching at the university level in 1989. In addition, I do research unrelated to my specialization fairly frequently and present conference papers on a regular basis.[30] However, I realize—as part of my anxiety about graduating—that work presents a real problem: I cannot work full-time because I am too tired; I still have days of complete incapacitation; I have limited periods during which I can function well; I still have panic attacks; I actually make myself physically ill when I contemplate interacting with other people on a professional level; I still occasionally have manic episodes during which I act inappropriately and embarrass myself. As I stated in a recent conference paper, "My brain tells me that I am inherently unlovable and worthless and that others know this about me. My brain tells me that I am a failure in every aspect of life and society" (Guenther 2018). Furthermore, as I search for employment opportunities and read the lists of qualifications, I quickly find myself feeling queasy. I would not hire a crazy, incompetent, and unreliable person, so why would anyone else?

Despite my academic achievements, my own Madness narrative, which has internalized academic sanism, tells me I am not worthy of scholarships, postdoctoral fellowships, or employment because I am mentally ill. When I was in the sciences, I would never have dared to suggest I had a mental illness, yet there was some room for acceptance of the mad scientist or nutty professor—or perhaps "the eccentric." In literature, there is definitely a place for those who study weird texts or niche areas and for the belief that mainstream culture is a negative creative space. Perhaps in those caricature images of scientists and bookworms, I see myself as fitting in. And I am aware of signs of mental illness in literary characters, students, and colleagues in ways that, I hope, make me more humane. But I have to accept that I can do only what I can do.[31] And that is part of

---

30. One of the reasons for researching and writing outside of my own field is that I find it less frightening, and so my thoughts and actions more easily function. As for conferences, I use them as a sort of renewal—I can be a different person, a person who is not mentally ill, when I am away from home.

31. However, my family physician has provided me with a positive lens through which to view the undeniable fact that I can do intellectual work only about five or so

Mad resistance—I am not going to drive myself crazy to fit into what an academic is supposed to be, act, or think like. I can break institutional barriers through stoic silence, stony resistance, and self-care. Further, in telling my narrative in various fora, I can express my resistance to the medical model of scholarship that denies my capability because I have an illness.

Conclusion

On its website, UNICEF (2021) states that the United Nations Convention on the Rights of Persons with Disabilities (CRPD) is a legally binding international agreement by countries to help ensure children and adults with disabilities enjoy the same rights as others and are treated fairly and with respect (par. 1). For me, as a student, an academic, and a Mad activist I see several major ways I can contribute to the foregrounding of the need for such a framework within university culture. As a mentally ill person, I am open and loud about my challenges, a shift in my voice and action that has arisen out of sheer desperation: when a person feels there is nothing left to lose, failure does not present a significant threat. Fear is weaker than misery, especially when that misery leads to suicidal ideation. For my own survival, I need to make my voice heard, demand shifts in policy and culture, and inspire others to do the same. John Donne exclaimed during his own fight with self-homicide that we must "deliver ourselves from the tyranny of this prejudice" against people with mental illness ([1608] 1982, 26). As a literary critic, I am self-conscious about the cultural and academic narratives of mental illness, and my voice adds to the rewriting of those texts.

Further, I am aware of the situations that university students at all levels face. I can build disability studies and mental health awareness into my basic pedagogical practices—particularly in the literary texts I

---

days a month now. She claims that I can accomplish so much in those days that if I could do the same thing all month, it would be unfair to "normal" people. As silly as this might sound, there is a kernel of truth here. I could research, absorb material, and write faster than any other graduate student in my department. That was my payoff—I knew I had a limited space of wellness in which I needed to complete tasks, so I did them in a somewhat manic (or expedient) way.

choose—not only by opening the conversation and implementing practical solutions but by illustrating the benefit of Madness as a creative force and as a different perspective of understanding. As for doctoral studies, many of my friends who are in or who have just finished PhD programs tell me one has to go Mad because part of the program is surviving mental torture by one's own mind and by the system that lacks any understanding of what it is doing to people.[32] Intellectually, we know this "go Mad" theory is bunk.[33] We need to destabilize forced definitions of academic capability not only to provide a healthy institution and equity but also to include the various processes of resilience, strength, and creativity that people with mental illness live and experience.[34]

Works Cited

American Psychiatric Association. 2013. *Diagnostic and Statistical Manual of Mental Disorders (DSM–V)*, 5th ed. Arlington, VA: American Psychiatric Association.

Arsenault, Jane [Shawna Guenther]. 2020. *Crazy Little Thing Called Mom*. N.p.: Self-published. Kindle.

Donne, John. [1608] 1982. *Biathanatos*. Edited by Michael Rudick and M. Pabst Battin. New York: Garland.

Gilbert, Sandra, and Susan Gubar. 1979. *The Madwoman in the Attic: The Woman Writer and the Nineteenth-Century Literary Imagination*. New Haven, CT: Yale Univ. Press.

Guenther, Shawna. 2018. "Renegotiating Utopia: Where Is the New Harmony for the Marginalized?" Paper presented at the Utopia Studies Society (Europe) Conference, Tarragona, Spain, July.

---

32. Price also acknowledges that "how we learn, how we work to develop new ideas that point toward a better society for all" is mandatory in academia (2011, 8).

33. Although I am intellectually aware that I can change my own narrative, enacting that change is still, even after twenty-five years of psychotherapy, extremely challenging.

34. The disability justice movement covers a number of physical, mental, and emotional disabilities. Its praxis, however, overlaps Mad activism: defining mental illness under the umbrella term *disability* is a significant advance in recognizing mental illness as a medical illness and, more specifically, a medical illness that is truly disabling.

Kafai, Shayda, and Melanie Jones. 2019. "Mad Scholars Anthology Call for Papers." At https://call-for-papers.sas.upenn.edu/cfp/2019/07/20/mad-scholars-anthology.

Pickens, Therí Alyce. 2019. *Black Madness :: Mad Blackness.* Durham, NC: Duke Univ. Press.

Price, Margaret. 2011. *Mad at School: Rhetorics of Mental Disability and Academic Life.* Ann Arbor: Univ. of Michigan Press.

Samuels, Ellen. 2017. "Passing, Coming Out, and Other Magical Acts." In *Negotiating Disability: Disclosure and Higher Education*, edited by Stephanie L. Kerschbaum, Laura T. Eisenman, and James M. Jones, 15–24. Ann Arbor: Univ. of Michigan Press.

UNICEF. 2021. "About [the *Convention on the Rights of Persons with Disabilities (CRPD)*]. Malé, Maldives: UNICEF. At https://www.unicef.org/maldives/documents/convention-rights-persons-disabilities-crpd.

Valle, Jan W., Santiago Solis, Donna Volpotta, and David J. Conner. 2004. "The Disability Closet: Teachers with Learning Disabilities Evaluate the Risks and Benefits of Coming Out." *Equity and Excellence in Education* 37, no. 1: 4–17. At https://doi.org/10.1080/10665680490422070.

Wolframe, PhebeAnn M. 2013. "The Madwoman in the Academy, or, Revealing the Invisible Straitjacket: Theorizing and Teaching Saneism and Sane Privilege." *Disability Studies Quarterly* 33, no. 1. At https://doi.org/10.18061/dsq.v33i1.3425.

World Health Organization. 2019. "World Mental Health Day 2019." Oct. 10. At https://www.who.int/news-room/events/detail/2019/10/10/default-calendar/world-mental-health-day-2019-focus-on-suicide-prevention.

———. 2022. *Mental Disorders.* Geneva: World Health Organization. At https://www.whoint/news-room/fact-sheets/detail/mental-disorders.

3

Complaint as a Maddening Practice

Moving through the University as a Mad Grad Student

Rebecca-Eli M. Long

Content notes: gender-based violence, verbal violence,
abusive behavior, sexual violence

Meeting Up with Madness

I left what was at least the fifth meeting in the past week, this time with a caseworker in the Dean of Students Office. *I am a case to be managed,* I joked with my friends. It was an acknowledgment of how I felt as if I had become a problem, the solution to which could allegedly be located in one of the many institutional offices I had visited. Somewhat of an intractable problem, given that meetings with my adviser, the Disability Resource Office, the university ombudsman, and an associate dean, along with one desperate walk-in "crisis" appointment to the counseling center, had not accomplished anything except to create more meetings. Instead of my complaining about a problem, the situation morphed into my becoming the problem. I was now a case. Probably a red flag on some university monitoring system.

I had ended up at the Dean of Students Office exhausted but vaguely hopeful that this would be the meeting that finally accomplished something. My anxiety was swirling as I fidgeted with the phone-cord bracelet around my wrist. I tried not to think about the last time I was in this office, during my first year of undergrad, when I had been asked to come in to discuss my seemingly chronic suicidal ideation. Now, as a graduate student, I thought things might be different. I moved through university spaces much more smoothly these days. There had just been a little bump on the road: a professor whose class I no longer felt safe attending.

The caseworker outlined my options. I could talk to the professor involved, technically the first step in most complaint procedures. *But I don't feel safe doing that. How am I supposed to tell the professor that I think his behavior is inappropriate when he yelled at me the last time I was in his office?* Then you can try to talk to the department chair. *He wants me to follow the procedure by meeting with the faculty member first. Besides, I don't really trust him not to defend his faculty and his department.* You could hang in there; classes end in a few weeks. *I'm having panic attacks at the very thought of going near the building.* Well, then you could take a psychological withdrawal and drop the class. *Then I'd have to pay another semester's tuition. Besides, I'm passing the class. I don't think my mental health is what's causing the problem here.* As it became clear that no good course of action would be offered, I became withdrawn and reticent, my answers dwindling to just a couple of words. In the end, I received some platitudes about how the university was there to support me and a printout of anxiety self-help resources.

I took the bus across campus back to my office. I laughed so I wouldn't cry. I texted pictures of the self-help tips to my friends, who agreed that a reading list and smartphone apps wouldn't solve anything. Among the resources was the suggestion to utilize the counseling center, which had referred me to the Dean of Students Office in the first place and had a well-established history of providing inadequate services to students (Long and Stabler 2022). Particularly insulting was the suggestion of mindfulness because I was already acutely aware of what was going on. I knew I had been dismissed and was seen as irrational. The rift between my story of what was going on and university officials' story was insurmountable. I was angry. I was crazy. I was Mad.

Framing Complaint

According to Elizabeth Brewer, "Coming out as mad, rather than mentally ill, makes a statement about how one views their experience and the nature of mental difference" (2018, 16). I first claimed Madness out of anger. That is, I was Mad in multiple meanings of the word. Like Margaret Price (2011), I was "mad at school"—both a Mad person existing in academic spaces and someone who was deeply angry with systemic processes of higher education that fail to live up to claims of diversity and inclusion. My Madness and coming to identify as Mad were intertwined with the process of complaint. In this chapter, I build on Sara Ahmed's (2021) work on complaint as feminist pedagogy to discuss from a Mad perspective the difficulties—and the possibilities—of complaining.

Positions of Madness and disability complicate the already complicated process of complaint. Mad individuals are denied the ability to be legitimate knowers because our attempts to represent ourselves can be reduced to disordered symptoms of mental illness (Liegghio 2013). My efforts to complain became a symptom of my disabilities, not an indication of the ableism I encountered. Because of the difficulty of representing myself in the complaint process, I turn here to autoethnography, seeking to tell stories that show the social complexities in concrete moments of lived experience (Ellis 2004). This chapter could also be characterized as "autistethnography" (Grace 2013), a genre that shows how autistic people reclaim narrative authority in telling our stories (see Van Goidsenhoven 2017). These vignettes, a concatenation of my time as an undergraduate student and my experiences in graduate school, situate my education within a larger conversation among those in the margins who search for new pathways in and through academia.[1]

If Madness matters in academic practice (Church 2013), then the ways in which we come to identify with Madness also matter.[2] Though I

---

1. Both complaint and autoethnography are risky. I write this chapter knowing that these are things I am not supposed to write about. I have been cautioned against such public disclosure. However, "that there is so much pressure not to complain tells us something about what complaint can do" (Ahmed 2021, 286). I take these risks hoping that Madness can create a space to tell truths that otherwise go ignored and to contribute to projects of imagining other ways of studying together, outside and within the limited pathways of higher education (Meyerhoff 2019).

2. Here, Kathryn Church details developing a Mad studies component to the university curriculum and how this component affected activities and relationships across the university.

had previously identified as neurodivergent and disabled, this complaint process was the first time I felt a sense of familiarity with *Madness* as a self-descriptor. I "came out" as Mad in an actual closet, which had been converted into my campus office.

Rather than viewing Madness as an immutable fact of my neurology or as a simple result of living in a sanist society, I approach it through Rosemarie Garland-Thomson's concept of "misfitting" to describe a more complex interaction in which mental divergence and the social world co-create each other. Garland-Thomson uses misfitting to "elaborate a materialist feminist understanding of disability by extending a consideration of how the particularities of embodiment interact with their environment in its broadest sense, to include both its spatial and temporal aspects" (2011, 592). Such an approach moves far beyond a deficit approach to mental difference or disability, instead positioning Madness as a generative force. The friction of misfitting allows Madness and complaint to become a form of resistance.

Complaint is about experiencing the world differently, perhaps differently than you should if the university were to truly live up to its promises of diversity and inclusion. Complaint attempts to bring attention to the more subtle dimensions of misfitting. The domain of complaint is primarily affective, relying on feelings of frustration, compassion, and grief. The process of the complaint wears you down, likely by design, using "exhaustion as a management tool" (Ahmed 2021, 93). Yet I contend that complaint also offers a Mad tactic for building collective knowledge and imagining the university otherwise.

Care and Constraint

When the caseworker handed me the sheet of self-help anxiety-coping strategies, I was reminded of the facile nature of the university support system and all the perfunctory let-me-know-if-there's-anything-I-can-do-to-help-yous. As people in those meetings told me to reach out if I needed anything, I flashed back to my first year as an undergrad, when I learned how empty the university's promises of care were. By the end of my first semester, I had been labeled a "care and concern" issue precisely because I did as I was instructed and reached out for help.

My transition into college was rocky. The downward spiral once I arrived on campus was predictable yet unpredicted. I reached out to my roommates, academic advisers, and the dorm's resident assistants for support. More often than not, each request for help ended up with an after-hours call to the school's counseling center and on one memorable occasion an involuntary trip to the campus police station—all of which was meticulously documented in my student record without my knowledge.

Care became a disciplinary tool. I was referred repeatedly to the counseling center, even though staff refused to offer me even the standard ten sessions per academic year because of my preexisting diagnostic labels. The most help they provided was a list of off-campus mental health professionals who might take my insurance. Despite messages on the flyers posted in the hallway of my dorms, claiming in bold letters that my school cared, I was skeptical. Instead of providing meaningful care, referrals to the counseling center's care were nothing more than an expansion of the "barely acknowledged zone of quasi-psychiatric surveillance, risk assessment, and preventive intervention" that extends from the classroom to other facets of student life (Reiss 2010, 27). Student support services, which frame mental distress and disability as "crises," rely on rhetorics of resilience that attempt to discipline individuals rather than address structural injustices (Aubrecht 2012).

Care, as the university enacts it, is also coercion. Because the university had a record of just how much it "cared" about me, the dean of students threatened to expel me for being a drain on university resources. Similarly, the Disability Resource Office decided that this record was evidence that my accommodations were not effective and could therefore justifiably be revoked. In such situations, "care" is a threatening practice that glosses over a paucity of institutional support. In my first year of college, I learned that care masked threats. As a graduate student, I have now learned that care becomes a way to perpetually deflect complaints and further the exclusion of Mad bodyminds.

Complaining While Mad

The circumstances leading up to a complaint often become clear only in hindsight. I had long been familiar with academic ableism, but this particular spring semester of graduate school was worse than usual, pushing me closer to understanding the sanist ways in which the academy operates. I made routine trips to the Disability Resource Office to complain about the inaccessibility of campus infrastructure and professors' attitudes, including when a professor in a community-development course presented "mental disability" as a threat to community well-being. As the semester moved on, my experiences escalated from frustrating to unbearable as I realized the environment of my research methods class was deeply hostile to my bodymind.

It took time for me to trust myself. I had learned to see myself the same way as university administrators: anxious, uncertain, and even a liability. Over the coming weeks, classroom interactions that could at first be brushed aside as a professor's peculiarities formed a broader pattern as my access requests were repeatedly blocked and met with verbal violence. My friends and even other professors in the department confirmed that I should do something, but no one was sure what path I should take. As I navigated my way through policy documents and eventually met with administrators, the instances of discrimination that mattered most to me were dismissed, while university officials latched onto happenings that I thought to be unimportant.

My complaint was dissected. The Disability Office supposedly cared about implementing academic accommodations but did little to enforce them or address concerns of bias. Bias or harassment was not seen as an access issue. Some offices, such as that of the ombudsman or dean of students, seemed to exist only to excise particular facts and redirect me to more offices. They cared about locating a single instance of injustice or at least assuring themselves that whatever I experienced wasn't enough for me to claim gender-based discrimination. Sexual misconduct and gender-based violence are often notoriously swept under the rug, yet they also seemed to be the litmus test for the baseline validity of a complaint. On some days, I hoped there would be enough evidence to lodge a Title IX grievance because at least then there would be a clear path forward.

I found I didn't have the words to explain my visceral reaction to traumatic memories raised by my experiences that left me lying on the floor for entire afternoons, unable to write. My past experiences were not sufficient proof that I knew what abusive behavior feels like. In diagnostic language, I'm prone to intense and inappropriate emotions, but what is the appropriate response to inappropriate circumstances? The appropriate options for engagement were limited in ways that pathologized and excluded my Mad bodymind. The available pathways for reporting a complaint replicated existing institutional biases that prioritize so-called rationality, verbal dialogue, and narrow avenues for reaching what the university considered a "solution," all of which were separated from power dynamics and bodymind differences that made these practices untenable.

As I attempted an appeal to the rationality of the university, I began to suspect that behaving reasonably is part of what had gotten me into this situation in the first place. I made the mistake of assuming that this professor's classroom would be a space that challenged institutional norms, but as I moved through the complaint process against him, I learned that we were supposed to talk about justice only in a theoretical sense. In the first half of the semester, we read Linda Tuhiwai Smith's *Decolonizing Methodologies* (2012). I latched onto ideas of survivance (Vizenor 2008) and testimonio (Beverly 2004) as methods—methods that I employ here.[3] As this professor lectured at length about how academia is complicit in producing hegemonic forms of positivist knowledge, he seemed unaware of how his abusive tactics in the classroom reproduced these norms, creating the circumstances for my complaint. In my final paper, I got a shred of bitter pleasure out of reminding him that "decolonization isn't a metaphor" (Tuck and Yang 2012, 3).

I also noted the value of disabled people taking up space. This statement emerged organically when I was writing up my ethnographic observations

---

3. The term *survivance* is the combination of *survival* and *resistance* and indicates survival as a form of resistance. Testimonio is a Latin American literary method for making sense of collective oppression. I find these Indigenous, decolonial methods especially generative for working against the hegemonic power of the university and critiquing a curriculum that gives these concepts only lip service. Though colonialism and ableism are connected, I am not conflating these forms of oppression and acknowledge the privilege I have as a white settler, currently writing on Cherokee land.

on disability-service spaces. Yet it also applied to my experience in the class, where I was both physically and rhetorically denied space. When I told the university ombudsman about being asked to sit separately from the class, he replied, with no irony whatsoever, *So the professor doesn't give you a seat at the table?* My adviser had to explain why I started laughing at this statement, a common metaphor for inclusion. If the table represents sanism and ableism, I don't want a part of it, anyway, though it would have aided my notetaking. Complaint teaches us about how spaces are occupied and who is expected to occupy them.

As I moved through such meetings, I learned I was expected to provide the solution to my own complaint. Furthermore, my complaint was valid only if it was ultimately actionable. The only solution I could suggest was using my accommodation that permitted extra absences for "disability-related reasons" so that I could skip class for the rest of the semester. Though I also asked that potential disciplinary action toward the professor be considered, I have no doubt that my complaint ended up being filed away. I'm not even sure if the professor read my final paper, if my "A" in the class reflected my work, or if the department wished to avoid a grade appeal—a way of silencing future complaints from a student now designated "the problem." Responses to complaints are often less about reparative action and more about inaction, silencing, and misdirection. In cases of Mad complaint, scrutiny can only too easily be turned back on the complainer through networks of care and surveillance.

The Work of Complaint

Complaint is part of the broader complex of diversity work. It is an endlessly frustrating and often fruitless process, yet it is also a tactic that I turned to when the more conventional practices of what the neoliberal university euphemistically terms "self-advocacy" failed to effect meaningful change. I found complaint to be especially potent from a Mad perspective because it exemplifies Ahmed's claim that "diversity work is hard because what you come against is not revealed to others" (2017, 138). This effort is a double-bind: we approach diversity work from our own position of lived difference, but our difference also hinders the efficacy of any attempts to enact change. Our very presence provokes the need for shifts in how universities operate, yet despite having developed extensive knowledge of higher education through having to navigate it, we are rendered as unreliable witnesses to our own experiences. Nevertheless, for all its pitfalls, complaining keeps us from being ignored and continually generates resistance against the sanist university by reminding others how things could be different. Even as the university tries to push me out, I guest-lecture about disability justice, lead student groups, and meet with administrators to suggest ways in which the university could be different. These forms of politicized labor are often catalyzed through complaint.

While the inherent sanism of academia will likely continue, I hope for a future with what Mia Mingus (2011) terms "access intimacy"—that illusive feeling where someone "gets" your access needs. In practices of complaint, access intimacy would mean not having to explain why certain actions are harmful, why your communication style may vary from day to day, or why the labor of complaining while also trying to keep up with graduate education is so enormous. I am encouraged by those who build Mad access intimacy, including my fellow contributors to this volume. I am also encouraged by the undergraduate students who echoed my complaints about this professor the following semester as well as by the classmate who read a draft of this chapter and affirmed my experiences. Complaints can be how we come to form "collectives that keep us going" (Ahmed 2021, 282). As we reconceptualize what academia might look like, I contend we need to pay close attention to the spaces of "support" services, such as advising, disability resources, conflict mediation, and student affairs. They will not truly offer support until they engage with Mad experiences within the university.

For Mad scholars, the difficulties of self-representation are immense. As long as our experiences are doubted and pathologized, we cannot truly participate in academic communities. In this chapter, I have provided an autistethnography as a counternarrative to emphasize the ways in which Mad complaints are made illegitimate. It draws attention to how Madness is managed in academia: not only in the classroom but also through networks of referral and surveillance that discipline, limit, and misdirect Mad complaints.

Works Cited

Ahmed, Sara. 2017. *Living a Feminist Life*. Durham, NC: Duke Univ. Press.

————. 2021. *Complaint!* Durham, NC: Duke Univ. Press.

Aubrecht, Katie. 2012. "The New Vocabulary of Resilience and the Governance of University Student Life." *Studies in Social Justice* 6, no. 1: 67–83. At https://doi.org/10.26522/ssj.v6i1.1069.

Beverly, John. 2004. *Testimonio: On the Politics of Truth*. Minneapolis: Univ. of Minnesota Press.

Brewer, Elizabeth. 2018. "Coming Out Mad, Coming Out Disabled." In *Literatures of Madness: Disability Studies and Mental Health*, edited by Elizabeth J. Donaldson, 11–30. London: Palgrave Macmillan.

Church, Kathryn. 2013. "Making Madness Matter in Academic Practice." In *Mad Matters: A Critical Reader in Canadian Mad Studies*, edited by Brenda A. LeFrançois, Robert Menzies, and Geoffrey Reaume, 181–94. Toronto: Canadian Scholars' Press.

Ellis, Caroline. 2004. *The Ethnographic I: A Methodological Novel about Autoethnography*. Walnut Creek, CA: Left Coast Press.

Garland-Thomson, Rosemarie. 2011. "Misfits: A Feminist Materialist Disability Concept." *Hypatia* 26:591–609. At https://www.jstor.org/stable/23016570.

Grace, Elizabeth. 2013. "Autistethnography." In *Both Sides of the Table: Autoethnographies of Educators Learning and Teaching with/in [Dis]ability*, edited by Phil Smith, 89–102. New York: Peter Lang.

Liegghio, Maria. 2013. "A Denial of Being: Psychiatrization as Epistemic Violence." In *Mad Matters: A Critical Reader in Canadian Mad Studies*, edited by Brenda A. LeFrançois, Robert Menzies, and Geoffrey Reaume, 122–29. Toronto: Canadian Scholars' Press.

Long, Rebecca-Eli M., and Albert Stabler. 2022. "'This Is NOT Okay': Building a Creative Collective against Academic Ableism." *Journal of Curriculum and Pedagogy* 19, no. 4: 288–314. At https://doi.org/10.1080/15505170.2021.1926374.

Meyerhoff, Eli. 2019. *Beyond Education: Radical Studying for Another World*. Minneapolis: Univ. of Minnesota Press.

Mingus, Mia. 2011. "Access Intimacy: The Missing Link." *Leaving Evidence* (blog), May 5. At https://leavingevidence.wordpress.com/2011/05/05/access-intimacy-the-missing-link/.

Price, Margaret. 2011. *Mad at School: Rhetorics of Mental Disability and Academic Life*. Ann Arbor: Univ. of Michigan Press.

Reiss, Benjamin. 2010. "Madness after Virginia Tech." *Social Text* 28, no. 4: 25–44. At https://doi.org/10.1215/01642472-2010-009.

Smith, Linda Tuhiwai. 2012. *Decolonizing Methodologies: Research and Indigenous Peoples.* 2nd ed. London: Zed.

Tuck, Eve, and K. Wayne Yang. 2012. "Decolonization Is Not a Metaphor." *Decolonization: Indigeneity, Education & Society* 1, no. 1: 1–40. At https://resolver.scholarsportal.info/resolve/19298692/v01i0001/nfp_dinam.xml.

Van Goidsenhoven, Leni. 2017. "'Autie-biographies': Life Writing Genres and Strategies from an Autistic Perspective." *Journal of Language, Literature, and Culture* 64, no. 2: 79–95. At https://doi.org/10.1080/20512856.2017.1348054.

Vizenor, Gerald. 2008. *Survivance: Narratives of Indigenous Presence.* Lincoln: Univ. of Nebraska Press.

4

Rest as Feminist Disability Praxis, or How to Write While Flaring, Depressed, and Totally Burned Out

Jess L. Wilcox Cowing

> *Content notes*: misogynoir, anti-Black racism, suicidality, self-harm

In November 2019, before the COVID-19 pandemic would shift white-collar work life to virtual interfaces, I interviewed on Zoom for a job I would never get. From the top of a dusty stairwell in my apartment building, I talked to a committee who eagerly asked about my research interventions and quoted directly from my writing sample. I made eye contact. I remembered to ask prescripted questions about their program. I demonstrated my preparedness by referencing information I clearly acquired from scouring their department's webpage. They assured me that they protect the time of their junior colleagues. I wanted desperately to be someone's junior colleague.

By May 2020, my November interview prep seemed as if it had occurred in a different lifetime. My experience, like that of so many other applicants interviewing for jobs that never come, now seemed surreal—almost as if it hadn't quite happened.[1] I considered composing a poem from

---

I thank Elayne Otstot for editorial support. I also thank Lydia X. Z. Brown, for whom there will never be enough thank yous.

1. Sabrina Orah Mark's essay "Fuck the Bread. The Bread Is Over" (2020) offered a way for me to write about my experience in navigating the job market at the beginning of the pandemic.

lines of rejection emails piling up in my inbox. *We received/Best wishes with/an unprecedented number of/the future/excellent applications such as yours.* I calculated my budget to see how long the tail end of a $25,000 fellowship stipend could last. If I continued eating two meals a day as I had trained myself to do for the past five years, could I make it until September before I had nothing left except debt? I typed in an email intended for my adviser: "Do you have any advice for how to finish a dissertation when you can't get out of bed?" I deleted it and sent instead: "Do you have any advice for how to finish a dissertation in the middle of a global pandemic?" They did not.

Graduate students, precariously employed instructors, and early-career researchers are deeply susceptible to the ableist pressures of academic productivity. They are also the least likely to have the resources to navigate those expectations without serious costs to their mental and physical health, even as they shoulder the additional responsibilities of mentorship and taking on additional classes. Professional development, including spending uncompensated time on writing projects and conference organizing, teaches graduate students early that being employable in an absurdly competitive job market requires doing endless unpaid labor at the cost of your research and your well-being. Moreover, academia is also an identity profession. You *are* an academic. And academic identity is based largely on adhering to, or at least being perceived to adhere to, the expectation that academics are simultaneously putting all of their energy into teaching, researching, university service work, and conference presentations to demonstrate their value and "success," without ever taking a break.[2] These experiences have been normalized as the expected costs of participating in academic life even as Mad and neurodivergent people have been pathologized for claiming exhaustion and depression as everyday lived experiences.

Thinking with feminist disability theory, this chapter examines Mad and crip explorations of rest as a way to disavow ableist cultures of academia that normalize burnout and pathologize those who dare to discuss

---

2. Margaret Price writes, "The notion of collegiality itself is regularly defined against mental disability" (2011, 114).

its manifestations. "Burnout" refers to a range of experiences such as exhaustion, depression, difficulty focusing and managing multiple tasks, and even a kind of apathy that stems from significant overwhelm. One of the most insidious aspects of academic burnout is that it affects *everyone*, but there is an unspoken norm to never acknowledge its effects on your ability to function in public—your breakdowns and inconsistencies should occur on your own time and at home. As feminist disability scholars have argued, neoliberal wellness initiatives have harnessed burnout to displace the harm of structural inequities and place the burden instead on individual people to bear for their own inclusion and survival.[3] In other words, academia as it is currently structured thrives on burnout as an expected cost of professional development.

I draw on my personal experience living with and self-accommodating a chronically ill and neurodivergent bodymind to argue for frameworks of care that intervene in the violence of ableist productivity standards. Writing in the wake of a PhD diploma conferral that felt anything but celebratory after the COVID-19 pandemic caused mass layoffs and hiring freezes, effectively collapsing the academic job market, I join feminist disability writers in foregrounding rest as a life-sustaining practice. Only through reclaiming our right to rest and rejecting burnout as a point of pride can we imagine more survivable and expansive conceptualizations of meaningful ways to work and live under capitalism.

Institutionalizing Burnout as an Academic Norm

Before the COVID-19 pandemic exacerbated the pressures put on graduate students in an already nonexistent job market, it had long become commonplace to see articles about the "alarming" and "epidemic" rates of depression and anxiety among graduate students. An article in *Inside Higher Ed* titled "Mental Health Crisis for Graduate Students" in 2018 cites a study that reveals 39 percent of graduate student respondents across disciplines and institutions reported having clinically significant depression

---

3. For more on crip time and a critique of how medical models impose linear time on disabled people, see Alison Kafer, "Time for Disability Studies and a Future for Crips" (2013).

in the "moderate to severe depression range," compared to only 6 percent in the general population (Flaherty 2018). The early-career researchers and graduate students I know would sometimes text these articles to each other with accompanying commentary along the lines of "Yeah, no shit."

One of the primary manifestations of academic burnout for me has been a depth of exhaustion that affects my ability to manage any kind of task associated with inquiry and communication—not just in academia but in all realms of life, including correspondence such as email (even to family members), writing and drafting abstracts (or even life updates), reading any long-form text (even in popular media), and writing with expected levels of complex thinking and organization. Burnout means that I can complete only one or two solid work-related tasks a day, and I will spend a whole week working up to writing a few paragraphs. As a recent graduate who has been on the job market, I am constantly expected to provide evidence of my teaching effectiveness and my ability to manage multiple projects. How do I convince a committee that I can manage their research projects or be a viable candidate for tenure when the reality is it took me a whole week to revise and update a cover letter for my application? As Margaret Price (2011) demonstrates, the very structures of academia are hostile to disabled and neurodivergent scholars, whose ways of thinking and working are perceived as slow and unproductive. And burnout only intensifies this perception of neurodivergent people as slow because it makes already Mad, disabled, chronically ill, and neurodivergent scholars seem even slower.

According to the World Health Organization, burnout is "an occupational phenomenon" but not "a medical condition" and occurs as a result of "chronic workplace stress that has not been successfully managed" (2019, par. 1). Yet this clinical definition emphasizes burnout as the result of improper "management," further reinforcing harmful assertions that burnout can (and should) be prevented by individual people if they only try hard enough. The advice that graduate students typically receive— from their programs, writing centers, advisers, workshops, and writing handbooks—typically tells them to build a routine, keep to that routine, and write every day. Work. Every. Day. Disabled writers have long critiqued this advice. "I hate the idea that you must write every day because I really can't do that," Keah Brown states. "Sometimes the aching bones in my body will not allow it" (2018, par. 5). The culture of hyperproductivity in academia does not allow for the nuances and realities of living in a disabled bodymind that Brown points out. Like most graduate students, I felt as though I should be working all the time to catch up to an arbitrary standard that few are able to reach. Despite my investment in feminist disability studies, I spent most of graduate school internalizing ableist standards of productivity, first by identifying my fatigue and anxiety as the problem and then acting according to what I thought would transform me into a better writer, a smarter thinker, an affable junior colleague. I expended an overwhelming amount of energy training myself to adhere to models of what other people called "being engaged and productive." The training never quite worked because eventually I would flare and be unable to type for days or weeks at a time without pain at every keystroke.[4] My depression would bring my momentum to a halt. There was no one particular moment that forced me to reconsider how I worked. It happened quietly, sometime after I moved to a different city and put a geographical distance between my address and campus. What emerged after a busy fall of conferences and chapter revisions was a persistent question: Why are we made to feel that we have to do things this way?

Embracing Crip Time

The structures of academia that normalize burnout necessitate a cultural and institutional shift, building on the work of Black, queer and trans, disabled, and other minoritized scholars of color who have sustained its most harmful impacts. My experience of burnout is hardly an anomaly. In fact, it is so crushingly ordinary that whole corners of Twitter, Reddit, and Tumblr are dedicated to sharing strategies for survival, all because the world in which we live and work was never intended to contain people with nap schedules and depression weeks. In a discussion of how anti-Black racism and ableism target Black women in the academy, Moya Bailey writes: "My

---

4. I use variants of the term *flaring* here to refer to periods when the symptoms of my chronic illness intensify and disrupt or totally upend my usual day-to-day activities.

overworking and overproduction prove necessary in a misogynoirist academic culture; however, the physical toll on my body and others like mine is palpable" (2017, par. 6).

Considering Bailey's critique of the impact of what she calls "misogynoirist academic culture" on Black women in the academy, the increasing pressures of the academic job market additionally place the burden on multiply marginalized academics to *do whatever it takes* to rearrange their lives for jobs that do not affirm their need for rest and life-sustaining care. I gradually began to shift the way I worked. The change began with acknowledging that I needed to rest before and after five days of conferencing. A friend who held a visiting assistant professor position told me that they blocked off most weekends for *not working*. I had never heard an academic friend or colleague even so much as suggest that possibility. "We can do that?" I remember asking. "Well, I just do it," they stated, a declaration that gave me permission to try. After coursework, when I had mostly shifted to writing and research at home, I started to deliberately embrace the time-honored disabled cultural practice of operating on crip time, or what Alison Kafer calls "a reorientation to time" (2013, 26). Put another way, I began to accept that I took longer to do things than nondisabled people. Kafer describes how crip time accounts for lived experience at tension with the ways in which the medical-industrial complex operates on linear, progressive time. For me, embracing crip time meant reading my bodymind and then acting accordingly.

In "Six Ways of Looking at Crip Time" (2017), Ellen Samuels reflects on crip time as a temporal portal for the grief that accompanies past selves and accumulated loss. Samuels writes about getting a PhD as a "solution" that, if it worked out, "was, and still is, the only way I could see to support myself in crip time" (2017, par. 18). Like Samuels, I often think that being an academic is the only way I can support myself with the flexibility to sleep in a way my bodymind insists, to take days and weeks off, and still belong to a community of thinkers and writers, even with the costs of burnout. Suspended in grief for the job market and anticipated loss to come, I would lie in my bed in between dissertation tasks and think, *Is this the only time in my life I will be able to work this way? What happens to me if I can't make it otherwise?* I was terrified of a future where I would have to sacrifice my bodymind needs to pay rent and care for my medical needs.

By the time Virginia was under a stay-at-home order at the end of March 2020, I had already been quarantining in my apartment in Richmond for more than three weeks. While others seemed to forge ahead with elaborate work-at-home routines they deemed a temporary respite from the demands of in-person schedules, I let myself be devastated, and I was. Like other disabled people in my life and on the internet, I had a sense that my world was about to be reordered in ways I could not yet predict but could sense acutely. Now, I cannot begin to count the ways my life lived in crip time had prepared me for quarantining at home. I also cannot begin to count the ways the pandemic has affected my professional life. A job market that dominated my thinking and working before COVID now feels like a job market that I pick up when I have time and then put away when I do not. The pandemic has laid bare all the unsustainable practices that prevent disabled people like me from working in the academy. At the same time, the pandemic has also revealed other avenues for organizing my life that may not have been available without its avalanche of disruptions. Unemployment prompted me to move in with another disabled friend, and our ways of working and caring for each other lifted me out of the worst parts of a depression that had set in before COVID-19 even started and worsened during the pandemic.

Rest Is Work, and That's Not a Contradiction

If I were honest about how I write and work, I would say that much of the time it looks like what we have been trained to recognize as not writing and not working.[5] I take a lot of naps. I sleep ten to twelve hours at a time when I am flaring, and I take two weeks to think about an essay before

---

5. Leah Lakshmi Piepzna-Samarasinha's book *Care Work: Dreaming Disability Justice* (2018) helped me to think about validating my own disabled experiences through contrasting them with how they "look like what abled people have been taught to think of as failure" (124). For more on writing and working from bed, see "Preface: Writing (with) a Movement from Bed" and "So Much Time Spent in Bed: A Letter to Gloria Anzaldúa on Chronic Illness, Coatlicue, and Creativity" in *Care Work*.

I write the first draft in forty-eight hours. I work in long, hyperfocused stints when I feel well and focused, and I take days and weeks off at a time to think and sleep. Leah Lakshmi Piepzna-Samarasinha's *Care Work: Dreaming Disability Justice* (2018) was the first text I read that validated my way of working and writing, sometimes from bed under a pile of ice packs, as a viable means of getting stuff done.

Feminist disability examinations of what Piepzna-Samarasinha calls "care work" and rest as work offer anti-ableist frameworks of care for disabled and neurodivergent academics. A feminist disability intervention into the insubstantial wellness models pervasive on college campuses names the subjectivities and Madness that scholars bring with them to campus and their academic work. On an episode of the *Imagine Otherwise* podcast, Aimi Hamraie explains what sustainability might mean when considering human capacity and limitations, especially during the COVID-19 pandemic: sustainability is "about being honest about our capacity and where we're at and honoring the limitations that we may face in terms of time and energy and just life and being alive in a time of a pandemic and being alive in capitalism" (Hannabach 2020). Hamraie's suggestion for academics to be more honest about our capacity and limitations in work is a needed intervention. At the same time, the ability to do so depends on existing hierarchies within academia. That is, the burden falls differentially on graduate students and multiply marginalized scholars to be honest about the amount of work they can take on and to what degree.

A more just concept of work in academia for precarious and minoritized Mad and neurodivergent scholars requires unpacking social and cultural assumptions about who deserves rest and who has access to restorative care. Tricia Hersey began her work with the Nap Ministry to "reframe rest" and "name sleep deprivation as a racial and social-justice issue" after her experience of profound exhaustion in graduate school. Hersey states: "I started sleeping all over campus. I was everywhere" (Hamblin and Wells 2020). Hersey's links between sleep and the historical extraction of labor from Black people resituates napping as a restorative practice that decenters overwork as the organizing principle for people's lives, especially for Black women, whom Hersey features in her writing and community art projects. Hersey's work is not explicitly an anti-ableist or disability-focused project, yet her theorization of rest as an anticapitalist intervention is in dialogue with the ways in which feminist disability scholars understand ableism as deeply imbricated with the legacies of enslavement and white supremacy.[6] For example, the Nap Ministry practices a framework of "rest as resistance" through acts such as the "Collective Napping Experience" that engage in radical acts of rest in places where we do and do not expect rest to happen, such as "parks" and "yoga studios" but also "churches" and "museums" (Nap Ministry n.d.). The Nap Ministry's Black feminist framework helps viewers and interlocutors recognize the continued legacies of racial oppression of Black people through the ways in which they have been historically and continue to be denied access to rest, even and especially through expectations to perform labor in social justice movement work (Hamblin and Wells 2020). Moreover, the Nap Ministry offers a pathway to imagine restful futures for everyone who sustains the harmful effects of racialized burnout within white-supremacist logics of ableist productivity.

Despite the devastations of the COVID-19 pandemic, it did force me to slow down—and ultimately to take a desperately needed break. By June 2020, I had no job prospects, and an apartment lease I could not afford to renew was about to run out. I switched my job search to almost exclusively nonacademic positions, and I slept. I moved in with a friend who helped me relearn how to cook and eat three meals a day and who later became family. I scaled down my workdays to only a couple of key tasks a day. An extended job search that had felt like a complete failure in June had begun to feel like a necessary pause by October. The process of initiating a cultural shift in academia toward access-centered work, toward capacious concepts of antiracist and anticolonial rest, necessarily begins with the least marginalized and most secure faculty. Only then will it be possible to extend the conditions of radical honesty to junior faculty and multiply marginalized academics as a practice without retribution and negative

6. For example, Talila "TL" Lewis defines ableism as "deeply rooted in anti-Blackness" (2020, par. 3). See also Sami Schalk's book *Bodyminds Reimagined: (Dis)ability, Race, and Gender in Black Women's Speculative Fiction* (2018) as well as Sami Schalk and Jina B. Kim's article "Integrating Race, Transforming Feminist Disability Studies" (2020).

consequences. My friend and colleague often asks people, "What would a more just world for you look like? What would access and justice look like for you?" (see L. Brown 2020). The academic world I dream of is one where the perspectives of Mad, disabled, and neurodivergent scholars engender meaningful engagement and change, where there are many ways of working well, including napping and taking two weeks off for flares and conference recovery.

A more just academic world would also look like a university administration that thinks first about protecting and supporting people instead of just reducing liability and like a separation of psychological counseling from university police to reimagine support and crisis as community issues, not punitive ones.[7] I imagine possibilities for chronically ill, Mad, and disabled people to transform academic institutions from sites that are merely survivable at best to ones that engender care. In that world, I dream of having Mad femmes, sick queers, and trauma survivors for university presidents, provosts, deans, and directors of student accessibility centers. In those positions, I want to see a trans dyke with scars on her wrists, and I want a person with a prescription for antidepressants or SSRI medication. I want a manic nonbinary femme who has been medically separated from college enrollment and had to skip class to beg for a ride to get three miles off campus to the closest therapist with a sliding-scale rate. I want a first-generation college student who failed half his freshman-year courses because he was doing care work for his bipolar mom. I want an anxious Black woman who naps in the library. I want an autistic international student who writes essays and answers emails only between midnight and 8:00 a.m. I want a transracial adoptee with a traumatic brain injury who had to learn how to appeal an insurance claim at the age of twenty-five. I want a sober trans man who has spent an entire semester between panic attacks and doing the bare minimum. I want a dyslexic butch for whom suicidality is rarely a crisis because that's just a Tuesday in February. I want

---

7. This concluding paragraph is informed by Zoe Leonard's poem originally written in 1992 under the title "I Want a Dyke for President" and published in 2006 as "I Want a President."

a chronically ill immigrant with attention deficit hyperactivity disorder who has had to question whether they should publish an essay or use identifying language in a public forum for fear that they will never get a job, will face retaliation from strangers on the internet, or will never be taken seriously as a rigorous scholar with a research agenda. But mostly I want to reconfigure what scholarly work (both the work we produce and the ways we function) might look like when we put access and care at the center without fear of repercussion and ask ourselves: How much can I actually do today? And what kind of care do I need?

Works Cited

Bailey, Moya. 2017. "Race and Disability in the Academy." *Sociological Review*, Nov. 9. At https://www.thesociologicalreview.com/race-and-disability-in-the -academy/.

Brown, Keah. 2018. "What Does It Mean to Be a Disabled Writer?" Interview by Alex Lu. *Electric Lit*, May 7. At https://electricliterature.com/what-does -it-mean-to-be-a-disabled-writer/.

Brown, Lydia X. Z. 2020. "Disabled Lives in Radical Imagination; Disability Justice in Freedom Work." Public talk for Fordham Univ. Department of English, Oct. 26.

Flaherty, Colleen. 2018. "Mental Health Crisis for Graduate Students." *Inside Higher Ed*, Mar. 6. At https://www.insidehighered.com/news/2018/03/06/new -study-says-graduate-students-mental-health-crisis.

Hamblin, James, and Katherine Wells. 2020. "Listen, You Are Worthy of Sleep." Interview of Tricia Hersey. *The Atlantic*, Apr. At https://www.theatlantic .com/health/archive/2020/04/you-are-worthy-of-sleep/610996/.

Hannabach, Cathy. 2020. "Aimi Hamraie on Sustainability and Disability Justice." Interview. *Imagine Otherwise* (podcast), Oct. At https://ideasonfire .net/121-aimi-hamraie/.

Kafer, Alison. 2013. "Time for Disability Studies and a Future for Crips." In *Feminist, Queer, Crip*, 25–46. Bloomington: Indiana Univ. Press.

Leonard, Zoe. 2006. "I Want a President." At https://www.lttr.org/journal/5/i-want -a-president.

Lewis, Talila "TL." 2020. "Ableism 2020: An Updated Definition." *Tu[r]ning into Self* (blog), Jan. 25. At https://www.talilalewis.com/blog/ableism-2020 -an-updated-definition.

Mark, Sabrina Orah. 2020. "Fuck the Bread. The Bread Is Over." *Paris Review*, May 7. At https://www.theparisreview.org/blog/2020/05/07/fuck-the-bread-the-bread-is-over/.

Nap Ministry. n.d. "About." At https://thenapministry.wordpress.com/about/.

Piepzna-Samarasinha, Leah Lakshmi. 2018. *Care Work: Dreaming Disability Justice.* Vancouver: Arsenal Pulp Press.

Price, Margaret. 2011. *Mad at School: Rhetorics of Mental Disability and Academic Life.* Ann Arbor: Univ. of Michigan Press.

Samuels, Ellen. 2017. "Six Ways of Looking at Crip Time." *Disability Studies Quarterly* 37, no. 3. At http://dx.doi.org/10.18061/dsq.v37i3.

Schalk, Sami. 2018. *Bodyminds Reimagined: (Dis)ability, Race, and Gender in Black Women's Speculative Fiction.* Durham, NC: Duke Univ. Press.

Schalk, Sami, and Jina B. Kim. 2020. "Integrating Race, Transforming Feminist Disability Studies." *Signs* 46, no. 1: 31–55. At https://doi.org/10.1086/709213.

World Health Organization. 2019. "Burn-Out an 'Occupational Phenomenon': International Classification of Diseases." May 28. At https://www.who.int/news/item/28-05-2019-burn-out-an-occupational-phenomenon-international-classification-of-diseases.

5

Diary of a Mad Black Woman
in the Academy

Sydney F. Lewis

> *Content notes*: institutionalization, anti-Black police violence,
> police brutality, verbal abuse, misogynoir, suicidality

Part I: Pathologized

On June 18, 2017, Charleena Lyles phoned the Seattle Police Department about a possible break-in at her apartment. According to Officers Jason Anderson and Steven McNew, Lyles was answering their questions normally when suddenly her face changed into an angry grimace; she pulled out a knife and drew her arm back "as if she was going to throw the knife" (Mackay 2017). Later, according to the officers, Lyles pulled out a second knife and lunged at the officers with a stabbing motion. That's when Anderson shot the five-foot-three, one-hundred-pound Lyles dead. Anderson didn't choose the less lethal option, his taser, because its battery had died. Lyles had been under mental health care after a previous incident in which she threatened someone with shears. She had been attending counseling but didn't take prescribed medication because she was pregnant (Bell 2019).

The day after Charleena Lyles was murdered by the Seattle Police Department, I shared her family's GoFundMe on social media and wrote:

> They are saying she was "mentally ill" (what does that even mean? You
> realize that's exactly what they would say about me to justify my murder).
> You know what you need to do and it's not just "share."

> I ate a lobster roll for dinner tonight. I can find twenty dollars. You
> likely can too. #CharleenaLyles

Four days, one hundred pills, and some morphine later, I was admitted to a local hospital after a suicide attempt—my third hospitalization in five years. At the hospital, I had my own run-in with authorities. On July 5, 2017, the day after I was released from the behavioral-health ward, I filed a complaint to the president and chief operating officer of the hospital. I put this account in here at length to center "real-time" Mad Black voices. This account, written while hospitalized, is copied here with few edits to demonstrate the life-threatening and life-altering abuses "Mad Black women" face when seeking assistance from authorities and the extent to which respectability, prestige, and the "badge of academia" will not offer assistance. From derision to death, the forces of misogynoir, homophobia, and anti-Black racism impair Black women's ability to ask for help.

Dear [name redacted]:

> I am writing to inform you of traumatic and abusive homophobia
> and direct violations of patient rights I, and another client, experi-
> enced at the hands of your staff. I can only speak from my direct
> experiences; however, I will be referencing another client [who
> I will call TC] as she is pertinent to the events. . . . While I was
> waiting to be transferred, I saw TC, who I had met the night before
> in the waiting room. I said good morning and asked her how she
> was feeling. She said she was not well because they were going to
> release her back to an abusive group home, and she hadn't received
> treatment. I told her to ask for a social worker or a patient advocate.
> The RN at the desk, Kelly W, a blonde, white woman, said that TC
> had seen a social worker, which TC denied. I asked that TC see
> a patient advocate since the staff was not listening to her and was
> being argumentative. A security guard, [Mr. O], demanded to know
> what "business it was of yours." I told him that I had been an LGBT
> advocate for over twenty years and the night before I saw TC being
> abused by the group home staff. Mr. O said, "Oh, so you're gay?"
> I replied "Yes." He said, "So are you accusing us of treating you
> differently because you're gay?" At this point, he was yelling. I said,

"No, but queer people are a marginalized and vulnerable population." He responded that he didn't know what that meant but that "everyone has problems" and that I "made a choice" (referring to my sexuality). He also stated that he has problems yet he "gets up and goes to work every day." He said that TC and I were "weak" and that we "needed to get a job." He concluded that I may have a PhD, but I was "clearly not all there." At this point I demanded a patient advocate for myself.

There were about 8 people behind the nurses' station including Mr. O and Kelly W. I repeated at least ten to fifteen times, "I want a patient advocate or Ombudsman." Mr. O said, "We don't have one of them," and then, "We have like ten. Give me the name of the one you want." He was smirking and laughing because there was no way I could know the name of the patient advocate and he wouldn't give me any information without a specific name.

I became frightened because of Mr. O's behavior and the laughing and smirking from the staff. It was clear that none of the staff were willing to intercede or assist me. I switched strategies and said, "I want to call my wife." The phone was arm's length from me, but I was afraid to touch it out of fear of retribution and physical harm. My wife did not know I was being transferred and I was scared due to the confrontation that was occurring while I was sitting on the stretcher. I repeated ten to fifteen times, "I want to call my wife." Kelly W stated that I could not call my wife because she "didn't want to deal with any drama."

I was crying. I told Kelly W that I was a voluntary admit, I did not feel safe, and I wanted to leave. She said, "You can't leave just because someone has a different political opinion." Ignoring that I had been taunted and denied my patient rights for the previous forty-five minutes, she resumed her business and refused to counsel me on the voluntary discharge process.

Another security guard whose name I did not catch because people were standing behind each other and concealing their name tags, said, while taunting and laughing, "What's her political opinion?" Kelly W replied, "Don't get her started again!" Meanwhile,

Mr. O sneered, "She's Miss PC [Politically Correct]. She thinks she runs this unit."

I was still crying and scared but sitting on the stretcher with my hands clearly visible. At some point, someone mentioned strapping me down to the stretcher. This threat, whether initiated or just to scare me, goes against the "Rights of Persons in Inpatient Psychiatric Program."

Eventually, the medical transport team got the approval to transfer. I made the ride to the other hospital in silence and traumatized stillness because I was so frightened. My wife didn't know where I was going and some of your staff's last provoking words were "They'll take care of her at [the other hospital], they'll handle her there . . ."

Charleena Lyles lost her life because her mental health assistance was inadequate, and her small, Black frame was considered a deadly threat. TC and I were labeled "weak" and threatened by Mr. O because we required mental health assistance. The strong/angry/Mad/crazy Black woman fuses into a single pathological archetype, and it's killing us.

Part II: Refusing to Suffer in Silence

In 2012, Utah State University Press published a groundbreaking anthology called *Presumed Incompetent: The Intersections of Race and Class for Women in Academia* (Gutiérrez y Muhs et al. 2012). Combining narrative and empirical studies, the text reveals the challenges faced by women of color as they navigate the demands of hiring, promotion, tenure, student and colleague relationships, and life/work demands. I'm struck by the nuances of that titular word: *incompetent*. In common parlance, *incompetent* refers to the lack of ability to do a task. However, the word is often judicially applied to someone deemed mentally unfit to stand trial. The dual meanings of the presumption of incompetence—to be considered not only inept but also mentally unfit—resonate with my "crazy-making" experience as an early-career academic.

Coincidentally, in 2012, the same year *Presumed Incompetent* was first published, I decided to leave academia. The final straw, after enduring a decade of microaggressions as a doctorate student and lecturer, was a mix-up in my course evaluations that resulted in the rehiring committee attempting to demote me to part-time status. This status would make me ineligible for the insurance I needed to continue my mental health care.

What started as possibly an innocent mix-up evolved into a full-blown encounter with academia's racism and misogynoir and proof that capitalism's hold on my means of health and survival was being wielded to maintain the academy's emotionally abusive control.[1] Even after I met with a contracts committee member and pointed out that the course evaluation numbers used did not reflect my actual course evaluations, my complaint was dismissed. Despite the use of incorrect data, the committee member stood by her assertion that my courses, emphasizing African American studies, were too easy, and that was the basis for my demotion. When I presented exams and assignments to argue otherwise, I was then told that the student workload was too light and that was the basis for my demotion. When I presented my syllabus to demonstrate a fair and rigorous workload, I was told that my grading policies were too generous, and that was the basis of my demotion. All charges were presented without evidence, and my rebuttal evidence was otherwise dismissed. Before I could utter that I believed I was being unfairly penalized, a committee member handed me an article she had written about being a white woman teaching with Black women in academia and told me about her upcoming trip to Africa to teach "poor African children." Her defensiveness belied her misogynoir. I left her office and cried.

Dismissal, humiliation, gaslighting, blame, and denial—the same tactics that buttress abuse—characterize this all too typical encounter. When I called my mentor, a gay man of color, he offered solace and a humbling truth: this was my woman-of-color "initiation to academia." The presumption of my incompetence was literally crazy making and triggered my first psychiatric hospitalization. I had been having panic attacks when I went

---

1. Originally coined online in 2008 by the queer Black feminist Moya Bailey, the "portmanteau term" *misogynoir* is used to show "the uniquely co-constitutive racialized and sexist violence that befalls Black women as a result of their simultaneous and interlocking oppression at the intersection of racial and gender marginalization" (Bailey 2021, 1).

to work, and after twelve hours of panic attacks in response to this encounter I took a handful of pills to make them stop. I was rushed to the ER and admitted to the psych ward. There, I decided that I could not return to academia.

This experience demonstrates a vicious, maddening cycle. Black women are pathologically produced as inept and crazy by the same institutions that create abusive conditions that lead to incapacity and craziness. This cycle continues when the abuse leads to interactions with the medical-industrial and prison-industrial complexes, which receive their power through the threat/use of state-sanctioned violence and abuse. As Katie Tastrom argues in "Disability Justice and Abolition" (2020), disabled people are routinely subjected to carceral systems "not just in jail and prison but [in] other manifestations of the carceral state like doctors, social workers, and other individuals and institutions" (par. 3). Talila "TL" Lewis confirms that "carceral systems medicalize, pathologize, criminalize, and commodify survival, divergence, and resistance." Although "disabled/neurodivergent people comprise just 26% of the United States population," they "represent up to half of the people killed by police, over 50% of the incarcerated adult prison population, up to 85% of the incarcerated youth population, and a significant number of those incarcerated in medicalized carceral spaces." In short, "whether under the pretense of 'care' or 'corrections,' disabled people are highly represented in all carceral populations" (2020, par. 5).

It was the prevalence of the aforementioned cycle that led to the "maddening" of Sandra Bland. In July 2015, twenty-eight-year-old Sandra Bland was violently taken into police custody after failing to signal a lane change. The terrorizing encounter, in which Officer Brian T. Encinia threatens her with his taser, proclaiming "I'm going to light you up," and rips Bland from her car, was recorded on the police dashcam, by a bystander, and by Bland herself. Three days later, Bland was found hanging from her jail cell, and her death was ruled a suicide. Buttressing this ruling were Bland's mental health history and her own words. On her blog *Sandy Speaks*, Bland wrote about her recent struggles with depression, her outrage over the killings of unarmed Black people, and her support of the Black Lives Matter movement. Reflecting on *Sandy Speaks*, the Black feminist Britney Cooper explains, "Unlike the race women of old, Sandy Bland did not dissemble. She shared her private struggles right alongside her political views" (2019, 104). Here Cooper is referring to the "culture of dissemblance" theorized by Darlene Clark Hines. In analyzing Black women's response to rape and domestic violence, Hines coined the phrase the "culture of dissemblance" to describe the "behaviors and attitudes of Black women that created the appearance of openness and disclosure but actually shielded the truth of their inner lives and selves from their oppressors." This strategy helped them to "resist the misappropriations and to maintain the integrity of their own sexuality." This "self-imposed invisibility" allowed Black women the "psychic space" to "harness the resources needed to hold their own in the often one-sided and mismatched resistance struggle" (1989, 912, 913, 915).

Though originally theorized in relation to sexuality, the strategy of "shield[ing] the truth of their inner lives and selves from their oppressors" is so prevalent among Black women that it has resulted in its own racialized archetype: the Strong Black Woman. Like dissemblance, the Strong Black Woman archetype has been described as an armor Black women put on to face the daily assaults of oppression (Manke 2019). Jasmine A. Abrams, Ashley Hill, and Morgan Maxwell describe the Strong Black Woman schema as "an amalgamation of beliefs and cultural expectations of incessant resilience, independence, and strength that guide meaning making, cognition and behavior related to Black womanhood" (2018, 518). The schema is not just an archetype but also an identity and an outlook, which means that "many Black women have mastered the art of portraying strength while concealing trauma" (518). Abrams, Hill, and Maxwell found that the more Black women adhered to the Strong Black Woman schema, the stronger the relationship between stress and depressive symptoms (522). According to Josephine Gurch (2019), the schema can also prevent Black women from seeking mental health treatment.

When Sandra Bland was pulled over and subsequently murdered, she was on her way to her new job at her alma mater, Prairie View A&M University. Though Sandra Bland was undoubtedly a strong Black woman, by refusing to dissemble she refused to succumb to the negative mental health effects of the Strong Black Woman archetype. As Cooper succinctly states,

"Caring for Black women's actual lives means sitting with the acuteness of our fragility. We break, too" (2019, 203). However, "breaking" is in sharp contrast to the stoic scholar who is the benchmark of academia. The trope of the all-consumed solitary scholar (usually white, usually male, usually heterosexual, usually nondisabled) is an academic trope for a reason. He is the most valued producer for the academic machine. Cooper, a Black academic feminist herself, describes the added pressure of maintaining the image of stoicism and strength for Black women. On her way to a speaking engagement at Harvard, she received a heartbreaking text from a former lover. Cooper describes, "As I stood at the podium doing my thing in that Harvard classroom, no one could tell that my fervent desire was to find somewhere to curl up and weep. . . . I couldn't fall apart like I wanted to because, well I'm a Black girl, and we don't get the luxury of doing frivolous shit like that" (2019, 100–101).

Academia, like other oppressive institutions, is structured through the logics of abuse. Nothing short of traumatic, this abuse deems Black women to be already professionally incompetent. Furthermore, Black women's strategies to navigate this oppressive abuse—dissemblance and the appearance of strength—augment the already negative mental health effects of oppression, while the demand to perform the Strong Black Woman is buttressed by the racialized, gendered, and ableist academic trope of the stoic scholar. The neoliberal academy is billed as a free idea exchange among a group of intellectuals. This idealistic and fantastical marketing belies a historical and present legacy of discrimination, theft, exploitation, and exclusion abetted by racism, sexism, heterosexism, classism, and ableism. Furthermore, the institution is founded on the gaslighting lie of freedom in and through education. This lie profoundly affects Black women. In 2015–16, Black women earned 70 percent of master's degrees and 66 percent of doctorate degrees awarded to all Black people (National Center for Education Statistics 2019, 149). Although Black women receive postgraduate degrees at higher rates than Black men and, indeed, at the highest rates within any race/gender group, this statistic does not translate to higher rates of Black women professionals within academia. In 2021, Black women accounted for only approximately 4 percent of full-time faculty in degree-granting postsecondary institutions (National Center for

Education Statistics 2023). With these abysmal statistics, academia embeds the conditions for Black women's racial and gender isolation. This phenomenon is supported not only by quantitative data but also by the anecdotal experiences of friends and colleagues. As a tactic of abuse, isolation prevents the abused from forming supportive relations with anyone outside of the abuser/abused dynamic. Isolation also forms the foundation for tactics of emotional abuse—gaslighting, humiliation, minimization, coercion, and threats. These tactics can aptly be called "crazy making." Once we are caught in this "maddening" cycle, it's a wonder we survive this institution at all.

I imagine Sandra Bland, mere miles away from her new career at Prairie View A&M University, as excited but also apprehensive about navigating the demands of an institution that was not built for her. If *Sandy Speaks* is any indication of the woman behind the headlines, I imagine Bland as open and vulnerable, outraged by the racism around her but refusing to hide behind an archetype of unyielding strength. The Bland of my imagination gives me strategy and renewed hope for my survival. However, the reality is that Bland was murdered, and both her refusal to dissemble and her openness about her inner struggle and life were used to justify her death. This is a cruel paradox with little room to break free. But if the Black feminist Cooper is right, and there is a "thin line between clarity and craziness, and sometimes clarity can be crazy-making" (2019, 107), then perhaps turning to the words of the "crazy" can provide clarity.

Part III: There Are No Answers Here, Only Love

Personal Journal Entry, July 2, 2017

> The hospital is punishment for refusing to suffer in silence. Rather than seeing the manifestation of your condition as a call for help, a last resort, begging to alleviate the pain, you're punished for breaking the unspoken pact:
>
> "We're all suffering, we're all miserable under racist cis-heteropatriarchal capitalism. . . .
>
> "How dare you think your suffering is worthy of a cry, a scream, some blood, an out? How dare you think you deserve more and would rather have nothing than less?"

I don't have the answers. I'm just an ambivalent academic and a Mad Black woman in the academy. I'm Mad—angry and crazy, more than a little unhinged. Despite my renouncement in 2012, I returned to academia in the fall of 2017, full of trepidation, first as an adjunct and now in my full-time position. The remembrance of the countless daily acts of racism and sexism and the academic trauma that I endured resulted in the psychiatric hospitalization in 2017, where I completed much of the writings presented here. I stand by these musings as they reflect the real-time crazy-making conditions of my hospitalization and the clarity and solutions I arrived at during that time.

I wrote the following "Mad manifesto" during my hospitalization:

> The first thing Dr. Kane said to me when I entered his office at the University of Washington Mental Health Clinic was, "Ms. Lewis, it is 9:05, you are five minutes late. Don't let it happen again." The second thing he said was "Love yourself more." It wasn't until now, after almost a decade of trauma and violence, that I was able to understand and implement the meaning of "Love yourself more."
>
> A stern, but boisterous man with an infectious grin, Dr. Kane could also be irritating, overly blunt, and egotistical, but, as he said, he didn't worry about it because he loved himself more.
>
> Loving myself more extends beyond interpersonal relationships into my interactions with institutions and their representatives. I love myself more than racist systems which demand that I, as a Black woman, should be content with less. I love myself more than patriarchal values which dictate that my supposedly "natural" role is that of a caregiver and nurturer regardless of my individual desires and needs. I love myself more than the minimal value that capitalism puts on my labor and knowledge, and I certainly love myself more than any representative of real or imagined power who believes their position permits them to denigrate me with impunity. This simple, but pivotal decision has deepened my relationships with my family and friends and enabled me to form more sustainable and impactful relationships with my communities.

When I talk about loving myself more, I'm talking not just about self-care but also about collective and community care. Collective care requires a systematic shift from independence to interdependence. Coming from a disability justice framework, interdependence is a liberatory strategy that sees "the liberation of all living systems and the land as integral to the liberation of own communities," where we "attempt to meet each other's needs . . . without always reaching for state solutions that inevitably then extend its control further over our lives" (Berne 2018, 28).

Translating principles of interdependence and collective care into the isolating ivory tower is not an easy task. Loving myself more, my holistic self, means rejecting the culture of dissemblance. I practice disclosure of my mental health struggles with those who need to know—namely, my students and my department chair because I love myself enough to ask for help. I teach and write on subjects I feel passionate about and center Black, Indigenous, and people-of-color voices in my work because I love myself enough to want to see myself and my communities reflected. I work from an intersectional antioppressive politic because I love myself enough to want more from my community. And most importantly, I rest because I love myself enough to want my work to be sustainable, and I know I deserve to recuperate.

This strategy is not without its drawbacks. I am fortunate to have an understanding chair who grasps the importance of mental health for Black and Indigenous people and people of color in the academy. In a market where between one and three percent of Black women receive tenure, I know that this strategy does not put me on the path to security, so I remain a lecturer. Because managing my mental illness is its own full-time job, I am unable to keep up with the demand to publish or perish. I put in extra work to foster relationships with my students based on mutual vulnerability and whole-self recognition, so when I tell them I'm highly anxious or spacey because of my medication, they understand.

In closing, I recall the prophetic words of Audre Lorde: "Caring for myself is not self-indulgence, it is self-preservation—and that is an act of political warfare" (1988, 131). This proclamation "reminds us that [Lorde] comprehended how systems use Black mental health and distress as a way to de-mobilize us in the fight for liberation" (Higgins 2019, par. 9). Loving myself more can provide a roadmap to navigating these systems. I can refuse to dissemble and can instead practice radical vulnerability, interdependence, and collective care, and there put the Strong Black Woman to rest.

Works Cited

Abrams, Jasmine A., Ashley Hill, and Morgan Maxwell. 2018. "Underneath the Mask of the Strong Black Woman Schema: Disentangling Influences of Strength and Self-Silencing on Depressive Symptoms among U.S. Black Women." *Sex Roles* 80, nos. 9–10: 517–26. At https://doi.org/10.1007/s11199-018-0956-y.

Bailey, Moya. 2021. *Misogynoir Transformed: Black Women's Digital Resistance.* New York: New York University Press.

Bell, Carla. 2019. "Police, Power, Policy, and Privilege vs. the People: We're All Charleena Lyles." *Essence*, Feb. 13. At https://www.essence.com/news/police-power-policy-and-privilege-vs-the-people-were-all-charleena-lyles/.

Berne, Patty. 2018. "10 Principles of Disability Justice." In Leah Lakshmi Piepzna-Samarasinha, *Care Work: Dreaming Disability Justice*, 26–29. Vancouver: Arsenal Pulp Press.

Cooper, Brittney C. 2019. *Eloquent Rage: A Black Feminist Discovers Her Superpower.* New York: St. Martin's Press.

Gurch, Josephine. 2019. "The Mental Health Cost of Being a Strong Black Woman." Hogg Foundation, July 30. At https://hogg.utexas.edu/mental-health-cost-of-a-black-woman.

Gutiérrez y Muhs, Gabriella, Yolanda Flores Niemann, Carmen G. González, and Angela P. Harris, eds. 2012. *Presumed Incompetent: The Intersections of Race and Class for Women in Academia.* Boulder: Univ. Press of Colorado for Utah State Univ. Press.

Higgins, John. 2019. "BHM: Audre Lorde and the Blueprint for Navigating Mental Health." *Afropunk*, Feb. 18. At https://afropunk.com/2019/02/audre-lorde-and-the-blueprint-to-navigating-mental-health/.

Hines, Darlene Clark. 1989. "Rape and the Inner Lives of Black Women in the Middle West." *Signs* 14, no. 4: 912–20. At https://www.jstor.org/stable/3174692.

Lewis, Talia "TL." 2020. "Disability Justice Is an Essential Part of Abolishing Police and Prisons." *Level*, Oct. 7. At https://level.medium.com/disability-justice-is-an-essential-part-of-abolishing-police-and-prisons-2b4a019b5730.

Lorde, Audre. 1988. *A Burst of Light: Essays.* Ithaca, NY: Firebrand.

Mackay, Rob. 2017. "Seattle Officer in Charleena Lyles Shooting: 'The Knife Is Produced, It's the Oh My God Moment. . . .'" *Q13 FOX*, June 23. At https://q13fox.com/2017/06/23/seattle-officer-in-lyles-shooting-the-knife-is-produced-its-the-oh-my-god-moment/.

Manke, Kara. 2019. "How the 'Strong Black Woman' Identity Both Helps and Hurts." *Greater Good*, Dec. 5. At https://greatergood.berkeley.edu/article/item /how_the_strong_black_woman_identity_both_helps_and_hurts.

National Center for Education Statistics (NCES). 2019. *Status and Trends in the Education of Racial and Ethnic Groups 2018*. Washington, DC: NCES. At https://nces.ed.gov/programs/raceindicators/.

———. 2023. "Characteristics of Postsecondary Faculty." At https://nces.ed.gov /programs/coe/indicator/csc

Tastrom, Katie. 2020. "Disability Justice and Abolition." National Lawyers Guild, June 29. At https://www.nlg.org/disability-justice-and-abolition/.

Part Two

Researching the Self

Positing the self as research, the scholars in this part frame their intersectional identities as a nexus or as generative opening.[1] Madness here becomes a practice, a way to analyze scholarship, read theory, and reimagine rhetoric in order to distinctly trouble the "adept" ways academia "produc[es] . . . disciplined cognators" (Chen 2014, 178). Although scholars have written about the importance of incorporating Mad studies into curricula and pedagogy (Price 2011; Wolframe 2013; Castrodale 2017; Snyder et al. 2019; Ballantyne et al. 2020; Newman et al. 2022) and about "thinking from the critical, social, and personal place of disability" (Johnson and McRuer 2014, 134), part two uniquely posits a practice of *reading* and *writing* Mad. What might we create if we produce writing, grammar, and syntax that is singularly informed by our Madness and our neurodivergence? What new modalities

---

1. There is an expansive lineage of autoethnography, "critical self-reflection," and "disability life writing" (Jarman, Monaghan, and Harkin 2017) within disability studies, including books such as *Planet of the Blind* (Kuusisto 1998) and *My Body Politic* (Linton 2007). Mad studies also embraces this reflexive practice as a way to "locat[e] Mad people at the centre of their own narratives . . . illustrating people's capacity to change the world" (Menzies, LeFrançois, and Reaume 2013, 15). For examples of this centering, see *The Collected Schizophrenias* (Wang 2019), *Haldol and Hyacinths* (Moezzi 2014), and *Heart Berries* (Mailhot 2019).

of analysis might an embodied/enminded Mad reading provide?

Here, Mad scholars tread the often contradictory path toward self-crafted legibility. We arrive at a Mad, neurodiverse reckoning when we name ourselves outside of what Leah Lakshmi Piepzna-Samarasinha (she/they) identifies as "the ableist, racist academic- and intelligence-industrial complex." We challenge prohibitive, pathologizing practices; we step off the preconceived paths and amplify our deep knowing, as Piepzna-Samarasinha writes, that there are "a million brilliant ways to create, dream, think, . . . and fly." It is distinctly from this place that we employ an exploration of Mad studies that encourages a "pushing up against, and thereby [an] exposing" of neurotypical research (Aho, Ben-Moshe, and Hilton 2017, 294).

Encouraged by our neurodivergence, Mad research practices provide the opportunity for salvaging and potentially for flourishing. Here we consider, for example, how we might emerge as our rooted, Mad selves precisely from places of forced erasure, places where we are made illegible or unseen. For many of the contributors to this part, neurodivergent joy and community weaving create ways to thrive as Mad researchers. Sarah Cavar's (they/them) intervention into "epistemic injustice" (Fricker 2007) occurs online with the celebration of trans, disabled, and autistic pride in digital community.[2] From this place, we are encouraged to enact Madness as a research modality. Rua Williams (they/them) invites us to resist ableist and allistic writing by reclaiming autistic rhetoric and divergent articulations that value neurodiverse voice and

2. For more on the interconnections between sanism and epistemic injustice, see "Toward Epistemic Justice: A Critically Reflective Examination of 'Sanism' and Implications for Knowledge Generation" (Leblanc and Kinsella 2016).

grammar. We are urged to explore what it could mean to "read, madly," as Melanie Jones (she/they) encourages: to make connections across uncertainty, doubt, and nonlinearity in order to challenge fields such as literature that simultaneously provide a historic voice to Madness and do much to exoticize and efface Mad voices. We are forced to grapple with the opportunities we lose when we ignore the lived experiences of those we profess to study, when we are asked to reduce ourselves to just one thing.

As Mad scholars, we linger in our observations of Madness as verb and tool.[3] We recognize and nourish our neurodivergence, and it is through this creation that we together urge research, reading, and writing that is intrinsically Mad. When we resist, we resist academia's intention to "stifle" and "expel" us (Price 2011, 8), and, here, possibilities abound. We dream openings that invite, as "Madmotherscholar" Caché Owens (they/them) writes, new bodymind practices supported by care: Madmotherscholars can "remind us of the messiness of the human experience and push our places of learning to more radical and transformative ways of knowing." By centering our Madness, we cultivate pathways of resilience from our bodyminds outward. We exist despite: despite editor comments, despite the disciplinary red pen ushering us back to sanist, ableist modalities. We write and read Mad; we learn, teach, and create community despite sanist constructions of shame and guilt that shadow us. Together, we name and practice ways to proliferate research with compassion. Here, our Mad, neurodiverse subjectivity—an agentic, glittery location—prospers.

3. From disability studies and queer studies, there is a precedent for turning nouns into verbs—for example, *crip* (Sandahl 2003) and *queer* (Butler 1990; Sedgwick 1990; Puar 2007; Barnett and Johnson 2015).

Works Cited

Aho, Tanja, Liat Ben-Moshe, and Leon J. Hilton. 2017. "Mad Futures: Affect/Theory/Violence." *American Quarterly* 69, no. 2: 291–302. At https://doi.org/10.1353/aq.2017.0023.

Ballantyne, Elaine, Kirsten Maclean, Shirley-Anne Collie, Liz Deeming, and Esther Fraser. 2020. "Mad People's History and Identity: A Mad Studies Critical Pedagogy Project." In *Public Sociology as Educational Practice: Challenges, Dialogues and Counter-Publics*, edited by Eurig Scandrett, 25–36. Bristol: Bristol Univ. Press.

Barnett, Joshua Trey, and Corey W. Johnson. 2015. "Queer." In *Encyclopedia of Diversity and Social Justice*, edited by Sherwood Thomson, 581. Washington, DC: Rowman & Littlefield.

Butler, Judith. 1990. *Gender Trouble: Feminism and the Subversion of Identity*. New York: Taylor & Francis.

Castrodale, Mark Anthony. 2017. "Critical Disability Studies and Mad Studies: Enabling New Pedagogies in Practice." *Canadian Journal for the Study of Adult Education* 29, no. 1: 49–66. At https://cjsae.library.dal.ca/index.php/cjsae/article/view/5357.

Chen, Mel Y. 2014. "Brain Fog: The Race for Cripistemology." *Journal of Literary & Cultural Disability Studies* 8, no. 2: 171–84. At https://muse.jhu.edu/article/548849.

Fricker, Miranda. 2007. *Epistemic Injustice: Power and the Ethics of Knowing*. Oxford: Oxford Univ. Press.

Jarman, Michelle, Leila Monaghan, and Alison Quaggin Harkin, eds. 2017. *Barriers and Belonging: Personal Narratives of Disability*. Philadelphia: Temple Univ. Press.

Johnson, Merri Lisa, and Robert McRuer. 2014. "Cripistemologies: Introduction." In "Cripistemologies: Part I," edited by Merri Lisa Johnson and Robert McRuer. Special issue, *Journal of Literary & Cultural Disability Studies* 8, no. 2: 127–47. At https://muse.jhu.edu/article/548847.

Kuusisto, Stephen. 1998. *Planet of the Blind: A Memoir*. New York: Dell.

Leblanc, Stephanie, and Elizabeth Anne Kinsella. 2016. "Toward Epistemic Justice: A Critically Reflexive Examination of 'Sanism' and Implications for Knowledge Generation." *Studies in Social Justice* 10, no. 1: 59–78. At https://doi.org/10.26522/ssj.v10i1.1324.

Linton, Simi. 2007. *My Body Politic: A Memoir*. Ann Arbor: Univ. of Michigan Press.

Mailhot, Terese Marie. 2019. *Heart Berries: A Memoir*. London: Bloomsbury.

Menzies, Robert, Brenda A. LeFrançois, and Geoffrey Reaume. 2013. "Introducing Mad Studies." In *Mad Matters: A Critical Reader in Canadian Mad Studies*, edited by Brenda A. LeFrançois, Robert Menzies, and Geoffrey Reaume, 1–22. Toronto: Canadian Scholars' Press.

Moezzi, Melody. 2014. *Haldol and Hyacinths: A Bipolar Life*. London: Penguin.

Newman, Joanne, Kathy Boxall, Rebecca Jury, and Julie Dickinson. 2022. "Professional Education and Mad Studies: Learning and Teaching about Service Users' Understandings of Mental and Emotional Distress." *Disability & Society* 34, nos. 9–10: 1523–47. At https://doi.org/10.1080/09687599.2019.1594697.

Price, Margaret. 2011. *Mad at School: Rhetorics of Mental Disability and Academic Life*. Ann Arbor: Univ. of Michigan Press.

Puar, Jasbir K. 2007. "Introduction: Homonationalism and Biopolitics." In *Terrorist Assemblages: Homonationalism in Queer Times*, 1–36. Durham, NC: Duke Univ. Press.

Sandahl, Carrie. 2003. "Queering the Crip or Cripping the Queer? Intersections of Queer and Crip Identities in Solo Autobiographical Performance." *GLQ: A Journal of Lesbian and Gay Studies* 9, no. 1: 25–56. At https://doi.org/10.1215/10642684-9-1-2-25.

Sedgwick, Eve Kosofsky. 1990. *Epistemology of the Closet*. Oakland: Univ. of California Press.

Snyder, Sarah N., Kendra-Ann Pitt, Fady Shanouda, Jijian Voronka, Jenna Reid, and Danielle Landry. 2019. "Unlearning through Mad Studies: Disruptive Pedagogical Praxis." *Curriculum Inquiry* 49, no. 4: 485–502. At https://doi.org/10.1080/03626784.2019.1664254.

Wang, Esmé Weijun. 2019. *The Collected Schizophrenias: Essays*. Minneapolis, MN: Graywolf Press.

Wolframe, PhebeAnn M. 2013. "The Madwoman in the Academy, or, Revealing the Invisible Straightjacket: Theorizing and Teaching Saneism and Sane Privilege." *Disability Studies Quarterly* 33, no. 1. At https://dsq-sds.org/article/view/3425/3200.

6

I'm Too Crazy for a Job

*Thoroughbreds, Fuckups, and Autistic, Mad, Disabled,
Femme Grassroots Intellectual-Freedom Portals*

Leah Lakshmi Piepzna-Samarasinha

*Dedicated to my younger weirdo genius self. You were always of worth, when you
were scoring high on the SAT verbal and when you were fucking up, making
mistakes, and being a regular kid. And to all the grassroots intellectuals, especially
the BIPOC crips and NDs, with all our fuck-it audacity and disabled dreaming.*

> *Content notes*: intimate-partner abuse, sexual
> and physical abuse, allistic supremacy

My people

My people are the fuckups,
the runaways, the ones who waited to tell their parents
till they were over 21,
so they couldn't be committed
the ones whose therapy
is backpacks and shoplifting and silence

The ones who grew as much of their own food in the backyard as they
    could
as a survival mechanism   not a fun green hobby,
the ones who whisper *I will beat you with a pipe*
I am feral as fuck

and even though I am now somehow an unexpected success
I still don't know how to adult or tame:
I'm always this close to walking into the woods
with everything I own in a ripped up white plastic bag

(Piepzna-Samarasinha n.d.)

Thoroughbreds, Fuckups, and Tickets to Ride

I have always and forever been both the smart kid and the fuckup. I was raised to excel and give my gifts to the state as one of the small number of outlier exceptions the state can use. I defected into another way of being smart and useful that could exist outside of the ways the white-supremacist, capitalist, colonialist, ableist, ageist patriarchy (WSCCAAP) farms neurodivergent others. That's what this essay is about.

For me as a working-class/lower-middle-class/straddling- and passing-class (a term I use to define people who are working hard to mask and pass as a more privileged class than we are), neuroweird, survivor, mixed brown and white, nonbinary, femme kid, my relationship to the educational/academic system was never chill. It was my "ticket to ride," my one shot at economic stability and survival. Not just for me, but also for my parents, one of whom was a first-generation sort of out of the Rust Belt working class, working a teaching job and side hustles with a degree from Worcester State; the other a middle-class, back-home, neurodivergent fuckboy and master scammer, surviving by creating elaborate long-term cons with all his hustler's and mixed-race survival skills, which worked until they didn't, and he was unemployed and on the couch again.

For them and me, and for all their long-term hopes and hustle that my smart exceptionality would eventually land us solidly and finally in the middle class, safe and saved, I had to keep being a thoroughbred, pumping out effortless A's, 4.0s, and gushing recommendations about how gifted and exceptional I was. If I did it flawlessly, it would keep me on a class/intelligentsia escalator that would lead to my—yes, even weird, little, brown, nonman me—becoming part of the intellectual elite. Not crazy and locked up or working minimum wage at Supercuts. Those were the two options, and there was no middle ground or room for mistakes.

Often when describing how I was viewed by my family, community, and the private school I attended on scholarship (one of two working-class/mixed-class scholarship students to be admitted), I call myself a *thoroughbred*. By that, I mean that breed of lower than middle-class kid who is tracked as "smart/gifted" and raised in a poor, blue-collar, Rust Belt neighborhood, rural area, town, or city to think of ourselves as "the one who's getting away." I was raised to believe that books and smartness and constantly maintaining a high standard of "excellence" was what would get me away—into class stability, a life of the mind, into being the one who saved my family and bootstrapped my way into us being "safe."

Thoroughbred horses are built for speed and a single purpose—running, outpacing everyone else, and winning. They are nervous, highly strung, filled with anxiety that fuels them down the track. After they run their race, they often collapse. Thoroughbred scholarship kids are raised with a single-minded focus—to use our brains to get the fuck out and not pay attention to anything else, whether it be friends or our home community. As an adult autistic person, I now see with perfect clarity that, of course, this is about the educational and power system valuing hyperfocus, hyperlexia, and hypercalculia—the autistic skills of being able to be "in the zone" for hours, read and do math fast, come to quick and incredible conclusions—over all other states, including especially the crash that comes after using them. It is an ableist, capitalist intellectual economy that is inherently extractive and unsustainable.

Being a thoroughbred means being taught that you are "different" from the other kids and that there's nothing good in where you and they are from. To stay where you come from might mean alcoholism or addictive drug use, illness, disability, HIV; a shitty job in a shitty place with shit relationships. Achieving escape velocity means not caring about or seeing that you have things in common with or a responsibility to the other kids on your block who aren't marked as the special exception. They have "wasted lives"; you, you can be different.

Kids who are some combination of light-skinned, racially ambiguous, and/or non-Black often get tracked hard into thoroughbredness because the system views our lightness as making us doubly "special." We are raced as "exotic," not threatening, presumed quiet and loyal. However, that marginal acceptance can turn on a dime, and we can be kicked out the moment we fight back or refuse to obey. I've also seen thoroughbredness be offered to dark-skinned, non–racially ambiguous, and/or Black young people. All of us, to differing degrees, are asked to be quiet, obedient, and grateful; darker-skinned and Black kids are policed harder and thrown out of elite institutions faster for perceived resistance, anger, or disagreement.

Thoroughbredness is a seductive mindset for certain kinds of neuro-divergent freak kids who do indeed score high on tests. It's a promise that our "difference" will be valued someday, that we won't just be the freak who never gets it. But the cost of accepting thoroughbred identity means embracing meritocracy, the idea that the smart and good prosper, and if others in our poor and working-class communities—or us—don't, it's our own fault.

Thoroughbredness pushes us into isolation, into hating where we are from and thus hating ourselves. It pushes us to believe we are only valu-able for how much we can speedily, intellectually produce, not for our bodies, our feelings, our pleasure, our vulnerability. It means believing unquestioningly that there is only one way to be smart and that every other way of being is stupid.

I was tracked into the gifted program for the first time at age six and simultaneously was someone teachers and parents threw up their hands at in consternation. "What's the matter with you?!" was a phrase that got thrown at me a lot. Although the terms *high functioning* and *low function-ing* weren't used to describe me because I wasn't recognized or labeled as autistic, I was still caught in and affected by the "high/low function-ing" binary. The high/low functioning binary of autism is a classification system that the academic- and medical-industrial complexes have wea-ponized against autistic and neurodivergent young people to categorize some of us as "savant/genius" autistic people and others as "dumb, bad, defective, or special ed." (This binary has implications for all people be-cause, as Talila "TL" Lewis [2022] writes, ableism also affects abled and neurotypical [NT] people—in this case I would argue because abled and NT people also learn ableist ideas of the "smart/stupid" binary and are impacted by them.)

I'm Too Crazy for a Job   111

For me, all of these dynamics meant that I was praised lavishly for my "high-functioning/savant" traits—the me that could read a book in two hours, write a straight-A paper in twenty minutes on the bus, memorize the textbook and regurgitate it for a high score on a standardized test. I was told I was a small adult, brilliant, would surely go to Harvard. I was simultaneously shamed for the parts that read as "low functioning"—the parts that struggled with balance, spatial knowledge, face blindness, overwhelm, that were and are nonspeaking, with selective mutism when stressed or scared. The parts that walked and moved differently, struggling to understand how to ride an escalator, taking the stairs by waiting till both feet are on each step before continuing. There was a lot of yelling, hands thrown up in confusion, and angry, impatient disgust at me. If I was so smart, why couldn't I walk down the stairs like "everyone else"? Why couldn't I stop crying, start talking? I must just be lazy, spoiled, manipulative, or not trying hard enough. Did I belong in the gifted program or special ed?

Those "failures," mixed with my being typed as precocious—a small adult, not a child—were also weaponized as reasons not to protect me from the sexual, physical, and other forms of abuse I survived in junior high and high school—a lack of protection from abuse that is common for many autistic young people. To the adults around me, my hyperlexia meant I was really an adult, not a child, and thus not an innocent victim deserving of protection but a freak who brought the abuse on myself by virtue of my "strange" traits.

Thirty-five years after I almost flunked out of first grade for being a smart failure who walked up the stairs differently, twenty years after I graduated from college with both honors and a full scholarship and a checkered academic record filled with weeks of missed classes when I was too depressed or overwhelmed to make it there or remember where the class was, queer, BIPOC (Black, Indigenous, people-of-color), autistic friends would bring me out into autistic identity and community. I would discover that my autistic story of education—of being a smart, weird person who might both excel and struggle without the right kind of access tools—is one (not the only) very typical autistic story. As Julia Bascom (2021), autistic organizer and executive director of the Autistic Self Advocacy

Network, young people who seem high and low functioning actually have a lot in common with each other. But back then, I just knew that my primary value was being a "smart kid" and that it made up for all the ugly, awkward, queer, brown other parts—and sometimes I was failing at it.

Recently when a friend asked me if I knew I was allowed to make mistakes after I received and was processing critical feedback about a form of access falling short at events I had produced, I winced. At forty-seven, I realized that one of my core wounds as a neurodivergent, autistic person is that I still have a core belief that I am only good when I get it perfectly right the first time. I was seen as ugly, weird, and annoying as a kid—a mixed-race kid with Tamil hair and features seen as "weird," an autistic, traumatized survivor kid of two autistic, traumatized, disabled parents who hadn't had much opportunities to heal. My allisticly defined "smartness" was the only good thing about me, the only begrudging reason I was allowed to stick around. I'm still healing and still unlearning that belief.

Getting to university on that fought-for full scholarship I'd worked for my entire childhood was supposed to be liberation, and in many ways it was. I was out of my parents' abusive house and free of the people at school who had sexually and physically abused me for years. But with no structure or autistic support, thrown into the world on my own, I floundered. I was depressed at a time when there was little language, understanding, or community for Mad students, besides many suggestions that I go on that early '90s first-generation Prozac. When I refused, there was just a big shrug from peers, my adviser, and teachers.

The things I was dealing with at nineteen—a mother diagnosed with stage-four cancer; a girlfriend I loved passionately, whose relationship lived in letters, not making out, who was suicidal and who I was pretty sure had died for years; being raped and threatened with death by a queer survivor lover who understood kink and depression more than most people I knew but was still incredibly violent and being dismissed by the anarchist political community we both belonged to after the relationship exploded; disassociation so thick it felt like a thick wool blanket—were not seen as things worthy of care, softness, understanding, or access. Or as things that were connected to me as a thinker, as someone who had wild, wonderful ideas and loved reading, thinking, and plotting. Instead, I was seen as a downer who talked about depressing things, one who just couldn't keep up with academic work or activism.

While I was blessed in being able to transfer to a smaller (and thus more accessible) liberal arts college that still gave me full funding, where I was able to attend smaller, seminar-based classes with some incredible Black, queer, feminist scholars, I still struggled in undergrad with studying theory that felt divorced from practice. Despite a lifetime of reading widely, I, like many working-class and poor students, didn't know what words like *problematize* and *hegemonic* meant, and I felt too embarrassed to ask for fear of exposing myself as "stupid." I remember trying to look them up in the dictionary, failing to find them, and feeling crushed; I was supposed to be smart, right? The ADA was signed into law in 1990, but I had no idea during my undergraduate years in the mid-1990s that I could request accommodations for mental health or neurodivergence, and I probably would've been denied them if I'd tried. I had made it to the promised land of college, but I was failing at being the best, shiniest student. Depression, suicidality, disassociation, and struggles without structure or access were fucking with my "performance." What was wrong with me? Who was I if I wasn't a smart, fast brain?

Dropping Out, Fucking Up, and Running Away to an Organic Intellectual Garden

I wouldn't have had friends who loved and accepted me, a community that felt real and supportive, meaningful work, accessible food, and pleasure—what the medical-industrial complex calls a "mental health support system" (Mingus 2015)—if I hadn't visited a close friend I met on an old-school riot grrrl listserv in Toronto in the summer of 1996. I fell in love with the city and all the ways it supported me and others: the abundant green spaces of its alleyways and small and big parks and railroad tracks and community gardens, three-dollar parties, friends who made me tea and listened when I was having a hard time, affordable housing, public transit and food, poor peoples, antiracist and anticolonialist activist communities. Perhaps most significantly, I found a rich psychiatric-survivor community, the first place I had ever encountered other Mad people building community with each other, organizing and articulating a political activist vision as people who were Crazy/psychiatrized/neurodivergent. Mad activist community is rare now, but it was even rarer then. Finding that community of older nuts who accepted me, loved me, and were being Crazy in public at organizing meetings for Psychiatric Survivor Pride Day and against forced treatment saved my life. I visited Toronto all through fall 1996, moved there during my last semester of undergrad in February 1997 with two bags of my things on the Greyhound, did all my final classes as independent studies, faxed in my thesis, and didn't leave Toronto for ten years.

I fought to stay in Toronto as a disabled immigrant sponsored by a partner who became abusive, even when people didn't understand why I didn't go back to the United States and when I didn't quite have the words to explain why, either. But it was simple: Toronto was neurodivergent, Mad access. The quiet, railroad-track neighborhood where I could afford to live alone was autistic access, trauma-survivor, psych-survivor access. The psych-survivor activist and cultural community—interwoven with local prison-justice, anticolonial, and antiracist organizing, so they understood Mad people issues as real and connected and respected us, with room to be leaders and speak at rallies—was access. The friends I had who were young, queer, Mad survivors of abuse, who would make tea and cornmeal porridge and stay up late talking, were access.

All of this access was made possible by some structural economic and political justice. Toronto in the late 1990s had more horizontal and accessible higher education than anything I'd ever seen in the United States. There are no private universities in Canada, and tuition in the late 1990s was $3,150 a year, not $25,000 (what New York University, my first college, would've charged if I hadn't had an almost full ride). As a result, many low-income/poor and working-class kids I knew went to university, and because of how affordable higher education was, there was less of a sense of fiendish competition between students—especially low-income students—to get into a handful of elite universities or prove themselves the one exceptional person worthy of one of a handful of scholarships. Canadian higher education was far from an antioppressive paradise, but these class realities created a baseline of a horizontal intellectual space, with room for students and academics who weren't straight, rich, white,

I'm Too Crazy for a Job 115

abled guys to talk about ideas. This horizontality and economic access in turn created porous spaces between campus and community intellectual spaces. For example, it was common for on-campus groups to leverage their privilege to bring radical writers or activists as speakers to campus and promote it widely to people who didn't go to university. I remember vividly attending a reading by Makeda Silvera, Chrystos, and Patrick Califia (a Black Caribbean writer and publisher, an Indigenous Two-Spirit poet, and a white working-class trans SM erotic writer) in a Ryerson (now Toronto Metropolitan) University auditorium packed mostly with people who didn't go to college there. "This event is open to all" is something many private US campuses might pay lip service to, but mostly only university-affiliated people attend.

Toronto's horizontal intellectualism also had rich community-based arts, education, and grassroots intellectualism supported by city, provincial, and federal arts funding that was easy to access. Instead of the National Endowment for the Arts giving out twenty-five $25,000 literature grants a year to the whole country, in Canada many smaller city/regional, provincial, and national arts councils gave out grants to emerging and midcareer artists and thinkers. It felt much easier to get money—including if you didn't have a spotless academic record. My first $1,500 Toronto Arts Council Grant to Emerging Writers in 1997 was the most money I'd ever had in my life. I'd submitted an application on recycled paper (like it had an old résumé on the other side) because I couldn't afford new paper, and my publication credits were mostly zines and the underground newspaper I worked on. It was common among the radicals I knew to get a small $2,000 grant to write a book or start a grassroots arts project, to know your friends had too, and to work together. There were plenty of community-based places to think and talk about ideas: the one-room, roach-filled apartment where me and my partner read and discussed Black and Indigenous activist writers and revolutionaries Assatta Shakur's, John Trudell's, Lee Maracle's, and Kuwasi Balagoon's writings; the prison-justice and psych-survivor shows on the community radio station; and the laundromat in Kensington Market where we held the meetings of the prison-justice newspaper I worked at because it was wheelchair accessible and no one was going to charge us money for hanging out there. In community spaces

116   Piepzna-Samarasinha

like Sistah's Cafe, the queer woman-of-color bookstore/café on Queen Street founded by Sister Vision Press, the first queer woman-of-color bookstore/café I'd ever experienced, and A Different Booklist, run by two queer Caribbean men who were partners, we read and argued ideas and could hang out and drink coffee for free for hours. There always seemed to be a free lecture coming up with land defenders and feminists of color. At the prison-justice paper, our organizing strategies included leaving copies on the bus, at prison waiting rooms, and at the free clinic and having them on hand to offer to people we fell into conversation with on the street. We identified as lumpen, cadre-based grassroots or organic intellectuals.

But what's a grassroots/organic intellectual? *Organic intellectual* is a term originally coined by the Italian Marxist theorist Antonio Gramsci in his prison notebooks in the early 1930s (see Gramsci 1992). He defined traditional intellectuals as those who see themselves as autonomous and independent from the ruling social group but who still believe they stand for truth and reason and the "objective." Organic intellectuals, on the other hand, are embedded in an oppressed social class or group (usually a working-class or poor one), are not separate from that communual knowledge, and use their labor to change the world that oppresses their community.

I learned the term *organic intellectual* at age twenty from Dr. Jerma Jackson via a core text in her "Intro to African American History" course, *A Life in the Struggle: Ivory Perry and the Culture of Opposition* (1988) by George Lipsitz. Ivory Perry was a working-class, rural, southern Black freedom organizer who did liberatory thinking and organizing work outside of academic contexts in the 1950s, 1960s, and 1970s. Not an academic, not someone viewing himself as exceptional, Perry invented thinking and practice while and by doing freedom work within his community. Lipsitz defined *organic intellectuals* as people who, unlike traditional intellectuals, "learn about the world by trying to change it and change the world by learning about it from the perspective of the needs and aspirations of their social group. Organic intellectuals succeed only when their organizing efforts articulate and activate ideas already present in the community, and when they tap existing networks of communication and action" (11). This is a wildly different idea of success and being smart.

I'm Too Crazy for a Job   117

Jumping forward a few years after I read about Perry, queer, disabled, Puerto Rican Jewish Communist elder writer and scholar Aurora Levins Morales would build on Gramsci and go in a wildly different, queer, brown direction when she called herself an organic intellectual:

> When I call myself an organic intellectual, I mean the ideas I carry with me were grown on soil I know, that I can tell you about the mineral balance, the weather, the labor involved in preparing them for use. In the marketplace of ideas, we are pushed towards the supermarket chains that are replacing the tiny rural colmado, told that store bought is better, imported is best, and sold on empty calories in shiny packaging instead of open crates and barrels of produce to which the earth still clings. The intellectual traditions I come from create theory out of shared lives, instead of sending away for it. (1998, 27)

A few years after Levins Morales would write these words, I would shoplift Joe Kadi's working-class Arab queer text *Thinking Class: Sketches of a Cultural Worker* (1996), where he would echo Levins Morales's description of the extractive marketplace of ideas in writing his own experiences as a working-class disabled Arab trans first-generation scholar trying to survive grad school (words I would read over and over when I returned to grad school after a decade's absence and needed to survive it):

> Middle and upper-middle class academics have traditionally sought out the experiences and stories of working-class/working-poor people for use in shaping theory. That is, we provide the raw material of bare facts and touching stories; they transform these rough elements into theory. Sound familiar? Gosh, it sounds like an exact replication of factory activity. Academics have approached me after I've given presentations on class, and said, "The stories about your family are so interesting" (Oh, *thank* you so much). "Don't you think they'd be stronger if you let them stand on their own?" Unedited translation: give me your stories, I'll write the theory. Leave it to the experts. *It's time to forget that shit.* (40, emphasis in original)

A decade later, queer Black troublemaker and independent scholar-writer-teacher Alexis Pauline Gumbs dug deeper into the soil and bloomed the fruit of what organic intellectuals can be and need in her Brilliance

118   Piepzna-Samarasinha

Remastered project, founded in 2012 as a space for rebel BIPOC academics and dropouts striving to survive the violence of academia and stay accountable to the communities they are part of. Gumbs coined the term *community-accountable scholars*, and Brilliance Remastered's original tagline was "Take Your Degree Home Whole and Keep Your Soul." Gumbs wrote: "Brilliance Remastered is a wellspring for remembering that as Audre Lorde said, the master's house is not our only form of support. As community, we are our primary and most valuable sources of support . . . It is my intention that . . . you will be able to choose to continue your passionate inquiry on your own terms in ways that prioritize and support strategies of power for the communities you love" (Gumbs n.d.a; original statement rearranged here).

As organic or grassroots or community-accountable scholars, we *stay close to home*, even if we go into the master's house. We bring and find home as we travel all over the world—to the ancestors, the future, and the stars. We are rooted in, learning *with* (not just "from"), and accountable to the communities we are part of—not separate from them, studying them from afar, having rocketed off someplace else. We are connected to land, our bodies, and our lineage. We are not competitive.

The idea that you could be smart outside of formal academia: that you could think and argue about ideas through action and talking with other people, also outside of academia, who already also had their own wisdom and knowledge (and who might also be you.) That you could be doing all this not as the one special one but as part of a community was thoroughly against what I had been raised on: the concept of an intellectual elite, thoroughbred, top or one percent, running like hell without looking back, or at the most going back and seeding knowledge to the masses and "saving" them. These rebel ideas of being a community-based thinker saved my life. I knew that that was what I wanted to be. The idea that I could form my own ideas of what smart was and that it could be working class, brown, neurodivergent, organic, alive, and embodied—that it could save and heal not destroy me, and that it could give back to all the other BIPOC disabled broke-ass weirdos out there—came from all these moments of contacting rebellious, Black, brown, feminist, working-class, and disabled/psych-survivor ways of taking apart the WSCCAAP's ideas of "intelligence" and "scholarship" that were killing me.

Moving to Toronto meant rebelling against the track I'd been put on at age six. I didn't do what was expected of me: graduate and go straight into grad school, complete advanced degrees, and excel as an academic while being grateful and not making waves, either by questioning the system, doing activism, or being inconveniently depressed and neurodivergent. Instead, I dropped out, and it was a big fucking deal. I chose a different life. I didn't take the GRE or go to grad school. I stepped off the path. In doing so, even and especially when it looked "crazy" to others, like I was ruining my life, I was making a brilliant disabled, neurodivergent brown life choice.

I lived in Toronto, inhabiting that space for a decade, and I thrived. Everyone I knew worked day jobs to make enough to live on, but we didn't see our paid jobs as our real work, just as a means to an end to buy time to do our real, mostly unpaid writing/creating/organizing work. It was normal that I was telemarketing and cleaning houses and landscaping to make rent and buy groceries *and* I was also writing poems, working on the prison-justice newspaper, being an activist. Being professional and getting a degree weren't a requirement to have a thinking, creating life.

Our creative ways of surviving capitalism while doing intellectual, teaching, and creative work were vast, and not separate from the work. We supported each other through mutual aid, way beyond the current popularization of the word; there was always food and often transit tokens at OCAP (Ontario Coalition Against Poverty), CARPV (Coalition Against Racist Police Violence), Bulldozer Community News Service, and Psych Survivor Pride Day meetings. I was able to access grants through the arts council system, where I would get a few thousand dollars to buy me time off work to stare at the wall and move words around. I started teaching writing as a community-based writing teacher working with LGBTQ youth, API (Asian and Pacific Islander) BIPOC youth, and youth in shelters and community spaces, and although I often felt like I was flying by the seat of my pants, I had peers, and we were developing our own thinking and practices around teaching by talking with each other. I co-created a school for radical Asian poetry and history with a bunch of other Asian queer radicals and won a City of Toronto Award for my work creating and teaching a writing program for queer, trans, and Two-Spirit youth. I wrote and got my first book published on a small, radical South Asian press. All of this work and space gave me what academia promises: a place to think, argue, create, and piss each other off. And I did it while sick, working class, poor, brown, queer, and Crazy.

By the time I went back to grad school a decade later, as much as I wanted it, I also knew I didn't need it. I referred to grad school as something I did in my spare time. When I first sat in on classes at Mills College's MFA program, specifically queer Malaysian literary superstar Justin Chin's memoir class (and was shocked by the mediocrity and racism of many of his students), Justin looked at me at the end of class and said, "Why do you want to go here? You're already doing stuff. You'll be bored. And they'll resent you because you've already published your book." I answered, "I want to maybe have your job someday." He nodded.

Grad school both made me a better writer in spite of itself and was a place where I cried in the bathroom because I felt so alienated from all the weird white people with money who'd never done anything on their own. I snuck off every class break to watch and rewatch my friend Gabriel Teodros's music video for his "No Label" rap on the computer in the grad lounge because it reminded me of where I came from, my community in Toronto: a bunch of working-class, Black and brown people dancing in front of an ordinary house in South Seattle as Gabe rapped about defying labels and binaries and being a diasporic mixed-race Ethiopian while wearing a homemade "I heart my melanin" T-shirt. I read and re-read the working-class queer Arab writer Joe Kadi's essay "Stupidity 'Deconstructed,'" about being working class in grad school to keep myself going. I reminded myself that universities don't own smart and that I could define my own version of smart as I ventured back to uni after a decade of community-based scholarship. I clutched Kadi's words close to my chest:

> I've figured out I belong in the university. Not just when they need a janitor, or a cook, or a construction worker. But when I want to go. If I choose to study there, I won't let anyone make me feel stupid; I'll

remember why it's so important they try. I won't let them turn me into
an assimilationist, a fraud, a middle-class-identified polite (person)
who's grateful for all the help these nice rich people offer. I'll stay true
to my roots. I'll use my brains, and my hands, to take this system apart.
I'll use my brains, and my hands, to get your feet off my neck. (1996, 56)

Working-class freak survivor neurodivergent weirdos deserve to be wherever we want to be, inside or outside the system, and we can be our best,
smartest selves without being either middle class or NT aspirational.

Disabled Visiting Schoolteacher Uncle: You Can Go Your Own Way

I didn't end up getting Justin's job, though. I had been doing college gigs
for years as a visiting performer, keynote, and workshop teacher, a strategy
taught to me by other grassroots queer artists (one of whom told me, "If
you call what you do performance art and add a workshop, you can get
$2,000!"), and after I got my MFA, I just kept right on going. I didn't go
get the lecturer job. It just didn't make sense to me, access-, spoons-, and
money-wise. Friends who had also graduated with MFAs were working
four different adjunct community college freshman-composition classes
in four different exurbs of the Bay, driving hours a day, correcting hundreds of essays, and still were on food stamps. This was the path we'd been
taught: you had to do adjuncting in order to get offered the slightly better
associate professor lecturer gigs.

But I knew I couldn't do that with the spoons I had as a chronically ill
and disabled person whose disabilities involve frequent illness, pain, and
energy crashes: working that kind of schedule and commute would land
me straight on my ass with double pneumonia. Instead, I pursued a path
of making the most money I could in the least hours possible, just like I
had in Toronto in the 1990s and 2000s. These strategies allowed room for
sickness and Madness, which a deficit model of disability would see as lack
but which I saw as spaces of both pain and generative possibility. My pain
days were often also the days I wrote my best essays. Gigging allowed me
time to do the hours and hours of unpaid (but gorgeous) labor of sitting
at a kitchen table or bed, making poetry, memoirs, and essays happen. I

kept my lucrative hours teaching sexual health, breast, and pelvic exams to medical students, being a visiting lecturer/performer/keynote speaker/ workshop teacher on the college gig circuit, reading tarot cards in my bedroom. Even with the hours of setup labor, I could make in one or two weekend campus visits what friends made in a whole community college freshman-comp semester.

And more than that: I could say and do more than what a lot of the professors who taught me could do. They might get fired or harassed or be denied tenure if they said some of the things I said: I didn't have tenure or a salary to lose, so I could shoot my mouth off more. We both were doing essential work, just different kinds, that supported each other. And I was still teaching writing and literature—but online and independently. Years before the 2020 COVID-19 Zoom boom of online content, I created and taught my dream writing classes, among them "Frida and Harriet's Children," a writing class by and for disabled queer and trans BIPOC writers, in a text-only, non-sensory-overload format that was accessible to Deaf and neurodivergent students. Everyone could write from bed, on a heating pad, in their wheelchair-accessible house, and a long-access check-in was how we started and centered every class.

Alisa Bierria, the Black feminist scholar and cofounder of INCITE! Women of Color Against Violence, writing of her work as cofounder of the radical feminist-of-color rape crisis center Communities Against Rape and Abuse (CARA) in the anthology *The Revolution Will Not Be Funded* (2007), describes CARA's audaciously creative strategies to fund it using nonstate and noncarceral approaches to abuse. In the face of Seattle city cuts to antiviolence funding and scrutinization of CARA because of its explicit Black feminist politics, CARA used a "dual identity" strategy, where, "for example, in all materials designed for city officials, we replaced the phrase 'community organizing,' which seemed overtly political, with the phrase 'community engagement.' . . . This kind of 'doublespeak' and 'dual identity' is a common practice among people of color and poor people who spend time and spaces dominated by white people and middle-class and wealthy people" (157–58).

In pursuing a strategy of always being a guest lecturer, never a bride, I have relied on a similar strategy as a disability justice thinker and writer without a trust fund. I continually and imperfectly ask myself: How am I hustling the system to make the sweetest equation of spoons plus impact plus money plus freedom plus free-zone time plus the work I was made to do? Is it still working? Do I need to evolve my strategies? This continual re-evaluation of hustle is a disability justice survival and intellectual strategy, fueled by disabled self-determination: *How is this survival strategy working and changing as my bodymind changes and grows? What strategies give the most power to my disabled BIPOC thinker-writer-self?*

By being a perennial visiting writer/scholar, I gave up on some things I could really use: a regular paycheck, health insurance, and retirement paid for by a university. I honor my friends who decided the university is the best solution for them because it provides those things, and I do not think they are wrong. But I look at what I've gained: the ability to work at my own disabled and autistic brilliant snail-and-lightning pace, to write and teach freely, to be my sick and neurodivergent self with more autonomy, and not to be slowly sickened by micro and macro aggressions/ oppressions to the point where I get cancer or more PTSD, like so many disabled BIPOC academics I have known. The disabled and neurodivergent wildmind insists: *There is no one correct disabled strategy. We do not control the system, but we are struggling to make a million brilliant shape-shifting cripple ways to hack the system.* We work inside universities, we work outside, we coach, we throw our own classes, we dip in and out, we make our own schools.

Alexis Pauline Gumbs has written extensively about her experience as a brilliant Black queer feminist student and choosing to turn down plum offers of academic jobs to instead be an independent scholar, "walking in the legacy of black lady school teachers in post-slavery communities who offered sacred educational space to the intergenerational newly free in exchange for the random necessities of life" (Gumbs n.d.b). Her Black queer grassroots scholarship strategies are ones I've studied and learned from as I sibling my brown queer disabled ones. I am also supported by disability justice spaces that believe that interesting ideas are not just the provenance of people who are "smart" as anointed by the academy or the medical-industrial complex's racist and ableist IQ tests. In disability justice online spaces like Sick and Disabled Queers, a long-running Facebook group founded by disabled and Mad Mizrahi writer and organizer William Maria Rain in 2010, someone could use their one spoon to share a great, weird idea they had at 3:00 a.m. and that was valid, even and especially if that idea was their only offer. Nobody was fancy or official—we all were just regular sick crips, disregarded by official society as kooks and people who took too many sick days lying in bed typing to each other. DJ spaces have created horizontal spaces of creative and thinking, away from stardom, birthing so many good ideas from a space of collective disabled brilliance. It's Cripple U, and there's no prerequisites or high SAT scores required.

There's a thing I call the *audacity of autism*. One of the great things about being autistic is the sense we have of *you can go your own way*. Even though allistic society relentlessly punishes us for doing this, a lot of us persist in creating amazing life structures we do *our way*. When the world is set up to shut you out and fuck you over, sometimes you go, *"Well, I might as well just do what the fuck I want."* Both poor and autistic people (and people who are both) have particular kinds of wild-ass genius where we just make shit up that works for us. It's something that confuses the hell out of NT and middle- or upper-class people: they assume we must be secretly rich to take the risks we do. What they don't understand is that when you're already pushed out on a limb, sometimes you might as well jump off and try to fly.

What I want is nothing more or less than the dismantling of the ableist, racist academic- and intelligence-industrial complex and the creation of spaces where there are a million brilliant ways to create, dream, think, lie down, and fly. Where survival is divorced from ableist allistic definitions of intelligence. Where the choices for survival lie beyond being a thoroughbred or being dead and we all have what we need. Where autistic kids are loved as we are, however we are. I offer these stories as testimony, memory, and possibility models toward our creating this future and as testament to the work we are doing to make it happen right now. And most of all, as an honor song to the kid I was, that ordinary, Worcester's own, freak, weird, genius, regular kid who loved learning and writing and thinking with all their heart. They are one of many epitomes of what we long for in decolonized, antiableist thinking and creating.

You can go your own way. Let's.

Works Cited

Bascom, Julia. 2021. "Interview: Julia Bascom." *Neurodiversity News,* Jan. 7. At https://neurodiversitynews.net/interview-julia-bascom/.

Bierria, Alissa. 2007. "Pursuing a Radical Anti-violence Agenda inside/outside a Non-profit Structure." In *The Revolution Will Not Be Funded: Beyond the Non-profit Industrial Complex,* edited by INCITE! Women of Color Against Violence, 151–64. Boston: South End Press.

Gramsci, Antonio. 1992. *Prison Notebooks.* Vol. 1. Edited with an introduction by Joseph A. Buttigieg. Translated by Joseph A. Buttigieg and Antonio Callari. New York: Columbia Univ. Press.

Gumbs, Alexis Pauline. n.d.a. "About." Brilliance Remastered program (website). At http://brillianceremastered.alexispauline.com.

———. n.d.b. "Biography." Conscious Camp. At https://consciouscampus.com /talent/dr-alexis-pauline-gumbs/#:~:text=Dr.%20Alexis%20Pauline%20 Gumbs%20is,the%20random%20necessities%20of%20life.

Kadi, Joe. 1996. "Stupidity 'Deconstructed.'" In *Thinking Class: Sketches from a Cultural Worker,* 39–58. Boston: South End Press.

Levins Morales, Aurora. 1998. "Certified Organic Intellectual." In *Medicine Stories: History, Culture and the Politics of Integrity,* 27–32. Boston: South End Press.

Lewis, Talila "TL." 2022. "Working Definition of Ableism—January 2022 Update." *Talila A. Lewis* (blog), Jan. 1. At https://www.talilalewis.com/blog/working -definition-of-ableism-january-2022-update.

Lipsitz, George. 1988. A *Life in the Struggle: Ivory Perry and the Culture of Opposition.* Philadelphia: Temple Univ. Press.

Mingus, Mia. 2015. "Medical Industrial Complex Visual." *Leaving Evidence* (blog), Feb. 6. At https://leavingevidence.wordpress.com/2015/02/06/medical -industrial-complex-visual/.

Piepzna-Samarasinha, Leah. n.d. "My people." Unpublished poem in "The Way Disabled People Love Each Other," poetry manuscript in progress.

7

Embrace the Lie

Seeking Truths through Reading, Madly

Melanie Jones

Content notes: gun violence, eating disorder, biphobia, suicidality

People get Mad studies. At least, they do eventually. Sooner or later, I have buried them under enough evidence, bombarded them with enough terminology, bared enough scars. It becomes clear, or at least plausible, that what a culture decides is not "right"—not appropriate, not rational, not real—fluctuates through time and space, carrying the flotsam of the Mad in its wake. People see more and more how we drown in the discursive current: how being labeled "crazy" denies us the right to be heard in any language but objectification.[1] They can trace the costs of dehumanization once the dam breaks: the millions marginalized, brutalized, unhoused, or stripped of rights because of the voices they hear, the worlds they travel, the demons with which they grapple.[2]

1. Mad speakers are often positioned "within a rhetorical black hole." The very act of claiming a Mad positionality casts the speaker as unauthoritative when declaiming anything but iterations of disease and lack. When it comes to Mad speakers discussing our realities, identities, and minds, anything resembling a challenge to the status quo has already been dismissed as warped, inaccurate, or deficient based on our diagnoses—or abstracted into something so otherworldly and transcendent, so outside "normal" cognition, that the humanity of the speaker ends up erased anyhow (Prendergast 2001).

2. As intersections of race and ethnicity, gender and sexuality, and class and citizenship converge around Mad identity, the statistics become exponentially grimmer. For an in-depth look at how homelessness and a diagnosis of mental illness converge, see

What they often *don't* get is why I choose to work in literature. This bafflement can extend even to my colleagues. If my goal is to explore new ways of engaging with lived experiences of Madness, then why do I operate in a discipline dedicated to fiction? If I want to advocate for the most vulnerable siblings in our Mad network, why not work in sociology or law, where I could still "do" fiction on the side?

At the root of such questions is the assumption that literature finds purpose only in the service of concrete aims; that literary study, in turn, has value only when linked to the study of something else. And the courses I teach do call on students to consider fictional texts in conversation with other fields. As a comparatist working across Anglophone, Russophone, and Francophone worlds, I must often do explicitly transdisciplinary work. I must grapple with the cultural narratives I interrogate, unpacking the gaps and exploring the tangles that come from Mad fictions' reciprocal interactions.[3] Like the literary theorist Rita Felski (2011), I have little patience for theorists who contend that engaging with other fields will diminish the singularity and alterity of literary form.

Nonetheless, I also join Felski in my dissatisfaction with approaches that serve largely to "highlight literature's relationship to what it is not," reducing fiction to an ideological slogan or a stepping-stone to "real," quantifiable data (2011, 6). The suffocating nature of that approach is particularly noticeable when one is working on literatures of Madness. Attempts to embrace "questioning and destabilizing dominant discourses" of race, gender, or sexuality and to "expos[e] their normalizing and essentializing functions" often come to an abrupt halt where psychiatric categories

---

Who Qualifies for Rights? (Failer 2018). For a discussion of overdiagnosis and negative outcomes for racial minorities, see *Eliminating Race-Based Mental Health Disparities* (Williams, Rosen, and Kanter 2019).

3. In practice, such interdisciplinary work is little different from that of a dear friend in philosophy, who must necessarily draw on disciplines such as history and economics to make a moral case for reparations; nor is it far off from work by experimental psychiatrists who use resources from the humanities to supplement their therapeutic approach. Literary studies, however, has been so thoroughly denigrated by the machinery of neoliberal capitalism—and so thoroughly tarred by its own elitist heritage—that it must, even within the embattled humanities, fight tirelessly to justify its very existence.

are concerned (LeFrançois and Diamond 2014, 40). Moralistic reasoning and rigidly biomedical interpretations continue to dominate medical humanities programs, which approach fiction overwhelmingly as a how-to guide for clinical empathy or a practice run for patient visits (Sparks 2014).

When Felski warns that deterministic readings flatten our "dialogue with literature" to "a permanent diagnosis" (2011, 1), her choice of words is telling. If literary study must increasingly defend its existence through recourse to "what it is not," so too am I often pressed to pin down what is mutable in me if I am to make my perspective on Mad literature appear valid. And if Mad literature's readers must continually resist both opaque alterity or flattening diagnosis, so too must I constantly reposition myself to avoid reducing my subjecthood to sterility and silence.

This chapter traces my ambivalence about being Mad while working in Mad fiction and the value I ultimately draw from that ambivalence. Fiction frees me to occupy multiple, contradictory, and at times equally valid truths without fear or restraint, even as that immersion also forces me to ethical action, calling on me to make and take stands. As a scholar, I seek to return the favor by reading, madly: I commit myself to an endless dance between certainty and uncertainty, seeking and refusing explanation or origin, so that the truths of questioning and conversation are not lost in our bid for ends and answers.

> The final belief is to believe in a fiction, which you know to be a
> fiction, there being nothing else. The exquisite truth is to know that
> it is a fiction and that you believe in it willingly.
> —Wallace Stevens, "Adagia I," in *Opus Posthumous*
> (1990)

Reading fiction requires us to embrace a lie. We take up a book knowing it will lie to us—that its pages contain worlds that, in all the ways we are used to divvying out realities, must be classified as false. And yet that "must" is, if only temporarily, laid to one side. Walls against the unlikely, impossible, and unacceptable come tumbling down. We indulge ourselves in a paradox of immersion at a safe distance. In suspending our disbelief, in agreeing to fiction's terms, we open ourselves to meanings rarely allowed outside its bindings. We yearn for whatever truths we might guess at, what

Embrace the Lie 129

imaginings we brush against, how to exist in suspension a while longer even as we are driven on by the desire for revelation. We may even rejoice in the questions that remain unanswered on the final page.

What is an intellectual exercise to some is an ecstatic permission to others.[4] Never has my yearning for multiplicity, my desire to embrace mutability, been stronger than when I navigate my own cognitive divergence. Never have my reading experiences been richer than when I am overtaken by the strange colors shading my mental-emotional world. Literature's ravenous need to seduce speaks so strongly to what has felt dangerous or rejected in me, what has been shamed for overwhelming excess or dismissed as unbearable lack. The production of fiction and its reproduction through each reader carve out a space where we might, even for a moment, escape myopic, tyrannical definitions of truth.[5]

Reading, teaching, writing Mad fiction let me feel my own openly contradictory identities—as ill, as traumatized, as making myself sick, as teetering on crazy—to be coexistent, perpetually held in a suspension of manifold beliefs. There lies in so many of my students, so many of my peers, the same desire I feel to lay down the weight of a static, dominating vision of the world that so rarely matches up with what we see, what we feel: the desire to play in the text and allow it to play with us. Literature does not place me outside epistemological authorities and their attendant claims. Yet it can make the more rigid and arbitrary among them turn fluid, allowing alternative readings to slip through the cracks. Under the cover of literary exploration, I can claim a kind of rebellious credulity.

4. What we can imagine, what we can dream, is also a tool of resistance. "We are always dreaming and have always been dreaming," Leah Lakshmi Piepzna-Samarasinha asserts, "way beyond what we are allowed to dream" (2020, 253)—visions beyond facile discussions of tolerance and cure that take us to whole worlds just out of our grasp.

5. This is the beauty of Gérard de Nerval's autofictional *Aurélia* (1855; see de Nerval 2006), where readers are baited with the promise of biographical revelation only to be led through a world, as a student once remarked, where *truth* and *reality* are no longer synonymous; it is the intoxication of Gisèle Pineau's *Chair piment* (Skin on Fire, 2004), which continually blurs the lines between magic and medicine, curse and trauma, revelation and hallucination.

130   Jones

Yet reading while Mad is rarely just about the ecstasy of belief. We may also rejoice in a defiant form of doubt. For so many of us, our particular brand of truth is constantly under siege. We are dragged down by distrust: of our experiences, our processes, our functions, our faiths. Yet one of the hallmarks of Mad fiction is its commitment to testing the limits of our convictions. It floods us with unreliable narrators, shifting temporalities, baiting half-truths, and so it frees us to acknowledge uncertainty as something not unique to us but fundamentally omnipresent. In overlapping genres such as horror, magical realism, and especially Black speculative fiction, which often "take for granted multiple forms of cognition [and] mental engagement," readers' "understanding of the world must [repeatedly] be engaged—in order to be confirmed or disrupted" (Pickens 2019, 12, 14). These works don't just attempt to fool us; they bring the tenuousness of any concrete, collective understanding of realities and truths to a head.[6] At its most rebellious, Mad fiction asks not so much the question "Who 'knows' and who doesn't 'know,' but what does it mean to 'know'?" (Felman 1978, 12). Yet the authors also show us, often in the starkest of terms, that we must grapple with our doubts if we are ever to move forward. We must seek solidarity across our uncertainties. There is triumph for the Mad reader in delving into a different shade of doubt and in seeing others confront it for the first time. There is freedom in embracing the gaps a book refuses to close.

In this intoxicating space, this flow of discourse, we can accept how much we do not know and how very little we fundamentally are. "Incomprehensibility has an enormous power over us in illness," Virginia Woolf notes, "more legitimately perhaps than the upright will allow." We can begin to push back once "the police are off-duty," and we are allowed to "grasp the meaning" of something that has not yet been silenced (1926, 41). You will not accept my truth? You make me doubt whether it is a truth at all? Then fine, it is all a lie, if admitting that is what it takes for me to

6. Anna Starobinets's short-story collection *Perekhodnyi vozrast* (*An Awkward Age*, 2008) is a masterclass in such disorientation. Each story ends either in the genre of dark fantasy or medical realism, but it is near impossible for readers to determine that outcome until the end.

play within it—but still, all this may be true, regardless. How do you really know for sure?

> Poetic knowledge is born in the great silence of scientific knowledge.
> —Aimé Césaire, "Poésie et connaissance"
> (1944, my translation)

This is a truth. It is not all of them.

Another truth is that I do still want to know what it means to be Mad. What it means to be a Mad scholar working in maddened, maddening texts.

When I first disclosed to a mentor, she laughed. "Oh," she chuckled reassuringly, "but you're not really crazy!" It stings to have an identity taken from you just as you've begun to claim it, no matter how uncomfortably it sits under your skin. And I have claimed it. I have slung it across my shoulders as I climbed the academic ladder. That conversation was not the first time a disclosure was met with disbelief. It would not be the last. These moments force me repeatedly to recognize that the flavor of my thoughts, the quiet self-cannibalism of my moods, siphon me off from the "problem children" in the eyes of my culture: the vilified psychotics, the demonized schizophrenics. My status as cis-passing and white, my upper-class childhood, my educational advantages—all permit me to wander halls that might otherwise be barred, to go through doors that might otherwise swiftly be shut and locked. When I take up the label *Mad* as a researcher or instructor, it is primarily as a form of strategic essentialism. It is a way to build solidarity under a politically expedient alliance while still recognizing its limitations (Spivak 2014). Mad-as-such, at least in public, is something I can shrug on and off—so long as its more extreme manifestations stay behind closed doors and its costs are kept off official records. It is a state of quasi-invisibility, of ever-ready accompliceship.[7] I taste its promise. I feel the weight of its opportunity.

7. Whereas *ally* denotes general support, *accomplice* suggests active participation. Sometimes this accompliceship looks like campaigning against police presence on campuses; sometimes it looks more like unpacking a teaching assistant's ableist rant under the guise of being a "normal" colleague so they take my critique seriously. For the term *accompliceship*'s indebtedness to antiracist movements, see *Taking Sides* (Milstein 2015).

132   Jones

Still, I feel an insatiable desire for an identity where my nature is not always in doubt, my experiences so often fraught, and my positioning so deeply ambivalent. It took me a decade to embrace my bisexuality; it took much longer to accept both the essential fluidity and sociocultural construction of sexual labels.[8] Nonetheless, being queer has been an overwhelmingly liberatory experience for me. Even as I remain closeted to most family members, even amid the biphobia I have witnessed and experienced, I can clearly differentiate between external shaming and my own evolving sense of gender and sexuality. My Madness is different: far less easy to categorize as positive or negative, as embodying suffering or pointing toward liberation.[9]

Questions of identity, meanwhile, quickly dovetail into questions of origin.[10] I cannot believe that biomedical determinism has led to all the many disorders listed in my chart, especially when they feature such

8. Unsurprisingly, Mad studies is deeply indebted to queer theory in its understanding of identity as performative and of truth as something constructed and sustained through repetition and citation. Both fields seek ways to reincorporate what society casts as deviant or inferior, but without replicating hierarchical binaries (Spandler 2017).

9. As I weigh these seemingly clear-cut differences, however, I am reminded that high depression and suicide rates in the LGBTQ+ community were historically blamed on inherent deviancy rather than on the tremendous stigma its members faced and the social traumas with which they grappled. Loving the same sex or being trans often could mean a life of self-loathing, failed relationships, and rejection by society, and this correlation was often treated as self-evidently causative (Bruckert and Hannem 2012, 80–85). It is essential that I do not romanticize how painful living while Mad has often been for me. Nevertheless, I have seen how radically life can change when one's world is no longer structured in such exact opposition to divergent forms of expression, experience, and knowledge. If I had been born fifty years later, how might a lessening of similar stigmas and traumas have woven my Madness in different forms and framed it in different terms?

10. This is near unavoidable as Western models of mental illness often lock horns precisely on the issue of an origin that determines essence. Those who attack biomedical models of mental illness often disparage psychiatric intervention precisely because they believe Madness is socially provoked and constructed. Likewise, many advocates of the biomedical approach ground their interpretations in the assumption of an essential difference in brain chemistry, even if they acknowledge the social factors at play (Donley and Buckley 2000).

Embrace the Lie   133

cultural chimeras as anorexia nervosa and an anxiety disorder that only emerged in graduate school. Yet nor can I accept the theory that trauma, even on the scale of capitalist catastrophe, is solely responsible for my major depression, hypomanic cycles, and the recurrent desire to die beginning from the onset of puberty. Even with the rise of biopsychosocial models,[11] I still feel pressured to privilege aspects and negate others, to incessantly parcel out these splintering categories along a spectrum of agency and blame, cause and effect, patient and scholar.

Clinical thought wants a way to track the truth of a disorder to its source in the body, to pin disability to an origin point. This act of diagnosing an entire consciousness all too easily becomes a form of cognitive shortchanging: once we have named something, we take it as a point of reference, and we believe we understand it (Donley and Buckley 2000, 171). Metaphors become literal; pathways become ends. Psychiatry has helped me to heal in some ways. Yet many of its practitioners continue to resist learning from or with Mad people. It assumes the need to cure what I consider parts of my own self.

The social model actively combats this reduction and flatly refuses the automatic designation of divergent bodies as abject or inferior. Yet in practice this model also often willingly narrows its own parameters of eligibility. Even Mad studies in its "march from shame to pride" can struggle to acknowledge those who "who refuse to orient themselves toward positive affect" (Miyatsu 2018, 50) and often privileges "survivors" who reject the tenets of psychiatry over "service users" who still embrace the idea of recovery (Spandler 2017, 6). It can even end up replicating the sane/

---

11. The biopsychosocial model, coined by George Engel in 1977, sees health as a kind of Venn diagram, built on an ongoing series of interactions between the biological realm of disability or pathology, the psychological realm of thoughts and emotions, and the social realm of economic, cultural, and environmental factors. This holistic model has been increasingly embraced by academic medicine and health advocacy groups in recent years. The fact remains, however, that the same biomedical essentialism Engel critiqued nearly half a century ago remains a pressing concern for Mad activists today. For more on the history and application of Engel's model, see "The Biopsychosocial Model 25 Years Later: Principles, Practice, and Scientific Inquiry" (Borrell-Carrió, Suchman, and Epstein 2004).

134   Jones

Mad binary in its efforts to resist pathologization, emptying psychotic or schizophrenic states of significance altogether rather than disorienting their positionalities. By rendering the very concept of Madness baseless, it "dismisses madness as a viable subject position, ensuring that those counted as such—either by communal consensus or psy-disciplines—remain excluded from conversations about disability because they cannot logically engage [in them]" (Pickens 2019, 32). What is lost when the vast discrepancies between conceptions of Madness, illness, deviance, and divergence continue to be resolved by emptying disability's potential, when "denigrated identities are 'rescued'" from accusations of inherent inferiority by "distancing them from the 'real' of physical or cognitive aberrancy projected onto their figures" (Mitchell and Snyder 2001, 3)?

Literature seems to step into the breach. The past three centuries have witnessed an explosion of Mad fiction: its writers, researchers, and readers have elevated divergence to its own religion, its own art. Madness haunts fiction's steps: the play between truths and lies, the proclaiming and crafting of realities within worlds, can assert Mad expressions at odds with dominant logics.[12] Some scholars have even claimed that it is only through the slippery permissiveness of art that Madness can lay claim to any voice, even if all that voice can relate is the void of understanding around that Madness.[13]

As a Mad reader, I know there is a freedom in fiction's pages that cannot be matched in the world outside. The "contradictory and equal truths" of literature rely on whether I, whether we, can be comfortable

12. The early twentieth-century Martinican writers Suzanne and Aimé Césaire, for example, advocated surrealist poetry and art as tools of political transcendence. Their quest to bring the il-logical and un-conscious to the surface as a way to wrench thought and feeling in new directions came in direct response to the Western intellectual tradition, whose brutality and sterility they blamed for the birth of both colonialism and fascism (Kelley 2001, 15–19).

13. Observing the simultaneous denigration of both psychoanalysis and fiction in the latter half of the twentieth century, Shoshana Felman charts an essential "contradiction" of our age: "At a time when we believe we have 'liberated' madness . . . we repress, we deny literature, the sole channel by which madness in history has called itself by its own name, or had at the very least spoken with relative liberty" (1978, 14, my translation).

Embrace the Lie 135

in believing through doubting—whether I, whether we, can embrace the revelation of not understanding.

But where in the expansiveness of this romantic concept, in this alleged voicing, does literature allow for a Mad subject to speak? Is there room for Mad voices amid this heady dream of a voiced Madness?

I cannot resist the push of immersion and the pull of doubt. Literature's profound ambivalence strikes at something deeper than a thousand lists of symptoms, than all my collected ecstasies and pains. Yet if scientific knowledge defines but too readily binds, then poetic knowledge expands but too readily abstracts. And in the end, the results can be dishearteningly similar. The ridges of my Madness flatten into metaphor: one that continually overflows and overempties. The old allure of communicating the unsayable, the intoxication of capturing the ineffable, has often lured literary scholars into replicating medicine's old sin: carving the "carrier" hollow so that Madness stands for all that the speaker can signify.

My advisers and mentors have expressed their doubts that there is anything left in Mad fictions but endless postmodern play or the ever-more minute dissection of symptoms.[14] Mad fiction's seemingly infinite variety, inescapable fluidity, and ineffable suspension between positionalities still operate based on the assumptions outside its pages.[15] It continues to denote those claimed to be Mad as dis-placed, il-legitimate, the moment we exit fiction for life.

I do not seek some essential self in literature, any more than I do in a medical textbook or sociological study. I have seen the dangers that come

14. The twenty-first century's emptying out of meaning and truth has encouraged the "rendering [of] insanity as at once 'ubiquitous and irrelevant'" (Prendergast 2001, 49). Either the subject is Mad, and so illness is all they can hold, or they are not Mad because we all are, and so it does not make any difference. Effacement is thus paradoxically enacted through the total embrace of doubt.

15. In her overview of critical approaches to Sylvia Plath's *The Bell Jar* (1963), for example, Rose Miyatsu notes that scholars rarely see Madness as "a piece of [Esther's] identity that she might build an identity or community around," instead viewing it as "a temporary step before a feminist awakening." The kinship that Plath's protagonist feels with her fellow inmates is similarly dismissed as an aberration, "to be replaced with more 'legitimate' identifications once she is 'healed' or reintegrated back into the larger society" (2018, 52).

from such identifications. I have heard of these dangers, from others far more vulnerable to the costs. Yet there still scratches in me a hunger to feel marked across the pages, allowed to recognize the power of metaphor without stripping away the flesh. I want to flip the table where our choices sit, between a false identity and a static one, between the endless labyrinth of *The Turn of the Screw* (1898) and the diagnostic confessional of *Prozac Nation* (2001). I want to scream: "Who cares if 'Mad transcendence' is gone? We are still here!"

> No, man is broad, too broad, even, I would narrow him down.
> Devil knows what to even make of him, is the thing!
> —Fyodor Dostoevsky, *Brat'ia Karamazovy*
> ([1879–80] 2017, my translation)

I still remember every catch in my throat. Every choked-down breath.

It is May 2014. Elliot Rodger has just killed six people and wounded more than a dozen others. It is a little more than a year since my boss died by suicide, less than a month after someone I love like a younger sibling has been released from an institution. It is May 2014, and I am on the phone with a relative, trying to convince her that newscasters shouldn't automatically label the killer as mentally ill.

I know what I would like to say. How I want to unpack the ways disability has historically been "the master trope of human disqualification" (Mitchell and Snyder 2001, 3), to lay out the devastating effect the false link between disability and violence has had on Mad people.[16] I want her to care about the population getting thrown under the tracks. But while this woman knows some of what I am, I have always downplayed the full reality of my experiences to her. I am reluctant to reveal myself and so lose the right to argue on such topics at all. I am scared to lose the unconditionality of her love.

So I argue. I take a different tact, one whose rhetoric is as well worn to me as the media pattern it attempts to unravel. This conflation of sanity and morality is fundamentally flawed, I explain. This knee-jerk response

---

16. Studies such as Heather Stuart's "Violence and Mental Illness: An Overview" (2003) have repeatedly found no link between those labeled mentally ill and violent behavior; in fact, as Stuart notes, studies indicate that the Mad are either somewhat or significantly more likely to be *victims* than perpetrators.

Embrace the Lie 137

divorces individual blame from cultural culpability and effaces the racial dynamics at play.[17] Think of the harm this response does to sick people, I cannot resist adding, parenthetically adding *"how people like you might label me, how I might have been."* We know Rodger is racist, misogynistic, hateful; we have no idea if he's mentally ill.

"Of course he's crazy, Melanie," she says, exasperated. "He killed six people!"

We keep trying to make things separable. To pare off parts of ourselves and others and trace them back to a starting point so all that follows makes sense. Across even a rhizomatic model of society, of self, there must still be anchoring points.[18] We need them, at least in the world we occupy now, and we cannot help but look for solutions, answers, ends. And so we stumble in the dark: tracing places where a disorder has latched, where a divergence has been born, where the radicals have taken root—desperate to determine agency, affix guilt, free ourselves from old chains. Which self is formed in the murk of belief and action, spoken out in endless, mutable metaphor? At which point in this twisted web shall we plant our flag, only to see it slip beneath the quicksand of endless unraveling or tangled in the vines of all other points of reckoning?

Literature cannot save me, but it can repeatedly and insistently bring the crises of material and metaphor, identity and essence to a fruitful head. If "no term in the history of madness is neutral" (Reaume 2006, 182), then I will let that subjectivity be continually highlighted. I will not forget it in a quest for medical determinism or sociological assertion. I will choose to

17. A shooter's race remains the strongest predictor of whether media outlets discuss the mental health of the perpetrator. White male shooters get armchair diagnosed, treated largely as individual aberrations to the status quo. Black and Brown shooters, by contrast, are often approached as homogenous products of a violent, sick, or twisted culture (Duxbury, Frizzell, and Lindsay 2018).

18. Gilles Deleuze and Félix Guattari (1972) offer the rhizome as a mode of knowledge and model of society in contrast to the arboreal, linear, originary fixation of the West. Rhizomes are a collection of simultaneous operations-assemblages that allow for multiple, nonhierarchical points of entrance and departure. They are always in the middle, between, and interbeing; all points are connected to something else, but there is no unity in the sense of a final or ultimate whole.

138   Jones

engage it head-on, working within a field equally and endlessly suspicious of, enamored with, and bedeviled by questions of origin and meaning.

A book is both a closed and an open thing. The words a text yields are freighted with intention, a life's blood further cast through the voices that birthed, surrounded, and fought within the author, outside their full knowledge and beyond our full ability to pinpoint them. Yet a book is also a creature of porous process, given new life as it is eternally (re)written with each (re)reading. We cannot ignore either aspect without losing the "human weightiness" that comes from engaging differences across our worlds, our minds: the crucial confrontations that fuel debates over reliability, trustworthiness, and resonance beyond its pages (Burke 2008). Yet to acknowledge those confrontations is to admit not only that what a book contains is both true (from a mind, rooted in a reality) and not true (from one's mind, rooted in another reality) but also that it both does and does not have an origin or essence—that the best way to parse its materiality is to grapple with the warp and weft of its metaphor. This is a familiar conundrum for the Mad: to be true and not real, to be constructed and essentialized, to be the essence and escape of narrative possibility.[19]

If I as a literary scholar hope to move beyond the binary of transcendent abstraction and dehumanizing pathology, I must engage my field—and its surrounding interlocutors—by reading, madly. I must dance between dreaming and doubt and must value context, contingency, and conversation as the best ways to break from old binaries without emptying out differences in the name of inclusion. This means allowing divergent perspectives to multiply and hold space for one another, to let my guard down enough to let unexpected questions challenge, reconceptualize, and transform what we know of our worlds in the "testing ground" of fictional exploration. But it also means slipping constantly between a

---

19. In making this link, I build on David Mitchell and Sharon Snyder's work, in which they assert that "disability inaugurates the act of interpretation" and "incit[es] the act of meaning-making itself" (2001, 6). In *Narrative Prosthesis* (2001), they argue that disability draws our attention to the "variable, vulnerable, and inscribable" nature of materiality. What spurs narrative invention is the tension generated by language, which "lacks the very physicality that it seeks to control or represent" (6–8).

"critical maddening" that strips bare the "material and discursive conditions" necessary to create categories of Madness (Wolframe 2018, 35), on the one hand, and a Mad criticality that asks how this "strategic" deviance does or does not translate from representative to realized, on the other (Mitchell and Snyder 2001, 9).

In practice, this Mad criticality can look rather like being a restless gadfly: flitting between literature and Mad studies, crossing the often stark lines between disability studies and the health humanities. My work is not bound to a particular theoretical tradition or political stance.[20] Reading madly demands continuous recognition of the unstable, mutable discursivity of the Anglophone, Francophone, and Russophone worlds in which I travel. It requires listening to polyphonies and charting polyvocalities across texts where "contingency . . . enables the ethical . . . to interrupt or suspend the epistemological" (McCarthy 2015, 27). To read madly is to highlight departures, to resituate conversations, to chart undercurrents, to expand inquiries.[21] It is to continually seek truths and never be satisfied with ends.

> No live organism can continue for long to exist sanely under conditions of absolute reality.
> —Shirley Jackson, *The Haunting of Hill House*
> ([1959] 2019)

20. People who have never read my work or heard me speak have preemptively introduced me at conferences as someone who "works in" trauma studies, psychoanalysis, queer studies, or the medical humanities, a description seemingly based purely on whatever all-encompassing theory is currently in vogue. I do gather insights from these fields, as I do from Black studies, Indigenous studies, and feminist studies. But I join Françoise Lionnet and Shu-Mei Shih (2011) in the assertion that the word *theory* should always have a lowercase *t* because its domination over an oeuvre can easily efface the conflicts, gaps, and fruitful misdirections that literature, especially comparative literature, excels at exposing.

21. In my current work at the intersection of mental illness and trauma, reading madly can mean laying out how sexual trauma challenges the spiritual architecture of Orthodox Christianity in a Dostoevsky text or asking how Soviet-era Mad fiction complicates the easy divide between victim and perpetrator. It can also mean questioning whether postcolonial fiction's metaphorization of disability effaces cultural neurodivergence or examining the ways the French Vietnamese writer Linda Lê appropriates Russian poetry to resist cultural essentialism, instead asserting a collective literary identity founded in endless wounding.

One of the costs of literature's postmodern turn, of literary study's embrace of interdisciplinary critique, is that the old transcendence of art is stripped away. As a result, scholars such as John Limon have argued that literature is an "undisciplined discipline" that "surrenders its ability to produce truth" in order to gain "the advantage of flexibility or critique that its anti-disciplinarity affords" (paraphrased in Mitchell 2002, 16). Certainly, literature sets itself at odds with scientific fields and their emphasis on concrete, reproducible findings. More so even than history or philosophy, both literary production and theory have increasingly sought "to demonstrate that truth is a variable and contextual phenomenon produced by the convergence of institutional power, ideologies, and influence" (Limon, paraphrased in Mitchell 2002, 16).

Yet some new truths, some repositionings that remake our world, can reveal themselves only in literary exploration through those moments when we choose to embrace the lie. Fiction gives us "'phenomenological' access to what makes of a thesis a thesis as such . . . a nonthetic experience of the thesis, of belief, of position, of naivety" (Jacques Derrida, quoted in McCarthy 2015, 27).[22] If we let this suspension work on us—if we follow Donna Haraway's advice to "stay with the trouble" and don't "hide our unease with the very catches in our thinking" (paraphrased in Soros 2018, 71)—then each author, each text, each tradition can present a new battleground, a new way to trouble a foundation or suggest a new start. Each work takes out a crowbar and pries out a little more space for a counterreading. Each work opens up new conversations within a vast heteroglot web that are never individual or isolated but come alive only through reciprocity, reflection, and response (Bakhtin [1963] 1994).

I do not claim that taking up a Mad identity enables me to glimpse some deeper truth about Madness. I have not cracked some hidden code;

---

22. Thetic expression (and, following Jean-Paul Sartre, thetic consciousness) is positive, aware, and often prescriptive, whereas the nonthetic is aggregate, not consciously attended to, open to variable connotations of use. When we read fiction, "literature does not so much obviate the question of belief as it allows us to experiment with it, trying out different positionalities (including the position of naiveté) in order to understand something of positioning itself" (McCarthy 2015, 27).

I am not supplying the final piece to some vast hermeneutic puzzle. Nor is this chapter about asserting that only the Mad truly "get" what a text means, know what literatures of, on, or by the Mad "should" say or are saying. What I *can* assert is that years of reading madly—reading while Mad, reading myself *as* Mad—has led to a productively maddening state of reading that helps me push Mad studies forward precisely through its ambiguities and frustrations. Tracing and reweaving the shades of my own psychosocial identity have made me hyperaware of the niggling doubts, the pivots in interpretation, the ethics of holding epistemologies in suspension that I might have otherwise ignored. It has encouraged me to follow side streets that curve away from the dominant interpretive path. And it has reaffirmed a belief I have held since I was nine, when I first realized fiction could offer more than just an escape: that literary study, this dance of doubt and dreaming, this tug between perspectives, this imagining of a thesis-as-such in action, is an essential aspect of remaking our world for the better.

I approach literary study as I approach my Mad self: as a relentless and far-flung search.[23] For answers that must, if the search is to be worth anything, yield up only more questions. For questions that must, if they are to have any value, be urgent in the answers they suggest, in the people they might help, in the gaps they might fill. Questions and conversations, not just the answers and ends we label as such, are truths in themselves. They hold what is so crucial and so hard to grasp: our stories, our choices, our living lives.

Works Cited

Bakhtin, Mikhail. [1963] 1994. *Problemy poetiki Dostoevskogo*. Reprint. Moscow: Next.

Borrell-Carrió, Francesc, Anthony L. Suchman, and Ronald M. Epstein. 2004. "The Biopsychosocial Model 25 Years Later: Principles, Practice, and Scientific Inquiry." *Annals of Family Medicine* 2, no. 6: 576–82. At https://www.annfammed.org/content/2/6/576.

---

23. In doing so, I draw on the pioneering work of Therí Alyce Pickens (2019), who urges literary studies—and especially those studying Madness—to shift from assertions of meaning to explorations of value.

Bruckert, Chris, and Stacey Hannem. 2012. *Stigma Revisited: Implications of the Mark.* Ottawa: Univ. of Ottawa Press.

Burke, Seán. 2008. *The Death and Return of the Author: Criticism and Subjectivity in Barthes, Foucault, and Derrida.* Edinburgh: Edinburgh Univ. Press.

Césaire, Aimé. 1944. "Poésie et connaissance." *Cahiers d'Haiti* 2, no. 5: 14–19. At https://doi.org/10.2979/ral.2010.41.1.109.

Deleuze, Gilles, and Félix Guattari. 1972. *Capitalisme et schizophrénie.* Paris: Editions de Minuit.

De Nerval, Gérard. 2006. *Aurélia.* In *Selected Writings*, translated and with an introduction and notes by Richard Sieburth, 265–316. New York: Penguin.

Donley, Carol, and Sheryl Buckley. 2000. "The Tyranny of the Normal." In *Teaching Literature and Medicine*, edited by Anne Hunsaker Hawkins and Marilyn Chandler McEntyre, 163–74. New York: Modern Language Association of America.

Dostoevsky, Fyodor. [1879–80] 2017. *Brat'ia Karamazovy.* Seria "Ekskliuziv: Russkaia klassika." Moscow: Izdatel'stvo ACT.

Duxbury, Scott W., Laura C. Frizzell, and Sadé L. Lindsay. 2018. "Mental Illness, the Media, and the Moral Panics of Mass Violence: The Role of Race in Mass Shootings Coverage." *Journal of Research in Crime and Delinquency* 55, no. 6: 789–91. At https://doi.org/10.1177/0022427818787225.

Failer, Judith Lynn. 2018. *Who Qualifies for Rights? Homelessness, Mental Illness, and Civil Commitment.* Ithaca, NY: Cornell Univ. Press.

Felman, Shoshana. 1978. *La folie et la chose littéraire.* Paris: Seuil.

Felski, Rita. 2011. *Uses of Literature.* Hoboken, NJ: Wiley.

Jackson, Shirley. [1959] 2019. *The Haunting of Hill House: A Novel.* Reprint. New York: Penguin.

Kelley, Robin G. D. 2001. "Introduction: A Poetics of Anticolonialism." In *Discourse on Colonialism*, edited by Aimé Césaire and Joan Pinkham, 7–29. New York: Monthly Review Press.

LeFrançois, Brenda A., and Shaindl Diamond. 2014. "Queering the Sociology of Diagnosis: Children and the Constituting of 'Mentally Ill' Subjects." *CAOS: Journal of Critical Anti-oppressive Social Inquiry* 1, no. 1: 39–61. At https://caos.library.ryerson.ca/index.php/caos/article/view/98.

Lionnet, Françoise, and Shu-mei Shih. 2011. "Introduction: The Creolization of Theory." In *The Creolization of Theory*, edited by Lionnet, Françoise, and Shu-mei Shih, 1–34. Durham, NC: Duke Univ. Press.

McCarthy, Anne C. 2015. "Suspension." In *Jacques Derrida: Key Concepts*, edited by Claire Colebrook, 23–30. New York: Routledge.

Milstein, Cindy, ed. 2015. *Taking Sides: Revolutionary Solidarity and the Poverty of Liberalism*. Chico, CA: AK Press.

Mitchell, David T. 2002. "Narrative Prosthesis and the Materiality of Metaphor." In *Disability Studies: Enabling the Humanities*, edited by Sharon L. Snyder, Brenda Jo Brueggemann, and Rosemarie Garland-Thomson, 15–30. New York: Modern Language Association of America.

Mitchell, David T., and Sharon L. Snyder. 2001. *Narrative Prosthesis: Disability and the Dependencies of Discourse*. Ann Arbor: Univ. of Michigan Press.

Miyatsu, Rose. 2018. "'Hundreds of People Like Me': A Search for a Mad Community in *The Bell Jar*." In *Literatures of Madness: Disability Studies and Mental Health*, edited by Elizabeth Donaldson, 50–68. London: Palgrave MacMillan.

Pickens, Therí Alyce. 2019. *Black Madness :: Mad Blackness*. Durham, NC: Duke Univ. Press.

Piepzna-Samarasinha, Leah Lakshmi. 2020. "Still Dreaming Wild Disability Justice Dreams at the End of the World." In *Disability Visibility: First-Person Stories from the Twenty-First Century*, edited by Alice Wong, 250–61. New York: Vintage.

Pineau, Gisèle. 2004. *Chair piment*. Paris: Gallimard Education.

Prendergast, Catherine. 2001. "On the Rhetorics of Mental Disability." In *Embodied Rhetorics: Disability in Language and Culture*, edited by James C. Wilson and Cynthia Lewiecki-Wilson, 45–60. Carbondale: Southern Illinois Univ. Press.

Reaume, Geoffrey. 2006. "Mad People's History." *Radical History Review* 94:170–82. At https://doi.org/10.1215/01636545-2006-94-170.

Soros, Erin. 2018. "Writing Madness in Indigenous Literature: A Hesitation." In *Literatures of Madness: Disability Studies and Mental Health*, edited by Elizabeth Donaldson, 69–85. London: Palgrave MacMillan.

Spandler, Helen. 2017. "Mad and Queer Studies: Shared Visions?" *Asylum: The Magazine for Democratic Psychiatry* 24, no. 1: 5–6. At https://www.research gate.net/profile/Helen-Spandler/publication/345940467_Mad_and_Queer _Studies_Shared_visions/links/5fb263e492851cf24cd5c9d3/Mad-and-Queer -Studies-Shared-visions.pdf.

Sparks, Tabitha. 2014. "Literature in Medical School: Why, How, and If." *Hektoen International: A Journal of Medical Humanities* 6, no. 2. At https:// hekint.org/2017/01/29/literature-in-medical-school-why-how-and-if/.

Spivak, Gayatri Chakravorty. 2014. *In Other Worlds: Essays in Cultural Politics.* New York: Routledge.

Starobinets, Anna. 2008. *Perekhodnyi vozrast.* Moscow: Molodaia Gvardiia.

Stevens, Wallace. 1990. *Opus Posthumous: Poems, Plays, Prose.* Rev. ed. Edited by Milton J. Bates. New York: Knopf Doubleday.

Stuart, Heather. 2003. "Violence and Mental Illness: An Overview." *World Psychiatry* 2, no. 2: 121–24. At https://www.ncbi.nlm.nih.gov/pmc/articles/PMC1525086/.

Williams, Monnica T., Daniel C. Rosen, and Jonathan W. Kanter, eds. 2019. *Eliminating Race-Based Mental Health Disparities: Promoting Equity and Culturally Responsive Care across Settings.* Oakland, CA: New Harbinger.

Wolframe, PhebeAnn M. 2018. "Going Barefoot: Mad Affiliation, Identity Politics, and Eros." In *Literatures of Madness: Disability Studies and Mental Health,* edited by Elizabeth J. Donaldson, 31–49. London: Palgrave Macmillan.

Woolf, Virginia. 1926. "On Being Ill." *New Criterion* 4, no. 1: 32–45.

8

The Madmotherscholar in Academia and Beyond

Caché Owens

Content notes: sexual assault, fatphobia, anti-Black racism, violence, self-harm, eating disorder

---

To be a mother living mad(ly) is to straddle several worlds simultaneously, to have your mind fractured so it can be thirty places at once. To be a Mad mother is to be a body stretched. I shouldn't have to be as resilient as I am, but as a Mad mother I can "make it" only in this way, and for me to make it is for my son to make it. More than this: the skills I use to thrive as a Mad and disabled mother serve me well in many contexts. My impressive multitasking, attention to detail, nurturing, and creative problem solving may have developed as a means for my survival, but they are still assets I possess.

I am a geographer studying the intersections of place and body justice, and my lived experience only enhances my technical skill. So why does the academy, a place of critical thought and innovation, relegate me to the margins? Refuse to see my value? Place so many barriers in my path? During a global pandemic, when systems are crumbling, there is no better time for all sectors, especially the academy, to embrace a subset of people who have no choice but to center care. It is time to embrace nurturers who move slowly and intentionally, reject universalism, and keep access and inclusion at the forefront.

I ground this work in Cheryl Matias's notion of the "motherscholar." Matias's term alludes to a body so stretched across borders that it ultimately becomes borderless. Rather than straddle a duality, the motherscholar is both, neither, and something new altogether. Matias purposefully does not put a hyphen between *mother* and *scholar* because both terms equally inform each other to create something unique. Matias writes, "The motherscholar is both a mother that draws from her practice of mothering to inform her research and pedagogy as much as she is a scholar who draws from her activism to inform her practice of mothering" (2022, par. 4).

What happens when the motherscholar is Mad, too? The Madmotherscholar shakes things up even further, disrupting the neat boundaries of both academia and parenthood. The Madmotherscholar is often in the precarious situation of being expected to give care (be a mother) and create with care (be a scholar/teacher/researcher) while needing care (be Mad/disabled). Madmotherscholars can teach us so much about care, boundaries, guilt, and acceptance. As time passes, I am becoming more and more certain Madmotherscholars are needed to disrupt academia's rigid, cold, competitive, and exploitative nature. We are care connoisseurs. Care for us means more care for everyone.

A Scholar, a Mother, and Mad

In 2008, I graduated high school, packed up my childhood bedroom, drove two hours south, and moved into the dorms at the University of Wisconsin–Milwaukee. The day I won a full-ride scholarship, my mother and I jumped for joy in our living room. The relief was overwhelming; we screamed at the top of our lungs for an hour. My first semester of college challenged me intellectually and allowed me to blossom socially. When I had a solid group of friends by December, I felt like the world was my oyster.

While back home for winter break, my life changed. I became pregnant unexpectedly following a sexual assault. In an instant, my future went from bright to foggy at best (the fact that motherhood signals the end of life for so many people is a different essay for another book). I told the scholarship coordinator the news when I returned to school for the spring semester. I was hoping she would have all the answers. Parental housing, university childcare, trauma counseling? I hoped there would be something she could point me to that would allow me to stay in school.

The Madmotherscholar in Academia and Beyond   147

Unfortunately, I was met with only pity and well wishes. At the end of my first year of college, I had to give up my scholarship and move back home with my mother and grandmother. The message was clear: the university is no place for mothers.

Following the birth of my beautiful baby, I couldn't bear to think about the future. I was almost thankful for the sleepless nights and constant chaos of new motherhood. It distracted me from pondering my bleak outlook. I had previously experienced depression and anxiety, but never in such a manic and all-consuming way. Pregnancy and childbirth altered me in ways I didn't anticipate. For months, I felt as if I couldn't catch my breath. I would fantasize about falling asleep and never waking up again. I hadn't experienced such a drastic change in my mental health. The Madness (of both my mind and my motherhood) was creeping in and taking over.

I use the phrase "creeping in" because at the time becoming Mad felt like a gradual process. As I look back, I see it less like a creep and more like a jarring, furious flood. It started with constant insomnia despite my being devastatingly tired. The tiniest of noises would send me leaping from my seat. My family and I chalked it up to new-mom jitters. My body felt as if it were taking longer than "normal" to recover from childbirth. Back, pelvic, and knee pain started to feel chronic, but I blamed my fat body and didn't think much of it. Suddenly, my son was six months old, and I was barely sleeping, crying almost every day, riddled with widespread pain in my body, and obsessing about self-harm. I was stuck in a cycle of obsessive optimism (I'll get a Fulbright and take the baby to South Africa! I'll move to New York City and audition for *Saturday Night Live!*) and overwhelming depression (I would leave the baby with my grandma and aimlessly drive around, debating with myself if I should crash the car). I felt empty. When an eating disorder took hold of me, it felt normal. I ate no solid foods for ninety days, and everyone was happy for me. Nobody is alarmed when a fat person stops eating, any more than when a mother is struggling. People complimented my son's chunky cheeks and my weight loss in the same breath.

Motherhood seemed to push me over the edge. Yet it also cradled me and kept me safe. To keep this baby alive, I had to stay alive. It's mentally exhausting to continually be reminded of the fact that the very thing that seems to be killing you is keeping you alive. I don't remember much from those early days, but I remember the immense confusion, million-mile-an-hour obsessive thoughts, and debilitating pain. And for more than a decade, I was away from my body. I dissociated, blinked, and ten years later had moved across the country with my tween son, completed a master's and a doctorate in geography, held a full-time position at a flagship university, and married my wife. I tried to feel proud of myself. I couldn't help but feel as if it all were meaningless. My body was absent.

Drew Leder's (1990) concept of the absent body suggests, as revisited by Carla Finesilver, Jennifer S. Leigh, and Nicole Brown, that "unless we are injured, sick, in pain or—at a lesser level—hungry, cold or needing the toilet we pay little or no attention to the inner workings of our bodies" (2020, 143). However, in my case the opposite was true. To protect myself from caving under the weight of my pain (mental and physical), my body wandered off. In a sadly sweet (or sweetly sad) sort of way, I am thankful for the disembodiment. To have been fully present for the extreme turmoil and obsession I was experiencing could have been the death of me. I wasn't centering my care, but nor was anyone else. So the same bodymind that I hated scooped me up and sent me away, leaving an empty body behind. There are vast chunks of time missing from my memory. Was I there even for a moment? Did it matter? After all, my body wasn't that important when I was trying to make a name for myself in the academy. In most instances, academic work is explicitly designed to make our bodies seem invisible and unimportant (Finesilver, Leigh, and Brown 2020, 144).

If we faithfully produce written research outputs and win accolades that can be leveraged for resources, we are good academics, even if we destroy ourselves along the way. This became clear when I was applauded for going seventy-two hours without food when I locked myself in my office and wrote for three days straight. A fatphobic, ableist, task-oriented capitalist society will continue to celebrate me if I complete my work even if I am pale, dizzy, and nauseated by the end of it. Only now, six months after leaving academia, have I started to fully appreciate what I accomplished in a setting so hostile to the realities of my being. Only now am I coming back to my body.

The intense stress I carried for a decade is starting to ease now that I can openly express the day-to-day impact of being Mad, disabled, and a mother. This reflective essay has allowed me to unpack the traumatic experience of becoming a Madmotherscholar. For ten years, I have been Mad, a mother, and a scholar all at once. I am finally realizing that this experience didn't have to be so excruciatingly challenging.

The day-in and day-out of parenting consistently bring my disability, my Madness, into focus.[1] In the early years of my son's life, I internalized deficit-based language around disability. I was preoccupied with my body's failures and frustrated by my "limits" and my deviation from the "norm." I lacked language or knowledge about the radical and transformative ways I could think about my disabilities. I slowly learned about the social model of disability, which suggests that the concept of disability results from society's failure to accommodate the breadth of the human experience meaningfully. I started to be a part of disability communities.

When I found the language of "Madness," an evocative term that rejects the idea that I am somehow broken, I viewed myself through a new lens. The wonderfully weird ways my bodymind functions became parts of me that I could celebrate and admire lovingly. Mad studies and Mad communities gave me permission to embrace both the beautiful and haunting parts of being mentally "ill." I started to view my body less and less through a deficit lens and more and more through a positive lens as a work of art. Limits became care needs that I refused to apologize for. When I learned to insist that my care needs be considered, it became easier to be in my body. There are days when I still feel limited, but those feelings are the result of inaccessible environments, not my failings. *Disabled* for me now means "society is not accommodating me," not "I am disabled," as in "I am lacking."

---

1. I reflect on my lived experience using the words *disabled* and *Mad* interchangeably not because they are synonyms but because the way my bodymind internalizes and reflects upon concepts of "disability" and "Madness" is in constant flux. Simply put, there are days when I feel Mad, days when I feel disabled, days when I feel both, and days when I feel nothing at all. My use of both terms here also pays homage to the personal growth, self-forgiveness, and community teachings that have come from engaging with these linked communities.

Care-less Environments: How Academia
Excludes Motherhood and Disability

Motherhood and disability, two identities that are seen as opposites in our ableist society, can manifest in commonalities and parallel lived experiences. Both are viewed as inherently challenging and burdensome. Both mothers and disabled people are often excluded, disregarded, or judged in academic spaces. Yet by centering the marginalized experiences of Madmotherscholars, we could operationalize care in academia to create radically supportive and inclusive environments.

The list of things that I admire about mothers is very long.[2] They are nurturing multitaskers, selfless shapeshifters, and endlessly creative problem solvers. They are also often expected to give themselves to motherhood with little complaint or reward. To be a mother often requires constantly reminding the world of your value.[3] It is not surprising that some mothers cave under all the pressure.

Similarly, I have a deep love for people with disabilities. Those of us with "wicked" bodies or "Mad" minds are quietly and not so quietly living beautiful lives in communities and spaces not built for us. Out of

2. My discussion here is rooted in the concept of motherhood as "a socially constructed set of activities and relationships involved in nurturing and caring for people," not as an essentially gendered position (Collins 1994, 56). Historically, mothering has been entangled with the concept of the feminine and is often used to reinforce binary gender identities. For better or for worse, *motherhood* thus becomes synonymous with *womanhood*. As a nonbinary person, I uplift the fact that anyone can be a mother.

3. I focus specifically on motherhood rather than on parenthood for a few reasons. First, like other motherscholars (Huopalainen and Satama 2019), I argue there is power in being reflexive about our subject position. That is, there is value in scholarship that contextualizes identity and positionality. To focus on my lived experience as a Mad mother, educator, and researcher, I aim to highlight my intersectional experiences and reject the urge to universalize. Others have discussed the power in making room for the "multiple becomings" (Braidotti 2011, passim) that emerge from the margins and cracks; rejecting a universal frame "support[s] the construction of solidarities and alliances of care across difference" (Amsler and Motta 2019, 86). Although also important, the experiences of fathers and other types of caregivers are outside the scope of my lived experience and would necessitate a different kind of reflection.

necessity, the disabled and Mad life is often one of meticulous planning, constant self-advocacy, and strategic maneuvering. If we try to live without these strategies, the world would erase and silence us. To live a crip life often requires constantly reminding the world of our right to be.

As Cheryl Matias highlights, "The feminine, soft, emotional, and caring archetype so deeply embedded in the stereotype of the mother . . . can be viewed as at odds with the ivory tower's brute, controlling, and cutthroat need for publications and prestige" (2022, par. 2). Regardless of gender, mothers experience a disproportionate amount of the negative impacts of parenting across all areas of life compared to fathers. Academia is based on an outdated model where (male) professors are seen as having a wife at home who takes care of domestic duties (Coe 2013).

Conversely, research shows that academic mothers report greater academic and family stress, less partner support in parenting, and perceptions of less institutional support for the balance of work and family compared to fathers (O'Laughlin and Bischoff 2005). Others have highlighted how the term *working mother* is a juxtaposition of oppositional language in which the social status, norms, and expected commitment to being a "good mother" are in direct conflict with the expectations of effort, competence, and authority required to be an "ideal worker" (Gonçalves 2019). Sarah Amsler and Sara Motta write, "Mothers often face a choice of assimilation or denial in workplaces. The ideal-type mother cannot be an ideal-type neoliberal subject (careless, disembodied, and disengaged from the messiness of non-economic life) or an autonomous, flexible 'entrepreneur' of the self" (2019, 82).

To be both an academic and a mother is to straddle competing worlds. I will never forget when at seven my son loved to do impressions of others. When I asked him to do an impression of me, he laughed and immediately said, "Jonah, go play. I need to do my research. I'm a researcher. All I do is research." I laughed, but inside I winced. To him, I was putting the work first. To my adviser, I was slacking and failing to carry my weight. I was trying to win for myself and my family, but the only thing I saw was a loser—doing many things poorly instead of one thing well.

Academic work is to always be "researching, writing and publishing in a manner that blurs the boundaries between life inside and outside the ivory tower—but only in one way" (Munn-Giddings 1998, 58). The performance of academia often requires researchers to act as though their work exists in a vacuum and is "not embodied in concrete lives" (Amsler and Motta 2019, 90). In a comparable way, high-stress environments rooted in competition and scarcity disregard those living on "crip time"—the day-to-day temporal shifts that often occur in a disabled person's life (Kafer 2021). In the neoliberal academy, there is no room for ebbs and flows. Disability and illness are supposed to be static and constant (Dolmage 2017). A culture of being always on paired with a disregard for crip time creates especially hostile conditions for the Madmotherscholar.

If mothers, especially disabled mothers, dare to acknowledge their realities as problems outside the scope of a course or research project, that acknowledgment is viewed as a threat to the rigidity, objectivity, and professionalism that dominate the neoliberal campus (Puwar 2004). Agnes Bosanquet describes this opposition best when she writes, "The ideal academic subject is unencumbered by caring responsibilities and succeeds as an individual within a managerialist-audit system of performance measures, research outputs, impact metrics, and funding targets. Disrupting this, here she is—a mother and an academic—leaking all over the place and making academia messy" (2018, 66).

Conversations about "leaking" and the fluids and functions of the body bring up images of disability. Discussing bodies and personal needs is taboo in the workplace. Anything outside the norm must be justified by an increase in personal productivity. "Living problems" become relevant only if they become "work problems."

There is constant pressure to be "the best and perfect mother" *and* the ideal, nonproblematic disabled colleague.[4] Internalized shame and self-berating can overwhelm us with the feeling of "never being good enough" or "always being at the wrong place at the wrong time" (Amsler and Motta 2019, 90). It is not uncommon for mothers to feel forced to choose motherhood or the academy, for the Mad to be forced to choose between their

---

4. For more on perfection, femininity, and mothering, see McRobbie 2015.

well-being and a career. In both instances, the world has decided we don't get to have or be both.

Universities have a clear image of the type of person that belongs on their campuses. People with disabilities are not included in that ideal. Nor are moms. Mad mothers? We are certainly not what they have in mind. It is overwhelming (insane even?) to think about the endless well of wisdom and innovation we all are missing out on with these exclusions. The university *could* be a leader in revolutionizing the culture of work. We can ask the right questions if we listen to those on the margins. How can we replace a culture of suffering with one of gentleness and support? Where is there room for slowness? For intentionality? For flexibility? For care?

Lived Experience amid the (In)Sanity of Academia

During graduate school, I had fewer accolades than all my peers. I lacked a supportive community. I was generally ignored regarding professional-development opportunities. Nevertheless, I thought my personal story had value. I didn't have any peer-reviewed publications about equity in education or community organizing in marginalized communities, but I *was* the type of person our "progressive" geography department was researching. In our interdisciplinary department, I studied community organizing, participatory action, and urban planning with an emphasis on both food systems in Black communities and educational inequity within the context of the New South, *while* I was a fat, Black parent battling with school staff to operationalize equity for the sake of my Black, disabled child in the New South. My life was the embodiment of merging theory and practice.

Nonetheless, I failed to "balance" all the extras required of a graduate student. Personal research projects, teaching, office hours, conference travel, campus service, and evening meetings were nearly impossible to keep up with. For the very reasons we were discussing in my classes, I was struggling to conform to the norms of a graduate program. Anti-Blackness, mass incarceration, lack of affordable housing, failing schools, ableism, and medical discrimination had been seminar discussion topics that were directly affecting my daily life and my mental health. I was certain that connection would count for something.

I was instead constantly reminded of all the ways I was falling short. I was told I would never be hirable. I was told I was "lucky to be there." I learned very quickly that my presence was tokenized and my lived experience was not anyone's priority. It was insane to me to watch a professor empathize with a theoretical person from an article and then dismiss my very tangible need for support.

They wanted me there, but not in my entirety. At all three of the institutions I've been affiliated with, I have experienced this jolting realization. My presence is tolerated, even welcomed, if I don't try to disrupt the status quo. The logic I thought I had was repeatedly challenged by the insanity of academia. The insanity just made me madder—angrier and iller. As much as I am Mad, I am sane, too. Why is there no room for *my* Madness in this mad system?

The broad strokes of my story are not new or unique. Many have extensively documented how universities make little effort to accommodate people with disabilities *or* mothers (Dickson 2018). Black people with disabilities are continually undersupported and overpoliced. We have only recently begun to acknowledge the way we fail Black mothers in medical, work, and community settings. Those at the intersection of these identities find even less support and care.

So many things confused me about academia. In a wildly subjective world, the cardinal rule of objectivity made no sense. As a first-generation college student, I continually encountered hidden norms, expectations, *and* the consequences of not being "up to speed." Interdependent systems of oppression compounded by pervasive ableism and sanism made it easy for others to dismiss, criticize, and ignore me. At the same time, I was trying to reckon with my privilege as an educated, light-skinned, documented person who worked in proximity to whiteness—so much negotiating of swirling, conflicting thoughts in my already overactive and obsessive brain.

Multidimensional oppression and privilege exacerbated the difficulties of being a Madmotherscholar. I gaslit myself more times than I can remember, went several nights without sleep after overanalyzing every interaction, and internalized the oppressive behaviors of others. To my peers, I tried to continually downplay my responsibilities as a mother as a sort of "penance" for my being. I had not yet read Sonya Renee Taylor's

(2021) work that so eloquently reminds us that "the body is not an apology." Academia currently tells us that we must choose: mother or scholar? Mad person or scholar? You cannot be both.

And then, after months of going to therapy, creating, being in community, reading, writing, laughing, crying, and healing, I asked myself a question: "Do you believe that the refusal to choose is itself a choice?" I decided I did. There are days when I am irrational and manic and must sit with two conflicting ideas. During some of my most difficult moments, I temporarily believe I must be the most amazing, perfect mother or must harm myself as penance. The refusal to choose between these extreme choices creates a push and pull that forces me to ask for and accept care, keeps me alive, and fuels my creative soul. It shows me again and again how to center concepts of care that cultivate abundance. We all deserve care not because we earn it but because we are.

Coming Undone and Back Together: A Madmotherscholar

Disabled mothers offer counternarratives to the "highly constrained and constraining images of maternity-as-attainable-perfection" (Cooper 2020, par. 10). When we welcome them into the university, they also interrupt images of perfection in the professoriate. They remind us of the messiness of the human experience and push our places of learning to more radical and transformative ways of knowing. They guide us past the constraints of sanism and toward more expansive forms of critical thought. I am eager for more intersectional stories of Mad mothers like me, stories that are vital if we want to disrupt the influence of dominant norms created by white, thin, cisgender, sane, able-bodied narratives.

Hyperindependence and self-sufficiency will never be able to care for the whole person. We are forced to fracture. I know this because I compartmentalized myself into discreet parts—a mother, a scholar, and a Mad person—until all that was left were bits and pieces. Despite being widely dismissed in professional spaces, these complementary and conflicting parts of me (motherhood and Madness) have a significant bearing on my personal and professional life. Motherhood and Madness are both beautiful and ugly. In today's reality, motherhood is often an all-consuming experience that demands more than you have.

The Madmotherscholar is entangled in several "love–hate" relationships. Although I love my child, I often hate being a mother, in part because of the ugliness of my mental illness. There are days (many more than I would like) when I get irrational and spiral, and I don't shower or leave my bed. The guilt and the shame that come from acknowledging that my mental health sometimes prevents me from getting up to eat dinner with my family make it hard to be a mom. There are few things I am better at than teaching. Yet there are days when it is impossible to stand in front of a room of students because I'm in too much pain or I can't stop crying.

When I am the "best" motherscholar, it is often because I am ignoring my care needs. I rush things that I know are best done slowly. I don't eat despite knowing that a nourished body is best. I self-isolate and forget about my caring community that wants to support me. I get tunnel vision and put self-preservation on the back burner. When I inevitably reach my breaking point, it's easy to blame myself. Rest eludes me, and stress mounts, resulting in debilitating mental health for days and weeks.

I have strategies that help me cope and build resiliency, but these strategies are frowned upon in our current systems of work. My tools are place based and involve nature, play, rest, quiet, and adventure. It is so common for academics to lose touch with the very things I require for survival. Notions of failure are plentiful. Ableism tricks us into thinking disabilities are failures of the body.[5]

There are days when I am on the brink of giving up, but suddenly my son learns something new or kisses me on the cheek, and I am in awe of his beauty. Motherhood and Madness can be beautiful, too. In a manic state or sitting with an obsessive thought, I find new art projects, new questions, and new answers. I can expand my mind to intimately connect with my child's most outlandish ideas. I have extraordinary patience for my son's depression-fueled fits of rage. My body and mind make demands

5. For a Madmother to a Madchild, the looming suggestions of personal failure have resulted in many of these self-blame spirals. Dominant narratives suggest that having a child with a disability is due to an inability to "mother well" (Colker 2015, 1205). There have been many moments when I've wondered if I could sustain my existence as both Mad and a mother.

The Madmotherscholar in Academia and Beyond   157

of me that I have no choice but to honor. So, too, I honor the demands my son's body makes and embrace the positives. *Madmother.* This reframing reminds us that there are ways of being where disability and motherhood coexist peacefully—where these identities are assets instead of hindrances. If I can find peace as a Madmother, radical imagination shows me a world where I can thrive as a Madmotherscholar.

Most environments operate in ways that frame both disabilities and motherhood as "limiting"—holding you back, weighing you down (Cooper 2020).[6] We fail to acknowledge that these frustrations are not inherent to disability or motherhood or to the coexistence of the two. They result from systemic oppression born of the ableist, individualistic, capitalist, white-supremacist patriarchy (hooks 2020). The social model of disability forces us to reckon with how individuals with disabilities are relegated to the margins and how "handicaps are made out of characteristics" (Jones 1996, 349). This same model can be applied to constructs of motherhood. Motherhood is not innately limiting. Motherhood feels like a constraint under the hyperindependent, self-sufficient, and competitive ways of being we project onto motherhood. A reality where motherhood is viewed as collaborative, interdependent, and fluid is possible.

In service of this alternate reality, I spend time reflecting on the gifts of motherhood and the joy of my Madness. I share my reflections with others through my public scholarship. Madmotherscholars can give us insight into how to care for the whole person. The more I reflect, the more I can identify how these seemingly competing parts can work together in my favor if I let them. My familiarity with mothering helps me to nurture patience within myself, *for* myself. This is especially helpful during times when my disability feels insurmountable. Equally, my disabilities, inconsistent mental health, and chronic pain help me accept the imperfections in my mothering. I won't ever be *the* perfect mother (there is no such thing).

6. Harriet Cooper recalls Clare Quallman's example of "losing the freedom of easy mobility" and the freedom that those who have mobility take for granted. Her example draws a parallel between wheelchair users and mothers with strollers, diaper bags, and extra "stuff." Both realities share a "frustrating negotiation with the physical world" (2020, par. 7).

The best way for me to be a mother is to welcome care when I need it. When it feels difficult to trust this asset-oriented reframing of myself as a Madmother, my community reminds me. There are more ways of being than those with power want us to believe. *We are not failures.*

Creating the Care-centric Academy

Our systems fail us by neglecting to see our value. Although these oppressive and exclusionary systems have persisted, we can create spaces that uplift Mad and disabled mothers through radical imagination and mutual support. Centering care allows us to make room for Madmothers, a shift that ultimately benefits everyone. Madmotherscholars can teach us to embed principles of collaboration and nurturing into virtually all aspects of daily life. Madmotherscholars offer a new paradigm of teaching, learning, and working together. A big part of this shift is propelled by shifting mindsets rather than establishing new programs, policies, or services (although there is a place for those, too).

We first need a reconceptualization of how we frame help and care. There are times when the best way to be a Madmotherscholar is to rely on your community for support. This requires us to reject the language of help for an ethos of care. Help is an action; care is a value. Considerate scheduling of meetings, flexible deadlines, and accessible childcare are examples of necessary care that should "just be." Chimamanda Adichie urges us to "shake off anxious feelings of guilt and shame" when it comes to requesting what we need from others (2017, 10). Abandoning the language of help affirms that Madmotherscholars existing at various intersections have the right to thrive, despite societal norms that seek to "render our most basic needs undesirable, untenable, unreasonable, or 'special'" (Eales and Peers 2021, 165). Providing marginalized people with the support they need to ensure their survival is not "going above and beyond." It should be considered the standard.

The language of help often elicits paternalistic, bureaucratic, and/or burdensome responses. The decision to offer help is a choice that often occurs at the individual level amid unequal power dynamics. Don't "help us" based on a warped sense of altruism. I am not asking for help. Care for *me* so that I have a chance to contribute what I know about creating

The Madmotherscholar in Academia and Beyond   159

systems that care for *you*. A value speaks to the core of how something is designed, implemented, and evaluated. When we create a system of care, there are structures in place that ensure care is given and received as needed. There is less need to make "exceptions" or justify "requests" because this new system affirms that all our care needs are valid.

This shift requires each of us to reimagine what makes a successful academic. I have started to clandestinely evaluate my students against their own self-care goals.[7] I provide care by following their lead. This kind of evaluation is not encouraged at most universities. Individualized care is often viewed as an exception for those with "special needs" and as a less rigorous approach. Madmotherscholars interrupt this deficit mindset by prioritizing our needs and modeling this for our students. We do this often out of necessity. On some days, the only way to survive is to honor our care needs. To loudly require care is a challenging skill that Madmotherscholars can show us.

Those of us with relative privilege, power, and access must challenge ourselves to be more unapologetically vulnerable and introspective. Vulnerability is more dangerous for those on the margins. When someone in a relative position of power normalizes naming their care needs, that makes it easier for someone else to do the same. Sitting with the ways internalized capitalism, patriarchy, white supremacy, ableism, fatphobia, and so on show up in each of us is a *good* first step. Naming these reflections externally to others is a *great* first step.

Thriving care systems also reject the urge to universalize. The kind of care I crave is not concerned with "norms." Some people may be uncertain of what their care needs are. What would a college experience look like that first guided new students to reflect on their care needs and to

---

7. I had a student share with me that they were more focused on making their first friend than on getting good grades. An A– in my class and zero new friendships may seem like a success to me but wouldn't have fulfilled this student. In my role as a "care-full" teacher, I spent the rest of the semester supporting this student by focusing on opportunities for meaningful connection first and on the course content second. The student engaged with the content when it was positioned as a social activity and was pleased with their progress. Who am I to challenge their version of success for themselves?

return to those reflections for guidance? Operating from a place of abundance, we can consider that there are as many care needs as there are people. Conflicting care needs will undoubtedly arise. However, within this paradigm even conflict becomes a source of care. When we become invested in each other, there is no choice but to continue to question, reflect, and experiment until we all are cared for. Care becomes boundless, a space to express and explore creativity as well as a source of innovation and critical thought.

Furthermore, we must question our relationship with rules, consequences, and fairness. Before COVID, I regularly called into a research team meeting rather than attending in person. I was consistently "breaking the rules." I hadn't proved that I was "worthy of help," and there was no system of care that showed others how to support me in the way I needed. My adviser assumed I was taking advantage of the "flexibility" and scolded me over coffee, but the truth was that I was sitting alone in a dark room, my anxiety too intense to leave. My son, having just been suspended from kindergarten after a behavioral outburst, sat outside my door playing with his Legos. Once he went to sleep at night, I would log back into my email and try to catch up on what I had been too distracted to digest earlier. I contributed to the project differently than the rest of the team, but I was still offering valuable insights. We didn't have the tools or space to unpack our conflicting care needs. Instead, highlighting the rule I had broken was much easier for my adviser. I started attending every meeting in person. I checked out mentally and physically. I did the bare minimum and grew resentful.

Rules are often established to avoid conflict, robbing many of us of the chance to explore new and messy ways of being in community with one another. By no measure are rules 100 percent bad. However, they can easily become means of control, punishment, and profit. Radical care systems encourage us to meet people where they are.

Centering care guides us to a more transformative place. A culture of collective care reminds us that we must care for each other not because we "should" but because the care of another is bound up with my care. If anyone is left behind, we all are at risk of being left behind. The exclusionary nature of higher education leads us to forget how much we rely on the lived expertise of others. How can the expertise that comes *only* from living in a disabled body inform us if we make no space for it? While conducting a qualitative interview with a colleague, only I, the Madmotherscholar, could recognize and gently redirect an applicant stuck in an obsessive thought spiral. My lived experience as a Madmotherscholar led to the development of a new approach to data collection. We have yet to figure out how to fully value and celebrate the knowledge that comes from lived experience.

Border bodies at the liminal intersections of socially constructed identities remind us of our fluidity. Border bodies remind us to reject simplistic binaries and embrace nuance. Under this framework, the "Mad mother, bad mother" and "good mother, bad academic" binaries fail to be adequate. There were semesters in which I did little research, and my "output" was meager. The university doesn't know how to quantify the way my life as a Madmother enriches my scholarly endeavors.

To resist Mad mothering is to be "complicit in neoliberal-ableism, neoliberal-sanism, and neoliberal-patriarchy" (Douglas et al. 2021, 45). Madness challenges reason, and universities love reason! If we make room for Madmotherscholars, we will be thankful we did so. We will be rewarded with a shake-up of academia as we know it. Madness scrambles up what we think we know into something completely new. Motherhood teaches us how to nurture and care for something in a way that allows it to blossom and evolve into something more impressive than we could have imagined. Madmotherscholars are both storytellers and creators. It is exciting to think about all the things Madmotherscholars can teach us about care. Might a transformed university rooted in care influence the rest of the world around us? Are we willing to find out?

Works Cited

Adichie, Chimamanda Ngozi. 2017. *Dear Ijeawele, or a Feminist Manifesto in Fifteen Suggestions.* New York: Vintage.

Amsler, Sarah, and Sara Motta. 2019. "The Marketised University and the Politics of Motherhood." *Gender and Education* 31, no. 1: 82–99.

Bosanquet, Agnes. 2018. "Motherhood and Academia: A Story of Bodily Fluids and Going with the Flow." In *Lived Experiences of Women in Academia:*

Metaphors, Manifestos and Memoir, edited by Alison L. Black and Susanne Garvis, 65–75. New York: Routledge.

Braidotti, Rosi. 2011. *Nomadic Theory: The Portable Rosi Braidotti.* New York: Columbia Univ. Press.

Coe, Alexis. 2013. "Being Married Helps Professors Get Ahead, but Only If They're Male." *The Atlantic,* Jan. 17. At https://www.theatlantic.com/sexes /archive/2013/01/being-married-helps-professors-get-ahead-but-only-if-theyre -male/267289/.

Colker, Ruth. 2015. "Blaming Mothers: A Disability Perspective." *Boston University Law Review* 95:1205–24. At https://www.bu.edu/bulawreview/files /2015/05/COLKER.pdf.

Collins, Patricia Hill. 1994. "Shifting the Center: Race, Class, and Feminist Theorizing about Motherhood." In *Representations of Motherhood,* edited by Donna Bassin, Margaret Honey, and Meryle Mahrer Kaplan, 56–74. New Haven, CT: Yale Univ. Press.

Cooper, Harriet. 2020. "The Fantasy of Maternal Autonomy and the Disabled Mother." *Studies in the Maternal* 13, no. 1. At https://doi.org/10.16995/sim .296.

Dickson, Martina. 2018. "The Joys and Challenges of Academic Motherhood." *Women's Studies International Forum* 71, no. 6: 76–84.

Dolmage, Jay Timothy. 2017. *Academic Ableism: Disability and Higher Education.* Ann Arbor: Univ. of Michigan Press.

Douglas, Patty, Katherine Runswick-Cole, Sara Ryan, and Penny Fogg. 2021. "Mad Mothering." *Journal of Literary & Cultural Disability Studies* 15, no. 1: 39–57. At https://muse.jhu.edu/article/781813.

Eales, Lindsay, and Danielle Peers. 2021. "Care Haunts, Hurts, Heals: The Promiscuous Poetics of Queer Crip Mad Care." *Journal of Lesbian Studies* 25, no. 3: 163–81. At https://doi.org/10.1080/10894160.2020.1778849.

Finesilver, Carla, Jennifer S. Leigh, and Nicole Brown. 2020. "Invisible Disability, Unacknowledged Diversity." In *Ableism in Academia: Theorizing Experiences of Disabilities and Chronic Illnesses in Higher Education,* edited by Nicole Brown and Jennifer S. Leigh, 143–60. London: UCL Press.

Gonçalves, Kellie. 2019. "'What Are You Doing Here, I Thought You Had a Kid Now?' The Stigmatisation of Working Mothers in Academia—a Critical Self-Reflective Essay on Gender, Motherhood and the Neoliberal Academy." *Gender and Language* 13, no. 4: 469–87. At https://doi.org/10.1558 /genl.37573.

hooks, bell. 2000. *Feminist Theory: From Margin to Center*. London: Pluto Press.

Huopalainen, Astrid, and Suvi Satama. 2019. "Mothers and Researchers in the Making: Negotiating 'New' Motherhood within the 'New' Academia." *Human Relations* 72, no. 1: 98–121. At https://doi.org/10.1177/0018726718764571.

Jones, Susan. 1996. "Toward Inclusive Theory: Disability as Social Construction." *NASPA Journal* 33, no. 4: 347–54. At https://doi.org/10.1080/00220973.1996.11072421.

Kafer, Alison. 2021. "After Crip, Crip Afters." *South Atlantic Quarterly* 120, no. 2: 415–34. At https://doi.org/10.1215/00382876-8916158.

Leder, Drew. 1990. *The Absent Body*. Chicago: Univ. of Chicago Press.

Matias, Cheryl. 2022. "Birthing the Motherscholar and Motherscholarship." *Peabody Journal of Education* 97, no. 2. At https://doi.org/10.1080/0161956X.2022.2055897.

McRobbie, Angela. 2015. "Notes on the Perfect: Competitive Femininity in Neoliberal Times." *Australian Feminist Studies* 30, no. 83: 3–20. At https://doi.org/10.1080/08164649.2015.1011485.

Munn-Giddings, Carol. 1998. "Mixing Motherhood and Academia: A Lethal Cocktail." In *Surviving the Academy: Feminist Perspectives*, edited by Danusia Malina and Sian Maslin-Prothero, 56–68. New York: Routledge.

O'Laughlin, Elizabeth, and Lisa G. Bischoff. 2005. "Balancing Parenthood and Academia: Work/Family Stress as Influenced by Gender and Tenure Status." *Journal of Family Issues* 26, no. 1: 79–106. At https://doi.org/10.1177/0192513X04265942.

Puwar, Nirmal. 2004. *Space Invaders: Race, Gender, and Bodies out of Place*. Oxford: Berg.

Taylor, Sonya Renee. 2021. *The Body Is Not an Apology: The Power of Radical Self-Love*. San Francisco: Berrett-Koehler.

9

In-Cite

The Mad Possibility of Interethnography

Sarah Cavar

[I] support the radical idea that the ICD and DSM—medical authorities—don't determine what communities I belong to.
—metapianycist, "I Support the Radical Idea . . ." (2020)

Content notes: anti-Black police violence, murder, transphobia

The Project

I learn I am autistic at eight, on the internet. After beginning my research on WebMD, I graduate to sites on Asperger's syndrome, a term whose contestation by autistic activists I learn later on. I find comfort in a community in which problems become shared, positive features. While my family believes me "subclinically" weird, these online spaces prove a balm to my loneliness.

I move from symptom lists to YouTube videos and finally to written narratives. I consume, with uninformed horror, the content of antiautistic organizations such as Autism Speaks, often stylized by others as "Autism $peaks" to indicate its prioritization of profits over autistic people. Years and Google searches later, I find the fringes of what I later discover to be a vibrant autistic community online. But my real entry point into autistic community and into what I term "trans disabled" (TD) digital space is a blog post: "Quiet Hands" by Julia Bascom (2011). This post, which ultimately went viral, addressed a scene on the TV show Glee. In it, Will Schuster reaches out to "quiet" his obsessive-compulsive lover Emma's wringing *hands. Bascom writes that this scene, although seemingly forgettable, also shows a site of trauma for autistic survivors of abusive "therapy." Emma's quieted hands bring back years of restriction by professionals bent on controlling autistic people's self-stimulatory movements, or "stims," which are perceived as unsightly and abnormal. Thus begins my academic study of diagnostic essentialism, pathologization, and bodymind self-determination.*

I have been doing TD research since 2011, yet I have been recognized as doing so only since January 2019, when I became research assistant to Dr. Alexandre Baril, who was involved in work on TD intersections across a range of mediums, including blogs. When I joined him, I was eager to put my years of experience as a TD blogger-scholar to work but feared the implications disclosure might have for my hardly begun academic career. I feared, to paraphrase Robert McRuer (2006), "coming out Mad"—that is, disclosing psychological disability in a landscape that prioritizes reason and acuity. When Dr. Baril also offered me lead authorship of the chapter on the trans–disabled intersection in the second edition of *Trans Bodies, Trans Selves* (Erickson-Schroth 2022), which I enthusiastically accepted, my fear and excitement only grew.

While honored to be partially entrusted with the story of my community, I felt the weight of responsibility. I would research TD digital communities who are facing what Miranda Fricker (2007) calls "epistemic injustice" in both its testimonial (denial of authorship) and hermeneutic (denial of language) forms. The blogs I had long followed and planned to study anew were routinely dismissed even by fellow bloggers, who considered gender self-determination and self-diagnosis "idiotic" and "attention seeking," imploring users to "leave the house." Trans, disabled, and other marginalized knowledges face rejection rooted in ableism, and epistemic injustice is inherently tied to the presumed "incapacity" (disability) of the speaker. Ironically, this is the same process by which self-diagnoses are invalidated: metaphoric accusations of "delusionality" dot claims made against self-diagnosed and gender self-determined people. And, of course, the phrase "leave the house" carries with it the presumption that to frequent only digital publics is to be inherently inferior to those who live "in real life." Likewise, "internet diagnosis" and "internet gender" are subordinated to their real-life, doctor-prescribed counterparts.

In the comments section of Bascom's post, I find other autistic bloggers, including those who used the microblogging/social media platform Tumblr (which I had previously used only to participate in fandom) to build community. I enter a new social milieu, following the hashtag #actuallyautistic and its offspring, #actuallybpd, #pseriouslypsychosis, #actuallydisabled, and others (henceforth the "#actually hashtags or tags"). Rather than being spoken for, over, and about by parents and "professionals," we speak for ourselves in these tags.

Some people using the #actually hashtags (the most popular of which remains #actuallyautistic) are teenagers; others are adults. Most are queer. Some are trans; the tags' trans memberships grow, as does shared knowledge of trans existence. Some are professionally diagnosed, others self-diagnosed, a difference that led both to conflict and collaboration. Legitimacy battles aside, however, most users in the #actually tags are in favor of self-diagnosis. Participation in the tags, after all, reflects an understanding of the importance of disabled self-determination and a commitment to speaking beyond medically dominated narratives of self.

With limited chapter space in *Trans Bodies, Trans Selves*, I decided to focus on neurogenders, which I describe elsewhere as "genders specific to particular modes of neurodivergent experience . . . contextualized through enminded difference" (Cavar 2021, para. 6). I included *autigender*, defined as "autism as part or whole of gender identity [and/or] a gender that can only be understood in context of being autistic" (mogai-archive and autigender-culture-is 2021) and the result of a robust autistic pride movement attentive to the well-populated trans/autistic intersection I encountered on #actuallyautistic. This community-created term allows many autistic people to think critically about the relationship between autism and gender experience and, further, between autism and selfhood. For those of us proud to be autistic, autigender constitutes another iteration of LGBTQ+ difference to be celebrated rather than pathologized. Established and emergent neurogenders as well as Mad genders themselves remove the onus of the critique embedded in the diagnosis of "broken brains" by the psychiatric system and turn shared "symptoms" to sites of belonging.

In the chapter, I liberally cited blogs as TD resources and sites of scholarly collaboration rather than of information extraction. I decided to call this digitally generated knowledge *emblogged knowledge*, a nod to Emily K. Abel and C. H. Browner's concept of "embodied knowledge" (1998, passim). I used the term *emblogged knowledge* to refer to knowledges resulting from and intertwined with digital subjectivities and communications. In bringing emblogged knowledge into "real" (legitimate) life, I would move our scholarship "out of the house" and into public discourse. More specifically, I would reveal blogs as both sites of discourse and bodies of knowledge, both selves and the battlegrounds on which selfhood is won.

Lack of In-Cite: Trans Mad Sourcing

As my identities solidify, as evidence of my autism mounts, and as I accumulate various "professional" psychiatric diagnoses, I remain embedded in TD digital spaces. I learn the ins and outs of "#survivingpsych," what to say to get the treatment I want and retain autonomy. I receive an autism diagnosis and clearance for trans medical intervention, a welcome change after an adolescence of pathologization and forced treatment. I didn't change fundamentally when my labels moved from the internet to my medical chart. Yet, somehow, this movement made me real in the eyes of medicine. I, as a knower, have become obsolete.

I am a trans disabled person. I know who I am among. Yet I am valid only by the doctor's pen stroke. The very communities that made me who I am today are marked illegitimate by the same stroke as medical/psychiatric authority becomes law. Simultaneous curiosity and anger lead me to my present interest in the expansive, subversive identificatory possibilities that these "illegitimate" digital spaces hold, hybridizing self and scholarship, study and subjectivity. As a nascent scholar, I am intellectually and emotionally indebted to the shared counterknowledge of those in these spaces. My research must be noncompliant.

I anticipated confusion and ridicule at my research interests, having had similar experiences while explaining "Mad studies" to peers unfamiliar with it. I felt as if I had to nudge and wink my ideas across, even to others concerned with trans/disability studies. "I'm going back to Tumblr," I would say, laughing strategically. "They actually have really profound things to say."

Internally, though, I would cringe, as if we bloggers hadn't long benefited from this TD experiential oeuvre. At fifteen, I read the words *gender* and *discursive construct* and somehow understood. Bloggers produced new genders simply by *naming* them; neogenders, like other genders, were merely oft-repeated words (Cavar and Baril 2021). We were both earnest and playful in our adoption of new gendered language, acknowledging both the importance of salient terminologies for our identities and the entertainment such experimentation can provide. We knew that the lines between *real* and *fake* genders and disabilities were drawn in the mountainous power disparity between doctor and blogger. Indeed, anxieties around falsified identity are still often explained as concerns about internet trolls impersonating actually disabled people and thus hurting our collective reputation; these impersonations carry echoes of ableist offline accusations lobbied at disabled people for everything from service animals to welfare benefits and in truth only further harm the disabled community writ large.

As I accumulated diagnoses offline, this reality became personal. The status of my apparent ailments depended not on my personal experience but on my ability to meet or fail to meet abled, sane norms, especially "productivity." All names I claimed were unreal without a doctor's signature, but names once signed were indisputable. Contestations reflected a "lack of insight." My undiagnosed transness was at best speculation, at worst "malingering." This overlapping terrain of struggle is doubly disabling for TD self-scholars, who are now reduced to perpetual patients. Our bodies turn to bibliographies in need of beefing up, peer review, and the assignment of legible language. A doctor's note, whether from an MD or a PhD, turns "unstable crips" into orderly data. As a graduate student, I, too, am implicated in the university's violent demands for epistemic "compliance."

Think: Lack of insight.

Insight.

In-sight. In-cite.

What could we incite?

Following the Blogger: Doing Interethnography

From 2012 to 2015, Tumblr sees a renaissance of TD self-diagnosis and self-determination. Much like earlier autistic communities, TD bloggers resignify diagnostic labels as markers of community belonging. Meanwhile, self-created "neogenders" and "neopronouns" constitute novel approaches to gender identity. The blogger Margot Orbitsing first introduces me to the practice, creating a "list of pronouns [xe] had seen in no particular order" (Orbitsing et al. 2013) based on xir knowledge and aesthetic preferences; many remain in wide usage today. One popular set, fae/faer/faerself, *is created by blogger Shadaras, whose gender is "somewhere between angel and fae-creature," and aims to give a "giant fuck you" to the gender binary (Orbitsing et al. 2013). TD bloggers continue this ethos, using* fae *to reclaim the myth of the "changeling child," a designation to whom autism diagnoses are often retrofitted.*

My digital cotheorizers and I are evidence of each other, our stories entwining in complex citational chains. I name this theoretical dance *interethnography*, a word with two meanings. *Interethnography* is a lesser-known synonym for *netnography*, which Charlotte Aull Davies (2010) describes as observing community behaviors within a given cultural (in this case virtual) context. However, the prefix *inter-* promises the potential for more than mere observation. Beyond its reference to the internet, I use the word *netnography* to suggest *intersubjective* ethnography, storytelling that destabilizes the boundary between "my" story (reflexive) and "their" story. Sometimes, as I have done in this chapter, this means citing my experiences and theirs as proof of each other. Other times, braiding self-texts is involved, wherein theory takes the form of emblogged, lived, conversation.

I "follow" the TD blogging methodologies of reblogging and community hashtagging. Reblogging copies one blogger's original post, with credit, to one's own blog. Other bloggers can add their own commentary to these posts and respond to questions. For TD bloggers, reblogged and commented-on posts are often bibliographic, sources we store in our archives of self. These posts can be found using community hashtags, including the #actually tags, whose self-determining context and ethos inaugurated my membership in TD communities. Thus, we collaboratively resist hermeneutic injustice even as some of us are not term creators. We undermine medical authority by wielding the tools of identification rather than passively receiving diagnoses, thus gaining agency over the ways we are read.

Interethnography also reflects the ongoing, affirmative conversation crucial in TD emblogged theory. Early in my digital education, pro-neogender bloggers actively encouraged me to read and reblog conversations that with each successive iteration further redefined trans identity. Other trans bloggers, including me now, advocate a big-tent definition of transness to advance widespread community access. For example, the trans blogger Aaliyahbreaux writes that "just wanting to be [a different gender] makes [one] transgender" (Aaliyahbreaux et al. 2019), advancing a desire and community-based ethos for belonging rather than a reliance on medical diagnosis. For blogger Cowboyslovingboys, Aaliyahbreaux's post constitutes a form of assisted self-disclosure: "This is one of the posts I can explicitly pinpoint as helping me realize that I might not be cis. *The biggest symptom of being trans is wanting to not be your gender.* It can also be dysphoria, it can also be euphoria, it can also be presentation, but wanting to be something else is all you really need" (Aaliyahbreaux et al. 2019, italics added). Belonging becomes a matter of desire rather than of diagnosis, identification with other trans people rather than over-identification by a diagnostic checklist. Cowboyslovingboys resignifies "symptom," refusing medicalized dysphoria as a sole qualifier for trans identity. Aaliyahbreaux's post provided him an inroad to and model of trans counterdefinition, which other bloggers in the chain could reaffirm and add to. Here, as in assertions of self-diagnosis as community belonging rather than individual pathology, there is a challenge to medical hegemonic notions of illness and autonomy. Sometimes this challenge is direct, and bloggers critique a psychiatric system that renders their knowledge always-already untrustworthy. Other times, however, the critique is embedded in the very interethnographic process that resists it: what was once a site of individual condemnation becomes a community conversation.

Interethnography is already happening via community-based language reclamation and self-diagnosis. In our participatory, citational practice of self-naming, we resist objectifying and hierarchical approaches to diagnosis. In contrast to the professional diagnosis that conveys an individual as ill and reifies TD people as objects of observation, I have experienced the empowerment that comes with the assertion of self-knowledge. In stark contrast to the isolation of the clinical encounter, we find our strength in numbers. Our emblogged archives blur the boundary between scholar and subject, provider and patient. Our methodologies carry the power to resist medical, psychiatric narratives of TD life; our collective voice, matched with the power of an attentive trans Mad studies, can liberate and reconceptualize stories written *about us* yet *without us*.

At first, I only observed, unsure if I belonged. Since then, traumatic experiences with medicine and psychiatry as well as a "formal" autism diagnosis at age eighteen have situated me firmly inside the "actually." I am a trans #actually blogger, whose defiance of identificatory norms traverses both gender and diagnostic landscapes.

We have already seen the impact of interethnographic self-identification and resignification both online and offline. I write this in the midst of the COVID-19 pandemic and in the shadow of global calls to abolish the police. In 2020, the COVID-19 pandemic drove us online en masse; then, the murders of Breonna Taylor, George Floyd, Elijah McClain, and countless others drove us into the streets. Digital scholarship entered mainstream discourse, and for a moment so did collective calls for prison and police abolition. While conditions continue to change regarding recognition of the ongoing pandemics of COVID and of police violence, we continue to use digital storytelling to narrate the insufficiency of these violent systems in addressing harm and delivering "justice" and to continue calling attention to those voices deemed inherently criminal, threatening, and untrustworthy. Each act of reclamation refutes and (thus) refuses institutional definitions of "deviance," disputing the epistemic violence of the category itself. In light of these acts, testimony by all affected by the penal system, shared through now essential digital channels, prefigures and pushes toward a better world.

We Mad scholars also share much in common with oft-criminalized abolitionists now demanding societal transformation (if not already among them). We certainly share common goals, even beyond our calls to abolish medical and psychiatric policing. We, too, refuse to cede the power of self-naming, instead engaging in a scholarly practice that resists the diagnostic alchemy that turns person to patient (or prisoner). Many of us, including me, owe our lives and our freedom to underground, online, highly decentralized skill-sharing strategies. Collective, counterepistemic archives are crucial to our discursive and material freedom.

I anticipate the need for recognition, promotion, and citation of emblogged knowledges only to grow since the beginning of the COVID pandemic as we continue to relearn what sociality, safety, and isolation look like. Blogger-scholars, in conjunction with prisoner-scholars, sex worker–scholars, and others whose legitimacy is undone by epistemic injustice have much to teach fellow scholars and activists, particularly in terms of creating anti-institutional sites of community and self-determination. Interethnography poses exciting possibilities for these groups, too, for former—and current—community members who find it crucial to close the academic/participant epistemic gap.

Following Merri Johnson and Robert McRuer's text-message-coined term *cripistemologies*, I consider the citational possibilities in "remote locations, styles, and modes of transmission for prohibited knowledge about disability" (2014, 130). As Emmanuel David refers to "bodies, practices, and identities that inhabit the archipelagic coastlines" of trans experience (2018, 335), Johnson and McRuer refer to an epistemic "backwoods" far from the R1 campus (2014, 128). Wandering the digital backwoods, I prioritize not only emblogged *scholarship* but also emblogged *scholars* them/ourselves. I follow the Cite Black Women Collective, which calls upon scholars to "reconfigure the politics of knowledge production by engaging in a radical praxis of citation that acknowledges and honors Black women's transnational intellectual production" (n.d., par. 3), for which they have been denied both credit and access. I step beyond the critical ethnographic practice of contextualizing subjects' voices (data) and instead cite the contexts provided by bloggers themselves on sites of mutual influence. To do so is to resist transphobic, ableist norms of simultaneous surveillance and invisibility.

For scholars accustomed to collecting citations, cross-referencing quotations, and placing pieces across space–time in conversation with one another, my process proves both new and familiar. Yet my "archipelagic," cripistemic practice, unlike traditional approaches to ethnography, does not "neutrally" observe and interpret subject behavior through the lens of outside research, with or without the self-reflexive ethos now popular in the field; it is not an autoethnography, a meditation on the contexts and meanings surrounding my lived experiences. Instead, I challenge the binaries self/other, scholar/subject, text/context, and sane/insane. I need the words of others to make words for myself. This story is mine to tell only as told through others, whom I present not as subjects but as researchers like me. As a blogger, I take their stories, study them, and integrate them with my own in a chain of interdependent, unruly self-scholarship. While I can provide here only this brief, static account of an ever-growing field, I hope other Mad scholars might see bits of their own coming-of-Madness in my own words and in those of my sources. We are necessary to the form and contents of the knowledge that Carrie Sandahl (2003) and Sky Cubacub (2015) call "queercrip" as well as to that which I call "transMad" (Cavar 2022). I thank my forebears, my Tumblr friends, my followers, and those I follow not only for making me think but also for helping to make *me*. "Your story is the same as mine. Thank you for expressing everything I've been struggling to find words for."

Works Cited

Aaliyahbreaux, Aceofsquiddles, Jasminethegothbunny, Cowboyslovingboys, Accept-nothing. 2019. "I Wonder How Many. . . ." Tumblr, July 21. At https://acceptnothing.tumblr.com/post/186414686448/i-wonder-how-many-gaypeople-are-actually.

Abel, Emily K., and C. H. Browner. 1998. "Selective Compliance with Biomedical Authority and the Uses of Experiential Knowledge." In *Pragmatic Women and Body Politics*, edited by Margaret Lock and Patricia M. Kaufert, 310–26. Cambridge: Cambridge Univ. Press.

Bascom, Julia. 2011. "Quiet Hands." *Just Stimming* (blog), Oct. 5. At https://just stimming.wordpress.com/2011/10/05/quiet-hands/.

Cavar, Sarah. 2021. "Xenogenders, Neopronouns, and the transMad Toolbox." *Queer Disability Studies Network* (blog), Oct. 20. At https://queerdisability studies.wordpress.com/xenogenders-neopronouns-and-the-transmad-toolbox/.

———. 2022. "Toward TransMad Epistemologies: A Working Text." *Spark: A 4C4Equality Journal* 4. At https://sparkactivism.com/toward-transmad-epistemologies/.

Cavar, Sarah, and Alexandre Baril. 2021. "Blogging to Counter Epistemic Injustice: Trans Disabled Digital Micro-resistance." *Disability Studies Quarterly* 41, no. 2. At https://doi.org/10.18061/dsq.v41i2.7794.

Cite Black Women Collective. n.d. "Our Praxis." At https://www.citeblackwomen collective.org/our-praxis.html.

Cubacub, Sky. 2015. "Radical Visibility: A Queercrip Dress Manifesto." *Radical Visibility Zine*, Apr. 22. At https://rebirthgarments.com/radical-visibility-zine.

David, Emmanuel. 2018. "Transgender Archipelagos." *TSQ: Transgender Studies Quarterly* 5, no. 3: 332–54. At https://doi.org/10.1215/23289252-6900724.

Davies, Charlotte Aull. 2010. *Reflexive Ethnography: A Guide to Researching Selves and Others*. London: Routledge.

Erickson-Schroth, Laura, ed. 2022. *Trans Bodies, Trans Selves: A Resource by and for Transgender Communities*. 2nd ed. Oxford: Oxford Univ. Press.

Fricker, Miranda. 2007. *Epistemic Injustice: Power and the Ethics of Knowing*. Oxford: Oxford Univ. Press.

Johnson, Merri Lisa, and Robert McRuer. 2014. "Cripistemologies: Introduction." In "Cripistemologies: Part I," edited by Merri Lisa Johnson and Robert McRuer. Special issue, *Journal of Literary & Cultural Disability Studies* 8, no. 2: 127–47. At https://muse.jhu.edu/article/548847.

McRuer, Robert. 2006. *Crip Theory: Cultural Signs of Queerness and Disability*. New York: New York Univ. Press.

metapianycist. 2020. "I Support the Radical Idea. . . ." Tumblr, May 15. At https://metapianycist.tumblr.com/post/618197583016411136/.

mogai-archive and autigender-culture-is. 2021. "Auti(s)gender." Tumblr, June 28. At https://autigender-culture-is.tumblr.com/post/655259399896563712/.

Orbitsing, Margot, askanonbinary, rocketrissa, and Shade Shadaras. 2013. "Pronouns I have Encountered in No Particular Order." Tumblr, Nov. 9. At https://archive.is/keNEY.

Sandahl, Carrie. 2003. "Queering the Crip or Cripping the Queer? Intersections of Queer and Crip Identities in Solo Autobiographical Performance." *GLQ: A Journal of Lesbian and Gay Studies* 9, no. 1: 25–56.

10

The Subject Is Mad

Rua Williams

To all the Mad folk who dare to bring change to the world
Like the ocean brings change to a rock.
We have a secret. Even erasure leaves a mark.

Content note: neurotypical supremacy, anti-Black racism

In this chapter, I deploy echolalic, hebephrenic, and muted narrative devices to explore a neurodivergent, Mad practice of remembering, reflecting, and reimagining academic and life experiences—(hyper)connecting the personal to the academic to diffract hegemonic power into new patterns of transformation and coliberation. A Mad rhetoric embraces hyperconnection, hyperverbosity, and hyperrecalcitrance as valid sites of meaning making and embodied expression.

Remi Yergeau (2017) explores the concept of "demi-rhetoricity" as a position of narrative precarity. All neurodivergent voices can be dismissed, denied, and deflected by hegemonic authority as either functionless, unintentional, unrepresentative, or otherwise devoid of credibility or credulity. Autistic and Mad speech acts are both clinically classified and pathologized as involuntary, ineffectual, or defiant. For example, the term *selective mutism* is used to define a person's inability to speak as a deliberate, often defiant act of refusal. Yet as soon as we are not "too silent," we become "too noisy." *Echolalia* is a term for utterances that are repetitions, or echoes, of words or phrases, usually deemed "nonfunctional" or "involuntary." But to autistic people, echolalia is always an expression—an echo of affect, a pattern of soothing, communication via allusion. Similarly, *hebephrenia* connects seemingly unrelated words or concepts. This characterization is deployed against schizophrenics to classify their speech acts as symptomatic of delirium or paranoia and therefore to be ceased and dismissed.

Influenced by the work of Leah Lakshmi Piepzna-Samarasinha and Stacey Park Milbern (2018), Julia Miele Rodas (2018), Remi Yergeau (2017), Nirmala Erevelles, Elizabeth Grace, and Gillian Parekh (2019), Therí Alyce Pickens (2019), and others,[1] I explore divergent notions of authorship, kinship, and inheritance. There is much left unsaid and unexplained. I leave it up to you to make some connections for, and to, yourself. I invite you to parallel my narrative of struggle, exploration, and discovery. It is my hope that these explorations encourage others to adopt their own ruptured, diffracted, noisy sensibilities of scholarship, pedagogy, and relation.

They say the definition of insanity is doing the same thing again and again and expecting a different outcome. Obviously, "they" never met water. Never met erosion. Never met an echo.

"Who Is Your Audience?"

"If the authors want the [journal] readership to support their call to move forward, they need to carefully consider how they are speaking to the readers" (reviewer).

> *Our readers will not respect your humanity unless you can learn*
> *to ask nicely.*

"You can't keep writing this way. You must communicate your message in an appropriate voice so that people can actually hear you" (well-meaning mentor).

> *You must carve yourself into a shape that is more appropriate.*
> *More publishable.*

"This manuscript needs substantial re-writing and re-structuring. In its current form, it is not clear which community of scholarly readers this manuscript is speaking to" (reviewer).

---

1. I foreground these scholars here as an act of citational justice and an accounting of my chosen ancestry.

The Subject Is Mad   177

> *You must carve the space into which your readers are to be poured.*
>
> *How else will they know where to direct their attention?*

I never realized that the reason I look up at the trees was because they asked me to.

> *The sycamores are barking.*

"The paper is not too 'reader-friendly'" (editor).

Why is it that only *certain people* have narratological difficulty counted as evidence of their genius?

"It's as though the autistic individual is looking through a shoe box filled with random handfuls of pictures and cannot organize them into a photograph album that tells a story" (Brown 2010, 21).

"Collections favored by autistic children appear like soulless possessions. . . . The autistic individual just stacks boxes full of useless junk" (Asperger 2009, 82).

"All of these words, numbers, and poems . . . could hardly have more meaning than sets of nonsense syllables" (Leo Kanner in Rodas 2018, 243).

Cascading echolalic connections, hebephrenic collections, "soulless," recursive, enfolded transmissions.

"Within this theoretical matrix, there is no real person doing the writing or speaking. *No tadpoles in the house.* And the idea that autistic language might as well be machine language is reinforced by researchers" (Rodas 2018, 61, italics added).

Perhaps all my memories are just the automated output of a dysfunctional neural network; my writing just the fractured, splintered, split, schizoidal echoes of input. And yet . . .

"Rhetoricity itself should not remain contingent on a rhetor's intent, or, more pointedly, on the perceptions of a rhetor's intent" (Yergeau 2017, 32).

"Maybe nothing is something after all" (Rodas 2018, 114).

"Demi-rhetoricity holds potential as a reclamatory strategy" (Yergeau 2017, 33).

"Refusal to satisfy a profound social desire for straightforward, transactional, and communicative language . . . the unwillingness or the inability to accede to language as transaction" (Rodas 2018, 141).

I compulsively collect the data in. I compulsively splice, cut together-apart, out (Barad 2007). This, too, is rhetorical articulation.

The very act of constructing a reader can be a violent practice of exclusion—constructing certain people as belonging to the category of "people for whom this text is intended and for whom the epistemic value of meaning making is granted," necessitating the corresponding category of "I didn't write this for you, and thus you are not allowed to make meaning from it or any meaning you construct can be invalidated as it was not made possible for you to properly understand it."

I'm told I can't critique interventionist science—the research that seeks to save us from ourselves, to deliver us from disability—because I'm too disordered to understand its necessity. I madly refuse to construct the boundaries of my text's vocal range. To do so would be to force demi-rhetoricity upon any who came to read it.

So, in writing that is for no reader, anyone can take meaning from it. At the same time, no one can claim interpretive authority over it.[2] The sense I make doesn't have to be the sense you take. To assure that equivalence would be an interpretive violence unto ourselves and others.

"To trouble notions of how a text speaks is to allow for the possibility that cognition, communication, and ability upend or cocreate said text" (Pickens 2019, 10).

Like Therí Alyce Pickens, I take for granted that Mad, divergent, Black, decolonial, and/or queer reading acts are necessarily participatory (2019, 14). As someone from a group for whom agential action is constantly called into question, I take for granted that I have no agency over the practice of your participation.

"Autistic invention can be a long game, or a joke without a ready audience, expressing itself 'without [addressing] anyone in particular' (Bosch, *Infantile Autism*, 9)" (Rodas 2018, 186).

"What do you mean, 'violence'?"

"What is all this talk about violence, anyway?" She is not the first person to ask me that today.

An email in my inbox also reads: "What do you mean when you talk about violence? Are people actually hitting you?"

---

2. See Rodas 2018, 174.

My hip twinges in memory of a former encounter. I had been allowed to present a personal essay on academic violence in assistive technology and on using passion to combat the uncritical objectivity that naturalizes societal inequities. My empirical work was rejected as unrigorous, and my essay became little more than a spectacle for mockery. No room for autistic testimony that contradicts curative projects.[3]

You can't keep writing this way. . . .

It's a little funny how STEM people go on about rigor and then constantly confess they don't understand all these big words—*silencing, harm,* and *violence.*

I think about a conference earlier that year and how a woman shoved me and threatened my friend with a chair, irritated that we dared to be critical of operant conditioning. I think about another friend who was stabbed at a conference as retaliation for her advocacy. I think about lunch that day, when a cofounder of this very conference shoved me out of line. I guess my disability really is invisible after all.

"Maybe the paper makes more sense than I do out loud," I offer, shrugging. *Maybe you should read it every day until it makes sense,* I stew silently.

"What's a panopticon?," chirps a cybersecurity researcher.

"I'm not sure I understood a word she said, to be honest!" She turns to our colleagues to guffaw. All our badges have pronouns on them. She used the wrong pronoun for me. No one corrects her.

There's a lump in my throat.

The Jewelry Box

"Many of the products they make at the workshop have to be thrown away. They aren't coordinated enough to make the edges clean." The speaker shows the audience a workspace on his slide. Disabled folks, young adults with cognitive disability mostly, arranged in a row.

"The autistic individual just stacks boxes full of useless junk" (Asperger 2009, 82).

---

3. See Kim 2017; Stramondo 2019.

They are making jewelry boxes.

On the next slide, the speaker shows the laser-cut guide tracks he made to help the disabled "workers" achieve clean edges. I am struck by how mechanical it all is . . . like an assembly-line robot without the gears.

Oh.

Oh.

He passes a laser-cut box around the room. The balsa wood is cut at angles and would fold into a perfect prism. The inside is covered in a soft, navy felt. The smell and the feel remind me of all the jewelry boxes stacked and lined up and spilling over every surface in my grandparents' room. Soft like velvet. Soft like dust. Smelling of balsa and sandalwood and the patina of oxidizing precious metals.

I see my grandfather's brothers, stacked and lined up in the institution. Smelling of balsa and felt and the patina of segregation.

They made the sheltered workshop more efficient. By turning my kin into gears.

These Thumbs Are a Landmark, My Inheritance

My grandmother's thumbs are a landmark.

They are wrapped around my hand as she pulls my small body up, bobbing in the sea. They tuck the blankets around my cold body, dabbing warm teabags on my red raw shoulders. They thumb through the yellowed, thinning pages of a book. They stick up, triumphant, as she places another piece in the puzzle that is always scattered over her dining-room table. They twiddle with her other fingers as they drip fluid sand down into fantastic bubbly castles on the shore.

"*A shoe box filled with random handfuls of pictures . . . cannot organize them into . . . a story*" (Brown 2010, 21).

Her hands, soft and creased, cup the shore where the tide pulls away, leaving moist sand and periwinkle mollusks dancing back down, chasing after the foam. Down, Down, Down, she scoops away until a pool of Newtonian slip-sand waits. Her thumbs pass idly around the tips of her fingers. Soupy goopy sand drip, drip, dribbling—stack, stack, stacking up into bubbly teeter-totter spires. Those sandcastles were like magic to me.

Magic castles spun from magic thumbs. Thumbs that were blue and purple-tinged from the skin she pulled away with her teeth, idly frittering away her anxiety.

Her thumbs are a landmark.

> *Madness was here, they whisper.*
> *Madness is your inheritance.*

Madness can be love, scratchy blankets, and bubbly dolloped castles by the sea.

The "Evidence Base" Is a Palimpsest

Nirmalla Erevelles, Elizabeth Grace, and Gillian Parekh (2019) describe the parenthetical in pedagogy, the palimpsest in analysis, and the practical in practice as conceptual interventions to imagine disability as a meta-curriculum, a phenomenon that, through these conceptual interventions, can teach us about how we teach and what results from that teaching.

Their deployment of the palimpsest in analysis is particularly appealing to my notions of resistant illegibility in Mad scholarship and Mad life. The palimpsest is a text on which "the original writing [has] been erased or rubbed out to make place for the second" (*Oxford English Dictionary*, qtd. in Erevelles, Grace, and Parekh 2019, s.v. *palimpsest*). Erevelles grasps the imperfection of this erasure as a space of conspicuous absence that can be traced as a cartography of displacement, revealing not a pristine account before erasure but a testimony of the erasure itself (in Erevelles, Grace, and Parekh 2019).

"Maybe nothing is something after all" (Rodas 2018, 114).

I encourage a palimpsestuous analysis of "the evidence base" in research of neurodivergent subjects. Within the text of the very methods and results, there can be found moments of elision, of deflection—the overwriting of autistic agency with a recoding of involution. I argue that research into disability and what is required to "ameliorate" disability are a project of interpretation, translation, displacement. Interpretation is an intent to make something legible in one's own epistemic frame, often without regard to the material consequences of that forced legibility. That which is made intelligible is haunted by the exclusion necessary to construct that legibility—a palimpsest.

The stories told by "the evidence base" are transmuted by a lens that traces the consequences of normative interpretation as deflection and displacement. An alternate dimension. An unreality. A hallucination. A vision that disrupts the dominant, creating fissures from which a sealed agency can escape.

The Space Between

My hand is the last part of me to descend. The meniscus seals around my fingertips. My hair splays around my head, my Leo's mane. The last bubbles escape the rim of my nostrils.

I am enveloped. Is this what it feels like in space? Is this what it feels like to disappear?

I can hear only my own heart, beating in syncopation with the drum-song that large vessels of water make, even when they are at rest.

I can see the clouds above me through the multifaceted fluid prism of the water's surface, rimmed by a broken mosaic of sapphire, azure, and cerulean. A portal.

It's the closest I come to seeing in real life what it feels like to live in my body. Infinitely far away. Infinitely close. Slightly blurry. Slightly muffled. If I touch you, will you break? Will I?

"If people squeeze, they'll bust."[4]

Have I come here to disappear? Why does my heart always shout, "I want to go home!," even when I'm already there?

I imagine inhaling.

Years later I will learn that it isn't "normal" for a child to wish, with all the intensity of a dying star's density, that they could just—wink, blink, burst, dissipate, vanish.

The demi-rhetor is demi-drowned.

---

4. For more on echolalic repetition, see Julia Miele Rodas's book *Autistic Disturbances* (2018), where the author repeats echolalic phrases of patients found in Leo Kanner's notes, interleaving these utterances throughout the book, allowing their previously classified "functionless" speech to have a new context for narrative function. "If people squeeze, they'll bust" can mean many things and have different affective charges depending on the moment.

> *They're drawn to water.*

My body will always remember what it feels like, enveloped underwater—in the space between rest and daring myself to breathe.

Drowning doesn't look like drowning.

"Do you feel like you are drowning?"

I had been trying to describe how I feel. All the tension built up in my chest—like my body is trying to scream without my permission. Like the flexion before a good dry heave. I am literally a walking wretch.

My cheeks are prickling, cold hot buzzing. My jaw is numb.

I would never have said I felt like I was drowning. As usual, the way I express my embodied sensations is never quite satisfactory to the clinical gaze. They are always trying to adjust my metaphors—to put metonymy where specificity is more accurate. Like ~~my body is~~ trying to scream without ~~my~~ permission . . .

"Autistic language might as well be machine language" (Rodas 2018, 61).

But it did remind me: "Drowning doesn't look like drowning."

My father wrote that (Vittone 2013). As a trained Coast Guard rescue swimmer, he knew something about drowning that other people knew differently. Drowning isn't what we are shown by media and collective imagination. Drowning isn't splashing and shouting and screaming for help. Drowning is *silent*.

The article circulates internationally every June. It was June when my psychiatrist asked me if I felt like I was drowning. The following June, I started drafting this chapter.

I thought about how very deeply, hauntingly ill I was. I thought about how absolutely no one asked if I was OK. I may never know if they were just too afraid or if they genuinely never thought anything was wrong.

Drowning really doesn't look like drowning. The collective imaginary of what drowning should look like is based on our own fear of what drowning might feel like. Similarly, *there is a collective imaginary of what Madness is supposed to look like, based on a collective fear of Madness itself.* But the Madness imagined by the clinician is not the Madness embodied by the Madfolk. What looks to the clinician to be the manifestation of psychic torment can be Mad joy. What the clinician does to relieve the Madfolk is usually psychic torment.

184 Williams

Maybe dispelling fallacies of normative perception is my inheritance. We must learn to notice when we are watching people drown.

Diffraction Is Also a Verb

In critical scholarship, the concept of diffraction has been taken up to navigate and negotiate the ways in which the modes and mechanisms of measurement inherently determine the possible interpretations of reality (Kaiser and Thiele 2017). In the two-slit experiment, light cast between two slits projects a pattern that can be analyzed to "prove" light is a particle or a wave or both based on the means of measurement used to observe the phenomenon. This diffraction is understood as the entanglement of reality with means of observation. Through a diffraction lens, it is easier to see how dominant cultural biases shape the direction and purpose of research inquiry and public policy.

In computer science, particularly computer vision, diffraction is *applied*. For example, the diffraction pattern of infrared light as captured by a camera is used to calculate the structure of the surfaces off which the light reflects. Here, the fact that the means of measurement produce an artifacted reality is known and is in fact *intentionally* deployed to calculate a representation of that reality.

Likewise, *cripistemologies*, a portmanteau word made up of *crip* and *epistemologies*, refers to a fluid network of understandings of disability that are driven by a resistant interpretation of that embodied relationship to society (Johnson and McRuer 2014). Cripistemologies refuse to naturalize disability as tragedy or as pride—demanding attention to the inherently conflicted reality of disabled life. Through this attention, the theory and practice of crip technoscience imagine disabled people as sites of "possibility, adaptation, and creative reflection" (Nelson, Shew, and Stevens 2019, 1) and refuse "to treat access as an issue of technical compliance or rehabilitation" (Hamraie and Fritsch 2019, 22).

Taken together, then, if diffraction is the phenomenon of measurement determining how reality is perceived, then *applied diffraction patterns* are the practice of using this artifacted measurement to build new ways of perceiving and being. Crip technoscience may be interpreted as the practice of intentionally diffracting one's onto-epistemic essence with the matter, measurement, and meaning of mechanical and digital strata—harnessing the diffracted nature of a cyborg embodiment to create and become new meanings.

"All of these words, numbers, and poems . . . could hardly have more meaning than sets of nonsense syllables" (Leo Kanner in Rodas 2018, 243).

Diffraction undoes the positivist conceit that "reality" is confined to that which can be perceived by senses unobstructed by substance or Madness. All our measures put us "under the influence." *All our tools are Mad.*

All Mad perception is unreality, all Mad testimony is not merely suspect but manifestly unintelligible.

Do you feel like you are drowning?

"Drowning doesn't look like drowning."

Madness can be an applied diffraction pattern. Repetition, ripples, echoes . . . these are the resistant neurodivergent praxis that generate perturbances, erosion, change.

Erosion Shapes the Whole World

It is late-early, the witching hour on the New York City subway. We sit, twenty-something "tech entrepreneurs," bleary-eyed, rocking with the tracks, waiting for the magic bullet to leave us at the airport.

A Black man, his face leathered and weathered by poverty, stumbles into the car with us. There is a bottle clutched in a paper bag in his left hand. He turns to the door. Places his palm on the cold-tempered glass. He begins to hum.

THUMP, he raps the glass.

Chugga chugga, answer the tracks.

Hmmmmm, the rumble in his throat turns into a melody. Distant, yet it reverberates in my chest like the train itself.

THUMP, SMACK, he begins to drum on the glass with his right hand. It's percussive. Both startling and rhythmic.

My companions ask if we should leave.

THUMP, SMACK.

I do not move. I am remembering my own musical bouts of Madness. The neighborhood adults whispering as I passed, wishing me to leave. My song projecting a shimmering halo diffracting me out of focus. The man is looking out through the watery portal of his own reflection. The subway is his instrument. His stone.

THUMP, SMACK.

The rhythm goes on. I am not really the sort to keep track of time.

THUMP, CRACK.

The glass splinters—a spider's web beneath his hand. He inhales sharply. He is not hurt. But perhaps he is a little afraid. Twenty years later, Jordan Neely would be murdered on a similar train for being hungry, Mad, and Black.

He transfers to another car before he leaves, sober enough to know he shouldn't be seen walking out of a door with a broken window.

I remember him. A loop in my mind. The little dot on the *i* of "Jeremy Bearimy."[5]

They say the definition of insanity is doing the same thing again and again, expecting a different result.

But he broke the window.

"Autistic invention can be a long game . . . without a ready audience"
(Rodas 2018, 186).

Was he autistic like me? Was he schizophrenic? Is there any difference other than our skin, diffracting others' fear and determining which of us is allowed our little bouts of Madness?

I hope he got the chance to break more windows.

The privilege of my boldness.

"It's just . . ."

My lab mate pauses, turns their face back to their screen. I am standing caddy-corner to their desk. They have given me good feedback on my prelims. But . . .

"But . . . it's just . . . I'm not sure it's such a good idea to disclose in your work like that."

"Demi-rhetoricity holds potential as a reclamatory strategy"
(Yergeau 2017, 33).

---

5. This reference is from "Jeremy Bearimy," *The Good Place*, season 3, episode 4, NBC, aired Oct. 18, at https://thegoodplace.fandom.com/wiki/Jeremy_Bearimy_Timeline.

"I know. That's why I do it. I know I'm not going to survive hiding behind a mask waiting for tenure. I have to make sure I don't even get interviewed by a place that would be hostile to me."

They look down. Bite their lip. Nod slowly. "I guess."

They are Black, and I am white. And if the tingling I get in the back of my neck when I speak to them is anything to go by, they are not altogether "normal" either. And I recognize then that my "strategy" of constantly uncloseting myself is a privilege. I hope I can barter the privilege of my self-endangerment for a shovel to scoop out space—so someone like my lab mate doesn't have to choose which closets to keep shut.

Chosen Families, Chosen Ancestors, Kinships of Affinity

People who are used to being discarded learn a lot about choosing family. Sometimes we even learn to reclaim family, knowing that even the communities we forge can splinter, fracture, and break. I write this in the wake of the disability justice advocate Stacey Park Milbern's death. I did not get to choose her as my family. I knew her only peripherally. She was, at best, a distant cousin, though in so many ways she was a matriarch of the broader kinship network that sustained me.

I live with a copy of Leah Lakshmi Piepzna-Samarasinha's *Care Work* (2018) on a shelf by my bed. I dream disabled dreams, imagining the love and the conviction in its pages guide me through the ether. At the end of this book, Leah and Stacey share a conversation about crip kinship and lineage (Piepzna-Samarasinha and Milbern 2018). It is a conversation about choosing family, about forging family as a public act of collective love and justice. And it is a conversation about choosing ancestors. It is a conversation about birthing, doulaing, people into a disabled community. In the wake of Stacey's death, it is a conversation about dying—doulaing disabled memory into disabled ancestry.

Care Work is a book by and for disabled queer people of color. There are details in this book that testify to the particulars of the struggles and community of the sick and disabled, the queer and trans, Black folks, Indigenous folks, and people of color. But I immerse myself in the work of disability justice activists because I wish to divest myself from the lineages of disability pride that rely on neocolonial logics, that enforce a supercrip respectability through capitalist value and biophilanthropy (Schuller 2017).

I want my scholarship to be a practice of doulaing people in the transition from hegemony to collective—through an identification with divergence. I wish to ferry my kin into a rebirth via divestment from able-normative white-supremacist kyriarchy.

"Through loving disabled people, I get to love myself" (Piepzna-Samarasinha and Milbern 2018, 256).

A *Madman finds answers everywhere* (Smith 2020).

A *Madman finds ancestors everywhere.*

As my ancestors, I choose all the Madfolk—spinning in the *i* dot of "Jeremy Bearimy." Everyone who was taken to an institution and never got out. Everyone who wanders about in plain view while everyone else casts their gaze away. Everyone who ever fissured a pane of glass into a spider-web. I choose the angry ghosts who haunt the institutions.

I choose every Mad soul who ever cast themselves tidally against the rocks, knowing not if they would shake off a few molecules or a few thousand tons of shale—knowing only it was right to try.

Mad, neurodivergent rhetorics are diffracted rhetorics. We are so well accustomed to living and dying through the gaze of those who demand we deny our own realities that we know better than most that you cannot know what you are looking *at* if you don't even know what you are looking *through*. Mad scholarship embraces the position of the demi-rhetor, of demi-interlocucity, by destabilizing the certainty of the *object* by madly protesting the clarity of the *subject*.

"Drowning doesn't look like drowning."

Protest with me. Tidally thrash with me. Break the windows. Release the ghosts. Find our ancestors.

. . . [6]

---

6. Do you feel as though I have left you hanging? I've been told autistic people are almost as bad at ending a conversation as they are at starting one. Of course, I am still talking, raging, ranting. . . . I've just wandered over to another street corner. Come and find me.

Works Cited

Asperger, Hans. 2009. "'Autistic Psychopathy' in Childhood." Translated and edited by Uta Frith. In *Autism and Asperger Syndrome*, edited by Uta Frith, 37–92. Cambridge: Cambridge Univ. Press.

Barad, Karen. 2007. *Meeting the Universe Halfway: Quantum Physics and the Entanglement of Matter and Meaning*. Durham, NC: Duke Univ. Press.

Brown, Julie. 2010. *Writers on the Spectrum: How Autism and Asperger Syndrome Have Influenced Literary Writing*. Philadelphia: Jessica Kingsley.

Erevelles, Nirmala, Elizabeth J. Grace, and Gillian Parekh. 2019. "Disability as Meta Curriculum: Ontologies, Epistemologies, and Transformative Praxis." *Curriculum Inquiry* 49, no. 4: 357–72. At https://doi.org/10.1080/03626784 .2019.1664078.

Hamraie, Aimee, and Kelly Fritsch. 2019. "Crip Technoscience Manifesto." *Catalyst: Feminism, Theory, Technoscience* 5, no. 1. At https://doi.org/10.28968 /cftt.v5i1.29607.

Johnson, Merri Lisa, and Robert McRuer. 2014. "Cripistemologies: Introduction." In "Cripistemologies: Part I," edited by Merri Lisa Johnson and Robert McRuer. Special issue, *Journal of Literary & Cultural Disability Studies* 8, no. 2: 127–47. At https://muse.jhu.edu/article/548847/pdf.

Kaiser, Birgit M., and Kathrin Thiele, eds. 2017. *Diffracted Worlds—Diffractive Readings*. Philadelphia: Routledge.

Kim, Eunjung. 2017. *Curative Violence: Rehabilitating Disability, Gender, and Sexuality in Modern Korea*. Durham, NC: Duke Univ. Press.

Nelson, Malorie K., Ashley Shew, and Bethany Stevens. 2019. "Transmobility: Possibilities in Cyborg (Cripborg) Bodies." *Catalyst: Feminism, Theory, Technoscience* 5, no. 1. At https://doi.org/10.28968/cftt.v5i1.29617.

Pickens, Therí Alyce. 2019. *Black Madness :: Mad Blackness*. Durham, NC: Duke Univ. Press.

Piepzna-Samarasinha, Leah Lakshmi. 2018. *Care Work: Dreaming Disability Justice*. Vancouver: Arsenal Pulp Press.

Piepzna-Samarasinha, Leah Lakshmi, and Stacey Park Milbern. 2018. "Crip Lineages, Crip Futures: A Conversation with Stacey Milbern." In Leah Lakshmi Piepzna-Samarasinha, *Care Work: Dreaming Disability Justice*, 240–57. Vancouver: Arsenal Pulp Press.

Rodas, Julia Miele. 2018. *Autistic Disturbances: Theorizing Autism Poetics from the DSM to Robinson Crusoe*. Ann Arbor: Univ. of Michigan Press.

Schuller, Kyla. 2017. *The Biopolitics of Feeling.* Durham, NC: Duke Univ. Press.

Smith, Phil. 2020. "[R]evolving towards Mad: Spinning Away from the Psy/Spy-Complex through Auto/Biography." In *The Palgrave Handbook of Auto/Biography,* edited by Julie M. Parsons and Anne Chappell, 369–88. London: Palgrave Macmillan.

Stramondo, Joseph A. 2019. "The Distinction between Curative and Assistive Technology." *Science and Engineering Ethics* 25, no. 4: 1125–45. At https://doi.org/10.1007/s11948-018-0058-9.

Vittone, Mario. 2013. "Drowning Doesn't Look Like Drowning." *Slate,* June 4. At https://slate.com/technology/2013/06/rescuing-drowning-children-how-to-know-when-someone-is-in-trouble-in-the-water.html.

Yergeau, Remi M. 2017. *Authoring Autism: On Rhetoric and Neurological Queerness.* Durham, NC: Duke Univ. Press.

Part Three

Disclosure and Disruptive Pedagogies

Mad pedagogy serves as a direct and deliberate response to the looming, oppressive specters of ableism, white supremacy, and cis-heteropatriarchy.[1] At the core of our pedagogical practices, Madness becomes a growing, ecstatic stance that resists the rigidity and conformity of the "normative educator." When we teach Mad, we envision education liberated.[2] We embrace Madness as

1. Although a distinctly Mad pedagogy has yet to be explored outside of pieces such as Margaret Price's *Mad at School* (2011) and Mark Anthony Castrodale's "Critical Disability Studies and Mad Studies: Enabling New Pedagogies in Practice" (2017), this part of our volume does build on existing literature on the intersection of disability studies and critical pedagogy. For more on this intersection, see Nirmala Ervelles's essays "Educating Unruly Bodies: Critical Pedagogy, Disability Studies, and the Politics of Schooling" (2000) and "Understanding Curriculum as Normalizing Text: Disability Studies Meet Curriculum Theory" (2005) as well as Cynthia Lewiecki-Wilson and Brenda Jo Brueggemann's collected volume *Disability and the Teaching of Writing* (2007).

2. Many of the contributors to the chapters in this part are informed by the traditions and writings of scholars who center liberation in their practices, including Paulo Freire's *Pedagogy of the Oppressed* ([1970] 2014), bell hooks's *Teaching to Transgress* (1994), Jeff M. Duncan-Andrade and Ernest Morrell's *The Art of Critical Pedagogy* (2008), and Zaretta Hammond's *Culturally Responsive Teaching and the Brain* (2015).

"an expressly political act," as a "plurality of resistances" (Menzies, LeFrançois, and Reaume 2013, 10).

Mad pedagogy must be moved from a liminal practice to one that is viscerally rooted in purpose, intention, and need. This shift does not arise just from disclosing a disability, though that can certainly be a component. It means moving to a practice of teaching that reimagines *how* we educate and *why*. Writing to her colleagues, Kelan Koning (she/her) describes how her Mad pedagogy creates love, solidarity, and support for students and other Mad educators: "Let us reimagine rigor and its tools." Teaching from this place of reimagining enables us to remake and refashion the normative restrictions of academic rigor and rationality so that our speech, our assignments, and the learning styles we celebrate become inclusive of the diverse ways we/people process and thrive. For Liz Miller (she/her), the heart of Mad pedagogy and its movement is in the creation and articulation of "caring methodologies" that empower multiply marginalized students. Within a sanist institution, we are moved to create classroom cultures that are constructed from the bodymind outward and that celebrate a panoply of Mad, neurodiverse knowledges.[3] For Samuel Z. Shelton (they/them), this also means explicitly centering Mad activism, wisdom, and kinship to "teach[] against normative rationality and reason." Madness as movement becomes a mechanism with revisionary potential, one that invites a reimagining of the educator as "care-full"

---

3. We locate these knowledges in the tradition of the Mad studies scholars Robert Menzies, Brenda A. LeFrançois, and Geoffrey Reaume, who declare that "Mad Studies is an exercise in critical pedagogy—in the radical co-production, circulation, and consumption of knowledge" (2013, 14).

(Piepzna-Samarasinha 2018, passim) and vulnerable, as championing neurodiverse practices and modes of knowledge production.

As Mad pedagogy moves us, we come to the realization that we, too, can move: *past, through,* and *without.*[4] Our pedagogy defies; it leads us to question what we know and to hold space for new ways of knowing. A-M McManaman (she/they) calls this application in literature courses a "dislodging," where students "develop[] their critique away from a diagnostic framework toward a Mad one." For Pau Abustan (they/siya), Queer Crip Pilipinx Bad Pedagogy invites a reclamation of "bad," so that we might create rebellious pathways out of the sanist, settler-colonial, and cis-heteropatriarchal standards of goodness and perfection. Mad pedagogy also becomes a place of reclamation, a place where we enter as Mad, multiply marginalized educators with the opportunity to address our past harms. For some, this means questioning the obligatory process of disclosing; for others, it means a deliberate and political engagement with disclosure as we are invited to refashion the classroom into the spaces we wish we had been a part of. For Jesse Rice-Evans (she/her) and Andréa Stella (she/her), the guiding principle of this Mad work is their "crazy femme pedagogy," which centers care and decenters white-supremacist and cis-heteropatriarchal standards: "If femme pedagogy that centers access needs and emotions is 'crazy,' then it's up

---

4. This practice of moving past, through, and without is informed by Mad studies scholars who advocate for a disciplinary "unsettl[ing]" and "troubl[ing]" (Spandler and Poursanidou 2019, 14, citing Bracken and Thomas, 2010) and for Mad claiming and movement as "memory work that can help liberate us" (Menzies, LeFrançois, and Reaume 2013, 15) from ideological and disciplinary structures.

to us, the Mad femmes, to do this work." In part three, we illustrate six ways to do the care-full work, the tending work, and the heart work that our students deserve.

Works Cited

Bracken, Pat, and Philip Thomas. 2010. "From Szasz to Foucault: On the Role of Critical Psychiatry." *Philosophy* 17, no. 3: 219–28.

Castrodale, Mark Anthony. 2017. "Critical Disability Studies and Mad Studies: Enabling New Pedagogies in Practice." *Canadian Journal for the Study of Adult Education* 29, no. 1: 49–66. At https://cjsae.library.dal.ca/index.php/cjsae/article/view/5357.

Duncan-Andrade, Jeff M., and Ernest Morrell. 2008. *The Art of Critical Pedagogy: Possibilities for Moving from Theory to Practice in Urban Schools.* New York: Peter Lang.

Erevelles, Nirmala. 2000. "Educating Unruly Bodies: Critical Pedagogy, Disability Studies, and the Politics of Schooling." *Educational Theory* 50, no. 1: 25–47.

———. 2005. "Understanding Curriculum as Normalizing Text: Disability Studies Meet Curriculum Theory." *Journal of Curriculum Studies* 37, no. 4: 421–39. At https://doi.org/10.1080/0022027032000276970.

Freire, Paulo. [1970] 2014. *Pedagogy of the Oppressed.* 30th anniversary ed. Translated by Myra Bergman Ramos. New York: Bloomsbury.

Hammond, Zaretta. 2015. *Culturally Responsive Teaching and the Brain: Promoting Authentic Engagement and Rigor among Culturally and Linguistically Diverse Students.* Newbury Park, CA: Sage.

hooks, bell. 1994. *Teaching to Transgress: Education as the Practice of Freedom.* New York: Taylor & Francis.

Lewiecki-Wilson, Cynthia, and Brenda Jo Brueggemann, eds. 2007. *Disability and the Teaching of Writing: A Critical Sourcebook.* Boston: Bedford/St. Martin's.

Menzies, Robert, Brenda A. LeFrançois, and Geoffrey Reaume. 2013. "Introducing Mad Studies." In *Mad Matters: A*

Critical Reader in Canadian Mad Studies, edited by Brenda A. LeFrançois, Robert Menzies, and Geoffrey Reaume, 1–22. Toronto: Canadian Scholars' Press.

Piepzna-Samarasinha, Leah Lakshmi. 2018. *Care Work: Dreaming Disability Justice*. Vancouver: Arsenal Pulp Press.

Price, Margaret. 2011. *Mad at School: Rhetorics of Mental Disability and Academic Life*. Ann Arbor: Univ. of Michigan Press.

Spandler, Helen, and Konstantina Poursanidou. 2019. "Who Is Included in the Mad Studies Project?" *Journal of Ethics in Mental Health* 10:1–20. At https://clok.uclan.ac.uk/23384/8/23384%20JEMH%20Inclusion%20iii.pdf.

11

Mad Lyrics

*Toward an Embodied, Community-Responsive
Pedagogy of Care in Academia*

Kelan L. Koning

And in the storm, what happens to that tree?
> —Jeff Duncan-Andrade, "All Together Now: Academic
> Rigor and Culturally Responsive Pedagogy" (2016)

> *Content notes*: gun violence, suicidal ideation,
> child abuse, natural disaster

---

i

Dear colleagues,

When COVID-19 hit, I imagined you might finally understand me, were joining me in my attic.[1] Colleagues, this is what Madness looks like in my world—a deep closet you step into, a threshold you cross without knowledge of an exit.

Dear colleagues,

I am not the person I appear to be. Some of you tell me, "You are an open book." I laugh, listen to your stories, your worries. And I really listen—without judgment, without expectation. But because you see an ear, an open book, you do not ask.

---

1. A reference to both Charlotte Brontë's *Jane Eyre* (1847) and Sandra Gilbert and Susan Gubar's *The Madwoman in the Attic* ([1979] 2000).

Dear colleagues,

When COVID-19 hit, I was forever changed already. A family of secrets that could not be shared. *You are an open book.* Sleight of hand, a deft magician. Imagine what it takes to seem that open. I tell you this without expectation, without hope. My students know me far better than you do.

Dear colleagues,

Revision. I tell you this without expectation for myself. But I have radical, boundless hope for our students. And if you are nodding your head, I am writing this for you. Because, dearest, dearest colleagues, I know I am not the only one.

Dear colleagues,

To be a Mad educator is to reclaim, even rewrite, the narrative of the (Mad)woman in the attic. *Jane Eyre* is a book I love to the core of my being, and still I had to look up the (Mad)woman's name—Bertha Mason. The label overpowers her narrative, her self. She does not get to tell her story. Not there.

Dear colleagues,

Sometimes I share the situation of my past, my body's journey, with you. You always seem a little puzzled, not sure what to do with the information, but also there is a tinge of pity. *You poor thing,* I imagine you thinking, *to have gone through so much.* Like reading *The Glass Castle* or *Educated.* We close the book and return to talk about the weather.

Although I may lay bare to you the situation of my childhood self, her body, I conceal the situation of my mind, my Madness. In this way, I closet the part of myself that seems dangerous, perhaps even career annihilating. To voice this Madness is to speak it into being, to cross a threshold. Like confessing to a crime. Your eyes on me now, a permanent lens.

Dear, dear colleagues,

It is with the greatest tenderness I say (to myself, to you), we owe our students, and each other, more. And so I open the door and share this Mad pedagogy with you.

ii

> Even in the writing of progressive educators, the notion of engaging students as embodied and integral human beings has received limited attention in the discussions of life in schools. And when such discussions are raised, they often are either shaped by concerns of deviance or notions that privilege individuality and subjectivity discourse at the expense of critical development and collective consciousness.
>
> —Andrea Darder, "It's Not Nice to Fool Mother Nature: Eco-pedagogy in the Pursuit of Justice" (2011)

Dear colleagues,

In my twenty years of working in education, from Chicanx studies tutor to writing center tutor coordinator to Educational Opportunity Program admissions counselor to faculty, I have engaged in what feels to me like the best kind of learning—through listening openly, sharing stories. To break down these hierarchies, to truly learn together, requires vulnerability. To be vulnerable, open, and responsive—this is at the root of my Mad pedagogy.

In *Teaching to Transgress* (1994), bell hooks writes, "The classroom remains the most radical space of possibility in the academy" (12). Although I agree with this to a point, I believe that what may be considered more informal spaces—such as the hallway, student commons, or my office where I have created opportunities for students to gather with each other and me in what I have come to call "community hours"—provide an equally radical space of possibility. And so my pedagogy involves what many consider hospitality—something as invisible as air—hallway check-ins before class, shared moments searching for a meeting place (the challenge of adjunct life), hours spent listening as students share with each other, engage in what neuroscientists describe as "productive struggle," in my office.[2] All these opportunities and spaces support one of students' most basic needs—a feeling of security in the academy, a space that was not

---

2. In *Culturally Responsive Teaching and the Brain* (2015), Zaretta Hammond discusses what neuroscientists describe as "productive struggle" in relation to culturally and linguistically diverse students.

designed for them,[3] the opportunity to be fully seen and genuinely cared for in this unfamiliar space.

Dear colleagues,

The academy feels to our students like a fixed point, something ivied, solid. Their lives, in contrast, are often fraught with fault lines.

"We're always getting constant reminders of racism in the world; there are always new shootings or new situations happening. So we try not to think about it because we all already have our own troubles to deal with. We don't always want to hear something that we still have no idea how to deal with" (reflection by a first-year student writer, expressed and written during community hours before the pandemic)

Dear colleagues,

Many students come to the university anxious and unsure of their place. While the practice of saying, "Look to your left and your right—one of you will not make it to the end of this class" may no longer be status quo, the sentiment remains like a stain.

I, too, have been stained. My counternarrative is simple: "Look to your left, to your right—this is your community."[4]

On our campus, low-income, first-generation students of color are the majority. They come from Pacoima, South Central, East Los Angeles, Watts. They take buses and trains. They pass through many neighborhoods, see many ways of living on their way to this university. They have often seen too much.

I turn off my video and cry.
I don't feel like I belong here.

---

3. On my campus, a majority of students qualify for full financial aid. Our classrooms are diverse ethnically, socioeconomically, and psychologically. Our students' history of trauma emerges in these spaces.

4. When I began my work as a classroom mentor with the Educational Opportunity Program, I was conflicted. What right did I have to be in this role? Didn't the students deserve a mentor of color, someone who looked like them? For all this difference, though, my Madness, my trauma, turned out to be not fissure but bridge.

Mad Lyrics 201

I am filled with an anxiety so strong I can't go to class.
I'm not sure I will make it.
I can't think.
I'm so lonely I'm afraid I will lose it.
No one knows.
This is my darkness, and I know it will never leave me.[5]

Dear colleagues,

Our students come to us with the weight of their lives on their frames, often without awareness of why they can't think, can't study, why they feel the fog descending. I often share with them that entering college can bring trauma of its own by providing more space for reflection, for new awareness of the conditions of one's life. This knowing might present itself as a feeling rather than a cognitive experience. We may not recognize its origins. This is amplified if the student must return daily to that environment.

I recall my own experience as a freshman, voraciously reading Alice Miller and engaging in what I referred to as "putting my finger in the wound"—peeling the scab of repressed memory back ever so gently to see if it still hurt.[6] It always, always did.

My journey has been shaped largely by listening, by noticing. In my work as an embedded tutor and writing center tutor coordinator in Chicanx studies, I learned that richer, often even astonishing work was accomplished when trust was established, when community was built, particularly for students whose neurodivergence or trauma was proving disruptive to their academic identity and progress.

As I moved into Educational Opportunity Program Admissions, I continued to find my way, often through my phone outreach

---

5. This is only a small list of what students have shared with me, either in writing or in speech. Most of these sentiments are shared frequently.

6. Miller's book *The Untouched Key* (1991) was as influential to me as R. D. Laing's *Knots* (1975) when I was a teenager. Miller clarified parental child abuse for me, while Laing made me believe that Madness was a rational response to an irrational world, something I found impossible to parse at the time. See also Miller's book *The Drama of the Gifted Child* (1981).

efforts. These connections, once established, offered rich benefits. People opened their lives to me—homelessness, abandonment, trauma of every possible kind. I became a lifeline to some, coaching them through the psychological rigor of their last year of high school—the hysterical call during the riots at Jefferson High School in 2005, the drive-by scares. And I connected to my own narrative—the murder trial, abuse, shoot-out, housing instability, hunger. I learned to share pieces of this narrative when the moment felt right, to move us beyond what felt like confession to a sense of community.

Dear colleagues,

When I entered the classroom as a faculty member in 2005, I carried this experience with me. For nine of the following fifteen years, my Mad pedagogy was developed and honed through an interplay between my admissions coaching work in the Educational Opportunity Program and academic coaching work in the classroom. I could not pretend, for instance, that a holistic approach was not needed in the classroom—not when I was simultaneously being made privy to student experience in high school and mentoring many college students who openly shared the experiences they were having in other classrooms and spaces across campus.

We have no way of knowing what our students have faced before they enter our classroom. Of what they carry. What we do have control over is creating the conditions for trust, sharing, and support.

Dear colleagues,

In my small office across a makeshift table, I learned in those years that deeply listening and sharing myself worked best as the students and I learned to navigate through the fire. What for many would be considered an act of disclosure for me is an intentional act of love, of solidarity. And I grew to understand that in this sharing powerful learning emerged.

Dear colleagues,

What is interesting about this act of sharing is, unlike in my interactions with you, the students take it in stride. They say, "Because you shared with me, I feel more comfortable with myself." They say, "I thought I was the only one." They listen with openness, with understanding. They see the mirrors, the windows, and together we move toward the threshold, the doorframe.[7]

Often my students will say, "You were my first friend on campus." They are not yet ready to say, "I need a space to tell my story. I need." They are often not yet aware that the darkness they live with has a name, that it can be treated.

Now I am rootless; my students and I "make do." Before the pandemic, we shared at the student center, in an empty classroom, in hallways. During the pandemic, when there is no physical space, we create one, learn the power of making space where there is none. And in this act we find our way also to trust, to learning.

Dear colleagues,

Don't think I've lost the thread. I am getting to the heart, the hard part. With students, it's easy. To listen and share as needed are almost medicinal. To gauge and give.

Dear colleagues,

I cry often with students. I do not try to control it, and I do not apologize. This is part of my Madness—the triggering of mood, the omnipresence of memory. Once, after a counselor began to cry when I shared my story with her, she said, "I have allergies." I do not want to be that person. I tell them, "You know I am always crying with you. I do not cry for myself, but I cry when I am proud of you, I cry

---

7. Emily Style uses the terms *windows* and *mirrors* in her work for the National SEED Project. She writes, "All students deserve a curriculum which mirrors their own experience back to them, upon occasion—thus validating it in the public world of the school. But [a] curriculum must also insist upon the fresh air of windows into the experience of others—who also need and deserve the public validation of the school curriculum" (1996, 5). I have added *doorframes* as a way to conceptualize the thresholds students cross as they realize their own potential and the beauty of their uniqueness, their Madness. This word also invokes Adrienne Rich's poem "The Fact of a Doorframe" in her collection of the same title (Rich [1984] 2002).

when I feel your pain, too." I am transparent. They are moved. Often we cry together. In this way, we normalize neurodivergence, trauma, find our way collectively. I am a window, a mirror, and at times a threshold to treatment, to relief.

iii

> It really boils down to purpose. If you're gonna do this work, if you're really gonna wrestle with this, you have to constantly revisit the question: *For what?* Public schools, *for what?* My classroom, *for what?* This curriculum, *for what?* This assessment, *for what?* And if the answer to that question is not about kids being connected to self-esteem, knowledge of self, self-love, their ancestors, then you are not community responsive, and you are not academically rigorous.
> —Jeff Duncan-Andrade, "All Together Now" (2016)

Dear colleagues,

As I continue to find ways to holistically support students inside the classroom, I have built check-ins on both a group level and an individual level and have created assignments that allow students to examine and explore their identities, to bring their whole selves into the work. And in this way, I have begun to reimagine rigor, too. To understand that it is not, as one student told me, "feeling as if I am going to fail" but instead high expectation with high support and ample space for reflection. To hold an ear to language, listen to it breathe.

Dear colleagues,

Let us reimagine rigor and its tools. In Andrea Darder's essay "It's Not Nice to Fool Mother Nature: Eco-pedagogy in the Pursuit of Justice" (2011), she explains the importance of an embodied approach to education, particularly for marginalized students: "In our efforts to understand the process of schooling, teaching and learning must also be acknowledged as human labor, that which takes place within our bodies. This also requires that we incorporate, consciously or unconsciously, the totality of who we and our students are, in and out of the classroom" (333). Therefore, to create truly rich learning experiences, we must recognize that teaching and learning are visceral and taxing and require us to recognize and bring our full selves to our shared learning spaces in all of our intersectional splendor, darkness, and light.

Dear colleagues,

Our Mad and neurodivergent students need to see themselves represented at the front of the classroom. And that representation needs to be normalized, made transparent, with intention.[8]

Sometimes we are missing the motivation from others in our household, so having it in this class made a significant difference for me. By implementing daily check-ins, everyone in this class can feel like they matter. Everyone in this class has a voice. Everyone in this class can eventually learn to trust their voice and ideas more in order to incorporate it onto their work (reflection by first-year student writer during the pandemic).

Dear colleagues,

I realize now I've unwittingly written myself object. Although I am a window, a mirror, and a threshold, I am also flesh and blood. In the fall of 2021, as I navigated grief and COVID-19, I chose not to perform wellness; instead, I chose to disrupt my own deeply ingrained image of what an educator looks like. "I am not OK," I shared. "Some of you are also likely not OK." And we held space for this feeling, found ways to tend to each other. Our daily check-ins became a lifeline for many of us; greeting each student individually

---

8. This call for representation demands a reckoning, a dismantling of the current white-centric, homogeneous face of Madness and neurodiversity. While in my classroom a majority of my Mad and neurodiverse students are Black folx, Indigenous folx, and people of color, the representation of Madness and neurodiversity (in both academia and society in general) continues to be white. In "I, Too, Sing Neurodiversity" (2020), Morénike Giwa Onaiwu points out that even at a summit on neurodiversity she was marginalized as a person of color: "Unfortunately, like the larger cross-disability community, the neurodiversity community is plagued with issues that remain embedded in our society at large. One notable problem is its failure to incorporate core tenets of intersectionality, especially with regard to race" (61). This critique of neurodiversity movements must extend to our approaches to Mad pedagogy as well.

and expressing gratitude became essential practices, and I no longer felt anxious about the time it was taking from the content. When a student didn't turn in a paper on time, we talked. They shared their anxiety, their pain. I invited them to write with me.

Soon a few students from different classes were regularly joining me outside of class across the screen, no expectations except to hold space together, to be present. As they wrote, I graded; periodically we checked in with each other, shared our progress, and shared more about ourselves. The students who joined me, unlike the ones who usually visit traditional office hours, were struggling. We built in mini check-ins. They shared their self-doubt, their fear, their desire to find the right words when their minds turned against them. I shared with them how much I wanted to do right by them, how I needed to take more breaks because of brain fog. They responded, "You got this, professor! Take your time." This interaction felt revelatory—a bridge built by language, by radical vulnerability. Because I couldn't not. They produced beautiful work, learned, and often aced the course. And I finally inhabited my Mad body, learned what collective care can be and do in the classroom.[9]

> I urge each one of us here to reach down into that deep place of knowledge inside herself and touch that terror and loathing of any difference that lives here. See whose face it wears. Then the personal as the political can begin to illuminate all our choices.
> —Audre Lorde, "The Master's Tools Will Never Dismantle the Master's House" ([1984] 1996)

Dear colleagues,

For many years I wondered at the connections I have been able to make with students across the cultural, socioeconomic, and

---

9. Loree Erickson, in "Thinking about and with Collective Care" (2020), describes collective care as "[putting] into visceral practice queercrip strategies that change the way we think about care, embodied difference, intimacy, and social organization. Collective care also makes practical interventions, building new practices to disrupt the disposability, commodification, and individualism that shape violent forms of state-based approaches to care and cultures of undesirability" (par. 9).

psychological spectrum. I do not share a cultural background with a majority of the students I have supported on their journeys, the ones who come back for recommendations to graduate school, who check in with joyous news as well as requests for advice. I often wished I had an easy answer, a bullet-point list like the ones I love reading in *Inside Higher Ed*. But only now have I begun to realize that although my ability to listen generously, my belief in my students' voices, is key, it is often my Madness, my trauma, that enables me to connect with them on a visceral level, even as our experiences may differ radically. To understand the way their minds sometimes fill with a thick fog, sometimes run at hyperspeed. Like mine.

Perhaps what I can offer in lieu of a list is this: we must leverage all that we have at our disposal and look at our wholeness through a different lens. Despite the vast differences in our lives, our needs, our beliefs, my Madness remains a pedagogical tool. Something authentic that I can offer with an open hand, open heart.

Dear colleagues,

When the earth shook our campus in 1994, thirty years ago now, we saw its vulnerability, the possibility for change. Roberto Sifuentes, the brilliant scholar and playful storyteller, used to say that after the earthquake faculty held classes under trees, and students ran naked in the quad. This is idyllic, peaceful to imagine.

During the pandemic, the campus stood vacant. In my dreams, it was overrun with weeds. Now our campus is buzzing with life again, but we are changed.

Dear, dear colleagues,

I leave you with this. So often our students see Madness, neurodivergence, as darkness, something that must be kept hidden. Let us open the window, the door, and show them the possibility of light.

Works Cited

Darder, Andrea. 2011. "It's Not Nice to Fool Mother Nature: Eco-pedagogy in the Pursuit of Justice." In *A Dissident Voice: Essays on Culture, Pedagogy, and Power*, edited by Andrea Darder, 327–42. New York: Peter Lang.

Duncan-Andrade, Jeff. 2016. "All Together Now: Academic Rigor, Social and Political Consciousness, and Culturally Responsive Pedagogy." Keynote address for Teach for America's 25th Anniversary Summit. YouTube video, 1:21:48. At https://youtu.be/OzNl4unAe20.

Erickson, Loree. 2020. "Thinking about and with Collective Care." Cultivating Collective Care. At https://www.cultivatingcollectivecare.com/post /thinking-about-and-with-collective-care?fbclid=IwAR22k_gMD4JrqbdV VnV8Wbp5q1XH-8vKq-8WW_jEd44-7VCNzRyIBFtJgHs.

Gilbert, Sandra M., and Susan Gubar. [1979] 2000. *The Madwoman in the Attic: The Woman Writer and the Nineteenth-Century Literary Imagination*. 2nd ed. New Haven, CT: Yale Univ. Press.

Hammond, Zaretta. 2015. *Culturally Responsive Teaching and the Brain: Promoting Authentic Engagement and Rigor among Culturally and Linguistically Diverse Students*. Thousand Oaks, CA: Corwin.

hooks, bell. 1994. *Teaching to Transgress: Education as the Practice of Freedom*. New York: Routledge.

Laing, R. D. 1975. *Knots*. New York: Pantheon.

Lorde, Audre. [1984] 1996. *Sister Outsider: Essays and Speeches*. Trumansburg, NY: Crossing Press.

Miller, Alice. 1981. *The Drama of the Gifted Child*. New York: Basic.

———. 1991. *The Untouched Key: Tracing Childhood Trauma in Creativity and Destructiveness*. New York: Anchor, Doubleday.

Onaiwu, Morénike Giwa. 2020. "I, Too, Sing Neurodiversity." *Ought: The Journal of Autistic Culture* 2, no. 1: art. 10. At https://doi.org/10.9707/2833-1508.1048.

Rich, Adrienne. [1984] 2002. "The Fact of a Doorframe." In *The Fact of a Doorframe: Poems 1950–2001*, new ed., 131. New York: Norton.

Style, Emily. 1988. "Curriculum as Window and Mirror." *Social Science Record*, Fall. At https://nationalseedproject.org/images/documents/Curriculum_As _Window_and_Mirror.pdf.

12

Mad Pedagogy in Disabling Academia

Liz Miller

Content note: eugenist thought

I begin writing this chapter ensconced in my living room, burrowed beneath blankets, amid the 2020 global COVID-19 pandemic crisis. This is what many of my days look like now. I leave the house I share with my partner (who, like me, is also neurodivergent, though not Mad) a couple of times a day to run or walk the dogs and even more rarely to visit the grocery store, stop by the pharmacy, or attend a medical appointment. It feels impossible to discuss my Madness—my diagnoses and the disarray they bring to my life—and my Mad theories and pedagogies outside the context of this pandemic. This holds true particularly in the United States, where citizens regularly protest mask mandates and folks everywhere attend cookouts and family reunions, bars, and crowded restaurants, while the rest of us isolate ourselves at home. This is the reality my students and I face, wondering which of our friends or colleagues will be the next to catch the virus.

As someone who isn't neurotypical, I hesitate to use the phrase "the new normal," as many have done since the first global lockdown began in March 2020 (e.g., CNN 2020; Fisher 2020; Florida 2020). This is because what is newly "normal" for many has already been a standard way of life for disabled people across the nation.[1] Chronically ill folks in particular have

---

1. A recent article published by Chime Asonye (2020) in the *World Economic Forum* further reminds us that what is "normal" has never accommodated people of color,

long known the challenges of avoiding sickness by disinfecting spaces and protecting themselves in situations that facilitate the spread of dangerous viruses and bacteria. Their bodyminds (Price 2015) possess the knowledge (and often the fears) that many people have only recently begun to acquire and that many conservative-minded individuals unfortunately continue to shun.[2] In saying this, I do not intend to invalidate the experiences of any person, disabled or not, who has suffered greatly during months-long isolation and quarantine. In fact, these pandemic circumstances have become fertile ground for new mental health issues as many of us struggle with loneliness, confinement, unemployment, fear, loss of productivity (however we wish to define this fraught term), and lack of adequate access to health-care resources, among other concerns. My purpose in drawing attention to disabled knowledges and knowledge making is to highlight how these epistemologies can fruitfully inform pedagogical practice, particularly in situations where issues of accommodation and equity come suddenly to the fore. Indeed, such a focus has become a central hallmark of my teaching in the English department of a large midwestern university.

In light of these recent global developments, I use this chapter to reflect upon how a Mad perspective inflected my teaching, largely in face-to-face, in-person settings, even before the COVID-19 pandemic. Importantly, though, I also offer my still-developing thoughts on Mad pedagogies in online spaces with students who did not necessarily want to sign up for digital learning, with students who may feel the stress and fear that attend a reopened American university during a global pandemic. I've spent a great deal of time reading, writing, and publishing about teaching and my personal pedagogical approaches, and I continue to do so now because COVID-19 inevitably shifts our paradigms in ways

---

the impoverished, and migrants across the globe. This holds especially true during the COVID-19 pandemic as Black, Latinx, and Native American populations are disproportionately affected by the virus due to "systemic health disparities" (par. 8).

2. Several people, such as Matthew Keegan (2020) writing for the BBC, have argued that many accessibility measures implemented during the pandemic, such as remote work, are accommodation needs that disabled people have asserted for decades.

Mad Pedagogy in Disabling Academia   211

irreversible—and perhaps for the better moving forward if we remember to meet our students where they are and offer them kindness above all else.

Pedagogically, I believe in "inviting disability in the front door," as Jay Timothy Dolmage (2007) calls for in his publication titled with the same phrase. Holding disability and disability knowledges as an organizing construct in my teaching, I and many instructors strive to make our courses and classroom spaces, both digital and physical, as accessible as possible. This may include negotiating accommodations with students based on their bodily knowledge and expertise and crafting welcoming syllabus accessibility statements (Wood and Madden 2013). In other cases, it could mean presenting material in many and multimodal formats (Yergeau et al. 2013) or offering students creative license in composing assignments and engaging course materials. Many of us who are disabled instructors and allies continually revise and reflect upon our teaching practices, frequently shifting processes according to students' needs.[3]

From a theory standpoint, I ground myself in disability studies pedagogy, drawing insights from scholars such as Dolmage, who figures the North American university as inherently ableist, and Margaret Price, who adds to this discussion by articulating the experience of mental disability within and around academic institutions, especially in her book *Mad at School* (2011). These scholars provide the initial framework for what I'm calling my "Mad pedagogy," a framework rooted in caring radically for my students by honoring their lived experiences; the identities they bring into my (physical and/or virtual) classroom, identities that inevitably tense against the racist, heteronormative, ableist, neoliberal violence of the capitalistic university; the needs, desires, and goals they bring to the course I teach; and their enmeshment within what has been called a "mental health crisis" in our universities.

---

3. Disability pedagogy, particularly within my discipline of rhetoric and composition, is a vast and storied corpus with too many wonderful thoughts and practices to enumerate in the present space. Anyone interested in reading more might begin with the edited collection *Disability and the Teaching of Writing* (Lewiecki-Wilson and Brueggemann 2007).

Indeed, we must ask ourselves whether we truly face a mental health "crisis" or—given the existence of the crisis since at least the time of my birth in the early 1990s—whether mental disability is and has been an inherent aspect of the university structure itself. In other words, I suggest that we face not a sudden crisis but rather a growing collective of students, faculty, and staff who experience mental illness by virtue of the very nature of academia. Not only are such spaces disabling, as Dolmage and Price contend, fraught with inequity and a lack of true concern for students' welfare, but they are also in fact inhospitable, given their normative expectations along axes of race, gender, class, and ability; the sheer steepness of tuition; the lack of meaningful access to health care, mental or physical; and the problematic teaching practices that make up so many of the courses in which students enroll, from draconian policies to the use of policing technology. In all honesty, it should not be surprising that so many of us suffer, as we will continue to do until the system fundamentally changes.

Teaching While Mad: Theoretical Underpinnings

In the coming years, I expect to see numerous publications musing upon the COVID-19 pandemic's influence on our pedagogies. I sincerely hope that many instructors and institutions will use that reflection to make greater use of the disability accommodations and practices illuminated through the pandemic, such as the need for remote work and the necessity of mutual-aid networks in circumventing dangerous capitalist structures. These violent structures compose what Kelly Fritsch has characterized as a "neoliberal biocapitalism" that thrives on exploited disabled bodies. It depends on most people considering themselves "not good enough" and therefore constantly needing to strive for betterment. Drawing on Jasbir Puar's articulation of "debility" in *The Right to Maim* (2017), Fritsch articulates how certain disabled and nondisabled bodies are rendered "well enough" to participate in society according to capitalistic tenets mandating productivity through gainful employment. People considered "too debilitated" to work must therefore self-improve until they reach the "capacity" to be exploited through labor. Importantly for Fritsch, even disability activism remains too entrenched within this violent system; many

Mad Pedagogy in Disabling Academia   213

organizations emphasize too heavily the "right" of disabled folks to work, often to the neglect of those unable to work and therefore not considered productive members of society. Significantly, she asks, "Who gets to have grievances about particular forms of disabled oppression and structural ableism" (2015, 15)?

Like Fritsch, I argue that university institutions are inextricably wrapped up in these notions of debility and capacity. For example, she notes, following Puar, "that a biopolitical shift has occurred focusing on the differential capacitation of all bodies, not the achievement of a normative able-bodiedness. . . . [T]here is a shift from regulative normality that cures or rehabilitates to ongoing biological control, where bodies are to be capacitated beyond what is thought of as the able-body" (2015, 27). Institutions such as colleges are absolutely at least partially responsible for mental health issues facing many members of their communities, thanks to their explicit participation in neoliberal biocapitalism. Rather than shifting to alternative models, they instead prefer to promote yoga or dog-petting sessions (only slight sarcasm here) as the solution to institutional harm that exponentially affects disabled people, people of color, poor folks, and queer minorities because such individuals are often viewed only as profitable labor machines. These students do not carry the same aura of success and wealth as their more privileged peers. However, I argue that there are tactics we can deploy to navigate the system in which we inevitably must participate. For me, Madness and caring praxis provide the entry points for such work. Embodied disability knowledges and caring practices seek to provide access and safety to folks left out of normative employment, health care, and social experiences. It is these knowledges that I try to incorporate into my teaching wherever possible, ever mindful of the fact that I nevertheless teach in a normative, hypercapitalist institution.

Early in *Care Work* (2018), Leah Lakshmi Piepzna-Samarasinha notes that "writing from bed is a time-honored disabled way of being an activist and cultural worker" (15). Had I written this chapter even a year ago, I would have struggled to imagine an academic reality that thrived in our bedrooms. Now, however, in a period where many work from home and I regularly "meet" with my students digitally, I get to Zoom in my pajamas, surrounded by pets, and my students do the same. And there is no need to apologize—not that there should be—because we're in a pandemic, and there's a tacit acknowledgement among many that we're all just getting by. Despite the mental and physical exhaustion COVID-19 has wrought and the health disparities plunged into stark relief, the current global crisis is simultaneously a potential experiment in disability knowledge, in radically shifting our priorities toward things that make us and others feel good. Perhaps this viewpoint is borne of necessity, as long hours of isolation and lengthy screen times have rendered me exhausted and headachy, but I love that folks can now spend hours a day baking or knitting or gaming or walking (or rolling) or lounging or happy-hour Zooming or social distance picnicking. In my mind, all these pursuits are forms of care work in the sense that they actively nourish us and take no part in white, normative capitalism. For me, teaching while Mad aligns with my commitment toward caring for others, or what Piepzna-Samarasinha calls "care work." Accessibility and access intimacy (a concept offered by Mia Mingus [2011]) are key. To a certain degree, these easy, low-budget activities are accessible to many and can nourish community and kin relationships. Importantly, Piepzna-Samarasinha highlights the phrase "to exist is to resist" (2018, 24). Existing is something that ought to be available to us all, and acknowledging and nourishing our existence and the existences of those around us can be a powerful tactic, even in disabling and debilitating institutional spaces.

I highlight Piepzna-Samarasinha's articulation of care for its emphasis on nonnormative bodyminds, its decentering of whiteness, and its use of knowledges and knowledge making that exist *beyond* the scope of academe. The simple truth is that I care about my students. Not only do I want to see them succeed and meet their personal, creative, and academic goals, but I want to see them thriving mentally and according to their differential needs. We may well be facing a new version of the "mental health crisis" in universities and across the nation—one exacerbated by marginalized identities, poverty, and structural oppression. I consider myself to have failed as an instructor to the degree that I exacerbate mental and/or physical distress in my students. I regularly tell them that if they're feeling overly stressed about my course, they shouldn't, and I'm happy to help them redirect and find alternatives for assignments. I want them to "protect their hearts," to borrow from Piepzna-Samarasinha yet again when she discusses the messy activist relationships folks have with themselves and with one another while navigating the world as trauma survivors (2018, 213–24).

However, I must acknowledge that not all teachers can easily institute this kind of pedagogical care work in their classrooms. I have the luxury of working in a fairly progressive English department, one that has encouraged me, even as a graduate student, to develop my own syllabi and wholly determine course content and activities. As a discipline, too, English more easily enables caring relationships and reflective practices. For example, when I teach composition, I can construct assignments in ways that facilitate communal relationships between students or enable students to tap into their needs and interests. There is great freedom in writing, and students often become personally invested in their work. The same is true when I teach disability studies courses because I'm easily able to address care and access work directly in course materials. Care work literally becomes the work of the class.

"Networks of care" is a concept I have begun theorizing in my work, most recently in my *Xchanges* article "Mental Health in a Disabling Landscape: Forging Networks of Care in Graduate School" (Miller 2020). In it, I argue, following Dolmage (2017) and Angela Carter and colleagues (2017), that universities are inherently disabling spaces, where graduate programs in particular foster mental illness diagnoses and mental health struggles among most of the folks I know and meet. As a means of combating this disablement imposed for the sake of survival, I call for what I term "caring methodologies": the strategic formation of networks of care to navigate oppressive institutional structures, stressful programmatic requirements, and isolation.[4] I further argue for underground connections and collaborations among graduate students. I build on what has colloquially been termed "whisper networks," wherein individuals with

---

4. In addition, I identify the following as supplementary to the work of networks of care: continued activism for mental health resources, livable wages, greater support for students of color and international students, and support for graduate students who are parents, among many other crucial concerns for graduate students today.

marginalized identities secretly and safely transmit knowledge to one another about how to navigate certain institutional structures and about which people may be trusted as allies and which need to be avoided.[5] My theorizing extends this line of thinking from a Mad/disabled standpoint and seeks to strategically mobilize it for the sake of all students' mental health and safety: "This collective responsibility becomes essential not only in ensuring the mental wellbeing of our fellow grad students, but also in literally navigating the workload upon us and the differential identities we claim" (Miller 2020, par. 8).

The onset of COVID-19 in the United States and university budget cuts will necessitate even more social support and fiercer activism. At the time of this writing, my home institution has slashed virtually all graduate student financial support, severely limiting our ability to pay our bills and engage in meaningful research opportunities, such as conference and archive travel. Peer-to-peer connections feel ever more pressing as institutional support mechanisms have fallen away. With no one checking in on us apart from a few individual professors, many of us are struggling to the extent that we fear we may not be able to complete our programs. No university commitments have been made to offer continued financial support to offset the pandemic, either. The only way many of us are surviving is by relying heavily on our existing care networks and mutual-aid groups.

What's more, I absolutely consider my students part of my network of care. I do not expect them to "take care of" me in the sense that they would offer me emotional labor. This they reserve, I hope, for one another and for folks existing throughout their various home, work, and social networks. I do encourage casual and friendly interactions when desired by all parties. Primarily, though, I include my students in my network in the sense that I care for them: in each class and through each assignment, I try my best not to overload them with tedious work that doesn't connect in any way to their academic or personal goals.

---

5. For example, students of color may inform one another about white faculty members who perform antiracism in meaningful ways, just as female, trans, and nonbinary folks may warn one another about which (often male) colleagues and authority figures are known to be dangerous.

Mad Pedagogy in Disabling Academia   217

If I contend that universities can be and are traumatic places—and I do—then I want to offer students the freedom to protect their hearts and find joy wherever possible. They don't need my permission to enjoy life or engage in self-care or mutual aid, but I strongly work to ensure my class *can* be a site of such work if students are comfortable and willing to engage. Some are, and some aren't, and that's OK. Universities are still spaces of oppression, and I'm still to some degree an arbiter of that harm. Students don't have to trust me to get by. I offer them spaces online to check in with one another honestly and share their own coping strategies, "fun" assignments such as film readings and Flipgrid videos, freedom to contribute to course curriculum through artifact presentations they compose for class discussion, and very few requirements for larger projects. Regarding the latter, I work closely with students to ensure their work is "rigorous" according to the standards with which they most closely align: academic, activist, community, familial, career, disciplinary, or otherwise.

Part of "caring" for my students entails direct concern for their mental health, a concern that I work to convey as strongly as I can through my discussions with them individually and as a group. Amid this ongoing pandemic, I send frequent messages exhorting them to spend time outside, take time off for hobbies and relationships, and make the most of the breaks I offer them throughout the semester. I also freely give extensions and opportunities to compose alternative assignments. These alternatives we determine collaboratively to arrive at the best option with their goals in mind. I also strive to leave assignments open-ended to allow students to tap into their "multimodal home places" (Cedillo 2017), to borrow a phrase from digital-media scholarship.[6]

Situating Mad Studies

If Mad studies can be defined as "a project of inquiry, knowledge production, and political action devoted to the critique and transcendence of psy-centered ways of thinking, behaving, relating, and being" (Menzies, LeFrançois, and Reaume 2013, 13), then I work to extend this project

6. Multimodal home places are the composing technologies students feel most comfortable using because of their life experiences.

beyond medical establishments and directly into the university locale. I find the work of Mad studies as a whole useful for its articulation of the issues that must be navigated in community building for Mad folks.[7] Many of these concerns remain relevant within the university classroom in general and provide insights into issues I and my students must navigate if we wish to build networks of care among ourselves.

Mad teaching practices in particular align with my specific beliefs and goals for interacting with other human beings. In the years that I have been teaching, I have noticed a sharp increase in the number of students who disclose mental health diagnoses and struggles to me. This is not altogether surprising considering the mental health "crisis" that exists on many college campuses today, combined with the political atmosphere following the election of Donald Trump in 2016. Such increased disclosure points to both the success of as well as the continued need for these networks of care.

Works Cited

Asonye, Chime. 2020. "There's Nothing New about the 'New Normal.' Here's Why." World Economic Forum, June. At https://www.weforum.org/agenda/2020/06/theres-nothing-new-about-this-new-normal-heres-why/.

Carter, Angela, Tina Catania, Sam Schmitt, and Amanda Swenson. 2017. "Bodyminds Like Ours: An Autoethnographic Analysis of Graduate School, Disability, and the Politics of Disclosure." In *Negotiating Disability: Disclosure and Higher Education*, edited by Stephanie L. Kerschbaum, Laura T. Eisenman, and James M. Jones, 95–113. Ann Arbor: Univ. of Michigan Press.

Cedillo, Christina. 2017. "Diversity, Technology, and Composition: Honoring Students' Multimodal Home Places." *Present Tense: A Journal of Rhetoric in Society* 6, no. 2. At https://www.presenttensejournal.org/volume-6/diversity-technology-and-composition-honoring-students-multimodal-home-places/.

---

7. For example, there are issues in agreeing on what identity terminology to use, such as *former patient, survivor, psychiatric inmate,* and so on. Debate also addresses what degree of connection should be maintained with government or medical bodies as well as how to conceptualize psychiatric oppression (according to race, class, ability, and so on). What kind of resistance or subversion ought to be engaged? Is it necessary to seek "proof" of diagnosis?

CNN. 2020. "Our New Normal, in Pictures." May 20. At https://www.cnn.com/2020/05/20/world/gallery/new-normal-coronavirus/index.html.

Dolmage, Jay Timothy. 2007. "Mapping Composition: Inviting Disability in the Front Door." In *Disability and the Teaching of Writing: A Critical Sourcebook*, edited by Cynthia Lewiecki-Wilson and Brenda Jo Brueggemann, 14–27. New York: Bedford/St. Martin's.

———. 2017. *Academic Ableism: Disability and Higher Education*. Ann Arbor: Univ. of Michigan Press.

Fisher, Max. 2020. "What Will Our New Normal Feel Like? Hints Are Beginning to Emerge." *New York Times*, Apr. 21. At https://www.nytimes.com/2020/04/21/world/americas/coronavirus-social-impact.html.

Florida, Richard. 2020. "The Lasting Normal for the Post-pandemic City." *Bloomberg*, June 25. At https://www.bloomberg.com/news/features/2020-06-25/the-new-normal-after-the-coronavirus-pandemic.

Fritsch, Kelly. 2015. "Gradations of Debility and Capacity: Biocapitalism and the Neoliberalization of Disability Relations." *Canadian Journal of Disability Studies* 4, no. 2: 12–48. At https://doi.org/10.15353/cjds.v4i2.208.

Keegan, Matthew. 2020. "Why Coronavirus May Make the World More Accessible." BBC, May 13. At https://www.bbc.com/future/article/20200513-why-the-coronavirus-can-make-the-world-more-accessible.

Lewiecki-Wilson, Cynthia, and Brenda Jo Brueggemann, eds. 2007. *Disability and the Teaching of Writing: A Critical Sourcebook*. Boston: Bedford/St. Martin's.

Menzies, Robert, Brenda A. LeFrançois, and Geoffrey Reaume. 2013. "Introducing Mad Studies." In *Mad Matters: A Critical Reader in Canadian Mad Studies*, edited by Brenda A. LeFrançois, Robert Menzies, and Geoffrey Reaume, 1–22. Toronto: Canadian Scholars' Press.

Miller, Liz. 2020. "Mental Health in a Disabling Landscape: Forging Networks of Care in Graduate School." *Xchanges: An Interdisciplinary Journal of Technical Communication, Rhetoric, and Writing across the Curriculum* 15, no. 1. At http://www.xchanges.org/mental-health-in-a-disabling-landscape.

Mingus, Mia. 2011. "Access Intimacy: The Missing Link." *Leaving Evidence* (blog), May 5. At https://leavingevidence.wordpress.com/2011/05/05/access-intimacy-the-missing-link/.

Piepzna-Samarasinha, Leah Lakshmi. 2018. *Care Work: Dreaming Disability Justice*. Vancouver: Arsenal Pulp Press.

Price, Margaret. 2011. *Mad at School: Rhetorics of Mental Disability and Academic Life*. Ann Arbor: Univ. of Michigan Press.

―――. 2015. "The Bodymind Problem and the Possibilities of Pain." *Hypatia* 30: 268–84.

Puar, Jasbir K. 2017. *The Right to Maim: Debility, Capacity, Disability.* Durham, NC: Duke Univ. Press.

Wood, Tara, and Shannon Madden. 2013. "Suggested Practices for Syllabus Accessibility Statements." *Kairos: Rhetoric, Technology, and Pedagogy* 18, no. 1. At https://praxis.technorhetoric.net/tiki-index.php?page=Suggested _Practices_for_Syllabus_Accessibility_Statements.

Yergeau, M. Remi, Elizabeth Brewer, Stephanie Kerschbaum, Sushil K. Oswal, Margaret Price, Cynthia L. Selfe, Michael J. Salvo, and Franny Howes. 2013. "Multimodality in Motion: Disability & Kairotic Spaces." *Kairos: Rhetoric, Technology, and Pedagogy* 18, no. 1. At https://kairos.technorhetoric.net/18.1 /coverweb/yergeau-et-al.

13

Teaching for Mad Liberation

Crip Dreaming toward a Transformative Pedagogy of Madness

Samuel Z. Shelton

> For people and organizations engaged in resistance against psychiatry, to take up "Madness" is an expressly political act. Following other social movements including queer, black, and fat activism, Madness talk and text invert the language of oppression, reclaiming disparaged identities and restoring dignity and pride to difference.
>
> —Robert Menzies, Brenda A. LeFrançois, and
> Geoffrey Reaume, "Introducing Mad Studies,"
> in *Mad Matters* (2013)

> *Content notes*: forced institutionalization, gun violence, racially motivated violence, police brutality, murder, anti-Black racism

---

I am both a Mad scholar and a scholar of Mad studies.[1] My experiences in higher education are filtered through Madness, and my Madness is one of the gravitational forces keeping me in higher education even when I feel the urge to withdraw. Mad people are those who experience and make sense of reality outside of the normative, compulsory forms designated as acceptable and desirable, forms largely carved out by psychologists/psychiatrists for the purpose of suppression, containment, and ultimately eradication. Our so-called disorders and conditions fill up the ever-swelling

---

1. In this chapter, I use *Mad* as an umbrella term meant to be inclusive of a wide range of identities, positionalities, and categorizations, including "crazy," "psychotic," "psych survivor," "mentally disabled," and "cognitively impaired," among others.

222   Shelton

pages of "professional texts" such as the *Diagnostic and Statistical Manual* (Burstow 2013), and some people devote their entire lives to studying us, trying to figure us out, and developing "cures" and "treatments" for us. My teaching pushes back against this framing by advocating for an understanding of enmindedment grounded in critical analyses of power instead of in assumptions of pathology (Kuppers 2014).[2]

As a result, the research and teaching I do often place me outside the dominant paradigms of the academic world, which continue to privilege individualism, rationality, and detachment above all. Even the presence of Mad studies within higher education seems like a paradox given how invested most colleges and universities are in the individualized, privatized discourse of mental illness and how hostile they continue to be to Mad scholars and scholarship. My chosen discipline, women, gender, and sexuality studies, which itself is invested in the reclamation of subjugated knowledges and subjectivities, offers moments of rest and recovery. Yet even here I have experienced challenges in gaining acceptance for research and writing that pushes back against the medical model of mental illness.[3]

What I am conveying is that becoming a Mad scholar is not something accidental or easy. My choice to follow this path has certainly been facilitated by my whiteness and other privileged social positions, which

2. The term *enmindedment* recognizes that the way we make sense of ourselves and the world around us—for example, the things we notice and reflect on, the sorts of thoughts we let ourselves have, the conditioned desire to have a "rational" mind— is surveilled, politicized, and governed. In other words, enmindedment recognizes that normativity creeps into our thinking beyond just the level of content to affect not only what we think about but also how, when, and why we think about things. Madness is an experience, a practice, and a mode of enmindedment that transcends the narrow, violent confines of sanity and rationality.

3. I make this assertion with the knowledge that women's studies, gender studies, and sexuality studies have historically had an uneasy relationship with disability studies; the field of feminist disability studies is the result of theorists who have actively crossed disciplinary and political boundaries to bridge these two worlds. I think, for instance, of Sami Schalk's work (e.g., Schalk 2013), which critiques the frequent presence of ableist metaphors in feminist writing.

have afforded me a degree of freedom not readily given to, for example, Mad people of color. Nevertheless, a Mad, proud identity is something I have had to claim intentionally for myself, often without the support of the institutions where I work.

Despite the obstacles I have faced in becoming a Mad scholar and scholar of Mad studies and in part because of them, I have been able to find a generative intellectual space for myself within these domains, a space where there exists abundance and possibility. Weaving Madness into my intellectual work has simultaneously opened new possibilities for critical thinking and enabled me to rest and recover from the weight of existing in stiflingly anti-Mad/sanist institutions. Indeed, although Madness and "mental illness" are often conceived of as hindrances to teaching and learning in higher education, even as they are identified as burgeoning "crises" (Snyder et al. 2019), experience has shown me that care-fully engaging with them in the classroom provides unique possibilities for transformative learning to take root. Moreover, whereas colleges and universities frequently frame Mad and "mentally ill" students in terms of a deficit to be overcome or risk to be mitigated, I have time and again seen the opposite: many of my most perceptive, knowledgeable students have been "mentally ill," and it is through their situated experiences of the world that they have developed skills for critical thinking and liberatory world building. I believe this observation is true because knowledge is rarely separable from experiences with power and oppression.

This is not to say that Madness can only be an outcome of inequity and injustice or that it is an intrinsically oppressed category. Rather, given that Madness is a critical sociopolitical position that questions dominant paradigms, Mad knowledge comes from refusal of *neuronormativity*. This term describes the ways that logics of power infiltrate our minds in an attempt to coerce us into particular ways of thinking about and interpreting reality. It conditions us to regard neurodiversity as dangerous and untrustworthy, whereas embracing a Mad position teaches us that multiple sorts of enmindedment are not just possible but also desirable and vital. In this sense, reclaiming Madness is a subversive act of *neuroqueering* (Egner 2019; Roscigno 2019)—of refusing assimilation to the oppressive psychiatric paradigms and social norms that uphold compulsory able-mindedness and neuronormativity. Consequently, engaging with Mad perspectives is an intellectual project through which we might gain access to the knowledges and understandings that neuronormativity suppresses.

In this chapter, I consider as a teacher what it means to conceive of Madness as something educators and students alike can learn with, from, and about as part of the collective labor of dismantling oppression and building liberated worlds. Calvin Rey Moen and Kaz DeWolfe maintain that "learning to discern what Madness is telling us is a lifelong task" (2019, 11). For teachers, embracing Madness supports us in this process of discernment by expanding the potential for us to *unlearn* internalized logics of power and discover radical new possibilities for togetherness. The following sections together provide three accounts of what I refer to as *pedagogies of Madness,* or critical approaches to teaching and learning in resistance to sanism and toward Mad liberation. Pedagogies of Madness emerge when educators actively refuse—as much as is possible—to subject ourselves or our students to "compulsory able-mindedness" (Kafer 2013, passim) or to neuronormative expectations underlying sanism by opting instead to center the experiences, perspectives, and needs of Mad peoples. Centering the most vulnerable and impacted both ensures equitable representation and generates opportunities to expand and fortify resistance through solidarity and coalition building. In the classroom, this centering helps teachers practice accountability to all of our students. This principle is borrowed from the disability justice framework and movement (Sins Invalid 2016).

Pedagogies of Madness, Take 1: Teaching for Mad Liberation

An interdisciplinary field of critical inquiry, Mad studies aims to understand the social, political, and historical conditions through which Madness is produced, constituted, and imbued with meaning, especially in relation to in/sanity and ir/rationality. Sarah Snyder and colleagues explain that "Mad Studies unsettles the logics of mental illness schemas that dominate how we comprehend and make meaning of Madness. . . . Mad Studies interrogates the construction of normalcy and subverts sanist research, knowledge, and practice paradigms" (2019, 486).

The term *Mad liberation* describes the ongoing, radical process of world building against sanist oppression, a process that is grounded in a deep yearning for alternative social arrangements and more just forms of togetherness. Mad liberation is about attending to the social, political, and historical contexts of Madness, organizing against the inequities and injustices Mad folks experience—especially the most marginal and affected among us (e.g., Mad trans people of color)—and advancing alternatives to the pathologization of mental difference that will sustain well-being rather than subjugation and eradication. Teaching for Mad liberation infuses these transformative goals into learning spaces in resistance to the sanist expectations and norms pervading higher education. This task includes teaching about histories of Mad oppression, such as histories of the asylum and the ongoing incarcerations of disabled people (Ben-Moshe, Chapman, and Carey 2014). It also means forming learning spaces against Mad oppression through inclusive, accessible, antisanist practice, which might entail such moves as changing grading or evaluation criteria, especially participation, and reimagining classroom activities through increased attention to neurodiversity.

As an example of teaching for Mad liberation, I often center two resources that provide counternarratives to the biological reductionism and pathologization of Madness within the dominant psychiatric scheme. The first resource is *Madness and Oppression: Paths to Personal Transformation and Collective Liberation* (2015), a mutual-aid publication by the Fireweed Collective. This resource offers useful definitions and clear examples for common social justice terms such as *oppression* and *transformation,* and it follows a workbook format that facilitates active learning. What I appreciate most about this text is how the authors situate various emotional and mental states relative to systems of power and oppression, which is helpful for broaching conversations about the danger and limitations of sanist worldviews. Using this work, my students and I have discussed how common terms within mental health discourses (e.g., *anxiety, depression*) are often reduced down to biology but are actually embedded in oppressive institutional and social contexts that create trauma (Cvetkovich 2012). I then connect this resource with other critical texts about care that turn away from an emphasis on "curing" individuals to advocate instead for relational transformations (e.g., Price 2011a, 2015; Piepzna-Samarasinha 2018).

The second text I center is Mia Mingus's "Medical Industrial Complex Visual" (2015), which "is offered as a tool for our work for collective liberation" (par. 1). The medical-industrial complex is the collection of interlocking interests, institutions, and structures that shape access to health care in the United States and other capitalist countries. It includes and grants power to sanist institutions, such as those in the mental health industry and prison system. Like *Madness and Oppression*, Mingus's work helps to demonstrate how discourses of mental "health" and "illness" are not apolitical but enmeshed in the histories of such social constructions as slavery, eugenics, colonialism, and capitalism. From her text, students and I can imagine how dominant, psychiatric perspectives about Madness contribute not only to sanism but also to the many other systems and structures with which it intersects and on which it depends. We can discuss, for instance, how involuntary medication of Mad peoples is connected to the carceral logics of the police and prison system, both of which exist to draw attention away from social problems through a reductive, neoliberal lens of individualism (Davis 2015). Building on this conversation, we then can collectively think about how the transformation of our ideas around mental health/illness are necessary for Mad liberation in addition to the multiple other social movements with which it is interconnected and interdependent.[4]

Doing this pedagogical work also means engaging students with Mad critiques and activism. Teaching for Mad liberation necessitates centering learning materials, discussions, and activities that call for intellectual transformation and expose ideologies underlying dominant, pathological paradigms operating to support compulsory able-mindedness or

---

4. Here I am thinking specifically about how the social construction of mental illness and processes of pathologization have been utilized to promote white supremacy, cis-heteropatriarchy, settler colonialism, imperialism, and capitalism. Pathologization is the repackaging of social and political issues and nonnormative differences between bodyminds (e.g., neurodiversity) into forms that can be isolated, surveilled, and governed by the medical-industrial complex (Rojas Durazo 2006).

neuronormativity. Pedagogies of Madness, in this sense, encourage the development of students' critical-thinking skills, both generally and more specifically in relation to sanist knowledge and belief systems, frameworks/schemas, and institutions. Much of the effort here is intended to open up space for students to disrupt internalized sanist thoughts and potentially recover a relationship to Madness that has been suppressed or made shameful. These pedagogies simultaneously engage students with marginalized and subjugated perspectives and provide students with the tools to question and unlearn the dominant paradigms so many of us are conditioned to believe. This unlearning is crucial because it opens up space for the exploration of alternative explanations and ways of thinking (Snyder et al. 2019). Unlearning empowers students to speak back to their colleges/universities, which oftentimes are more willing to provide generic mental health resources than to do the substantive work of building accessibility, equity, and justice.

Pedagogies of Madness, Take 2: Teaching against Normative Rationality and Reason

For me, becoming a Mad scholar and a scholar of Mad studies has been a process of learning how dominant discourses of rationality and reason, which continue to permeate the intellectual spaces of academia, have historically been weaponized against oppressed peoples to protect the power, wealth, and prestige of elite white men. The illusion of detachment cultivated by a narrow understanding of what is "reasonable" and "rational" means that many academics snub the open exploration of emotional and psychological investment—the "felt knowledge" we develop through active explorations of our emotions as sources of meaning making.[5] We inhabit an academic world where supposedly disinterested, ordered, and logical knowledge triumphs over the messiness of felt knowledges residing in our bodyminds—knowledges that for many people are essential to our survival and well-being in hostile families, communities, and societies.

---

5. "Felt knowledge" is a concept that comes to me from reading the powerful work of Audre Lorde, whose writings have been essential in shaping my understanding of knowledge, power, and emotion.

All people have a capacity for rationality and reason, but so too do all people come to interpret and live in the world through our emotions. The dominance of rationality and reason in academia makes it so that aspiring to achieve an appearance of detachment is seen as more desirable and acceptable than being accountable and honest about our emotional investments and reactions to that which we seek to learn about. Rationality and reason, as they are traditionally and narrowly defined, become weapons against embodied, emotional learning, especially that which asks students to explore and examine their feelings rather than to suppress them. Conversely, pedagogies of Madness engage students in questioning the supremacy of rationality and reason and in reclaiming a connection to their emotions and felt knowledges. For, as Margaret Price notes, there is a "popular conception that unsound minds have no place in the classroom," which exists "to protect discourse as a 'rational' realm, a place where emotion does not intrude (except within carefully prescribed boundaries), where 'crazy' students are quickly referred out of the classroom" (2011b, 33).

Pedagogies of Madness welcome intrusions of emotion into learning spaces, particularly where the embracing of emotion can lead to social transformation and/or the empowerment of oppressed peoples. Audre Lorde (1984), whose remarkable works have long inspired my own thought, teaches us that the suppression of emotions and felt knowledges, especially love and anger, is vital to the continuation of oppression because these knowledges can become crucial resources for the personal and social transformation of oppressed peoples. For instance, anger has been an undoubtedly significant emotion for propelling forward the Black Lives Matter movement, especially following the police murders of Breonna Taylor and George Floyd in 2020. It has also been imperative to queer, feminist, and disability justice movements, among others. The reclamation of emotions categorized as inappropriate, excessive, or Mad are vital for resistance because they fuel kinetic energies in our bodyminds that drive us to change our surroundings. Teaching for the reclamation of emotions such as anger is a resensitization process that can help students take ownership of their lives.

In making this claim, I am also cognizant of the ways in which emotions, rationality, and reason have been used to further oppression along multiple axes, in particular white supremacy. A significant aspect of Lorde's work around emotion is to recognize how people of color, especially women of color, have been subjected to violence and harm through constructed ideas or images of their emotionality. For example, some images of men of color portray them as emotionally volatile and therefore dangerous, especially to white people, and some images of women of color portray them as overly susceptible to emotions and therefore untrustworthy or immoral (e.g., promiscuous). Accordingly, reclaiming felt knowledge is not an identical process for all students, and questioning rationality and reason can have different outcomes based on students' unique positionalities. Part of the responsibility Mad teachers carry in opening this mental space is to know the potential for harm and to work with students to reduce the harm they experience. Honesty, transparency, and accountability are necessary practices here.

In teaching students to question rationality and reason and to explore felt knowledge, I often begin with small activities intended to help them become more conscious of, and attentive to, their emotional reactions. I ask them to talk about what they felt when engaging with particular learning materials. Depending on the context, we might journal privately, chat in small groups, or volunteer to share feelings with the class. As the term progresses, we engage in conversations about the connections between feeling and knowing as well as between feeling and action. I often include a reading that takes a critical position against rationality and objectivity, such as an essay by Lorde or an essay that examines how knowledge is embodied and partial. I make a point to ask students about what sorts of knowledge/understanding get left out when we neglect our emotions, identities, desires, and so on. We also reflect on how bias against emotions is connected to the marginalization and exclusion of different groups of people (who are assumed to be overly emotional) from intellectual spaces and projects, which, in turn, produces stereotypes and assumptions that bolster oppressive ideologies. Finally, I often ask students to consider what it means to learn about things that should be upsetting, infuriating, and/or wrenching from a place of assumed neutrality. What do we lose when we let go of our anger, Madness, and other emotional states?

It took me a long time to reconnect with my own emotions as an academic, and I experienced a great deal of harm because I was for so long so resistant to letting myself feel the things my bodymind needed me to feel. I understand now that reclaiming my Madness meant, in part, allowing myself to feel and to feel whole. Given that claiming Madness for oneself is a political act against neuronormativity, it then makes sense that Mad people ought to be mad—ought to be angry enough with the state of things to demand and struggle for something better. We also have much to grieve about, much to remember, and much to celebrate. But stereotypes and misunderstandings yield fear and hatred toward Mad people freely expressing our emotions, as they frequently do for people of color, queer and trans folks, and others. My practice of teaching prioritizes helping students to unlearn these stereotypes and misunderstandings so they can better witness anger, support people in grieving, and participate in joy. Developing these affective skills is a necessary part of ending Mad oppression and building liberated worlds for all kinds of Mad people.

Pedagogies of Madness, Take 3:
Teaching Crip Dreaming for Mad Kinship

Crip dreaming is the sometimes deliberate, sometimes not deliberate practice of longing for a "cripped" world—in this case, a Mad world—where the sources and conditions of oppression have been vanquished and relationships of equity and justice have been built in their place.[6] Dreaming in general carries an assumption of rest and recovery, and so crip dreaming means in part building worlds where rest and recovery are possible for all bodyminds, especially those that have been exhausted, depleted, bent, broken, or otherwise taken to the edge. Another way of thinking about crip dreaming is as the process of contributing to the Mad imaginary, which might be described as the collection of assorted thoughts,

---

6. My use of the term *cripped* here is meant to signal back to Margaret Price's definition of *crip politics* as a process of "infusing the disruptive potential of disability into normative spaces and interactions" (2015, 269). A cripped world is one in which ableism is continually subverted toward just social relations through the presence, radical inclusion, and centering of disabled bodyminds.

knowings, yearnings, questions, and possibilities that emerge from the reclamation of Madness and the refusal of sanism. At the center of the Mad imaginary is the promise of kinship and solidarity, which are radical ways of building relations and communities that honor neurodiversity by providing informed, life-sustaining care to all people on their own terms and with their consent. In other words, the Mad imaginary that I strive to generate with my students, through rest and through dreaming, is one that provides us with the inspiration and tools to collectively inhabit alternative ways of being in relationship with each other, formed around and through neurodiversities rather than against them. Crip dreaming is about recovering, discovering, and shaping a Mad imaginary that we can one day make real for ourselves.

For me, teaching in a way that nourishes crip dreaming is a largely creative process of guiding students to use their imaginations in resistance to the logics of sanism, for imagination is what allows us to question reality and long for freedom from hatred, tyranny, and injustice. In the words of Walidah Imarisha, "Once the imagination is unshackled, liberation is limitless" (2015, 4). Unshackling the Mad imagination is partly about promoting critical thinking and engaging students in active questioning of the dominant medical model of mental health and "illness," but it is also about more than unlearning. Imagination flourishes in the realm of possibilities, and its greatest benefit is that it empowers us to dream up realities different from those we have known. Teaching for Mad imagination requires, first, opening up the mental space for students to release internalized sanist beliefs and then supporting students in creatively thinking about what understandings could fill up that now emptied space.

Because I center my teaching around transformative justice, which prioritizes relationships and community building as tools for unmaking oppression and repairing harm (Mingus 2019), the imaginative work I perform with my students aims to foster Mad kinship, resilience, and liberation. Mad kinship means collectively envisioning alternative, Mad-centered modes of togetherness and then finding methods to build those restorative relationships. Mad kinship nurtures Mad resilience, our endurance for surviving oppressive conditions: we withstand oppression by holding each other close and extending love and care between us. Over time, kinship can yield liberation because our relationships have enough power to transform the world. Imagining possibilities for Mad kinship is an intimate act that asks us to explore stereotypes, prejudices, and other things we have internalized from living in a sanist society. Then we must commit to replacing such things with deliberate openness from which kindness, compassion, and friendship can grow. For me and for my students, I find that literature is especially useful for this task. I strive to provide stories by Mad people that are honest about the state of the world but ultimately focus on attachment and relational growth. I find that such stories offer guiding examples for Mad kinship that help students examine their own perceptions and arrive at new thoughts.

As a final example of my teaching practice, I often use Aurora Levins Morales's (1998) writing about *curandera* or medicinal histories to get students thinking about how the forms of kinship that people are familiar with today are neither universal nor timeless—how they are temporary and changing. She argues that dominant representations of history serve to make oppression seem unavoidable and natural, as if differences in power and access to resources between people are not the outcome of systemized assaults against oppressed social groups. Intervening in these histories by reimagining them from the "bottom up," from the perspectives of those who have been subjected to violence, inequity, and injustice, is a method for interrupting dominance and challenging hierarchies. For Mad folks, telling alternative histories can be a means of cultivating resilience through the knowledge that people like us have always existed and resisted—that our relatives and ancestors were never vanquished but continuously struggled to make the world better for themselves and for us. This knowledge itself can inspire Mad kinship by teaching that love and solidarity are as old as oppression, if not older still.

Conclusion

I believe the best way we can navigate the world and our extreme states is by loving our Madness. Instead of pushing it away, engage with it. To treat it with care and respect, learn whatever it has to teach us. In a world that was built for others, our Madness can guide us through the darkest times. . . . What we call Madness is a much

more reasonable reaction to the world than the way sane people
react to Madness.
— Jessie Stohlmann-Rainey, "Much Madness Is
Divinest Sense" (2019)

In this chapter, I discussed some of the ways that my Mad identity has informed my experiences within higher education and how I have attempted to infuse Madness into my teaching. I believe institutions of higher education are in desperate need of Madness and those who can channel it. I end this chapter with the quote from Jessie Stohlmann-Rainey because Madness has been a source of energy and life for me and because this quote represents the understanding I want to pass on to my students about Madness during the often too short time I know them. Pedagogies of Madness are ultimately about instilling the lesson that oppression and suffering make Madness "a much more reasonable reaction to the world" and something that we should embrace and seek to comprehend, for Madness can be an unmapped path to liberation that we choose to discover for ourselves.

Works Cited

Ben-Moshe, Liat, Chris Chapman, and Allison C. Carey, eds. 2014. *Disability Incarcerated: Imprisonment and Disability in the United States and Canada.* New York: Palgrave Macmillan.

Burstow, Bonnie. 2013. "A Rose by Any Other Name: Naming and the Battle against Psychiatry." In *Mad Matters: A Critical Reader in Canadian Mad Studies,* edited by Brenda A. LeFrançois, Robert Menzies, and Geoffrey Reaume, 79–90. Toronto: Canadian Scholars' Press.

Cvetkovich, Ann. 2012. "Depression Is Ordinary: Public Feelings and Saidiya Hartman's *Lose Your Mother.*" *Feminist Theory* 13, no. 2: 131–46. At https://doi.org/10.1177/14647001124426.

Davis, Angela. 2015. *Freedom Is a Constant Struggle: Ferguson, Palestine, and the Foundations of a Movement.* Chicago: Haymarket.

Egner, Justine E. 2019. "'The Disability Rights Community Was Never Mine': Neuroqueer Disidentification." *Gender & Society* 33, no. 1: 123–47. https://doi.org/10.1177/0891243218803284.

Icarus Project. 2015. *Madness and Oppression: Paths to Personal Transformation and Collective Liberation.* New York: Icarus Project.

Imarisha, Walidah. 2015. Introduction to *Octavia's Brood: Science Fiction Stories from Social Justice Movements*, edited by Walidah Imarisha and Adrienne Maree Brown, 3–6. Oakland, CA: AK Press.

Kafer, Alison. 2013. *Feminist, Queer, Crip*. Bloomington: Indiana Univ. Press.

Kuppers, Petra. 2014. *Studying Disability Arts and Culture: An Introduction*. New York: Palgrave Macmillan.

Levins Morales, Aurora. 1998. *Medicine Stories: History, Culture and the Politics of Integrity*. Cambridge, MA: South End Press.

Lorde, Audre. 1984. *Sister Outsider: Essays and Speeches*. New York: Ten Speed Press.

Menzies, Robert, Brenda A. LeFrançois, and Geoffrey Reaume. 2013. "Introducing Mad Studies." In *Mad Matters: A Critical Reader in Canadian Mad Studies*, edited by Brenda A. LeFrançois, Robert Menzies, and Geoffrey Reaume, 1–22. Toronto: Canadian Scholars' Press.

Mingus, Mia. 2015. "Medical Industrial Complex Visual." *Leaving Evidence* (blog), Feb. 6. At https://leavingevidence.wordpress.com/2015/02/06/medical-industrial-complex-visual/.

———. 2019. "Transformative Justice: A Brief Description." *Leaving Evidence* (blog), Jan. 9. At https://leavingevidence.wordpress.com/2019/01/09/transformative-justice-a-brief-description/.

Piepzna-Samarasinha, Leah Lakshmi. 2018. *Care Work: Dreaming Disability Justice*. Vancouver: Arsenal Pulp Press.

Price, Margaret. 2011a. "Cripping Revolution: A Crazed Essay." Plenary at the annual meeting of the Society for Disability Studies, San Jose, CA, June 18. At https://margaretprice.wordpress.com/presentations/cripping-revolution-2-28-13/.

———. 2011b. *Mad at School: Rhetorics of Mental Disability and Academic Life*. Ann Arbor: Univ. of Michigan Press.

———. 2015. "The Bodymind Problem and the Possibilities of Pain." *Hypatia* 30, no. 1: 268–84. At https://doi.org/10.1111/hypa.12127.

Rey Moen, Calvin, and Kaz DeWolfe. 2019. Introduction to *Much Madness: A Survivor's Guide to Extreme States and Self-Advocacy for Young Adults*, edited by Calvin Rey Moen and Kaz DeWolfe, 5–13. Morrisville, NC: Lulu Press.

Rojas Durazo, Ana Clarissa. 2006. "Medical Violence against People of Color and the Medicalization of Domestic Violence." In *Color of Violence: The INCITE! Anthology*, edited by INCITE! Women of Color Against Violence, 179–90. Durham, NC: Duke Univ. Press.

Roscigno, Robin. 2019. "Neuroqueerness as Fugitive Practice: Reading against the Grain of Applied Behavioral Analysis Scholarship." *Educational Studies* 55, no. 4: 405–19. At https://doi.org/10.1080/00131946.2019.1629929.

Schalk, Sami. 2013. "Metaphorically Speaking: Ableist Metaphors in Feminist Writing." *Disability Studies Quarterly* 33, no. 4. At https://dsq-sds.org/article /view/3874/3410.

Sins Invalid. 2016. *Skin, Tooth, and Bone: The Basis of Movement Is Our People: A Disability Justice Primer.* San Francisco: Sins Invalid.

Snyder, Sarah N., Kendra-Ann Pitt, Fady Shanouda, Jijian Voronka, Jenna Reid, and Danielle Landy. 2019. "Unlearning through Mad Studies: Disruptive Pedagogical Praxis." *Curriculum Inquiry* 49, no. 4: 485–502. At https://doi.org /10.1080/03626784.2019.1664254.

Stohlmann-Rainey, Jessie. 2019. "Much Madness Is Divinest Sense." In *Much Madness: A Survivor's Guide to Extreme States and Self-Advocacy for Young Adults*, edited by Calvin Rey Moen and Kaz DeWolfe, 83–93. Morrisville, NC: Lulu Press.

14

Learning and Teaching Bad as Resistance

Queer Crip Pilipinx Bad Pedagogy

Pau Abustan

Content notes: colorism, settler colonialism, genocide, murder

Through my Queer Crip Pilipinx Bad Pedagogy, I push back against deficit-based constructions of what's *bad* and simultaneously embrace our *bad* bodyminds.[1] I reflect upon and reexamine *bad* in a swirly, nonlinear, neurodivergent, queer, and crip manner, as in refusing society's limited expectations of multiply marginalized communities. My pedagogy captures my multiple, fluid, and changing experiences with *bad* throughout my learning, teaching, and activist life moments. My interactions with *bad* highlight the ways I and many of us are taught we are the *bad* ones in need of fixing, saving, and improvement instead of understanding and doing something about how greater societal systems are the entities in need of change and transformation.

As a queer, crip, gender-fluid, and Mad Pilipinx being, I experience *bad* and Mad operating together in that those who internalize and externalize *badness* and Madness are often located at the margins of society:

1. Margaret Price's *Mad at School* (2011) and Sami Schalk's *Bodyminds Reimagined* (2018) define a bodymind as one interconnected entity in resistance to mainstream culture's attempts to separate the mind from the body and to privilege the superiority of the mind over the body.

Learning and Teaching Bad as Resistance   237

those of us who are mentally ill, sick, disabled, neurodivergent, femme, nonbinary, transgender, queer; those of us who are Black folx, Indigenous folx, people of color (BIPOC); and those of us with low to no income. This chapter centers how communities in education and society can and should be proud of our sick, disabled, neurodivergent, queer, crip, and swirly *badness* and Madness. We are not the ones in need of fixing: the systems in which all people live are in need of transformation to support the wholeness of us all, especially those of us who internalize and externalize *bad*. Here, I embrace my reclaimed Mad and *bad* identity, trajectory, and community. *Bad* signals the urgent need for educators, activists, and community members to collectively embrace *bad* learners, teachers, community members whose lessons, perspectives, and pedagogies both inside and outside of the classroom never existed as good, perfect, and normal.

Many of us are taught to perceive ourselves as *bad* students and/or as *bad* educators instead of interrogating systems of oppression as the foundations of creating harmful *good/bad* binary systems. Margaret Price (2011) centers how education continues to perpetuate harm and toxicity, especially toward those who are Mad, mentally ill, sick, disabled, neurodivergent, and multiply marginalized due to growing productivity and performance expectations for both students and educators. Queer Crip Bad Pilipinx Pedagogy refuses the degradation of us and each other inside and outside of the classroom and instead fosters disability and transformative justice dreams of sustainable worlds of care, connection, gentleness, and accessibility. We embrace our Madness and *badness* as our experiences of not aligning with systems built to be broken move us toward worlds of wholeness and care for all.

Bad urges us to reimagine our world not through the confines of productivity, work, and activism but through an expansive disability and transformative justice framework where rest, joy, and community are prioritized over individualism, isolation, and overworking ourselves to make ends meet. Those who cannot work are taken care of in our future disability and transformative justice worlds. Devon Price (2021) highlights how our society distances itself from, resists, and avoids the label *lazy* as its connotations of less than are associated with not working and the corporate elite wish to overwork us. It is up to all of us to end these cycles of unattainable perfection and productivity in the workplace and in all aspects of our lives.[2]

As a PhD scholar-activist-educator, I resist the norms defined as "good" and embrace my work, activist, and life experiences with *bad* as they contribute to my *bad* pedagogy. *Bad* inside and outside of the classroom disrupts and unsettles our current work and productivity-driven world and instead moves toward our future world of swirly rest, where every bodymind is cared for and where we continuously learn and unlearn *good/bad* constructions in education and society.

From Internalized Oppressions to Externalized Dreaming Resistance

My pedagogy is deeply intertwined with my multidimensional, shifting, fluid, personal, and intimate life experiences with *bad*. My personal life experiences continue to reshape and redefine my Queer Crip Pilipinx Bad Pedagogy. I learned about *bad* and Mad as resistance through my existence because my queer, nonbinary, transgender, and femme-in-power Pilipinx ancestors and I were never supposed to thrive and flourish in our world: colonizers attempted to wipe us out, erase us, and minimize us, and yet we exist and we resist today.[3]

As a child, I began learning and internalizing oppressions from my family owing to the generational traumas that our ancestors encountered and we continue to encounter. When I was growing up, my immigrant Pilipinx parents would share with me, "Stay out of the sun; you will get too dark." My parents, grandma, and grandpa would pinch my and my siblings' noses with wooden clothespins, declaring that our flat noses needed to be molded to become pointier and more Euro-centric settler-colonial noses. My grandma shared her daily whitening soap with me to use every

---

2. Devon Price's *Laziness Does Not Exist* (2021) shows how society and work cultures shame laziness and nonproductivity when our bodyminds really require more rest in our current turbulent world.

3. In the introduction to her collected volume *Babaylan* (2010), Leny Mendoza-Strobel describes how Spanish colonizers attempted to wipe out Pilipinx women and genderfluid leaders by throwing them into waters with crocodiles (13).

morning and evening, stating it would make my skin fairer, smoother, whiter, and thus, according to her and my family, more beautiful. Through these everyday messages and actions circulated within my Pilipinx family, I was taught at a young age that my Pilipinx body was *bad*, inadequate, and needed fixing. In *Brown Skin, White Minds* (2013), E. J. R. David shares how many Pilipinx people internalize our minimization and the erasure of our communities as white-supremacist colonial education taught us and continues to teach us how our bodyminds are second class and less in not meeting constructed settler-colonial bodymind norms.[4]

Along with internalizing my Pilipinx bodymind as *bad* and in need of fixing, I internalized and externalized my gender to be *bad*, to need regulation. Throughout my youth, I internalized and externalized the term *tomboy*. According to Pilipinx culture, *tomboy* means a person assigned female at birth who dresses "like a boy" and plays with "the boys."[5] I loved wearing comfy clothes, running around, playing sports and video games, and biking around the neighborhood, which are activities often stereotyped to be "boy" activities. Because my hair was short, I was often perceived to be a boy. I remember a teacher yelling at me to "quit playing around" and "get back in the boy's line." Through these early childhood experiences of being policed within an imagined and constructed settler-colonial binary gender system,[6] I was taught my gender was *bad*, unclear, illegible, wrong, and needed to be assigned and regulated into one fixed gender category of either "boy" or "girl" even when I knew I was gender fluid at a young age—both girl and boy, in between, and no gender all at the same time.

4. E. J. R. David's *Brown Skin, White Minds* (2013) maps the history and ongoing internalized colonial mentality and oppression of Pilipinx communities.

5. Kevin L. Nadal and Melissa J. H. Corpus's "'Tomboys' and 'Baklas'" (2016) and Martin F. Manalansan's "The 'Stuff' of Archives" (2014) discuss unique lived identities of transgender, nonbinary, and queer diasporic Pilipinx communities.

6. Qwo-Li Driskill and colleagues' volume *Queer Indigenous Studies* (2001) and Deborah Miranda's article "Extermination of the Joyas" (2010) focus on how settler colonization attempted to erase gender and sexual diversity present in Indigenous communities across the globe. Gender and sexuality as they are widely known today are settler-colonial constructs and often erase the gender and sexual diversity of Indigenous peoples.

240   Abustan

As my race and gender continue to be marked as deficient and in need of fixing, my sexuality continues to be labeled and treated as monstrous, as *bad*, and in need of erasure. During my early and late childhood experiences, I crushed on both boys and girls. Every time these romantic and sexual feelings stirred up within me, I prayed to God to forgive me as the Catholic and Christian churches I attended every Sunday with my family preached about how being gay was a sin. As a young child, I internalized my queer thoughts, my queer heart, my queer sexual and romantic attraction, and my queer spirit to be not just defective *bad* but also deviant, monstrous, sinful, and dirty *bad. Bad* became synonymous both with feelings of lacking and with feelings and externalizations of my existence as terrifying, horrendous, and morally wrong.

In swirly connection to my race, gender, and sexuality bodymind experiences, my elementary school bodymind internalized and externalized *bad* in that I believed I was not smart enough when in performance-based school settings. I feared the teachers and other students would soon find out they made a mistake in selecting me for my school district's gifted program. Although teachers and fellow students called me "perfect," I was afraid they would soon find out I was far from excellent because I perceived myself to be *bad*, inadequate, and defective. I experienced my first panic attacks during third grade: my mouth would feel dry, and I would cough uncontrollably. I felt as if the room were closing in on me, and I could not breathe. I would feel hot and dizzy and helpless and would become frustrated and cry often. Even though others around me viewed and treated me as a *good* Asian American, a model minority, and "high-performing" student, I internalized that I was a *bad* student and thus externalized this belief through my panic attacks when feeling overwhelmed by high expectations others held of me. I began to emulate *bad* because I was not and could never be their perfect Asian American model minority.[7]

7. In Tracy Lachica Buenavista's "Movement from the Middle" (2007), Roland Coloma's "Disorienting Race and Education" (2006), and Anthony Ocampo's *The Latinos of Asia* (2016), constructions and lived material realities of diasporic Pilipinx identities and experiences are discussed in a complex manner. Diasporic Pilipinx do not fit neatly into constructions of first- and second-generation immigrant communities, are

Learning and Teaching Bad as Resistance   241

My experiences with internalizing oppressions and *badness* as a child led me to yearn for a classroom and world where we collectively unlearn our internalized oppressions. *Bad* grants us permission to love our body-minds, make mistakes, be messy, be swirly, and be far from society's expectations of us. Through various learning activities in my Queer Crip Pilipinx Bad Pedagogy, I invite my students to reflect upon their personal life experiences of internalizing oppressions. I ask them to name and write down the lyrics of a song and/or poem that relates to their experiences with internalizing oppressions. I prompt them to draw an iceberg; at the top is what others assume of them, and at the bottom is what is really going on, including what is hurting in their lives due to systemic traumas. These activities encourage me and my students to examine how society often categorizes us as less, as not enough, as monstrous, as *bad*. We disrupt and unsettle the *good/bad* binary together when we reimagine a world where we embrace our constructed *badness*. Our Mad, *bad*, swirly, unsure, anxious, and whole selves are enough. We commit to building a caring and sustainable education and world system that holds and takes care of all of us, especially those of us who are deeply intertwined with constructions of *bad*.

Through the naming and smashing of our internalized oppressions, I encourage my students to dream together new worlds where violent *good/bad* dichotomies do not exist, where all beings are free, liberated, whole, and loved in societies that do not attempt to erase us and/or define us. In this dream and future world, we do not internalize ourselves as wrong. My students and I draw, generate word collages, and/or piece together

---

underrepresented in US higher education, and are unable to fit into settler-colonial-defined categories of race, ethnicity, and Indigeneity because they can be of Indigenous and/or multiracial Chinese, Spanish, and other ancestry. Many Pilipinx share cultural connections with Latinx as both groups were colonized by Spain. Our multiple Pilipinx cultures are influenced by diverse cultures. Pilipinx do not have the same life and education experiences as those within the constructed Asian American umbrella, and although we are often grouped with and stereotyped to be high-achieving Asian American model minorities, we share similarities with other US-based BIPOC communities as we continue to survive structures of colonization, imperialism, racism, and more.

photos displaying our utopic worlds in which all aspects of our bodyminds are loved in our fullness. My students and I dream of worlds where our bodyminds are resting, making mistakes, slowing down, and thriving in our collective messiness, joy, sustainability, and community. When reveling in the swirly imaginations and dreams of my students, I am honored to know we are closer to disability and transformative worlds where we are not lacking, and, instead, we are brilliant because we are interdependent in connection with ourselves, with each other, and with our earth.[8] Resisting our internalized oppressions is needed for our dreaming of our liberation together.

Questioning Why

Reflecting upon our life experiences tied to world events, systems, and structures has led my students and me to externalizing dreaming resistance and questioning the why all around us. Questioning why we remain stuck within the confines of the *good/bad* binary is a central component of my pedagogy because naming and analyzing how deficit constructions of *bad* consume education and society prompt us to ask "Why?" Why do we categorize and regulate ourselves and each other according to the dichotomous pitfalls of *good/bad* in all aspects of our lives? Why is *bad* associated with deficiencies and monstrosities? Asking "Why?" invites us to situate our relationships with *bad* in greater histories and systems of oppression and resistance.

My students and I ask why we are labeling and treating ourselves and each other as deficient and/or monstrous. Instead, we embrace ourselves and those who are constructed as *bad* students and teachers, those who are late, those who are absent, and those who do not retain and enact knowledge learned in a neat and linear manner. We resist harmful constructions of *bad* and foster our reclamation of *bad* when we name how *bad* was forcibly placed on the bodyminds of people who fall outside of settler-colonial, cis-hetero-sexist-ableist-racist societal constructions of normalcy.

---

8. Leah Lakshmi Piepzna-Samarasinha's *Care Work* (2018) and Leanne Betasamosake Simpson's *As We Have Always Done* (2017) depict dreams of interdependent future worlds led by femme, two-spirit, transgender, and/or queer BIPOC.

Learning and Teaching Bad as Resistance   243

We embrace *bad* because our *badness* is our refusal to be trapped within unattainable education and societal norms and expectations. It is OK to mess up, forget, not understand, ask questions, and more. Naming and gravitating toward the *bad*, Mad, and messy are central to *bad* pedagogy.

Neurodivergent, swirly, nonlinear, and nonnormative ways of being, such as not talking, talking too much, interrupting, spacing out, thinking too slow and/or too fast, asking too few and/or too many questions, being "inappropriate" or "awkward" when conversing and/or writing, not remembering details, and more are traits widely labeled as deficit and as *bad* inside and outside of the classroom. Those with bodymind disabilities continue to be cast out to the margins of education and society, perceived and treated as less than. Queer and crip scholars and activists,[9] Mad scholars and activists,[10] disability critical race feminist scholars and activists,[11] and others showcase the ways in which education and societal norms were constructed to privilege the bodyminds and lives of an elite few.

Bad manifests worlds where the bodyminds constructed as other, inferior, deviant, unruly, and monstrous are honored and cared for.[12] *Bad*

9. Alison Kafer's *Feminist, Queer, Crip* (2013) connects feminist, queer, and crip issues and communities together. Robert McRuer's *Crip Theory* (2006) locates crip as resistance to neoliberal pushes for productivity and normativity. Jina Kim's "Toward a Crip-of-Color Critique" (2017) identifies crip not as an identity but as a process that actively resists harmful oppressive systems and constructed norms.

10. Therí Alyce Pickens's *Black Madness :: Mad Blackness* (2019) defines and situates Madness and psychiatric disabilities in the context of historical and ongoing white supremacy, a system that constructs Madness within Black communities who are surviving and resisting multiple forms of structural oppression.

11. Julie Passanante Elman's *Chronic Youth* (2014) connects race, gender, sexuality, and disability as constructions with lived material realities in youth popular-culture media, arguing that neoliberal projects reinforce disability as needing to be cured in order to construct productive citizens who will uphold capitalism and nation-states. Sami Schalk and Jina Kim's "Integrating Race" (2020) uses a critical race, feminist, disability studies framework to center the interconnectedness and simultaneous operations of racist, sexist, classist, and ableist systems in education and society and to show how our multiple and often separated academic disciplines are more interwoven than we think.

12. For more on the connections among constructions of race, gender, sexuality, and disability as deviant or monstrous, see Kim Q. Hall's edited volume *Feminist Disability*

reminds us of the core disability justice tenet of not leaving any body behind.[13] Throughout an academic semester, I prompt my students to share their favorite TV shows, animated stories, anime, movies, books, comics, manga, music, and celebrities that uphold or challenge *good/bad* binaries.

Instead of labeling and treating ourselves as deficient, we turn to critique the foundations of education and societal systems rooted in multiple systemic oppressions that force our unique bodyminds to perform and produce in one-size-fits-all unsustainable ways. We seek to transform ourselves to align with and embrace the *badness* of our brilliant bodyminds. We ask for assistance, ask for extensions, and ask for clarity. We create space to communicate in swirly ways, to interrupt, and to feel anxious.

Smashing Perfectionism

Simultaneously resisting and embracing *bad* within our everyday lives and questioning the why of *bad* prevents the cycle, myth, and illusion of normal, perfectionism, and flawless performance and helps us accept that our diverse and divergent bodyminds will mess up, get lost, become confused, unlearn, disrupt, and unsettle. Crip time is an example of how we can embrace *bad* in our everyday lives, learning, teaching, participating in activism, and more.

I live in crip time when refusing linear, neat, and binary timelines and expectations placed on my bodymind. Although I and many others live and thrive in crip time, the oppressions of settler-colonial, cis-hetero-sexist-ableist-racist linear time is often forcibly placed on us. Because I did not align with neat and fixed constructions of time, I was often and continue to be labeled and treated as *bad*—deemed unreliable, late, absent, unable to balance time and tasks, unable to learn and apply information,

---

Studies (2008), Nirmala Erevelles's *Disability and Difference* (2011), Rosemary Garland-Thomson's *Extraordinary Bodies* (2017), and Jaspir K. Puar's *The Right to Maim* (2017).

13. Patty Berne and Aurora Levins Morales's "Ten Principles of Disability Justice" (2018) was developed by majority sick, disabled, transgender, queer, nonbinary, femme, and BIPOC peoples involved with the disabled performance troupe Sins Invalid, which honors tenets of intersectionality, interdependence, cross-disability solidarity, coalitional and anticapitalist activisms, and more.

and more. Among family and friends, students and coworkers, and fellow organizers, I was and continue to be labeled as flakey, inconsistent, and *bad*.

I recall living in crip time during my childhood, unable to meet school and societal expectations. I found it difficult to grasp math, algebra, and calculus concepts and to retain and apply history and science lessons. My teachers shared with me how I struggled to write coherent essays with a thesis, evidence, flow, and connections. I felt *bad* because no matter how hard I tried, I could not learn how to sight-read music. It was difficult to participate and talk out loud in class. I was unable to fit the mold of linear and on-time progressive learning. I was *bad*; I was far from perfect.

As an educator today, I do my best to resist perfection inside and outside of my classroom. I do not assign exams and tests. I refuse to call on my students and ask them for on-the-spot knowledge recitation. I invite open-ended and at-your-own-pace sharing from my students either out loud in person or via Zoom chat. Attendance and participation are not graded or required. Weekly assignments of contributing a thought and/or question about lectures, films, readings, discussions, and activities have flexible due dates. Questions are always welcome. Midterm and final papers are a reflection of main ideas students engage with weekly throughout the semester. I do not grade for grammar and/or flow as it is my students' unique thoughts, storytelling, and questions that showcase our learning together. Students are encouraged to rest. Students are invited to be imperfect and what is constructed to be *bad* in academia.

I push back against and simultaneously embrace *bad* when our body-minds will not meet expectations for perfection. As crip scholars share,[14] we should not struggle to meet neoliberal and settler-colonial, cis-hetero-sexist-ableist-racist timeframes, and our societal clocks should be fully transformed to support our slow, fast, and in-between movements in crip time. Our learning, teaching, and lives will be nonlinear, not on time, and *bad* when not meeting constructed expectations for timelines. Educational

14. Alison Kafer's *Feminist, Queer, Crip* (2013) and Ellen Samuels's "Six Ways of Looking at Crip Time" (2017) describe crip time as resistance to neoliberal and ableist pushes for linear and consistent productivity.

246   Abustan

and social shaming of our lateness, our imperfection, and our inability to grasp and apply information is a reflection of how our education and societal systems were built for some of us, not all of us. Reclamation and embracing of *bad* teach me, my students, and our communities how being out of time and living at our own pace are welcomed. The prioritization of crip time and taking care of ourselves and each other is a reflection of the disability and transformative justice worlds of access intimacy described by Mia Mingus (2011);[15] the crip-centric liberated zones drawn by Patty Berne and Aurora Levins Morales (2018), Sins Invalid, and Shayda Kafai (2021);[16] and the dreaming of collective access to care work done by Leah Lakshmi Piepzna-Samarasinha (2018).[17]

Connecting with Ourselves and Each Other in Gentle Accessibility

In reflecting upon my reckonings with *bad*, I realize that so much of my embracing of my Mad and *bad* identity thriving in crip time was through the support of a community who empowered me to connect with myself and others. After taking my first critical disability studies class during graduate school, and after learning I was neurodivergent, my multifaceted experiences with *bad* began to make sense. I wished I had received support, understanding, and patience earlier in life. It was now clear why I struggled to label myself as *good* and why it was difficult for me to engage

---

15. Mia Mingus's "Access Intimacy: The Missing Link" (2011) brings forth the concept of access intimacy, wherein disabled people do not have to explain and/or reexplain their access needs. Disabled people practicing access intimacy show up for themselves and each other in the ways they can and do their best to ask for and honor each other's unique and interconnected needs.

16. See note 13 on Berne, Levins Morales, and Sins Invalid. Shayda Kafai's *Crip Kinship* (2021) further centers the crip-centric liberated zones of Sins Invalid that ask for and honor the unique and interconnected needs of disabled performers and audience members. Crip-centric liberated zones can translate into all aspects of society, such as educational settings.

17. Piepzna-Samarasinha's *Care Work* (2018) draws upon the disability-justice tenets of Sins Invalid to showcase how collective care and collective access can take place in society, beginning with honoring our own care needs connected to the care needs of others.

in linear thinking and actions such as organizing my emotions, interactions, writing, tasks, and calendar.

After learning about accessibility and my own neurodivergence as an educator and learner, I became gentler with myself and others for experiencing executive-functioning divergences in comprehending, remembering, and analyzing lectures, readings, assignment instructions, priorities, body language, social cues, facial expressions, and more. I accepted myself and others for being unable to grasp information, for forgetting meetings, deadlines, and details. I now realized why I was labeled a *bad* friend, a *bad* student, a *bad* worker, and a *bad* activist throughout my life. I began to seek access support and surround myself with intersectional crip, sick, disabled, neurodivergent, and Mad communities who practiced radical vulnerability, gentleness, and accessibility as they appreciated me for moving more slowly, thinking more quickly, feeling swirly, forgetting details, panicking, and spiraling.

Bad connects us with ourselves and each other as we imagine and enact futures of accessibility and gentleness. In a traditional and colonial sense, classrooms do not exist for building community, discussing, and feeling the spectrum of our emotions and bodyminds together. Working against this colonial construction, connection, gentleness, and accessibility are found throughout my Queer Crip Pilipinx Bad Pedagogy and classroom when my students and I facilitate check-ins. I begin class by sharing words and phrases in Tagalog and American Sign Language, such as *hello, how are you?, good morning, good afternoon*. I invite my students to share in their own and/or other learned languages to foster a classroom of gentleness and accessibility. Beginning class with learning and appreciating our community of communication diversities together encourages me and my students to expand and share with each other in an accessible manner.

Witnessing our learning community for who we are, where we come from, and who we are becoming is a form of connecting ourselves to each other in gentleness. Queer, crip, *bad*, and Mad are our collective play, joy, tears, and more inside and outside of the classroom. As we drop our masks and break down walls built within ourselves and between each other, we create blueprints for a world without structures that will suppress our collective gentleness. I invite our learning community to share anything.

How are we feeling? What supports are we seeking today? What questions and announcements would we like to share? Asking open-ended questions allows us to cultivate a caring, gentle, and accessible community.

Learning more from the collective wisdom, joys, fears, and dreams of our learning community allows us to cultivate a world where *bad* is welcomed. *Bad* is called in when my students and I begin to feel at home, to share that we are not perfect academic productivity machines: we are happy and hurting, we are excited and fearful. Gentleness and accessibility invite us to share the spectrums of our joys, our mistakes, our anxieties, our confusion, and more. We name together our pleasures, our cathartic moments, and our paradigm shifts. We revel in the scholarship, poems, art, music, and activism of intersectional scholars and activists who challenge the one-size-fits-all productivity mandates of colonization, imperialism, neoliberalism, and capitalism.[18] We reimagine our dreams for gentle and accessible futures where we can feel, where we can be goofy, and where we can experience the wholeness of ourselves. Cultivating *bad* in our classroom allows us to honor our *bad* bodyminds in connection, gentleness, and accessibility against education and societal systems that were built to disconnect and overwork us.

Conclusion

Through my Queer Crip Pilipinx Bad Pedagogy, my students and I challenge our internalized oppressions, question the why of *good/bad* constructs, smash expectations and the desirability of the normal and perfect,

---

18. Our communities are interconnected and need to eradicate interconnected systemic injustices locally and globally. Aurora Levins Morales's *Kindling: Writings on the Body* (2013) discusses how our bodyminds are affected by multiple systemic oppressions, such as the pesticides in our food and how farmworker and migrant communities are highly susceptible to illness and disabilities owing to systemic inequities and lack of protection for working-class, low-income, and migrant communities. Levins Morales's *Medicine Stories* (2019) illustrates the ways in which systemic global violences produce disabilities through the examples of state-sanctioned wars, genocides, and the trafficking of girls and women. Alice Wong's collected volume *Disability Visibility* (2020) showcases the stories of diverse disabled peoples who resist the ableist stereotypes and systemic discrimination found in education and society.

and connect with ourselves and each other in gentle accessibility. This *bad* pedagogy arose from my experiences with the *good/bad* dichotomy of internalizing and externalizing myself as *bad*, as other, as deviant, as imperfect, as inferior, and as monstrous. Naming how *bad* arose from histories and systems of oppression allows me and my students to dream externalized resistances to *bad* and reclamation of our *bad* bodyminds and pedagogies of teaching and learning together. I continue to embrace, cultivate, and invite *bad* inside and outside of my classroom because good, perfect, and normal are settler-colonial, cis-hetero-sexist-racist-ableist constructions. I revel in the constructed *bad*, messy, odd, imperfect, deviant, and other because the *bad* is me and the *bad* is all of us. It is up to all of us to dream of *bad* worlds and *bad* pedagogies together, where all beings are free from the *good/bad* binary and where we thrive in swirly disability and transformative justice futures of connection, gentleness, accessibility, and care.

Works Cited

Berne, Patty, and Aurora Levins Morales. 2018. "Ten Principles of Disability Justice." *WSQ: Women's Studies Quarterly* 46, no. 1: 227–30.

Buenavista, Tracy Lachica. 2007. "Movement from the Middle: Pilipina/o 1.5-Generation College Student Access, Retention, and Resistance." PhD diss., Univ. of California, Los Angeles.

Coloma, Roland Sintos. 2006. "Disorienting Race and Education: Changing Paradigms on the Schooling of Asian Americans and Pacific Islanders." *Race, Ethnicity and Education* 9, no. 1: 1–15. At https://doi.org/10.1080/136133205 00490606.

David, E. J. R. 2013. *Brown Skin, White Minds: Filipino -/ American Postcolonial Psychology.* Charlotte, NC: Information Age.

Driskill, Qwo-Li, Chris Finley, Brian Joseph Gilley, and Scott Lauria Morgensen, eds. 2001. *Queer Indigenous Studies: Critical Interventions in Theory, Politics, and Literature.* Tucson: Univ. of Arizona Press.

Elman, Julie Passanante. 2014. *Chronic Youth: Disability, Sexuality, and U.S. Media Cultures of Rehabilitation.* New York: New York Univ. Press.

Erevelles, Nirmala. 2011. *Disability and Difference in Global Contexts: Enabling a Transformative Body Politic.* New York: Palgrave Macmillan.

Garland-Thomson, Rosemarie. 2017. *Extraordinary Bodies: Figuring Physical Disability in American Culture and Literature.* New York: Columbia Univ. Press.

Hall, Kim Q., ed. 2008. *Feminist Disability Studies.* Bloomington: Indiana Univ. Press.

Kafai, Shayda. 2021. *Crip Kinship: The Disability Justice & Art Activism of Sins Invalid.* Vancouver: Arsenal Pulp Press.

Kafer, Alison. 2013. *Feminist, Queer, Crip.* Bloomington: Indiana Univ. Press.

Kim, Jina. 2017. "Toward a Crip-of-Color Critique." *Lateral* 6, no. 1. At https://doi.org/10.25158/L6.1.14.

Levins Morales, Aurora. 2013. *Kindling: Writings on the Body.* Cambridge, MA: Palabrera Press.

———. 2019. *Medicine Stories: Essays for Radicals.* Rev. and exp. ed. Durham, NC: Duke Univ. Press.

Manalansan, Martin F. 2014. "The 'Stuff' of Archives: Mess, Migration, and Queer Lives." *Radical History Review* 120:94–107. At https://doi.org/10.1215/01636545-2703742.

McRuer, Robert. 2006. *Crip Theory: Cultural Signs of Queerness and Disability.* New York: New York Univ. Press.

Mendoza-Strobel, Leny. 2010. "Babaylan Work Begins in the Body: Where Is Your Body?" Introduction to *Babaylan: Filipinos and the Call of the Indigenous,* edited by Leny Mendoza-Strobel, 1–58. Santa Rosa, CA: Center for Babaylan Studies.

Mingus, Mia. 2011. "Access Intimacy: The Missing Link." *Leaving Evidence* (blog), May 5. At https://leavingevidence.wordpress.com/2011/05/05/access-intimacy-the-missing-link.

Miranda, Deborah. 2010. "Extermination of the Joyas." *GLQ: A Journal of Lesbian and Gay Studies* 16, nos. 1–2: 253–84. At https://doi.org/10.1215/10642684-2009-022.

Nadal, Kevin L., and Melissa J. H. Corpus. 2016. "'Tomboys' and 'Baklas': Experiences of Lesbian and Gay Filipino Americans." In *Contemporary Asian America: A Multidisciplinary Reader,* 3rd ed., edited by Mi Zhou and J. V. Gatewood, 291–331. New York: New York Univ. Press.

Ocampo, Anthony Christian. 2016. *The Latinos of Asia: How Filipino Americans Break the Rules of Race.* Stanford, CA: Stanford Univ. Press.

Pickens, Therí Alyce. 2019. *Black Madness :: Mad Blackness.* Durham, NC: Duke Univ. Press.

Piepzna-Samarasinha, Leah Lakshmi. 2018. *Care Work: Dreaming Disability Justice.* Vancouver: Arsenal Pulp Press.

Price, Devon. 2021. *Laziness Does Not Exist: A Defense of the Exhausted, Exploited, and Overworked*. New York: Atria.

Price, Margaret. 2011. *Mad at School: Rhetorics of Mental Disability and Academic Life*. Ann Arbor: Univ. of Michigan Press.

Puar, Jasbir K. 2017. *The Right to Maim: Debility, Capacity, Disability*. Durham, NC: Duke Univ. Press.

Samuels, Ellen. 2017. "Six Ways of Looking at Crip Time." *Disability Studies Quarterly* 37, no. 3. At https://dsq-sds.org/article/view/5824/4684.

Schalk, Sami. 2018. *Bodyminds Reimagined: (Dis)ability, Race, and Gender in Black Women's Speculative Fiction*. Durham, NC: Duke Univ. Press.

Schalk, Sami, and Jina Kim. 2020. "Integrating Race: Transforming Feminist Disability Studies." *Signs: Journal of Women in Culture and Society* 46, no. 1: 31–55. At https://www.journals.uchicago.edu/doi/abs/10.1086/709213.

Simpson, Leanne Betasamosake. 2017. *As We Have Always Done: Indigenous Freedom through Radical Resistance*. Minneapolis: Univ. of Minnesota Press.

Wong, Alice, ed. 2020. *Disability Visibility: First-Person Stories from the Twenty-First Century*. New York: Vintage.

15

"The Deadly Space Between"

Toward a Mad Pedagogy and Mad Methodology

A-M McManaman

Though this be madness, yet there is method in 't.
—William Shakespeare, *Hamlet* ([c. 1599] 1992)

Now, in his heart, Ahab had some glimpse of this, namely: all my means are sane, my motive and my object mad.
—Herman Melville, *Moby-Dick* ([1851] 1981)

This piece of writing is emerging from a liminal space. Much like the woman who emerges from the yellow wallpaper, its momentum is generated from the in-between. It reverberates like laughter from an attic. It pursues white whales. Its chamber is a haunted one, though not a house. It sings songs while wearing floral crowns. It has believed as many as six impossible things before breakfast. Its temporality speaks endlessly of "tomorrow, and tomorrow, and tomorrow." And its author works in and from the abstract with the understanding that each of these allusions, whether they directly correspond with lived experience or not, will declare: "This object is Mad."

As a PhD candidate, genderqueer femme, and Madperson, I've been inhabiting this liminal space, the space between, for some time.[1] The story of the lonely, overworked, burnt-out graduate student wracked with anxiety and depression is probably as familiar as these literary allusions.

---

1. By the time this book is published, I will have become "A-M McManaman, PhD."

"The Deadly Space Between"   253

But the notion that the difficult conditions of graduate school will bring you within close proximity to the experience of "being driven mad" is different from openly declaring oneself a Mad scholar. Those of us who have lived in the in-between space of a PhD student (or in the even more liminal category of "candidate") and a graduate teaching assistant (who in fact occupies the space of instructor or "professor" whenever they are in the classroom) must forge complementary and contradictory identities. Our role is always in a strange flux, only further destabilized by the academic infrastructure of the modern university, in which an ever-decaying job market dictates our shelf life.

Living in-between these two states means never quite occupying one power structure—much in the way that my ability to pass as sane affords me the privilege of "function" and "success" but can never erase the internalized stigma. However, in this chapter I want to advocate that it is precisely in this space between that we as Mad scholars do our thinking, working, and teaching. In arguing for a Mad critical and pedagogical approach, this chapter explores the ways in which a Mad perspective and Mad studies more broadly may be conceptualized as a method of the space between, before discussing examples of the pedagogy of the space between in my own emerging Mad pedagogical practice.

Defining the Space Between and Reaching It Indirectly

I want to propose two things: (1) the space between is simultaneously the "thing" that emerges (and continuously is emerging) from the Mad experience of living "in between" and an articulation of the ways in which this in-between state is a dismantling of binary thinking; and (2) the ways in which we reach/work/dismantle from within the space between can be done only indirectly. Like the liminal literary spaces that I evoked earlier, the space between is a recognition of the ways in which a lived experience of Madness produces certain kinds of ambiguities that allow us to recontextualize our commitment to fixed certainties and definitions.[2]

---

2. I take the phrase "space between" from Herman Melville's *Billy Budd* ([1891] 2009), a text that narrates a crisis surrounding the emerging systems of social power that pathologize the body and mind. Not only is the text one of emergence, where the

To further define the space between, I draw on Shayda Kafai's concept of the "Mad border body." Illustrating through her lived experience, Kafai defines the Mad body as one of living "in-between" and offers this state as an alternative to the belief that "madness is one half of a static binary structure" (2013, par. 3). She argues that the Mad border body by its very nature is a "counter-narrative for madness and sanity" (par. 2). In seeking to dispose of the binary constructions of sanity and Madness, she demonstrates that Madness as an embodied experience is an ambiguous one that "affronts normativity" (par. 8) and "comfortably exists in the gaps" (par. 8). Drawing on queer theories of border bodies, she articulates the ways in which living in a Mad body, one that is in-between, deconstructs the binary and is always a "negotiation of sanity and madness" (par. 17). This in-betweenness gives us access to a way to recontextualize the binary because in embracing such fluidity, we are able to transform through "counter-narratives of madness" (par. 21).

The space between is the space from which such dislodging counter-narratives occur precisely because the Mad in-between body is counter to the notion that such concepts can't coexist. As Tanja Aho, Liat Ben-Moshe, and Leon J. Hilton describe, Madness is a "slippery and unruly object," and the "object" at the core of the emerging discourse of critical Mad studies brims with especially unruly, errant, contradictory, and even perverse potentialities. One reason for such unruliness, they note, is that Mad studies brings "together terms that in some ways are diametrically opposed" and pushes up against "the limits of protocols of academic practice" (2017, 294). In theorizing the space between, I follow from Aho, Ben-Moshe, and Hilton to suggest that Mad studies opens new and transformative spaces that acknowledge the often complex and often contradictory social and historical meanings of the experience and language of Madness.

---

emergent language of psychoanalytic pathology is in tension with older, competing models of the mind, but its narrator suggests that the means of reaching Madness is an indirect passage across "the deadly space between" (41). Notably, the narrator resists defining the space between, presenting it as an emergent, negated space of ambiguities. It is in this spirit that I evoke a theorizing of the space between.

"The Deadly Space Between"   255

Contrary to what we may understand as a "direct" method (the method of pathologizing, medicalizing, and reading heteronormatively and diagnostically), I see the space between not only as reached by indirectness but as an emerging *practice* of indirectness that is "highly critical of dominant constructions of *Madness, normality* or *sanity*, recognizing the flawed nature of simplistic dichotomous and oppositional constructions of difference" (Diamond 2013, 76). Where the direct method constructs an either/or dichotomy, the space between both collapses a fixed temporality and offers a spatialized counter to the rigid binary of sanity and Madness. Once such a collapse has occurred, to work and be in this space must *be* indirect, must be an enactment of negotiation, precisely because the position of the Mad border body destabilizes direct dichotomous structures. I invoke the concept of indirectness not only as a recognition of the liminal experience of in-betweenness but also as an assertion that we cannot produce transformative counternarratives by enacting methods that uphold a direct dichotomy between Madness and sanity.

Madness as an Always-Emerging Praxis

As Mad scholars, activists, and individuals who occupy and traverse the liminal experience of the space between, we theorize emergence continuously in our discourses of Madness. In their introductory manifesto to *Mad Matters*, Robert Menzies, Brenda LeFrançois, and Geoffrey Reaume outline the history of the "emergent field" of Mad studies, arguing and calling for a radical distance from biological determinism of the mind that will simultaneously value the diverse lived experiences and narratives of Mad people (2013, 1–2). Part of the conceptualizing of the space between is the movement, or working from, a kind of fluidity or an unfixed identity position. The space between evokes a transformative model that counters the crude medical model of the mind in which we are presented with symptom, diagnosis, treatment, and recovery. Mad studies asserts, through attention to our own lived experience, that the conditions of having Madness are world changing. This change is not only a temporal one but also one in which the temporality is interior and indirect. Once you have gone Mad, you are *always* Mad, not just Mad when you are symptomatic or diagnosed or when you cannot pass as sane. In this way, Madness is not a static, fixed occurrence or experience but one that continuously emerges and reemerges throughout our lives as Mad people. Madness changes the particular way our life is structured, and so we are caught in-between as a "dual inhabitant" in what Kafai calls a "border body" state (2013, par. 10, 2). But from this position as Mad scholars, we are able to admit a kind of vulnerability, a kind of messiness, within our own lived Mad experiences and within other scholarly fields.[3]

As a Mad literary scholar, I have always seen my own practice of literary criticism as reflective of the ways in which texts invite us to occupy and traverse liminal spaces. Close reading in itself, an essential tool of my trade, is a practice of the always-already emerging—one in which we explore a text's formal and stylistic choices as a means of attending to what emerges between the literal. My readings are produced in this close manner, which follows Anna Kornbluh's assertion that we should cultivate "reading methods that fathom the spatiality of the dialectic within criticism but also within literature itself" (2017, 406). Making the experience of Madness, of living in the space between, a pedagogical praxis and literary reading methodology allows for an exploration in and out of the classroom of the ways in which texts themselves are "Mad," by which I mean the ways in which texts reveal alternative forms—how they make alternative possibilities legible to us not merely as deconstructive resistance to systematic institutional forces but as transformative of those forces. In this way, I have also always considered my literary practice as "Mad" because both the texts themselves and the art of close reading are an attendance to the ways in which meaning continuously emerges and the ways in which such meanings may problematize and be problematic. Close reading is not the act of directly producing an absolute and fixed reading of a text

---

3. As Elizabeth Brewer notes in her recent account of the relationship between Mad studies and disability studies, these two fields have a long history together that for many expresses degrees of indebtedness as well as similar theoretical traditions despite the nuances between them. Brewer argues, "How one claims an identity reveals one's views on embodiment and on epistemology. Coming out as mad, rather than mentally ill, makes a statement about how one views their experience and the nature of mental difference" (2019, 12).

but a recognition of the ways in which close attention to the text reveals its contradictions—interpretation is the enacting of the space between.

Literary expressions and representations have long been investigated as sites of extremities of being, as producing and inducing liminal spaces in which the rational loosens (literature both describes, formalizes, and then becomes implicated in such production). Though lived experiences of Madness are socially taboo and stigmatized, literary representations of such experiences are abundantly discussed. As such, students are more willing to talk about Madness because the literary canon and literary criticism concern themselves with Madness repeatedly. Captain Ahab, the disabled monomaniac; Claggart, the deviant antagonist; Hamlet, the melancholic prince: these "Mad men" belong to a long historic, literary, and cultural preoccupation with Madness, alongside "Mad women" such as Ophelia, Medea, Lady Macbeth, and Bertha Mason. Through such fictional figures, often problematic and polarizing, we have formed a real-world representative discourse about how Madness is engendered, performed, embodied, and understood. These literary representations enact the in-between space precisely because they are not real and yet have very real effects as to how Madness is perceived socially and culturally. In this way, I think about how a direct approach to literary Madness that might consider literature only as emulating the normative social forces is counterintuitive to reading the complicated, contradictory, and counternarratives also contained therein.

Producing the Space Between through Disclosure

I am no stranger to the complicated and contradictory experience of traversing and occupying the space between as a PhD candidate. Though I never arrive at it directly, at some point in the semester, be it during the weeks dedicated on the syllabus to representations of Madness in literature, an entire literary course themed on Madness, or an extension of the conversations that occur in my classroom about normalization, a question inevitably emerges: When do I disclose my Madness, if at all? Claiming and using a word such as *Mad* can be a double-edged sword—in stating I am Mad, I choose not to lean against the diagnostic labels also attached to me but rather to be specifically and radically ambiguous and to produce the space between. By naming ourselves Mad, we situate Madness as distinctively nonpathological. But producing said space puts us at risk of producing a structure in which the listener may do the work of filling in the void we wish to leave ambiguous. As many scholars have noted, the act of disclosing one's identity (and more so when asking for accommodations) poses personal and professional risks as well as rewards (Price 2011; O'Toole 2013). However, our disclosure, our coming out, always does the work of transgressing what Katie Aubrecht describes as "the normative demand to remove and distance" ourselves from Madness and disability (2012, 34).

As my career has progressed, I now disclose myself as Mad most often when I'm introducing my students to the course and discussing my commitment to accessibility and accommodations. Disclosing my diagnosis has become an important act—holding space for my students and for Madness to exist without hesitation and shame. One compelling space emerges from such a disclosure—the atmosphere of the classroom changes, and mixed in with the discomfort is the possibility of a shift in perspective for both instructor and student. The reason why this happens is that Madness carries so much cultural and personal weight that it is impossible for us not to feel some degree of ambivalence about it. I see disclosing as an exercise of creating the space between because it disrupts the comfort students have in distancing themselves from fictional accounts of Madness. It is an act that is perspectively and atmospherically shifting precisely because it demonstrates to students, who often think of themselves as Outsiders and Others to such a space, that our unspoken commitment to the normative as academics is illusory.

By disclosing my Madness in the introduction to the course, I can encourage students to draw on their various encounters with words that describe psychic states. It also allows me to explain my choice to use the word *Mad* as someone with a lived experience whose aim is not to dismiss those who don't use it but rather to offer alternative perspectives to the dominant medical dichotomy through the study of literature. In my act of disclosure, the students are brought *inside* the in-between by their proximation to Mad texts and a Mad instructor. This space is not merely an abstracted atmosphere. Once I introduce them to these concepts and to

"The Deadly Space Between" 259

the possibility that Madness and sanity are not binary (thereby evoking the space between as a methodological tool), we can collectively and cooperatively generate and transform our discomfort, live in our discomfort, and seek to question our assumptions. In this way, Madness is not a distanced object of study but a method of inquiry via lived experience that the students may take as a critical position of study and thereby explore with it what new social forms might emerge from these Mad texts.

Pedagogy of the Space Between

In the fall of 2019, I taught my first course dedicated exclusively to Mad texts. It was limited to literature by women and femmes in part by the institutional and departmental course framework, "Introduction to Women and Literature."[4] I posed a series of crucial questions throughout the semester, using a variety of different literary texts to approach and reapproach each of these questions: How do texts tell us they are Mad? Do they? And why do we as scholars and critics feel inclined to take the critical position of the physician? It's not only important to invite students to consider themselves as active critical participants, already contributing to a larger field by their presence in a classroom discussion, but also to invite them to consider what critical tools—and, by extension, biases—they have inherited.

As a means of introducing students to a methodology of Madness that reimagines embodiment, we read Nellie Bly's *Ten Days in a Mad House* ([1887] n.d.), a text that presented students with a complex model of embodied Madness, institutional power, and the policing of gendered bodies. Bly's journalistic account of her masquerading as "Mad" to infiltrate an asylum and expose the conditions there makes Madness visible not only through accounts of the Mad patients but also through Bly's performance of Madness and the ease with which she was incarcerated. Students readily discussed her methods of "pretending to be Mad," and in rebuttal to the student consensus that they knew a person was Mad because the person

4. PhebeAnn M. Wolframe (2013) also discusses this kind of limitation and offers an account of Mad pedagogical methodology that becomes a totalizing praxis rather than just a method for Mad-specific courses.

acted a certain way (and, say, had a set of easily identifiable symptoms that mark the body in some way) I instead asked them: How do we perform sanity? How do you know someone is sane if they don't disclose it to you?

I considered this one of the most significant moments in the course, precisely because it caused students to shift from the position of the unspoken norm as they began to question how normality is proven and performed. *Ten Days* is exemplary of the ways in which binary constructions of sanity and Madness are enacted. As such, it is the ideal text to introduce the concept of the Mad body as an in-between one precisely because the suggestion that sanity might also be performed dislodges students' sense that sanity is an unquestionable normative state. These questions produced a series of revelations among students about just how *passive* we are to such invisible forces, and their responses to the concept that sanity might also be performative made for lots of messy, contradictory, revolutionary, confused, and impassioned critiques. In this way, my disclosure as a Mad scholar—seemingly bringing together the contradictory states of Mad woman and rational academic—reinforced such imperatives to question and allowed me to introduce the concepts of passing as sane and the bodymind as tools of analysis from the space between.[5] Not only was the in-between seen as the lived experience of Mad people (and the lived experience of their instructor), but I modeled it as a critical-reading perspective that conceptualized the uncertainties of sanity, the ambiguities of Madness, and the need to recontextualize the fixed notions with which students arrived to the classroom. With this framework in place, students began to articulate the ways in which texts complicate the dichotomy of sanity and Madness and to conceptualize the ways in which Madness is not just a mental experience but an embodied one.

Another way of decentering diagnostic readings (and thereby the "direct method") is to have students confront their immediate response to a text and ask why we so often diagnose characters even when a text itself is pushing against that power structure. To do such work, we read Charlotte

5. I work and teach with Margaret Price's definition of *bodymind* because this term accounts for the spatial and physical aspects of Madness that call into question the explicit division of body and mind (2015, 269).

Perkins Gilman's story "The Yellow Wallpaper" ([1892] n.d.), a staple of American literature and gender studies classrooms that is, tellingly, a text for which students and literary scholars readily wish to offer a diagnostic reading. After I prompted a discussion about why our immediate reaction to the text is to occupy the position of a diagnostician, students began trying to take the text on its own, Mad terms. This shift enabled a fruitful textual analysis of language used to describe Madness that was not limited just to symptomatic accounts, and I invited students to think about the ways in which the text demonstrated the engendered, embodied, and social aspects of Madness that it was also critiquing.

Once equipped with a language of Mad embodiment and the ways in which Madness destabilizes dichotomies, students could question what counternarratives were present within the text—and consider that not all counternarratives were formalized in the same way or worked the same ways. Students developed their critique away from a diagnostic framework and toward a Mad one, and they searched for moments in the text that enacted cultural and social representations of Madness. Pushing further and moving away from the immediate need to ask, "What is wrong with this character?" or "How might I diagnose them?," students stopped encountering the space between as something that occurred only in the act of disclosure or that was attached to representations by Mad literary characters and began to understand it as something also produced by the text itself. When students then encountered texts such as Sylvia Plath's *The Bell Jar* ([1963] 2005), Octavia Butler's "The Evening, the Morning, and the Night" ([1987] 2005), and the anonymously written "The Man Who Thought Himself a Woman" ([1857] n.d.), I invited them to explore and question why certain cultural images of the cis-white Madwoman were so pervasive. Introduced to intersections with queer studies, race studies, and trans studies, students were able to adapt their critical lens in order to articulate the ways in which Mad texts are not *fixable* or *fully definable* and may both problematize and be problematic. It is through consideration of these kinds of textual, historic, and social tensions that we can understand how texts may reveal alternative forms.

Perhaps my favorite assignment of the semester was a follow-up to Marge Piercy's *Woman on the Edge of Time* ([1976] 1985), a science fiction novel about an institutionalized Hispanic woman, Consuelo (Connie) Ramos, and her visions of a utopic future. Students were encouraged to write a utopian manifesto after they discussed the merits (and, more often than not, the problems) of the utopia within the novel. For this text about time travel, utopian futures, and institutional power, students quickly dispersed the "Is the character Mad or sane?" question as they began to explore how a Mad character (whose time travel and "visions" are diagnosed as delusions) both problematized and made problematic the legitimacy of a utopic vision. Connie's visions were a way to talk about what it would mean for us to see the in-between space as literally enacted and to consider time travel as traversing liminal possibilities.

As this text also imagines alternatives to institutions and offers a space for Madness to exist in future society, students eagerly discussed the utopian society—many of them keen to see elements of it as quite dystopic. In response to this view, I wanted students to see that the literary analytical tools we had been developing were not merely ways in which we could consider figurative and fictional objects but a way of conceptualizing and transforming our own world—a way of thinking not only about how we have received Madness through literary texts but about the way Madness fits in and is necessary to our own society. Because Piercy's text is a much more immediate call to action, a call to the readers to envision utopia, I wanted students to see themselves not merely as emerging critical readers but as emerging writers.

After a semester of performing Mad readings, penning a manifesto became a way of enacting and practicing the type of world-transforming work we had discussed was being done by Mad literature. As such, my students were working with their critical tools not just to produce readings about and then from the space between but also to see themselves as visionaries, participants, and writers of alternative narratives and to imagine that they could transform familiar institutions whose foundation is built on "rationale." The goal of this class had been to invite students not only to learn Mad studies but to do Mad studies. Once students wrote their individual manifestos, we dedicated an entire class to bringing all of those ideas together into one larger collective utopic vision. This goal not only required an attempt to bring together different viewpoints but was also a way in which we dislodged the binary of professor/student as we all became collaborators in the space between.

I close by means of indirectness and do so with reference to Melville's *Billy Budd* (whose very presence in this chapter begins in the liminal space of footnotes) and its narrator, who urges us to pursue "truth" with "its ragged edges" (Melville [1891] 2009, 100). The "ragged edges" of the space between are the ones that preserve and celebrate our liminal and indirect experiences as Mad bodies; they testify to the negative and to what we fear to disclose—for they are our messy, fluid, uncomfortable ragged truths. Just as my students ended with a manifesto and the spirit of resistance, I end here with the hope that the work in this volume about Mad scholars will allow us to revise our positions to and within academic and theoretic practice. This is not a closing at all, but an emergence.

Works Cited

Aho, Tanja, Liat Ben-Moshe, and Leon J. Hilton. 2017. "Mad Futures: Affect/Theory/Violence." *American Quarterly* 69, no. 2: 291–302. At https://www.jstor.org/stable/26360849.

Aubrecht, Katie. 2012. "Disability Studies and the Language of Mental Illness." *Review of Disability Studies* 8, no. 2: 31–44. At http://hdl.handle.net/10125/58522.

Bly, Nellie. [1887] n.d. *Ten Days in a Mad-House.* Univ. of Pennsylvania Digital Library. At https://digital.library.upenn.edu/women/bly/madhouse/madhouse.html.

Brewer, Elizabeth. 2019. "Coming Out Mad, Coming Out Disabled." In *Literatures of Madness: Disability Studies and Mental Health*, edited by Elizabeth J. Donaldson, 11–30. London: Palgrave MacMillan.

Butler, Octavia. [1987] 2005. "The Evening, the Morning, and the Night." In *Bloodchild and Other Stories*, 2nd ed., 33–70. New York: Seven Stories Press.

Diamond, Shaindl. 2013. "What Makes Us a Community? Reflections on Building Solidarity in Anti-sanist Praxis." In *Mad Matters: A Critical Reader in Canadian Mad Studies*, edited by Brenda A. LeFrançois, Robert Menzies, and Geoffrey Reaume, 64–78. Toronto: Canadian Scholars' Press.

Gilman, Charlotte Perkins. [1892] n.d. "The Yellow Wallpaper." Project Gutenberg. At https://www.gutenberg.org/cache/epub/1952/pg1952-images.html.

Kafai, Shayda. 2012. "The Mad Border Body: A Political In-Betweenness." *Disability Studies Quarterly* 33, no. 1. At https://doi.org/10.18061/dsq.v33i1.3438.

Kornbluh, Anna. 2017. "We Have Never Been Critical: Toward the Novel as Critique." *Novel* 50, no. 3: 397–408. At https://doi.org/10.1215/00295132-4195016.

"The Man Who Thought Himself a Woman." [1857] n.d. *Antebellum Magazine* Edition Project. At antebellummags.arizona.edu/knickerbocker/december -1857/ man-who-thought-himself-woman.

Melville, Herman. [1851] 1981. *Moby-Dick; or, The Whale*. Reprint. New York: Bantam Classics.

———. [1891] 2009. *Billy Budd*. In *Billy Budd, and Other Tales*, with an introduction by Julian Markels and an afterword by Joyce Carol Oates, 1–106. New York: Signet Classics.

Menzies, Robert, Brenda A. LeFrançois, and Geoffrey Reaume. 2013. "Introducing Mad Studies." In *Mad Matters: A Critical Reader in Canadian Mad Studies*, edited by Brenda A. LeFrançois, Robert Menzies, and Geoffrey Reaume, 1–22. Toronto: Canadian Scholars' Press.

O'Toole, Corbett. 2013. "Disclosing Our Relationships to Disabilities: An Invitation for Disability Studies Scholars." *Disability Studies Quarterly* 33, no. 2. At https://doi.org/10.18061/dsq.v33i2.3708.

Piercy, Marge. [1976] 1985. *Woman on the Edge of Time*. Reissue ed. Robbinsdale, MN: Fawcett.

Plath, Sylvia. [1963] 2005. *The Bell Jar*. Modern Classics. New York: Harper Perennial.

Price, Margaret. 2011. *Mad at School: Rhetorics of Mental Disability and Academic Life*. Ann Arbor: Univ. of Michigan Press.

———. 2015. "The Bodymind Problem and the Possibilities of Pain." *Hypatia* 30, no. 1: 268–84. At https://doi.org/10.1111/hypa.12127.

Shakespeare, William. [c. 1599] 1992. *Hamlet*. Edited by Barbara A. Mowat and Paul Werstine. New York: Simon & Schuster.

Wolframe, PhebeAnn M. 2013. "The Madwoman in the Academy, or, Revealing the Invisible Straightjacket: Theorizing and Teaching Saneism and Sane Privilege." *Disability Studies Quarterly* 33, no. 1. At https://doi.org/10.18061 /dsq.v33i1.3438.

16

Crazy Femme Pedagogies

Toward an Archive

Jesse Rice-Evans and Andréa Stella

| *Content note*: self-harm |

We are crazy femmes, but at times our Madness feels more like institutional gaslighting. We believe that though the university may forward short-term, piecemeal solutions, it will *never* center access because access directly challenges the frameworks of exclusion that the American university relies upon. In the face of this challenge, integrating femme frameworks of care, interdependence, and empathy into teaching is nonnegotiable. Expansive definitions of access are central to this ideology as institutional barriers for sick and disabled faculty and students are replicated in barriers for poor, working-class, nonnative English-speaking people; Black folx, Indigenous folx, and people of color (BIPOC); and trans and queer students and faculty.

We are instructors and collaborators. This accountability partnership means we rely on one another to take time off, communicate our needs to gatekeepers in the academic spaces we occupy, and ask for help. This chapter embraces a dialogic approach to teaching and writing by alternating the voices of the two authors. Jesse's words are in italics, and Andréa's are in nonitalic text. Many of our ideas emerge from each other's understandings and experiences. Allowing each author's voice to stand on its own yet in conversation with the other author's gives us opportunities to address not only our own subjectivities but also our own internal identifications of "crazy" and "femme."

265

We are especially conscious of our attunement to the identification *femme* (instead of *feminist* or *queer*): we find ourselves drawn to *femme* because of its slipperiness, its malleability, its messiness, the ways that femmeness mirrors craziness in its obsession with self- and collective care, radical (sometimes too much) vulnerability, and solidarity among nonmen and other marginalized embodied identities (Piepzna-Samarasinha 2018). Slippage is necessary for our autotheoretical framework to catalog an imperfect, messy archive of materials that mark our survivorship, failure, and care practices.

One essential consideration for us as authors: in this chapter and in our writing more broadly, we are unwilling to share details of the traumas our colleagues, peers, and mentors have experienced. They are not our stories to share. Instead, we share our own lived experiences and reflections as two white, autistic, Mad, femme graduate workers in precarious financial situations.

We know that all works of scholarship inevitably are shaped by their writer's specific subject position, a dynamic addressed overtly by Black feminist theorists such as Patricia Williams (1992), Barbara Christian (2007), and Patricia Hill Collins (2008), whose narratological innovations incorporate embodiment, reflexivity, and dialogue that exceed the university's narrow conception of "theory," "objectivity," and "academic writing." Indeed, as Sylvia Wynter (2006) and bell hooks (1994) note, if not state explicitly, the imagined speaker-author-scholar figure is by default conceived as white, male, cis-hetero, abled, and bourgeois. We explicitly and frequently address our own whiteness and other dimensions of our positionality in refusal of this invisibilization of subject position, which can ultimately replicate epistemic hierarchy and violence.

We also point to our whiteness and privilege throughout our piece to acknowledge that our stories are inevitably limited to our own narrow experiences and points of view. We know that modes of oppression are inherently intertwined (Collins 2008) and that solidarity across a multiplicity of identities is critical in achieving any semblance of justice (Harney and Moten 2013; Reed 2023), yet, ultimately, we can only narrate our own lived realities. We hope that though our stories are inevitably incomplete and emerging from very specific intersections of white privilege of disability, they might offer a kind of testimony that helps unveil and resist one dimension of academic ableism (Dolmage 2017).

Framings

Jesse: *Pedagogy is not an objective exercise, an abstract theoretical principle to be tested: it is an ethic of care, compassion, and antiracism, decentering white-supremacist cultural norms such as objectivity, worship of the written word, and paternalism. Again and again I have heard that my commitment to letting my students guide my teaching is "crazy," which is actually kind of perfect: if femme pedagogy that centers access needs and emotions is "crazy," then it's up to us, the Mad femmes, to do this work. In crazy femme pedagogy, intersectional feminism is crucial. We acknowledge, discuss, and center feminisms outside of these mainstream representations of mere representation and point to the substantive impact of white-supremacist feminism that dominates cultural representations of what feminism is and does.*

Andréa: When I see a rule, I see a wall. I immediately want to take a sledgehammer and bust it down, plant something new in its place, and fling the broken bits back at whoever put it there to begin with. Maybe I'm just deeply distrusting of anyone's best intentions, but the English Department loves to trumpet good intentions without ever consulting the people whom these policies affect. So I've gone ahead and changed my policies and procedures to support my students, and they are malleable; the language changes every semester as I hear more from my students about how my policies and the policies of others affect their learning. This recognition of personal access needs is an integral part of crazy femme pedagogy: it necessitates turning the lens on myself and sitting with my vulnerabilities instead of burying them and pretending that the structures in place are more appropriate than listening to my bodymind (Clare 2017).

If someone were to ask about my experiences, I would tell the truth. I have already done this many times. In white neoliberal spaces, I am rarely called anything to my face, but I see the glances and know the tones well: Just let her get through this, and we can talk after. When I bring up such experiences in therapy, I am asked if I might be projecting my own fears onto others, but I am not afraid. Craziness dilutes fear of my unprofessionalism, my inappropriate language and conduct, my unequivocal need to protect myself and protect an unknown other.

Embracing the Madness is especially difficult for a PhD student who is supposed to know the secret codes and discourses of the academic spaces I'm inside but doesn't. There are secret guidelines for how to do everything: ask permission, it echoes, when I know I have never asked permission except for consent, which is not what this is. I turn up in a hurricane of confidence and emailed confusion, my body taking up immense space in the depart- ment offices, my cane crashing off of the wall and into a table, the cubbies where paperwork appears, demanding responses from those well enough to show up in person regularly without the scrim of crazy coming too loose and retreating home to recover a mask of professionalism before the next time.

I feel feral. I hold shame for feeling feral. I turn primal around authority, like a cat whose fur stands on end in the face of a threat, ready to pounce and maul. I was raised by two psychiatrically disabled parents in the 1990s, when mental illness was not discussed openly. My father's bouts in psychiat- ric facilities were called "business trips" to the rest of the family. By the time he was homeless, I was old enough to tell people he was dead. My mother's hoarding disorder is still hidden from everyone except the landlords who evict her when she can no longer pay rent or they try to do routine main- tenance and witness the profundity of her compulsions. I am the product of manic whims and compulsive behaviors sewn together by erraticness. You can't blame me for being this way. But I am often given the benefit of the doubt because I am white, thin, cis-passing. My body is not coded as a threat, and that means I have privilege in many spaces that people who are systemically minoritized do not. Amid what Black studies scholars understand as a plantation politics that polices and sorts the bodies and spa- tial organization of Black people in institutionalized spaces (Shange 2019; Williams, Squire, and Tuitt 2021), I am not subjected to the same levels of surveillance, harassment, and carcerality as my BIPOC peers frequently are (Maldonado and Meiners 2021). Nor do I experience the severity of the kind of literal "pushout"—to use the words of Monique Morris (2016) and Eve Tuck (2013)—that multiply marginalized people are often subjected to. And I am specifically immune from the effects of the toxic nexus of anti-Blackness and ableism, which Talila "TL" Lewis describes as "mutually inclusive and mutually dependent" (2020, par. 7; see also Erevelles 2014).

Making an effort to lean into slurs I have been called hurts. I write a scathing course evaluation for a professor I was meant to work with. He harassed me, screamed at me in class for asking for more than five minutes to give a presentation I spent weeks developing. When I asked to see what my classmates write in their course evaluations, classmates who mostly ignored my obvious pain, I read that they marked "satisfactory" or "above expectations." They did not write, "Harasses the only queer, fat, disabled femme in our class." And now, because I have told the truth of my experience, I am crazy.

My Madness leaves me self-conscious in the academy and perpetually reflective of how my personal behavior might translate in the classroom. My thoughts are cacophony, my speech can be chaotic. I change registers quickly, gesture wildly, stomp around, and usually make my students laugh. The laughter isn't at my expense, though: the laughter is at my wild humanity, my transparency about the bullshit system we find ourselves functioning (or not) within at the expense of our bodyminds.

Here is a place for me to collect and collate some of those fragments: a crazy femme archive of navigating doctoral work while losing it completely, getting sicker and sicker, housebound, wrung out, jammed with catheters and muscle relaxers for my body spiraling into sickness. Here I can reject sense making and instead embrace nonsensical expression, planning without a net, sending ideas out into the formless void now made solid; here I have a space to contain the crazy, the femme abject, the content I make while lost in a pain-muddied astral haze.

If they were supposed to be *authorities*, then I never felt safe.

Receipts

Jesse: *I have spent every class session fully dissociated. I remember nothing. I instead ask a few friends:* What did I promise this time? How can I keep my word if I can't remember what I've done?

To be a crazy femme in academia means, for me, a devout therapy and self-care practice. Having access to some of the class privilege that accompanies academia—an access that is nonetheless often out of reach for disabled BIPOC academics—has translated into more care for my body-mind. Such care feels unsustainable because it is, but it's mandatory if I am to loosen trauma's incessant grip on my mind in order to write, read, or think.

We do not have to play-act being machines when we are not. I am not, though academia demonstrates again and again that this is the expectation. Instead, I should block off the fury, rage, apathy, pain, anguish, frustration—all the emotions that mark my craziness. What I know: craziness is not a switch I can flip. I can manage what I face through a practice of mutual care (Piepzna-Samarasinha 2018; Spade 2020), a practice I demonstrate to my students and colleagues through my care, my flexibility, my loud solidarity with anyone remotely marginalized by the institutions we must navigate.

My ethics: academia is an ableist, white-supremacist institution made elite through the myth of meritocracy and concomitant gatekeeping (Ferguson 2012; Guinier 2016). Those who survive believe they have earned their spot. Usually they have not.

Andréa: When I put together my second-year Portfolio Assignment and submitted it to the English Department reviewers, I wear my "I don't give a fuck how they see me" shield, feign brave, and click "send." Four months after submission, I receive an email that I failed a few sections, and my face immediately goes flush. I feel exposed. Here are some of the comments members of the committee made:

- "The annotations in the annotated bibliography are not real annotations, but a collection of dismissals charging these sources with advancing white supremacy."
- "The presentation of portions of this portfolio are too intensely personal to lead to a scholarly contribution."
- "The pedagogical account does not articulate its rationale clearly and within a scholarly body of work, which is especially disappointing for someone working in pedagogy."

I read these comments, ready to fight. I email Jesse and a couple of other femmes in my program, "wtf is this?," and they respond with the appropriate amount of actionable frustration. I can accept criticism, but getting called out for calling out white supremacy and being told that my writing is "too intensely personal to lead to a scholarly contribution" feel like acid poured over my most vulnerable parts. Following quickly behind the rage is a full-body exhaustion, the "I don't have the energy to fight these stodgy academics" exhaustion that renders me frozen for a couple of days. How many times do I need to be told I'm wrong before I believe it? How many times do I have to fight against an old guard's fixed and immovable beliefs before I surrender? Every time I get one of these bullshit/gatekeepy responses from my department, I think of my students. I cry a lot. If the department is willing to treat me this way, how do they treat my multiply marginalized peers? How do they treat my students? I cry more.

The semester when my professor screamed at me in front of the whole class, I self-harmed for the first time in twelve years. Life was happening fast, as it does, and empathy provided only a small cushion from the brutal reality of a PhD program. Being asked to work in a genre you cannot ethically support is a kind of harm. Continuing this work untethered from the department paying you to labor in its name is a kind of harm.

In truth, I feel guilt for the damage these harms have accrued in me. My whiteness shields me from the cruel white supremacy that permeates graduate curricula (Gutiérrez y Muhs et al. 2012); it contributes to my ability to slough off the labels I am assigned by department administration (difficult, demanding, entitled). My students often experience anti-Blackness, colorism, and racism (Kynard 2013), distinct from the discriminatory patterns that I experience as a white, autistic, fat, and physically disabled graduate worker. But wringing my hands over difference and privilege is its own kind of harm. I have to believe it is possible to acknowledge both this harm and the forces that insulate me from some of the worst abuses I have witnessed: the institutional, embedded structures organized against Black and trans women scholars, Brown and immigrant scholars, other sick and disabled scholars.

I am aware of my bodymind *because* of my Madness, not in spite of it. My Madness transmutes emotions, pain, and traumas into a way of knowing, deeply felt epistemologies of self and community care. This perspective is not widely accepted by faculty, who treat "emotionality and intellectuality as adversaries" (Price 2011, 51). This positionality comes at a cost; my jaw clenches, and the searing headaches begin, simultaneously numbing my neck and shooting pain through the right side of my face. I have always assumed that this pain signals that something is wrong with *me*, and I only recently realized that my pain is a response to being neurodivergent in a neurotypical-privileging field. I find comfort reading other scholars who have honored their emotionality, including Gillian Bayne (2014), Carmen Kynard (2019), and Aja Martinez (2020).

Even before the harassment and ableism I experienced in my doctoral program, I had bumped against constant messages that academia wasn't for me. Despite the privileges accrued by my whiteness, my class and financial privilege, and my parents spending many years as a faculty member and an administrator at a medium-size public university—not to mention the ease with which I breezed through coursework, my hair-trigger mood—my assertive speaking style and large body, my visible queerness and mobility aids marked me as Other enough to warrant near-constant gaslighting, resource withdrawal, and harassment from faculty and administrators. And then my less visible attributes—my anarchist, antifascist politics, abolitionist and pro-trans ethics, and public work against white supremacy—began to contribute material to the growing folio of my unprofessionalism, my noncompliance.

Of course, my noncompliance is manifold: my medical files, dispersed across distance and time, might also reflect my disagreement with misdiagnoses and refusal to participate in various treatments: an institutional history of pushback, self-awareness, shielding against institutional mismanagement of my bodymind. My embodied identities and subjective experiences—as a crazy, recently working-class, fat, southern, sick femme—have been weaponized against me again and again. At what point can I claim expertise in my own marginalization?

My list of official complaints has grown into an epic. Each new year of doctoral study, my access needs are denied and disrespected; my language is labeled too aggressive or intense; I am advised to "make eye contact" and to perform neurotypicality in the classroom. My body takes up too much space. I say "no" too much. I save emails and file complaints, crazily.

My course-observation report from a City College of New York (CCNY) English faculty member reads, "She clearly has a good rapport with her students but acts so lively it starts to come off as silly, like she is goofing off." Expressing authentic enthusiasm in front of my students gets interpreted as "silliness" instead of what it is: neurodivergence in action. I nervously laugh off this assessment. Good student rapport is not the valued marker here; preserving the standardized academic register is.

My intention is not to replicate the white-supremacist, sanist, and elitist logics of higher education. It is, instead, to illustrate that if being Mad in academia harms and silences me, a white, cis-passing femme with graduate-educated parents, deeming my words unsane, then the respectability politics that polices the discourses of those with less protections, less layers of privilege, must be immeasurably harmful and especially toxic for those navigating the intersection of anti-Blackness and ableism (Bailey and Mobley 2019). Crazy femme pedagogy calls for witnessing, for signal boosting, for speaking up in committee meetings, for holding space for others to speak, for practicing what Yanira Rodríguez (2019) calls a "pedagogy of refusal" in defiance of institutional silencing. I see you. We do not have to be afraid.

Classrooms

Andréa: I've started to imagine education and pedagogy nonlinearly as a refusal of white-supremacist Western linear logic (Wynter 2006) as it intersects with ableism. I started to imagine this a couple of years ago, before the call to remote learning was born out of COVID-19. My disabilities don't process neatly in chunks of written text such as essays or journal papers. I find myself more frequently scattered. Scattered on my hardwood living-room floor, legs splayed out, color markers everywhere, and some blank notebooks that could contain everything neatly if only I could get it all down. I lend some of this Madness to my Gemini sun—I can often be found out in the stratosphere—and rarely do I come back down to Earth on my own. The markers ground me. The notebooks ground me. But I bounce quickly between nascent projects, and the landing, the dismount, always feels like a crash.

All of my amended course policies and procedures were born out of my own necessity; I didn't yet have the vocabulary around centering access but retrospectively realized that is how I run my classroom. My pedagogy leads with femme intuition because I know that if my privileged (white, cis, disabled academic) self struggles with navigating the performance of academia, then my CCNY students, many of whom are multiply marginalized, must experience these struggles, too—a dynamic that Black feminist scholars such as Savannah Shange (2019) and Carmen Kynard (2013, 2019, 2020) attest to again and again. It feels unconscionable, harmful, to set expectations for them that I cannot accomplish myself—the expectation of biweekly in-person learning is really hard for me, even though when I get in the classroom, I love it.

I teach a couple of different composition courses, including Writing for Engineering and a first-year writing cohort course with Jesse called the Freshman Inquiry Writing Seminar (FIQWS), a themed first-year composition class paired with a "subject" course. In the course's ideal form, a collaboration emerges between the writing instructor and the "subject" instructor; unfortunately, the precarious position of many writing instructors often results in a power imbalance. Most of the "subject" instructors are full-time and/or tenure-track faculty with job security, and the hierarchical nature of the academy enables faculty with stability to assume that the writing instructors they are paired with will function as a kind of teaching assistant. The most successful FIQWS pairings are invariably between two part-time adjunct instructors, as in the case of Jesse, who taught the "subject" sections of our FIQWS courses, and me, the writing instructor. After initial pushback from the English Department, I now exclusively teach this course as a hybrid course.

Jesse: As a student, I have no choice but to embody crazy femme pedagogy: unable to respond to time-sensitive emails and requests for documentation except the one day a week when my meds work without the side effects of cognitive slowing and sleeping until 1:00 p.m. In class, I cannot avoid my endless questions, problematization, pushing toward liberation. An agentic force, I cannot even see another possible form of myself as student besides the one that I am. Those who practice crazy femme study don't make many friends and find themselves on the sharp end of complaint, the edges of disciplinarity, careening into other scholars' comfort. The pedagogy must not only become the praxis but also become praxis. Indeed, there isn't another way at all. The crazy femme pedagogue carries that anti-institutional ethos

Crazy Femme Pedagogies 275

away from the classroom, for better or worse for their loved ones, sometimes driving a languaged line between the femme pedagogue and others: those who have failed her extreme ethical standards of "femme 4 femme," "trust no institutional authority."

In the fall 2018 semester, while teaching "That's so Gay!,"—our hybrid composition and queer studies seminar, I am tasked with codeveloping a workshop on assessing student work on the open-pedagogy site I work for. I am no good at leaving out my biases: they're not really biases if they're objectively correct. I am not sleeping and am rippling with anxiety. In the middle of this work meeting, I realize that none of the words leaving everyone's mouths makes any sense, like when you say "cupcupcupcupcupcupcupcup-cupcup" until it's just sound, then nothing.

When it gets like this for me, I can't think big picture: the semester a blank, the year a melded pool, things that just happened slip far far down. I can still feel, but barely. Mostly it's rage, a primal kind of fury like a simmering trough from which I can drink, but never enough.

What a startling wall to run into: I feel as if I can no longer learn because I haven't learned yet while doing this graduate program, my brain waning and dissolving. I can't think if I am constantly getting sick, if I am up until 7:00 a.m. for no reason, if my medications can't stabilize, if my anxiety is choking, disappearing into things I know I can succeed at.

One of Andréa's students asks for clarity on the topic they've been discussing the entire class period. "I was in the ether," he says. I empathize.

Here are the instructions and expectations we are given as writing instructors to pass out to students:

> Students are expected to attend every class session of this course and be on time. If you miss five classes, your final grade will be dropped by one-half of one letter (a 90 to an 85 for example). If you miss six classes, your final grade will be dropped one full letter. If you miss seven classes, you will not be able to pass the course. Consistent late arrivals and early departures will have a negative impact on your grade. I will notify you by email if your course absences (for full or partial classes) are having an impact on your grade. If you have special circumstances, please see me. I am happy to work with you to help you complete this course.

Punitive assumptions aside, I read this, and I'm confused. I need to do math and surveille my students' in-person presence? And I am expected to privilege in-person learning when some mornings I can barely talk myself out of bed? Where should I even keep this record of attendance? On my phone? In a notebook? I toss out the policy because, in addition to being difficult to understand, it replicates all the institutional systems of harm (sanism, ableism, white supremacy) that I am working tirelessly to eliminate from my classroom. If I have to struggle to make it to class biweekly between navigating my other rent-paying jobs and my inconsistent mental health, then I deliberately give my students the same space and understanding that I need to make it through the week.

Once we pivot to a hybrid course, the in-person attendance falls away. I have discussions with my students about keeping up with the pace of class but also recognize that what I perceive as a benefit to seeing them in person might be more of a burden for them to accomplish—an 8:00 a.m. class two hours from their homes, followed by a full day of scattered courses, only to get home at 9:00 p.m.? Unsustainable—but the institution demands it anyway, and the students are quick to meet the demand despite whatever toll it takes on them. This model assumes that students don't also bear other responsibilities of caregiving and working, the administrative burden of being poor and working class, and the impact all this has on their emotional health and capacity.

Instead, I ask students to complete short low-stakes writing/reading assignments, which is already a typical request in a composition course. These "assignments" are often reflective-process prompts that they put in a repository such as Google Drive and I look over when I get a chance. I try to make instructions for the benefit of my students, not just for the benefit of me.

The first day of class, I assign three short readings that explain the purpose and goals behind our course projects: my "ungrade (no grade)" policy, which I adapt from Jesse Stommel's (2017, 2018) work; our weekly "labor logs" to track writing and reading, adapted from Asao Inoue's (2015) contracts and labor logs from the Antiracist Writing Assessment; and, finally, my own policies of not taking attendance or tracking punctuality, developed from my

Crazy Femme Pedagogies   277

own pedagogy with support from Margaret Price's book Mad at School: Rhetorics of Mental Disability and Academic Life *(2011).*

The following class we spend all of our time explicating the readings and these policies, discussing their goals and collaboratively brainstorming strategies for fulfilling the assignment guidelines while allowing room for creativity. Collaborating and embracing flexibility of genre, project, deadline, writing style are essential to crazy femme pedagogical praxis, which centers access needs and community responsibilities above the products created for academic courses.

Most CCNY students come for the school's STEM programs, a population of primarily Black and Brown New Yorkers who commute to campus from all five boroughs of New York City. Many students are first-generation Americans, visa holders, recently immigrated, and/or undocumented. These identities as well as my own as a queer disabled femme add to the complexity of the classroom experience because of the current precarity around all these intersections, but they shape my pedagogical approach, which centers access, intersectionality, and sociopolitical context.

That first day I also brought up that CCNY undergraduates will likely not have Black professors, queer professors, Brown professors. A young Black woman student said, "You just blew my MIND," and continued muttering her astonishment for several minutes. Although this woman and many of our students are feminists, these feminist embodiments are shaped by the overwhelming cultural impact of white feminism, which places considerations about gender and sex above considerations of race, class, disableism, and all of the other immense and powerful forms of oppression that mark us.

As an adjunct, I typically teach two courses a semester: one that my PhD fellowship pays for and one that I get paid for as faculty. Two courses at an overcrowded, underfunded public college means at least fifty-four students completing four or five major writing assignments, all of which include multiple draft submissions. If you do the math, it's an incredible amount of labor to review and offer comments, especially with a quick turnaround time. As I became increasingly incapable of reviewing student work at the pace it was coming in, I started to loosen my assignment-submission policy. Now I offer a few options to students: a formal deadline for students who want to move on to what they have in other, more stringent courses and a flexible deadline for students who might need more time. I often just tell the latter to get their work to me when they can; we don't need to negotiate dates unless the boundary is helpful to them. In response to this flexibility, I always hear "But it's more work for us!" from faculty who think hard deadlines will somehow relieve the overburden of student submissions. I can promise, after having done rolling submissions now as a disabled scholar over the course of a few semesters, that it is much easier to contend with than forcing myself to fit in the academic mold. What might seem like a small shift in classroom procedure, then, also reflects how my approach to teaching prioritizes flexibility and criticality of status quo pedagogical norms.

There are no penalties for feeling stuck, missing a deadline, spacing an assignment, missing a weekly response, misspelling a word, missing the hourly bus that lifts them from work to school, forgetting to schedule a meeting with me and Andréa. I, too, forget, and I am not penalized. Crazy femme pedagogy does not punish anyone for being human, for having needs, for caregiving, for failing. Students who are unable to prioritize their coursework above the rest of their complex lives are so often disciplined, a practice that embraces and centers surveillance culture and harms students. To admit my own flaws—even to embrace flaws as important characteristics of empathic, courageous, and complex humans—and to acknowledge that my emotions take up a large chunk of my internal life are to demonstrate a rhetoric of care, a femme pedagogy, that my students deserve, that I deserve from my own instructors but rarely get.

Teaching is its own therapeutic, challenging practice. Crazy femme pedagogy must be care oriented, adaptive, and access driven. Following M. Remi Yergeau (2018), Margaret Price (2011), and other disabled instructors and thinkers—Jay Timothy Dolmage (2005, 2014, 2017), Eli Clare (2017), Leah Lakshmi Piepzna-Samarasinha (2018)—as well as radical Black femmes (Barbara Smith [1977], Jacqueline Jones Royster [1996], Carmen Kynard [2013, 2019, 2020], Monique Morris [2016], and Audre Lorde [2020], among others), I integrate my own stories into my pedagogical work.

My students' experiences elsewhere in academia have trained them to function as academic machines; in my classes, we all are people doing our best under often impossible circumstances. When I disclose my undiagnosed neurological illness(es), it is both a request and a rhetorical choice: establishing our class as a space where generic fluidity, fluid capacity, and being bad at words are all part of a process of growing ourselves as curious scholars of our shared world.

Futures?

Jesse: After class, students drift up to my table, asking for a private word. It is midterm season, and their other teachers don't accept late work, don't do makeup exams or assignments. One student is the primary caregiver for her disabled sibling; another is celebrating her child's birthday, and she's stressed knowing how unforgiving full-time faculty are of their students' lives, citing their own demanding jobs and "tough love" pedagogies. Femme pedagogy sees no love in penalizing a young parent for celebrating her child's life, in students surviving.

The future I imagine is filled with students who care for themselves and one another first. Andréa and I have learned that our rest, our tiny community of texts and affirmations, the crystals and love notes we mail to each other are necessary for us to survive. If we can just model our crazy femme pedagogy for enough students, enough faculty, gently enough and with the correct tone and professionalism, we think it will be contagious. Institutional obsession with surveilling and punishing will melt away to reveal the spaces of radical care, vulnerability, and support that have existed in the undercommons all along.

Andréa: It feels funny/ironic to write this now, when it seems as if everyone has suddenly embraced the possibilities of technology—even though a year ago we were still being ostracized in faculty meetings for allowing students to use cellphones in class. Aside from allowing us to teach in a hybrid way, technology use has always been about student accessibility. The deliberate inclusion of these possibilities for attendance, technology, and assignments is essential to crazy femme pedagogy. Not all of my students have a computer, but most have a device. Why would I ban their technological tools and skills from my classroom? The policies become part of the praxis. My hope is that with the general incorporation of these policies into institutional documents (syllabi), the language of access and crazy femme pedagogy will begin to seep into the culture of the institution. Crazy femme pedagogy is rooted in care, and if we are able to discuss this framework transparently with our students, it is possible that they will take this language with them wherever they go throughout their coursework and implement it there.

I don't assume that students are late or absent because of their own mismanaged time; I assume subways, late coworkers, childcare difficulties, an additional shift on the day rent is due. I have witnessed other faculty and graduate workers make assumptions about CCNY students based on the twin pillars of ableism and anti-Blackness, a dynamic that disability critical race scholars such as Subini A. Annamma explicitly trace.[1] I wonder, based on my own struggles, about when my students last ate, how much they've slept, what chores they've put off to attend my class. I can't teach any way other than remotely now because of my own chronic pain and fatigue but also because I know my students need rest. Crazy femme pedagogy mandates rest, recuperation, breaks, care work.

I am deeply lucky: much of my resistance to this oppressive system comes from my proximity to a few other disabled scholars and allies in my academic community. We push back against the white-centered, individualistic/meritocratic framework by focusing on community and interdependence. Without my collaborator and work wife Jesse, I would have walked away or been kicked out (more likely the latter) because to navigate academia alone is to buy into the normative narrative of individuality and meritocracy that I just can't fit into. I need interdependence. I need to be able to ask for help and support. I need it to be OK to ask for help

---

1. For examples of this discussion in Annamma's work, see authored works such as "'When You Carry a Lot': The Forgotten Spaces of Youth Prison Schooling for Incarnated Disabled Girls of Color" (Cabral, Annamma, and Morgan 2023) and "Beyond Making a Statement: An Intersectional Framing of the Power and Possibilities of Positioning" (Boveda and Annamma 2023).

Crazy Femme Pedagogies   281

and support. In crazy femme pedagogical solidarity, support is a necessary form of care.

The greatest gift is discovering that my stripe of crazy actually matches some others': my coauthor and I became friends after laughing hysterically at an out-of-touch passage in an assigned text for a class we took. My discomfort often emerges as laughter, especially in charged authoritative institutional spaces, and so does hers. When neither of us apologized for these outbursts, I felt a kinship. We began sitting together, talking after class, meeting for late lunches and cocktails, cackling wildly over free bread at the Italian place on Amsterdam Avenue. She never apologized, and neither did I. We didn't have to.

Works Cited

Bailey, Moya, and Izetta Autumn Mobley. 2019. "Work in the Intersections: A Black Feminist Disability Framework." *Gender & Society* 33, no. 1: 19–40. At https://doi.org/10.1177/0891243218880152.

Bayne, Gillian. 2014. "Utilizing Insider Perspectives to Reflect Upon and Change Urban Science Education." In *Transforming Urban Education: Urban Teachers and Students Working Collaboratively*, edited by Ashraf Shady and Kenneth Tobin, 303–20. Rotterdam: Sense.

Boveda, Mildred, and Subini Ancy Annamma. 2023. "Beyond Making a Statement: An Intersectional Framing of the Power and Possibilities of Positioning." *Educational Psychology, Counseling, and Special Education* 52, no. 5: 306–14. At https://pure.psu.edu/en/publications/beyond-making-a-statement-an-intersectional-framing-of-the-power-.

Cabral, Brian, Subini Ancy Annamma, and Jamelia Morgan. 2023. "'When You Carry a Lot': The Forgotten Spaces of Youth Prison Schooling for Incarcerated Disabled Girls of Color." *Teachers College Record: The Voice of Scholarship in Education* 125, no. 5: 95–113. At https://doi.org/10.1177/0161468 1231181816.

Christian, Barbara. 2007. *New Black Feminist Criticism, 1985–2000*. Edited by Arlene Keizer, Gloria Bowles, and M. Giulia Fabi. Champaign: Univ. of Illinois Press.

Clare, Eli. 2017. *Brilliant Imperfection: Grappling with Cure*. Durham, NC: Duke Univ. Press.

Collins, Patricia Hill. 2008. *Black Feminist Thought: Knowledge, Consciousness, and the Politics of Empowerment*. New York: Routledge.

Dolmage, Jay Timothy. 2005. "Disability Studies Pedagogy, Usability and Universal Design." *Disability Studies Quarterly* 25, no. 4. At https://dsq-sds.org/article/view/627/804.

———. 2014. *Disability Rhetoric*. Syracuse, NY: Syracuse Univ. Press.

———. 2017. *Academic Ableism: Disability and Higher Education*. Ann Arbor: Univ. of Michigan Press.

Erevelles, Nirmala. 2014. "Crippin' Jim Crow: Disability, Dis-location, and the School-to-Prison Pipeline." In *Disability Incarcerated: Imprisonment and Disability in the United States and Canada*, edited by Liat Ben-Moshe, Chris Chapman, and Allison C. Carey, 81–99. New York: Palgrave MacMillan.

Ferguson, Roderick. 2012. *The Reorder of Things: The University and Its Pedagogies of Minority Difference*. Minneapolis: Univ. of Minnesota Press.

Guinier, Lani. 2016. *The Tyranny of the Meritocracy: Democratizing Higher Education in America*. Boston: Beacon Press.

Gutiérrez y Muhs, Gabriella, Yolanda Flores Niemann, Carmen G. Gonzalez, and Angela P. Harris, eds. 2012. *Presumed Incompetent: The Intersections of Race and Class for Women in Academia*. Boulder: Univ. Press of Colorado for Utah State Univ. Press.

Harney, Stefano, and Fred Moten. 2013. *The Undercommons: Fugitive Planning & Black Study*. London: Minor Compositions.

hooks, bell. 1994. *Teaching to Transgress: Education as the Practice of Freedom*. New York: Routledge.

Inoue, Asao. 2015. *Antiracist Writing Assessment Ecologies: Teaching and Assessing Writing for a Socially Just Future*. Anderson, SC: Parlor Press.

Kynard, Carmen. 2013. *Vernacular Insurrections: Race, Black Protest, and the New Century in Composition-Literacy Studies*. New York: State Univ. of New York Press.

———. 2019. "Administering While Black: Black Women's Labor in the Academy and the 'Position of the Unthought.'" In *Black Perspectives in Writing Program Administration: From the Margins to the Center*, edited by Staci M. Perryman-Clark and Collin Lamont Craig, 28–50. Champagne, IL: NCTE/CCCC.

———. 2020. "For Black Feminists Who Have Considered Solidarity When the Academy Is Enuf." *Education, Liberation, and Black Radical Traditions for the 21st Century* (blog), June 18. http://carmenkynard.org/for-black-feminists-who-have-considered-solidarity-when-the-academy-is-enuf/.

Lewis, Talila "TL." 2020. "Why I Don't Use 'Anti-Black Ableism' (& Language Longings)." *Talila A. Lewis* (blog), Aug. 17. At https://www.talilalewis.com/blog/why-i-dont-use-anti-black-ableism.

Lorde, Audre. 2020. *Audre Lorde: Dream of Europe: Selected Seminars and Interviews: 1984–1992*. Chicago: Kenning Editions.

Maldonado, David A., and Erica R. Meiners. 2021. "Due Time: Meditations on Abolition at the Site of the University." *Social Text* 39, no. 1: 69–92. At https://doi.org/10.1215/01642472-8750112.

Martinez, Aja Y. 2020. *Counterstory: The Rhetoric and Writing of Critical Race Theory*. Urbana, IL: Conference on College Composition and Communication.

Morris, Monique W. 2016. *Pushout: The Criminalization of Black Girls in Schools*. New York: New Press.

Piepzna-Samarasinha, Leah Lakshmi. 2018. *Care Work: Dreaming Disability Justice*. Vancouver: Arsenal Pulp Press.

Price, Margaret. 2011. *Mad at School: Rhetorics of Mental Disability and Academic Life*. Ann Arbor: Univ. of Michigan Press.

Reed, Conor Tomás. 2023. *New York Liberation School: Study and Movement for the People's University*. Brooklyn, NY: Common Notions.

Rodríguez, Yanira. 2019. "Pedagogies of Refusal: What It Means to (Un)Teach a Student Like Me." *Radical Teacher* 115:5–12. At https://www.jstor.org/stable/48694739.

Royster, Jacqueline Jones. 1996. "When the First Voice You Hear Is Not Your Own." *College Composition and Communication* 47, no. 1: 29–40. At https://www.jstor.org/stable/358272.

Shange, Savannah. 2019. *Progressive Dystopia: Abolition, Antiblackness, and Schooling in San Francisco*. Durham, NC: Duke Univ. Press.

Smith, Barbara. 1977. "Toward a Black Feminist Criticism." *The Radical Teacher* 7:20–27. At https://www.jstor.org/stable/20709102.

Spade, Dean. 2020. *Mutual Aid: Building Solidarity during This Crisis (and the Next)*. Brooklyn, NY: Verso.

Stommel, Jesse. 2017. "Why I Don't Grade." Jesse Stommel (website), Oct. 26. At https://www.jessestommel.com/why-i-dont-grade/.

———. 2018. "How to Ungrade." Jesse Stommel (website), Mar. 11. At https://www.jessestommel.com/how-to-ungrade/.

Tuck, Eve. 2013. "Neoliberalism as Nihilism? A Commentary on Educational Accountability, Teacher Education, and School Reform." *Journal for Critical*

Education Policy Studies 11, no. 2: 324–47. At http://www.jceps.com/wp-content/uploads/PDFs/11-2-10.pdf.

Williams, Bianca C., Dian D. Squire, and Frank A. Tuitt, eds. 2021. *Plantation Politics and Campus Rebellions: Power, Diversity, and the Emancipatory Struggle in Higher Education*. New York: State Univ. of New York Press.

Williams, Patricia J. 1992. *Alchemy of Race and Rights: Diary of a Law Professor*. Cambridge, MA: Harvard Univ. Press.

Wynter, Sylvia. 2006. "Black Education, toward the Human, after 'Man': In the Manner of a Manifesto: Framing a Transformative Research and Action Agenda for the New Millennium." In *Black Education: A Transformative Research and Action Agenda for the New Century*, rev. ed., edited by Joyce E. King, 357–59. Washington, DC: American Educational Research Association.

Yergeau, M. Remi. 2018. *Authoring Autism: On Rhetoric and Neurological Queerness*. Durham, NC: Duke Univ. Press.

Part Four

Mad Imaginaries
From Kinship to Community

As a collection of Mad scholarship, this anthology most urgently calls for a shift in how we construct and relate to academic community. If we are to truly thrive as Mad scholars, then our institutions must be profoundly transformed. To do this work, we need to dream collectively: What might a Mad academic future look like? What could these transformations motivate us toward? What new pathways might we create that support *all* our bodyminds?[1] Dreaming is a tool of change for multiply marginalized communities (Lewis 2018), and the Mad scholars in this concluding section dream us forward into robust kinship communities.

So much of this dreamwork is contingent on recognition, on our ability to construct communities where we can find one another. Sarah Smith (she/her) and Grace Wedlake (she/her) write that this kind of kinship creates "ongoing coalitions among Mad and disabled people that

---

1. Disability justice activists, led by the performance project Sins Invalid in the San Francisco Bay Area, developed and crafted one vision of moving forward with no bodymind left behind in *Skin, Tooth, and Bone: The Basis of Movement Is Our People* (Sins Invalid 2016). Such collectivity and cross-movement organizing are critical to our movement-building framework.

provide important alternative routes of care when institutions inevitably fail us." These routes become crucial outlets, the places we turn to in order to salvage and heal the parts of us that academia has diminished and restrained. For Sarah Arvey Tov (she/her), they embolden us to continue sensing our way forward as a collective: "Although Madness may come with hurt, indescribable mood shifts, and deep depression, Mad solidarity opens space for Mad joy in connectedness and belonging." In these pockets of solidarity, we are welcomed to cocreate, to imagine, to dream without shame.[2] We are urged to craft a "Mad anchor," as Tov describes it, that allows us to explore the beauty of our oceans and the wonder of their depths.

In many ways, Mad scholars find one another through our tenderness, our sensitivity, and our empathy. We also do so through humor and the liberation that can come from laughter amid pain. Kim Fernandes (they/them) charts such paths when examining how meme culture helps Mad students form online communities of support. These unorthodox pathways to community and solidarity help us feel seen, heard, and held in ways that are alien to the initiatives launched by university health programs. Yet much of the work of cultivating our Mad futures also occurs in the pause, in moments of stillness and reflection. When we slow down, or perhaps when we recline exhausted on our sofas, we reflect on the institutional practices that require the greatest shifting. For Shayda Kafai (she/her), this work begins internally with a Mad phenomenology: as "beings-in-the-world" (Toombs 1988, 202), we search for and create new orientations, tethers that urge us toward both self and communal homecoming.

2. Sharing needs without shame is central to the ninth principle of disability justice (Berne and Levins Morales 2018).

While some of these chapters explore political healing strategies within academia, others describe how Mad kinship exists only outside of the university. This divergence encourages us to think of how Mad kinship webs can coexist, of how we don't always find ourselves in the same ways, in the same places. While Diane R. Wiener (she/they) explores how uncovering as a "Mad professor" in the university, with all of its "enriching and troubling" effects, encourages community creation, Holly Pearson (she/her) argues that "what we are looking for" cannot be found in academia owing to its central tenets of hyperproductivity and privilege.

We hope that these lived experiences offer the seedlings for such messy, dynamic, transformative change. So much unlearning needs to happen; so many new networks of solidarity, of shared dreaming, of radical reimagining need to be grown. As you approach this closing part, dear reader, consider: What futures do you wish to forge, and who is there with you?

Works Cited

Berne, Patty, and Aurora Levins Morales. 2018. "Ten Principles of Disability Justice." *WSQ: Women's Studies Quarterly* 46, no. 1: 227–30. At https://doi.org/10.1353/wsq.2018.0003.

Lewis, Talila "TL." 2018. "the birth of resistance: courageous dreams, powerful nobodies & revolutionary madness." In *Resistance and Hope: Essays by Disabled People. Crip Wisdom for the People,* edited by Alice Wong, 56–66. N.p.: Disability Visibility Project.

Sins Invalid. 2016. *Skin, Tooth, and Bone: The Basis of Movement Is Our People.* San Francisco: Sins Invalid.

Toombs, S. Kay. 1988. "Illness and the Paradigm of Lived Body." *Theoretical Medicine* 9, no. 2: 201–26. At https://doi.org/10.1007/BF00489413.

17

Mad Resilience, Mad Kinship

Alternative Responses to Student Mental Health Crises

Sarah Smith and Grace Wedlake

> *Content notes*: suicide, police brutality,
> murder, racially motivated violence

Student mental health is at the forefront of many university initiatives as the call to recognize the overwhelming number of students in distress continues to grow. Queen's University in Kingston, Ontario, Canada, has been working on initiatives to support student mental health since the early 2010s, when a series of student suicides alerted the administration that further support was needed (Wong 2011). Despite ongoing awareness efforts, mental health support at Queen's and Canadian universities more broadly has remained entrenched within neoliberal ideology, which prioritizes student resiliency and fails to address inequities in order to maintain the status quo of the institution (Aubrecht 2019). We reject this formulation of student distress and these models of resiliency to instead forge a pathway to resilience for ourselves and others through our Mad kinship, relying on our interdependence rather than on the institution for support. Both of us enter this work as Mad-identified scholars and mental health advocates who have been failed in various ways by our university mental health services.

In this chapter, we acknowledge the key role of forming countercommunities and alternative approaches to mental health support spearheaded by Mad people in order to resist and challenge the shortcomings of university mental health initiatives. Specifically, we draw from our experiences crafting alternative crisis documents in the Department of Gender Studies in an effort to address the shortcomings around care for students at Queen's.[1] Through creating these crisis documents, we have crafted both Mad resilience and a "Mad kinship" to help each other survive within and against an institution that is actively working against our success. These alternatives—although unique to our university—provide just one example among the work of many other Mad people who are seeking to recognize broader structural and systemic harms as well as the critical role that community and collective care plays for Mad people in both resisting these harms and supporting one another when so harmed.

The Student Mental Health Crisis and the Neoliberal University

Over the past decade, there has been an increasing focus on the rise of mental health problems among college-age youth and a growing public discourse of concern over what has been labeled the "student mental health crisis" (Henriques 2014; Kao and Mason 2020; Treleaven 2022). In particular, there has been growing attention to the increasing number of student suicides on university campuses across Canada. In response to this crisis, universities have scrambled to improve access to mental health services. As demand continues to increase, many universities have adopted the Stepped Care model: "a system of delivering and monitoring mental health treatment so that the most effective, yet least resource-intensive treatment, is delivered first, only 'stepping up' to intensive/specialist services as required and depending on the level of patient distress or need" (Centre for Innovation in Campus Mental Health n.d.). In Canada, this model of care has been lauded by the Centre for Innovation in Campus Mental Health (CICMH), which argues that the Stepped Care model "prioritizes distribution of limited mental health resources in a way that maximizes effectiveness and best suits the needs of all students" (CICMH 2019, 6).

---

1. Grace worked on this project while completing their master's in the Department of Gender Studies at Queen's University. They are now a PhD candidate in the School of Kinesiology and Health Studies at Queen's. Sarah has graduated and is now a research associate in the Dalla Lana School of Public Health at the University of Toronto.

Mad Resilience, Mad Kinship   291

According to an article written in the 2017–18 academic year, during the previous five years requests for counseling appointments at Queen's had increased by 73 percent. At that time, the ratio of counselors to students was 1 to 1,225 (Dannetta 2019). Recognizing a need for improved services, Queen's turned to the Stepped Care model and implemented a number of policy changes: the reduction of appointment times from fifty to thirty minutes to create more slots for students as well as new partnerships with Empower Me, a "24/7 phone service for crisis situations and scheduled sessions" with counselors and life coaches (Queen's University 2020a), and Therapy Assistance Online, "an online, mobile friendly library of engaging, interactive programs that promote wellness and can help [students] bounce back from challenging times" (Queen's University 2020b). According to Dr. Rina Gupta, head of Counseling Services at Queen's, students at other universities have reported "high levels of satisfaction" with Stepped Care models, and she was confident that the model would operate successfully at Queen's (Danetta 2019).

However, the shift to the Stepped Care model at Queen's has not necessarily made it easier for everyone to access services. Not long after these changes were implemented, one of our university's papers, the *Queen's Journal*, interviewed seventeen students to discuss how the recent changes to the counseling system at Queen's had affected their lives. Overwhelmingly, the students cited new, added stress about competing for same-day appointments (Aiken 2019). While wait times are certainly shorter than the six-week average in previous years, the added stress of "competing" for appointments suggests that the shift to Stepped Care has not been as effective as the university had hoped.

These problems are also indicative of a larger issue. As we were writing this chapter in 2020, Black Lives Matter protests fighting against police brutality and the murder of Black and Indigenous people were taking place all across the United States and Canada. At the time of writing, at least four Canadians had been killed by police during "wellness checks," including Regis Korchinski-Paquet, a Black Indigenous woman living in Toronto; Chantel Moore, a woman from the Tla-o-qui-aht First Nation in British Columbia living in New Brunswick (Ibrahim 2020); D'Andre Campbell, a twenty-six-year-old Black man with schizophrenia living in

Markham (Cooke 2020); and Ejaz Ahmed Choudry, a Black man living in Mississauga (Cooke 2020). In the university context, Mona Wong, an Asian nursing student in Kelowna, British Columbia, was dragged across the floor of her apartment building and stepped on during a wellness check in June 2020 by a Royal Canadian Mounted Police officer, who went to the scene without a mandated mental health nurse due to staff shortages (Woodward 2020). As universities, mental health services, and the police continue to enact violence against Black folx, Indigenous folx, and people of color (BIPOC), we are reminded of the fundamental role that collective care and access play in imagining alternatives to responding to people experiencing mental health crises. The various alternatives to institutional care that we explore in this paper are grounded in the principles of collective care and social justice, organized largely by BIPOC.

What Does Mad Kinship Mean?

During our first year as graduate students at Queen's University, it became evident that the mental health supports available were failing us. While the local hospital and Queen's psychiatrists failed to offer Sarah support on multiple occasions, the Stepped Care counseling services at Queen's proved inadequate for Grace due to their inflexibility. However, this rejection of psychiatric care as problematic is not isolated to us. Mad people, in particular Mad people of color, experience structural and carceral violence through psychiatric care, which often includes forced treatment in the form of medication and involuntary hospitalization (Lebenbaum et al. 2018). Moreover, psychiatry is often unjustly biased against racialized people, labeling as deviant or pathological behaviors that would otherwise go unrecognized in white people, as is often the case with schizophrenia (Metzl 2010). Though the harms of Stepped Care programs may be more indirect than the violations committed by institutional psychiatry more broadly, the inadequacy of campus mental health supports means that many struggling students do not receive support until their crises have escalated to the point where they ultimately end up institutionalized, particularly if they are racialized, queer, and/or trans or take up other marginalized identities. Ableism and sanism are entangled in and upheld by racism, patriarchy, and other systems of oppression; psychiatry is informed

Mad Resilience, Mad Kinship   293

largely by heteropatriarchal and racist ideals of "normalcy," which is reflected in who is institutionalized for exhibiting "abnormal" behaviors (Metzl 2010).

Because of the various institutional failures during our first year at Queen's, we personally had to help each other foster resilience through our kinship. This kinship not only allowed us to survive the institution but helped us forge a new path forward that rejected nondisabled expectations placed on our Mad existences. Our kinship was formed first out of an emotionally intimate friendship—disclosing our Madness and how it affected our ability to navigate the institution. The gravity of this kinship was realized through recognition and understanding of ongoing coalitions among Mad and disabled people that provide important alternative routes of care when institutions inevitably fail us.

We repeatedly have returned to works on care webs and collective or crip-made access, such as Leah Lakshmi Piepzna-Samarasinha's *Care Work* (2018), to learn how communities of mutual care and support are built out of barriers to institutional care and how they are guided particularly by people of color, who have been doing this form of activism for centuries. As Piepzna-Samarasinha (she/they) writes, "Many precolonial (and after) Black, Indigenous and brown communities have complex webs and exchanges of care" (41–42). For example, they highlight several care collectives developed by people of color that they have been a part of, including Creating Collective Access and Sick and Disabled Queers (60). These care webs act as fundamental supports for disabled and Mad people where the systems and institutions have failed them.[2] She also shares the complexities of these care webs in efforts to navigate varying access needs and the reinforcing and overlapping dynamics of race, class, and gender that alter dynamics of care (66). Piepzna-Samarasinha reiterates the fundamental role that care collectives, despite their complexities, play in access for Mad and disabled people, and her work has been foundational to

---

2. Care webs are communities of collective access and mutual aid, usually composed of disabled and/or Mad people, with the goal of supporting people's physical and emotional needs outside of traditional avenues of "care" such as institutional medicine and psychiatry.

our own understandings of collective care. We also believe that part of Mad kinship involves the work of dismantling the very systems that cause distress and inaccessibility as a first step toward building a community of justice, which involves taking a serious look at how systems of power that contribute to and compound ableism, such as racism and colonialism, are part of institutional forms of care.

We recognize that this approach to care was created in response to institutional failures, so applying this framework to an institutional setting may run the risk of perpetuating the very issues it aims to address. Nevertheless, we have learned from those around us, in particular those in the Department of Gender Studies, that it is possible to resist institutional formulations of care with a framework developed outside institutional contexts and that this mobilization is in many cases necessary so long as we are careful—as we often see with antiracist and decolonial work—not to allow this framework to become co-opted or streamlined by the institution. We take up Piepzna-Samarasinha's idea of care webs in our approach to care, both in our personal relationships and within our department, and focus on the goal of *resisting* institutional forms of care, not just trying to change or adapt them to fit within the new framework.

As white people, we also want to acknowledge that in adopting these frameworks of care, we are indebted to those who have created them, specifically, disabled people of color. We use this framework because we recognize that ableism is intimately tied up with racism and colonialism. Thus, any form of resistance against ableist systems must involve the recognition of the intimate relationships between ableism and racism and work to dismantle these structures. We remain cognizant of our white privilege and how we might take it for granted when moving within these institutions while adopting forms of care that are rooted in the experiences and knowledge of disabled people of color. Doing so means committing ourselves to antiracist learning, engaging with the work of queer, disabled, and racialized scholars, naming racism when we see it in both our academic and medical institutions, and working to create cultures of care and support that are antipolicing and anticarceral.

In keeping these origins at the forefront of our understanding of care webs, our friendship has been based largely on the tenets of these communities of solidarity. Central to our Mad kinship is being open with one another about our experiences with Madness and working to understand each other's diagnoses and labels. We respect and support each other's choices of language to describe our experiences, including the adoption of psychiatric labels, whether these choices reflect our own or not. Moreover, we support each other's self-determination. We learn and know each other's needs and preferences for care to ensure that when we are not able to speak for ourselves—particularly in care settings—we can speak on behalf of one another, reflecting the self-determination of the person under care. When navigating formal supports, we fight for access to care on behalf of one another, and we share the therapeutic and professional knowledge we receive, particularly as we have access to different means of support. This approach, although not always perfect, works to protect us from the psychiatric and carceral violence we may be unjustly exposed to if we were without the support of an advocate seeking to ensure we are being cared for as we would wish to be. We advocate for one another for fear of the structural violence we may face otherwise and out of recognition that the neoliberal university structure was never made for us, regardless of the adaptations of care made by the university administration.

Crafting Alternative Approaches

Our project in the Department of Gender Studies came to fruition during the 2018–19 academic year due to our increasing support for one another as Mad colleagues as well as to our mutual criticism of the institutional mental health supports offered on campus. We were originally prompted by the discovery of the Green Folder, one of the guiding institutional documents for responding to mental health crises at Queen's. This two-page reference guide for students, staff, and faculty explains how to identify and respond to students in distress, specifically during emergency situations. As Mad people who understand the abuses that can arise from such interactions, the fact that this document was circulating in our department was distressing to us. Despite the comfort we found in one another, we were faced with and troubled by the complex position of being both the target of these carceral policies as students and the enforcers of this "care" as teaching assistants. The Green Folder was striking, outlining that, "regardless of the circumstances or context, ANY reference to wanting to die/suicide should be taken seriously, and a mental health professional should be contacted" (Queen's Student Affairs 2019). Under the list of emergency contacts were Counseling Services, the Emergency Report Centre, and 911.

As Mad people and as researchers involved in social justice work, we were uncomfortable with the idea that services should be contacted with or without student consent regardless of circumstances and in the case of any reference to suicide, especially with respect to students who are racialized, queer, and/or trans because these groups have historically been more frequently targeted by institutional violence. Though the policy was designed for "protection," calling 911 on a BIPOC student talking about suicide may actually lead to more harm. Thus, these Queen's policies remove the autonomy of the student in distress and fail to consider the complexities both of responding to suicide and of suicidal ideation in general. With this knowledge, we decided the Department of Gender Studies was the right place to begin advocating for a stronger culture of care and awareness about the realities of Mad students because gender studies operates under a disciplinary framework similar to that of Mad studies—one that is ideally grounded in critical theory and social change.

We began by writing a letter addressed to the faculty and staff of the department that highlighted the gaps we had noticed in recognizing Mad studies as a legitimate contributor to the field of gender studies as well as the gaps in support for Mad students and Mad ways of navigating the institution. We soon learned that the dilemma for the department was not that it did not *care* but that it did not have the resources or knowledge to resolve the issues we had highlighted. The faculty and staff shared with us their own concerns—how they, too, did not feel supported, nor did they feel that they were allowed to be openly Mad. Many people were misinformed about the nature of suicidality and the notion of risk and were interested to learn that suicidality or thoughts of self-harm do not always constitute an emergency. In contrast to the Green Folder, which directs those of us faced with a crisis to external "services," this conversation demonstrated that our department was willing to look within and reflect on the aspects of community care that could be incorporated and to better respond to the community's needs as a department made up of differing experiences, abilities, and access to support.

This kind of conversation would not have been possible without our mutual experiences in navigating a sanist institution as Mad academics. Although each of us experiences Madness differently and uses different approaches to combat the isolating experience of being a Mad academic, relying on our mutual support has encouraged us to imagine care for our students and colleagues beyond and outside of institutional services. In isolation, neoliberal institutional solutions become commonplace and difficult to resist or challenge as different obligations pull us in separate directions. However, our relationship as well as our conversation with the faculty and staff in the Department of Gender Studies have reflected the necessity of allyship and alternative means of community care for one another outside of those system structures that enact further violence.

Ultimately, these conversations led to some important changes. Learning that our community was concerned mostly about crises, we were able to turn our attention to specific resources created by Mad-identified folks. To address our community's needs, we created documents outlining information about suicide and how to navigate mental health crises as a community, adapted from similar documents produced by the Icarus Project (now the Fireweed Collective; see Fireweed Collective 2020). We also introduced the concept of personal-crisis directives to provide people with the opportunity to outline the aspects of their Madness that are personally distressing and that make them feel the most at risk and to state their preferences for emergency contacts.[3] For privacy reasons, we have no way to know if others have also used these documents with their supervisor or other faculty or staff members, but our hope is that by making this action plan available, we can not only create alternative practices for responding to crises but also help students, faculty, and staff have more autonomy in any future crisis situations.

---

3. These directives were informed largely by "Crisis Plan and Working through Hard Times" (Copeland 2015), a resource provided online by the Wellness Recovery Action Plan.

Beyond creating space for more open conversation, these alternative crisis documents reinforced our Mad kinship as we came to understand each other's "warning signs" and care preferences through the process of informing others about how these documents would work. Moreover, beyond our department and our kinship, this work acted as a crucial intervention in the university's current neoliberal approach to care, which prioritizes the values of profitability, liability, and productivity. Our hope is that in crafting this Mad kinship between us and working on alternative supports within the Department of Gender Studies, we can open up the space into a community of collective access and care both in and beyond our own university.

Conclusion

As former gender studies students, we have been encouraged to locate our research within actions for social change and to disrupt hierarchies between academic thought and lay knowledge. We believe that this value should extend beyond just research and that it is crucial to draw upon the knowledge of Mad people doing the work outside of academic spaces to help change academic culture. By creating academic environments that are more capable of holding space for difficult emotions and tough conversations, we can make university spaces more accessible for Mad people, which in turn can facilitate the growth of Mad studies scholarship.

Though we have sent our alternative documents to Queen's Counseling Services and hope to engage in more honest conversations with them, our work on these crisis documents has not yet resulted in a radical shift regarding mental health services at Queen's. What our work has achieved, however, is the recognition that we needed to foster Mad kinship with one another and a community of care within the Department of Gender Studies. Our problems are certainly not unique, and our strategies are by no means novel or exhaustive.

The solution to this problem does not lie in fighting for better mental health services, as mainstream discourses seem to suggest, but in crafting alternatives outside of the neoliberal regime. Though public opinion and media discourses surrounding the student mental health crisis are

Mad Resilience, Mad Kinship   299

based in discourses of reform, we believe that we can no longer depend on a system that continually fails us and puts both lives and livelihoods at risk, in particular the lives of those who are marked by racism, sexism, homophobia, and other forms of violence. Although our intervention in the Department of Gender Studies is a relatively small step, we believe that through this work we are creating possibilities for alternative ways to support one another through community and collective care.

As identified throughout this chapter, we are indebted to the work of Mad people, in particular Mad BIPOC who exist both inside and outside the academy, to help us articulate our needs to our department—and sometimes each other—regarding how to navigate mental health crises without involving police or psychiatrists. However, we do believe that sharing our *personal* stories of Mad kinship and how we have fostered Mad resilience is important because it offers an example of how Mad scholars have valuable experience and knowledge to contribute to our university communities. Our shared resilience also points to the importance of having Mad people in academia support one another when the services designed to care for us ultimately fail. We hope that in sharing our stories of Mad resilience and Mad kinship, we have provided an example of how alternative frameworks can work not only to support students, staff, and faculty experiencing distress but also to reject the neoliberal formulation of mental health care that currently dominates the university structure.

Works Cited

Aiken, Rachel. 2019. "Under New System, Students Compete for Same-Day Counseling." *Queen's Journal*, Nov. 21. At https://www.queensjournal.ca /story/2019-11-21/features/under-new-system-students-compete-for-same-day -counselling/.

Aubrecht, Katie. 2019. "The Nothing But: University Student Mental Health and the Hidden Curriculum of Academic Success." *Canadian Journal of Disability Studies* 8, no. 4: 271–92. At https://doi.org/10.15353/cjds.v8i4.535.

Centre for Innovation in Campus Mental Health (CICMH). 2019. "Stepped Care for Post-secondary Campuses: A Promising Model to Improve Access to Mental Health Care on Campus." Sept. At https://campusmentalhealth .ca/wp-content/uploads/2019/09/Stepped-Care-Guide-V13.pdf.

————. n.d. "Stepped Care Approach." At https://campusmentalhealth.ca/toolkits/campus-community-connection/models-frameworks/stepped-care-model/.

Cooke, Alex. 2020. "Recent Deaths Prompt Questions about Police Wellness Checks." *CBC News*, June 23. At https://www.cbc.ca/news/canada/nova-scotia/police-wellness-checks-deaths-indigenous-black-1.5622320.

Copeland, Mary Ellen. 2015. "Crisis Plan and Working through Hard Times." Wellness Recovery Action Plan, July 2. At https://www.wellnessrecoveryactionplan.com/crisis-plan/.

Dannetta, Luca. 2019. "Student Wellness Services Introduces New Model of Care." *Queen's Journal*, July 8. At https://www.queensjournal.ca/story/2019-07-08/news/student-wellness-services-introduces-new-model-of-care/.

Fireweed Collective. 2020. "Navigating Crises." Mar. At https://fireweedcollective.org/wp-content/uploads/2020/03/IcarusNavigatingCrisisHandoutLarge05-09.pdf.

Henriques, Gregg. 2014. "The College Student Mental Health Crisis." *Psychology Today*, Feb. 15. At https://www.psychologytoday.com/ca/blog/theory-knowledge/201402/the-college-student-mental-health-crisis.

Ibrahim, Hadeel. 2020. "Killing of Indigenous Woman Raises Questions about Who Should be Doing Wellness Checks." *CBC News*, June 6. At https://www.cbc.ca/news/canada/new-brunswick/chantel-moore-indigenous-woman-shot-by-police-edmundston-1.5601097.

Kao, Josie, and Zoë Mason. 2020. "How to Make a Crisis: Cracks in Mental Health Care at U of O and U of T." *The Varsity*, Apr. 30. At https://thevarsity.ca/2020/04/30/how-to-make-a-crisis-cracks-in-mental-health-care-at-u-of-o-and-u-of-t/.

Lebenbaum, Michael, Maria Chiu, Simone Vigod, and Paul Kurdyak. 2018. "Involuntary Psychiatric Admissions Have Increased Significantly in Ontario: Study." Centre for Addiction and Mental Health, Feb. 22. At https://www.camh.ca/en/camh-news-and-stories/involuntary-psychiatric-admissions-have-increased-significantly-in-ontario.

Metzl, Jonathan. 2010. *The Protest Psychosis: How Schizophrenia Became a Black Disease*. Boston: Beacon Press.

Piepzna-Samarasinha, Leah Lakshmi. 2018. *Care Work: Dreaming Disability Justice*. Vancouver: Arsenal Pulp Press.

Queen's Student Affairs. 2019. "Identifying and Responding to Students in Distress." Queen's Univ. At https://www.queensu.ca/studentaffairs/sites/webpublish.queensu.ca.vpsawww/files/files/19-0049%20Student%20Affairs%20Green%20Folder%20for%20web.pdf.

Queen's University. 2020a. "Empower Me." At https://www.queensu.ca/student wellness/empower-me/.

———. 2020b. "TAO—Therapy Assistance Online." At https://www.queensu.ca /inclusive/initiatives/student-experiences-survey/support.

Treleaven, Sarah. 2022. "Inside the Mental Health Crisis at Canadian Universities." *MacLeans*, Nov. 14. At https://www.macleans.ca/education/inside-the -mental-health-crisis-at-canadian-universities/.

Wong, Jan. 2011. "How Academic Pressure May Have Contributed to the Spate of Suicides at Queen's University." *Toronto Life*, Sept. 1. At https://torontolife .com/city/queens-university-suicides.

Woodward, John. 2020. "Mental Health Unit Wasn't Staffed on Night B.C. Student Dragged, Stepped on by Cop during Wellness Check." *CTV News*, June 24. At https://bc.ctvnews.ca/mental-health-unit-wasn-t-staffed-on-night-b-c -student-dragged-stepped-on-by-cop-during-wellness-check-1.4998993.

18

Anchoring in Mad Solidarity

Sarah Arvey Tov

> *Content note*: genocide mention and suicide mention

Tattooed on my right ankle is my anchor of Madness. I was in a hypomanic episode after deciding to go off my antidepressants, and my mom took me to the psychoanalyst Ann Ulanov's presentation "Madness and Creativity."[1] I took visual notes, frantically capturing my thoughts and feelings through dynamic shapes and images interspersed with words and phrases. Most prominently featured was Ulanov's metaphor of Madness as an anchor. I noted my heel, emblematic of strength and vulnerability and the force that literally grounds me and moves me forward. I scrawled, "my lowest self" and "site of transformation."

Ulanov proposed that Madness holds possibility for creativity beyond the trope of the Mad artist and that Madness can be used as an anchor to harness creative energy. I had previously heard Madness constructed only as a deficit. As such, it felt like endless dark, stormy seas. Huge waves engulfed me as I struggled to come up for air. There was nothing to hold onto, nothing in sight, and the only way out was to conquer the waves and get out of the storm. Safety in that scenario could exist only if I left Madness behind. Yet if I was struggling to get away from Madness, was I just struggling to get away from myself? How could I reconcile the ways that Madness lives within me without feeling drowned? What would it mean to explore alternative connections to Mad identity and community?

---

1. This presentation was based on her book by the same title (Ulanov 2013).

Anchoring in Mad Solidarity   303

At the time, I was also a special education teacher and designing a program for students classified with emotional disturbance (ED).[2] In other words, students who were deemed "mad at school."[3] As I explored my own Mad identity, I was also working to disrupt deficit conceptions of disability and Madness in school, especially in relation to intersections of race, disability, and Madness.[4] How could we transform schooling practices so that Mad youth are given space and time to create and utilize their own anchors of Madness for creative personal expression, refusal, and resistance (Annamma and Morrison 2018)?[5] How can we anchor together in Mad solidarity and Mad joy?

Although originally inspired by Ulanov, my conception of Madness as an anchor has evolved through my deepening of Mad identity and

2. ED is one of the disability classifications under which students can receive special education services through the Individuals with Disabilities Education Act of 1990. In 2020, the US Department of Education reported that Black or African American and multiracial students are significantly more likely to be labeled ED compared to all students with disabilities. In 2021, among Black, Native Hawaiian and Pacific Islander, American Indian and Alaska Native, and multiracial youth with disabilities, one in four boys and almost one in five girls received out-of-school suspension (Office of Special Education Services 2021). The overrepresentation of Black or African American and multiracial children among children identified with ED and the exclusion and disciplinary removals of disabled youth of color must be read as symptoms of the coercive nature of racism, ableism, and sanism based on white-supremacist hierarchies of intelligence and behavior and notions of normality (Connor, Ferri, and Annamma 2016; Lewis 2022).

3. In *Mad at School* (2011), Margaret Price discusses manifestations of Madness in higher education. I am interested in extending her analysis to include the social, cultural, and political construction of Madness in K–12 schooling.

4. As a teacher, I didn't yet have a name for these conceptions, but upon entering graduate school I discovered DisCrit, which brings together disability studies in education and critical race theory to "explore the ways in which race and ability are socially constructed and interdependent" (Annamma, Connor, and Ferri 2016, 13). DisCrit helps me better understand and explain my observations and experiences as a special education teacher.

5. I use the term *Mad youth* throughout this chapter to encompass students who may be classified as ED in school as well as those who are not classified but may identify with mental and psychological disabilities and/or Madness. All of their experiences of sanism contribute to the construction of Madness in school.

304   Tov

connections to Mad kin. On a literal level, the anchor is designed to keep a ship safe and secure in a desired location or help control the ship in nasty weather. Although Madness is typically considered to be unstable, unsafe, undesired, and out of control, I imagine the anchor of Madness as constructing a Mad identity that grounds a person in their wholeness and allows them to identify, express, and access what they need to uphold their safety and personhood on their own terms. Just as anchors are made to fit the specific size and dimensions of a boat, so is the anchor of Madness unique to each person and affected by intersectionality, context, and ongoing personal journeys. The anchor of Madness is not stagnant but shifting and dynamic as we navigate uncharted waters.

In these journeys, felt experience (Patsavas 2014), Mad community, and academic and activist theories of disability and Madness are intertwined and melded together. They inform one another and contribute to the ways our anchors are constructed and where and how we choose to drop anchor. I use "we" not to imply that "we" embody and experience Madness in the same ways but to write in connection to and solidarity with Mad kin even as we experience Madness uniquely based on our individual expressions and intersectional experiences.

The Complexities of Anchoring

The rope to my anchor runs through the many iterations of Madness that reframe and reimagine my identity, community, and educational justice for Mad youth, students, and educators. The noun phrase *anchor of Madness* thus transforms into the verb phrase *anchoring in Mad solidarity.*

For me, Madness as an anchor moves away from a deficit framework toward presence, beauty, and joy. Anchors ground the ship and connect with the earth. They are not confined to a single location. Madness is carried within us; it encompasses and grounds us in the full spectrum of being. There is no singular definition or experience of Madness; it's a mosaic of dynamic pluralities. Therí Alyce Pickens calls on Black feminist theory to explain the importance of the term *Madness* "because of the critical possibilities it offers in its vagueness," the way it "describe[s] impairments such as cognitive or mental illness [and serves as] a catchall phrase designed to reference those not behaving according to culturally prescribed norms"

(2019, 51). Utilizing this framing of Madness opens the Mad community to those who identify with a specific diagnosis, those who may feel stamped by a label, and those who share an affinity or experience of Madness regardless of a psychiatric classification. Where psychiatric labels can be a tool of pathologization, reclaiming Madness can extend to refusals to uphold socially constructed emotional and behavioral expectations.

Madness has been (and continues to be) used as a tool of marginalization, and I am critically reflective on the ways that my own identities contribute to my understanding and experience of Madness. While my marginalized identities (Mad, disabled, queer, Jewish, woman) set me outside of nondisabled, cis-hetero, Protestant norms, whiteness is my most apparent identity marker and affords me unjust power. Whiteness shapes my narrative, interactions, and the ways that people value my being and presence. Beyond being reflective of these experiences, I am committed to and always working toward dismantling white supremacy and intersecting systems of oppression on internalized, interpersonal, and institutional levels. This is especially relevant in education, where white females are the embodiment of many school traumas for Mad youth of color and their families.[6]

The intersectional nature of race, disability, and Madness manifests in the material differences between my experience of Madness and those of Mad students of color. When experiencing mixed episodes, I was offered support and a medical leave, while I watched Mad youth of color being hypersurveilled, controlled, and restrained. Intersections of systematic racism, ableism, and sanism define the educational experiences of Mad youth of color. Sins Invalid, an artist collective of queer disabled artists of color, provides social, political, and historical context:

> We cannot comprehend ableism [and sanism] without grasping its interrelations with heteropatriarchy, white supremacy, colonialism and

---

6. In a report issued in 2020, the National Center for Education Statistics found that 79 percent of public-school teachers in the United States are white. In my time as a middle school educator, families and youth of color regularly shared experiences of racism, ableism, and sanism from white female educators.

306 Tov

> capitalism, each system co-creating an ideal bodymind built upon the exclusion and elimination of a subjugated "other" from whom profits and status are extracted. 500+ years of violence against black and brown communities includes 500+ years of bodies and minds deemed dangerous by being non-normative—again, not simply within able-bodied normativity, but within the violence of heteronormativity, white supremacy, gender normativity, within which our various bodies and multiple communities have been deemed "deviant," "unproductive," "invalid." (2019, 111)

State-sanctioned schooling is one of the pillars that upholds white supremacy, ableism, and sanism through the normalizing processes of behavioral and instructional expectations. Schools create a seabed of normality and subjugation, attempting to cut ties to and eradicate Madness as an anchor. Mad youth are not given agency to create and explore their own waters or opportunities to find and choose ocean floors that foster a positive sense of self and community.

Furthermore, students' refusal to anchor in oppressive classroom structures has been coded as defiance rather than agency and self-preservation. I worked with a Mad Black student who regularly walked out of her social studies class due to the teacher's focus on a damage-based Black history curriculum,[7] which the student described as triggering and traumatizing. In response, school administration reprimanded the student for being defiant but did not hold the teacher accountable for her damaging curricular content or instructional techniques. Another student, a Mad Black Indigenous youth, flipped a desk after his language arts teacher made a racist comment. The teacher asked for his removal from the general education setting, invalidating his experience and using exclusion as punishment for nonconformity. Because the student was labeled with ED, the onus was put on his individual behaviors rather than on the racist, sanist environment. Outside of school, he had access to tribal therapeutic support

---

7. Eve Tuck describes damage-based research as "a pathologizing approach in which the oppression singularly defines a community" (2009, 413). I use the term *damage-centered curriculum* to surface the ways that curricula are similarly used to pathologize communities of color.

Anchoring in Mad Solidarity   307

for culturally sustaining wellness (Lee 2022), but in school colonial and assimilationist perspectives of his race, culture, and disability were deeply embedded and normalized in curriculum and instruction.

These are just two examples of the ways that schools negate and punish the experiences of Mad youth of color. They show the coercive nature of sanism and racism that make the school and classroom environment inaccessible for so many.[8] Whiteness and "sanity" are positioned as normal in schools, and therefore noncompliance is constructed as abnormal, as deviant, as Mad (Leonardo and Broderick 2011). When I spoke up against these injustices, I was told that as a Mad educator I was conflating the experiences of the students with my own and that I needed better emotional boundaries.[9] I was told to withhold my Mad identity and focus on student safety. However, student safety meant that the school isolated Mad youth in crisis and denied their meaningful participation in the school community. The coded language of "safety" deters Mad solidarity in schools and perpetuates silence and violence.

Due to the dangerous and deficit construction of Madness at school, it is no surprise that many Mad youth desire to distance themselves from the label and stigma of ED. Mad youth are not given agency to discover and construct their own anchors of Madness, and Mad educators are asked not to anchor alongside them. These restrictions ultimately inhibit finding and building a community and discourage solidarity between Mad youth and Mad educators. As a K–12 educator and teacher educator, I think about missed opportunities for Mad solidarity and Mad Pride and dream of ways that Madness as an anchor and anchoring in solidarity may contribute to educational justice.

8. Although students classified with ED are provided accommodations, modifications, and specially designed instruction as part of their educational rights through Individualized Education Programs, these services do not incorporate youths' community and cultural knowledge. Such services can also be abused as tools of marginalization when a disability classification, such as ED, is cited as justification for exclusion.

9. I chose to disclose my disability classification to my administrators because my mixed episodes required additional support. However, my disclosure was thereafter used by administration to undermine my professional opinions and perspectives.

Casting into Mad Imaginaries

> The saving of our world from pending doom will come, not through
> the complacent adjustment of the conforming majority, but through
> the creative maladjustment of a nonconforming minority. . . .
> Human salvation lies in the hands of the creative maladjusted.
> —Martin Luther King Jr., *Strength to Love* (1963)

From preschool to higher education, schools require conformity to institutionally racist, ableist, and sanist environments. What if instead we were emboldened by "creative maladjustment"? What would it look like to move from the threat of noncompliance to the possibilities of Mad imaginaries?

In schools, Madness is used as a reason to segregate and exclude those who are unable and/or unwilling to conform. However, I dream of the possibility in Mad youth and educators choosing to anchor together in the face of the inaccessibility and pain inflicted in schools. As I imagine new horizons for Mad youth and educators, I'm drawn to Polvora's description of the social construction of Madness and how it may be disrupted:

> Most mental illnesses are seen as disorders because they prevent the person from functioning properly in the social world we have set up for ourselves. People have become so indoctrinated into this reality that they fail to realize almost all of the expectations placed on us are arbitrary and unnatural. If our society had an established place, purpose, or outlet for "mentally ill" behavior, it would become normal. If the majority of the population was bipolar, things would be set up to accommodate them, and those without bipolar "symptoms" would struggle to fit in and understand the world. Is failure to hold up to the expectations of other people really a disorder? . . . It is true that people labeled mentally ill may engage in behaviors that are destructive to themselves or others, but people too often assume that these choices stem only from the thought patterns; without considering that the choices may instead be a reaction to the frustration, anger and alienation that are a result of society's refusal to validate those thought patterns. (2011, 4–5)

Polvora questions the very nature of Madness and its supposed (non)existence outside of social and cultural expectations. Mad-affinity spaces in and beyond schools hold opportunities to disrupt sanist expectations.

Anchoring in Mad Solidarity   309

Fostering Mad identity and creativity as well as affirming and sustaining youth's multifaceted social and cultural identities require a radical reimagining of school structures (Paris 2012). One way to do so may be through multimodal forms of meaning making and storytelling.

For instance, the first time I felt anchored in Mad solidarity was when I joined a psychodrama group. I had never been in a group of all Mad folks (including the facilitator), and that alone was liberating: I was in a space where Madness was expected and accepted. I had not thought it possible to feel at home among other Mad people, but we were witnesses to one another's truths and created solidarity through deep connections. As we went through various drama exercises, sharing our stories, traumas, and internal narratives, we became the directors of our own stories. In that space, there wasn't the dismissal of my reality that I experienced with psychiatrists, the medical system, and neurotypical people. I was able to embody my thoughts and feelings freely and spontaneously as I enacted my truths, imagination, challenges, and Madness. I was embraced as my full self; my felt experiences were validated and contributed to our collective Mad knowledge and care.

Psychodrama invited methods of storytelling and imagining that engaged my full bodymind. It offered new methods of access, processing, and supporting one another. The Mad solidarity I felt in psychodrama was in stark contrast to the sense of isolation and hiddenness I had always previously felt. For me, it contributed to what Mia Mingus calls "liberatory access." She states, "Access for the sake of access is not necessarily liberatory, but access for the sake of connection, justice, community, love, and liberation is. We can use access as a tool to transform the broader conditions we live in, to transform the conditions that created that inaccessibility in the first place" (2017, par. 30). Anchoring in Mad solidarity moves away from the myth of independence toward a liberatory future in which we can access and anchor in ocean floors attune to our fullness. Access is not related solely to Madness and disability but also to the affinity spaces that are created for community and survival amid intersecting systems of oppression and to the coalitional spaces we design across our diverse bodyminds.

Mad imaginaries are also intergenerational: they look back and dream forward. Sins Invalid describes disability justice as "a vision and practice of what is yet-to-be, a map that we create with our ancestors and our great-grandchildren onward, in the width and depth of our multiplicities and histories, a movement towards a world in which every body and mind is known as beautiful" (2019, 26–27). Mad imaginaries require learning about the ways that our ancestors used Madness as an anchor for their creativity and survival.[10] They make connections with Mad kin beyond the bounds of space and time and use those connections to delve more fully into the creative construction of the anchors that drop to bring us presence in self and community. Among the Mad ancestors is my great-great-grandmother. In bouts of mania, she would crochet blankets, table cloths, and doilies. We still have hundreds of them. When I look at them and hold them, I can feel her. I can feel the pain and trauma as well as the creative expression that sustained her and continue to manifest through my anchor of Madness.

Mad histories and imaginaries may contribute to liberatory access in education. Psychodrama and creative cultural expressions can transform narratives of Madness. I continue to learn from generations of Mad, disabled, and chronically ill queer communities of color that center creativity to cultivate and revive cultural practices and collective healing. Mad communities have extensive histories of mutual aid, care work, and community-based healing (Piepzna-Samarasinha 2018). Through leadership by those most affected, anchoring in Mad solidarity is a continuous commitment to collective liberation.[11]

10. Intergenerational experiences of and connections to Madness may differ widely based on familial, cultural, and personal ties to Madness and how they intersect with patriarchy, settler colonialism, and capitalism. In *How to Go Mad without Losing Your Mind* (2021), La Marr Jurelle Bruce describes lineages of Black radical Mad creativity in the United States from the centuries of chattel slavery into the present. Many Indigenous scholars and activists have also addressed Madness and mental health through a framework of "our culture is our treatment" and Indigenous lifeways as essential to healing from the intergenerational traumas of colonialism and genocide (Gone 2022).

11. As defined by Sins Invalid, collective liberation is when "we move together as people with mixed abilities, multiracial, multi-gendered, mixed class, across the sexual spectrum, with a vision that leaves no bodymind behind" (2019, 26).

At present, our educational system disconnects us from Mad histories and fails to creatively dream Mad imaginaries. Social emotional learning (SEL) is suggested to support Mad youth, but it is typically aligned with cognitive behavior therapy (CBT), which dismisses the role of systemic oppression and intergenerational trauma on mental and emotional well-being. Dena Simmons points out that the majority of the SEL curriculum used in schools is more like "white supremacy with a hug"—for example, "asking students to practice deep-breathing in response to systemic oppression is simply offensive" (2021, par. 17). CBT and SEL focus on Madness as existing only within an individual rather than on the social, cultural, and intersectional conditions that construct Madness as a deficit. Liberatory access would move beyond SEL to engage Mad folks' personal, intersectional, and intergenerational histories through a desire-based framework.[12] Mad imaginaries are the opportunity to dream beyond present circumstances and move toward creative possibility.

Creativity invites new methods to drop anchor on our own terms. When I hurt people during episodes of hypomania, there are multiple modes to apologize and repair relationships. When going through depression, I'm invited to explore the ocean caverns with curiosity instead of with judgment. Multiple ways of being and knowing could be assets to schools and the academy, yet they are dismissed because they are not deemed "rigorous" or "valid." What's overlooked is validity and worthiness of Mad perspectives and experiences and the intense rigor in dreaming beyond the normalized structures that confine us.

Mad imaginaries could embolden youth and educators and open new horizons for anchoring together in Mad solidarity. I had only a glimpse of Mad possibility in the classroom before Madness led to my need for a medical leave and change in position. I still think about the missed opportunities for solidarity in school and dream about the ways we could

---

12. In contrast to a damage-based framework, Tuck describes desire-based frameworks as "concerned with understanding complexity, contradiction, and the self-determination of lived lives . . . by documenting not only the painful elements of social realities but also the wisdom and hope" (2009, 416).

forge Mad communities in educational spaces. I remember one Mad youth entering crisis and throwing class materials and desks. While one paraprofessional led other students out of the room, I had to stop another paraprofessional from using physical restraint. I noticed that the student was moving desks together like a fort and sheltering himself under it to create a sense of safety. In previous conversations, he told me that the series *Planet Earth* calmed him, so I projected an episode, and he cried. We sat in silence, connected through codesigning a space in which we could anchor together.

On another occasion, one of my Mad students reached out to me in Mad solidarity. On that day, I could feel panic rising in me and an episode coming on, so I needed to leave campus immediately. I calmed my nerves enough to make a plan and check in with each of my students and administrators. One Mad student paused me before I left and asked if I was OK to drive. That small yet profoundly supportive question felt like a stronger sense of solidarity than I had ever experienced from administrators or coworkers. He saw my humanity, could relate to my experience, and cared for my well-being.

Years later, I found Mad studies and Mad Pride through my graduate studies and disability justice work in education, and I dream of ways to make them accessible to students from early childhood to higher education. When I find tools created for and by the Mad community, I imagine how they could contribute to a deeply relational Mad solidarity in general educational spaces. Youth could share their stories, identify their own needs, and create liberatory access through strategies for personal and community healing. Mad youth and educators could co-construct resources modeled after materials like the queer organizer Elliott Fukui's (n.d.) Mad Survival Tools. They could have opportunities to learn and connect with Mad histories of creativity and resistance. Mad educators and youth could use Fireweed's example of healing justice to discuss Madness and oppression as well as plans to support one another in crisis (Icarus Project 2015; Fireweed Collective n.d.). Mad youth could cast Mad imaginaries with Mad kin, artistically expressing their own stories beyond the damage-based narrative written for them (Tuck 2009). This work requires interdependence cultivated for and by Mad

Anchoring in Mad Solidarity 313

communities and creates sea floors of brilliance, imagining a yet-to-be in educational spaces.

Anchoring with Mad Joy

Mad solidarity and Mad imaginaries can manifest Mad joy. Mad joy is often lost amid shaming and the social and medical expectations to "cure" Madness. Anchors, despite their integral function on a ship, are most often hidden within the boat's structure or invisibilized beneath the water's surface, just as our Mad identities are often hidden from plain view. When I was first diagnosed, I was relieved to have an explanation for my bipolar episodes but also felt the stigma of an official classification. I felt caught in binaries: reality versus insanity, truth versus falsity, me versus Madness. Is my creativity part of my personality or a product of illness? Am I vivacious in character or living in hypomania? Is my fatigue from overworking or from depression?

For a long time, I was ashamed and felt I had to hide my Mad identity. Anytime I shared my bipolar diagnosis with someone, it felt as if I were coming out,[13] as if I were disclosing my anchor without an anchor line to ground me. I felt I had to examine my anchor alone, separate, and in secret. The process lacked healing and transformation. The psychiatric recommendations given to me were rooted in white capitalist individualism and Western medicine. It wasn't until I found Mad kin that I felt I could anchor without judgment or hesitation. I wasn't asked to change myself, be cured, or just get over it.

Mad kin showed me that Mad solidarity is not restricted to a common pain but opens space to create Mad joy. As opposed to drowning in the metaphor of Madness as stormy waters, anchoring in Mad solidarity

---

13. My experience of "coming out" as bipolar is in line with Ellen Samuels's description of how "coming out is primarily portrayed as the process of revealing or explaining one's disability *to* others, rather than as an act of self-acceptance facilitated by a disability community" (2003, 239). She discusses this common process in contrast with moments in which coming out is more associated with empowerment and political action. There are also limitations to the discourse of "coming out" as disabled, and it is not simply analogous to coming out as gay, lesbian, bisexual, trans, or queer.

opened my mind and spirit to imagine the possibility and beauty of Mad joy amid the complexities. Anchoring allows for full presence, a moment of pause, and the calm to simply watch the sunset. Here Mad joy centers wholeness in self and community. Although Madness may come with hurt, indescribable mood shifts, and deep depression, Mad solidarity opens space for Mad joy in connectedness and belonging. We're told that Madness is an illness, Madness is undesirable, and Madness leads to inevitable suffering. However, Mad joy reminds us that connection and transformation exist within our Madness. Mad joy does not always entail feelings of happiness but provides opportunities for healing. It involves shifting and swaying together and bearing witness to one another. I'm here with you. You are precious. I love you as you are.

I wonder about the ways that Mad joy may also open space to creatively meet one another's access needs. Leah Lakshmi Piepzna-Samarasinha asks, "What does it mean to shift our ideas of access and care . . . from an individual chore, an unfortunate cost of having an unfortunate body[,] to a collective responsibility that's maybe even joyful?" (2018, 33). Our access needs vary from person to person and moment to moment. In allowing us to creatively meet one another's access needs, Mad joy creates spaces to anchor together. Access and care may mean allowing the opportunity for verbally processing, taking a break, helping someone to access medication, or contributing to a care network for someone wishing to live without medication. Acts of care and access create a sense of Mad community, solidarity, and joy.

Mad joy does not decomplicate the experience of Madness but instead embraces a complexity in which sorrow and glee exist simultaneously. It means not limiting the Mad experience to a single narrative, emotional binary or epic tragedy. Mad joy does not equate Madness with damage; rather, it is expansive, living into the many iterations of ourselves and our communities. Mad joy is learning and sharing the collective project of solidarity, access, and belonging. It is celebrating one another even as we grieve Mad kin who have completed suicide. It doesn't mean always feeling cheerful, but it can be as simple as the warmth of sitting together silently when you can't get out of bed. It can be the meme a friend sends

Anchoring in Mad Solidarity   315

you when you haven't smiled in days. It can be in a daily phone call to remind you that you are amazing without having to do or produce anything. Mad joy is in the subtle moments of connection and the ongoing celebration of wholeness.

I dream of an academy and school system in which my anchor of Madness drops alongside Mad kin and in connection with Mad youth. In this not-yet-realized educational structure, I imagine Mad joy existing alongside Mad pain, the allowance of contradicting internal forces, the full expression of self. Mad theorizing through expressing and uplifting Mad experiences and perspectives will bring us together toward intersectional and intergenerational Mad solidarity.

But, and, Also . . .

Madness brings the beauty of "but, and, also"—the resistance to any binaries and the existence of multiple simultaneous and possibly contradicting truths. My feelings of and connections to Madness are ever changing and evolving. With every draft of this chapter, my perspectives shift, and I stumble on my words. It is a new experience to boldly claim Madness after years of hiding. Madness informed my practice when I was special education teacher, but I was deterred from sharing, and my Madness was used to discount my professional judgment. In contrast, in my experience as a Mad, disabled graduate student, my insider perspective is invited into disability studies and Mad studies, although I nevertheless constantly battle against what is considered valid and valuable in the academy. Through the tides, I've held onto my anchor of Madness and continue to learn new ways to anchor in Mad solidarity. I have infinite appreciation and admiration for my Mad friends, the editors of this anthology, my care team, my family, and my zubby (trans spouse), who have informed the construction of my anchor as well as anchored alongside me. We are so quick to want answers, something concrete, tangible, and definable. Yet that is the opposite of Madness, so, instead, I invite you into the murky exploration and depth of anchoring in Mad solidarity.

I am in deep gratitude for the anchoring together throughout this anthology. The vibrancy of mentorship from Shayda and Melanie has been sustaining and brightened my graduate experience with Mad joy. Reading other chapters of the book has made me feel seen and deepened my awe of our collective knowledge, wisdom, and lived theory. I'm honored to receive them as gifts of collective Mad care. You all greatly contribute to and expand my understanding of myself, my connection to the Mad community, and my sense of Mad solidarity and joy as we cast into the Mad imaginary that we can manifest only together.

Works Cited

Annamma, Subini, David J. Connor, and Beth A. Ferri. 2016. "Touchstone Text: Dis/Ability Critical Race Studies (DisCrit): Theorizing at the Intersections of Race and Dis/ability." In *DisCrit: Disability Studies and Critical Race Theory in Education*, edited by David J. Connor, Beth A. Ferri, and Subini Annamma, 9–32. New York: Teachers College Press.

Annamma, Subini, and Deb Morrison. 2018. "Identifying Dysfunctional Education Ecologies: A DisCrit Analysis of Bias in the Classroom." *Equity & Excellence in Education* 51, no. 2: 114–31. At https://doi.org/10.1080/106656 84.2018.1496047.

Bruce, La Marr Jurelle. 2021. *How to Go Mad without Losing Your Mind: Madness and Black Radical Creativity.* Durham, NC: Duke Univ. Press.

Connor, David J., Beth A. Ferri, and Subini Annamma, eds. 2016. *DisCrit: Disability Studies and Critical Race Theory in Education.* New York: Teachers College Press.

Fireweed Collective. n.d. "Crisis Toolkit." At https://fireweedcollective.org/crisis -toolkit.

Fukui, Elliott. n.d. "Mad Survival Tools: Stay Mad, Stay Together." Mad Queer Organizing Strategies. At https://madqueer.org/madsurvival.

Gone, Joseph. 2022. "Re-imagining Mental Health Services for American Indian Communities: Centering Indigenous Perspectives." *American Journal of Community Psychology* 69, nos. 3–4: 257–68. At https://doi.org/10.1002 /ajcp.12591.

Icarus Project. 2015. *Madness & Oppression: Paths to Personal Transformation and Collective Liberation.* Chico, CA: AK Press.

King, Martin Luther, Jr. 1963. *Strength to Love.* New York: Harper & Row.

Lee, Tiffany. 2022. "Educating for Wellness through the Practice of K'é." In *Transforming Diné Education: Innovations in Pedagogy and Practice,* edited by Pedro Vallejo and Vincent Werito, 77–84. Tucson: Univ. of Arizona Press.

Leonardo, Zeus, and Alicia A. Broderick. 2011. "Smartness as Property: A Critical Exploration of Intersections between Whiteness and Disability Studies." *Teachers College Record* 113, no. 10: 2206–32. At https://doi.org/10.1177/01614681111130100.

Lewis, Talila "TL." 2022. "Working Definition of Ableism—January 2022 Update." *Talila A. Lewis* (blog), Jan. 1. At https://www.talilalewis.com/blog/working-definition-of-ableism-january-2022-update.

Mingus, Mia. 2017. "Access Intimacy, Interdependence and Disability Justice." *Leaving Evidence* (blog), Apr. 12. At https://leavingevidence.wordpress.com/2017/04/12/access-intimacy-interdependence-and-disability-justice/.

National Center for Education Statistics. 2020. "Race and Ethnicity of Public School Teachers and Their Students." US Department of Education. At https://nces.ed.gov/pubs2020/2020103/index.asp.

Office of Special Education Services. 2021. "OSEP Fast Facts: Race and Ethnicity of Children with Disabilities Served under IDEA Part B." IDEA: Individuals with Disabilities Education Act. At https://sites.ed.gov/idea/osep-fast-facts-race-and-ethnicity-of-children-with-disabilities-served-under-idea-part-b/.

Paris, D. 2012. "Culturally Sustaining Pedagogy: A Needed Change in Stance, Terminology, and Practice." *Educational Researcher* 41, no. 3: 93–97.

Patsavas, Alyson. 2014. "Recovering a Cripistemology of Pain: Leaky Bodies, Connective Tissue, and Feeling Discourse." *Journal of Literary & Cultural Disability Studies* 8, no. 2: 203–18.

Pickens, Therí Alyce. 2019. *Black Madness :: Mad Blackness*. Durham, NC: Duke Univ. Press.

Piepzna-Samarasinha, Leah Lakshmi. 2018. *Care Work: Dreaming Disability Justice*. Vancouver: Arsenal Pulp Press.

Polvora. 2011. "Diagnosis 'Human.'" *Wax and Feathers: The Icarus Project Zine*, Apr. At https://nycicarus.org/images/waxandfeathers.pdf.

Price, Margaret. 2011. *Mad at School: Rhetorics of Mental Disability and Academic Life*. Ann Arbor: Univ. of Michigan Press.

Samuels, Ellen. 2003. "MY BODY, MY CLOSET: Invisible Disability and the Limits of Coming-Out Discourse." *GLQ: A Journal of Lesbian and Gay Studies* 9, nos. 1–2: 233–55. At https://doi.org/10.1215/10642684-9-1-2-233.

Simmons, Dena. 2021. "Why SEL Alone Isn't Enough." *El Magazine* 78, no. 6. At https://www.ascd.org/el/articles/why-sel-alone-isnt-enough.

Sins Invalid. 2019. *Skin, Tooth, and Bone: The Basis of Movement Is Our People.* 2nd ed. San Francisco: Sins Invalid.

Tuck, Eve. 2009. "Suspending Damage: A Letter to Communities." *Harvard Educational Review* 79, no. 3: 409–27. At https://doi.org/10.17763/haer.79.3.n0016675661t3n15.

Ulanov, Ann Belford. 2013. *Madness and Creativity.* College Station: Texas A&M Univ. Press.

19

Mad Laughter

*On Finding and Forming Graduate
Communities through Memes*

Kim Fernandes

Content note: forced institutionalization

Managing Madness?

In graduate school, my Mad peers and I experience the kinds of everyday realities that are explicitly dissonant with the university's reassurances that we could—and would—be well if we just tried the right combination of things.[1] Even before our graduate programs had begun, we were inundated during orientation week with clear expectations for the kinds of idealized, "healthy" lives we might construct as graduate students.[2] Over and over, the university offered an image of a successful graduate student as someone who can nip stress and anxiety in the bud through one of many initiatives that would support us in staying "well." As my Mad peers and I had been reminded many times over in our lives, we were told that when we are at

---

1. Throughout this chapter, I do not use "the university" to refer to a specific university; rather, I intend for it to serve as an amalgam, a composite of universities and the responses they have offered to the experiences of Mad students. This composite is also in acknowledgment of the university's role in upholding systemic, oppressive patterns and behaviors in higher education.

2. I use scare quotes around words such as *healthy* and *well* to mark them as intended to be read ironically rather than as direct quotations from other sources.

odds with the world around us or otherwise distressed, all of the resources that we can imagine are there—we just have to find the right ones.

Within higher education, madness is frequently managed by systemic attempts to stifle it.[3] As Shayda Kafai argues (2013), this stifling erases the "simultaneous" experience of Madness and sanity that the "Mad border body" often experiences, instead setting up a clear border between Madness and sanity. Although rarely explicitly discussed within the multitude of wellness initiatives that have mushroomed across the neoliberal university, the question of disclosure (Samuels 2017) is also central to the university's strategies around managing Madness to ensure "compulsory able-mindedness" (Kafer 2013). The university's positivist framing of disclosure—"Tell us so we know, and then we can help you"—is frequently at odds with students' experiences of disclosure amid an environment of academic ableism (Dolmage 2017).

Experiences of being Mad in the academy can be isolating and frustrating, especially against the backdrop of expectations of the typical graduate student as a bodymind (Price 2015; Schalk 2018) that is both productive and happy. Because university narratives around "mental health" are often heavily focused on what the individual student can do to be and feel better rather than on the pervasive sanist, ableist rhetorics and practices within academia, the formation of Mad kinship is also hindered. Pointing to the limits of these attempts to "fix" the individual rather than the system, a chronically ill Mad friend, K, once noted: "You can't just bring a puppy to the library at the end of the semester and tell me that I'm going to have better mental health or do better on my exams now—you have to make room for my ulcerative colitis, for my depression, and for how I'm not going to be the best student in your classes because you assume that no student in your classes could ever be this ill—or this kind of ill."

Despite the university's insufficient (and often violent) responses to Mad students, this chapter exists because my Mad graduate community

3. Although I use the capitalized term *Madness* elsewhere throughout the chapter to refer to students for whom Madness is a source of identity, community, and pride, I use *madness* (lowercase) here to underscore the university's reliance on biomedical models in approaches to health and well-being.

has made it possible. In this chapter, therefore, I write joyously, albeit from a mind/body space that the university has perceived and described as in need of fixing. I also write from the love and care that have emerged from shared activist-academic communities of Madness, none of which is present in the many university "solutions." These communities emerged from Facebook groups and Instagram pages for graduate students, in particular those that were focused on sharing memes about the graduate experience. This chapter—like (my) Madness—meanders. It does not fall into a linear rhythm or an outline that can be traced neatly from start to end. While I refer to several other graduate students with whom I am in community throughout the chapter, I introduce each person briefly, using only an initial and focusing on our conversations in community rather than on their locations and identities to ensure that they are able to stay anonymous.

I use this space to write about how a commonplace activity for so many graduate students—meme sharing—has enabled Mad communities to develop and flourish through shared joy and laughter. As I write about the communities of care that meme sharing has enabled, I also note the ongoing, enduring possibilities for these communities as personal and intellectual homes within an otherwise sanist, ableist academia. Memes play an integral role in enabling deeply accepting, transformative conversations about Mad (in-person and virtual) community among other graduate students. Amid academic spaces that attempt to quietly manage and silence conversations about owning and inhabiting Madness, these meme-based communities emerge as a crucial site through which Mad kinship continues to be cultivated.

The Impracticability of University Care

The university's purportedly well-meaning attempts to "help" rely on a binary wherein Madness is either invisible and therefore absent or made visible and therefore in need of management. During the beginning of my time in graduate school, I often found myself asking where the other (Mad) graduate students like me were. M, a graduate student in statistics, noted one night when we were walking home together from dinner that she had disclosed her bipolar diagnosis to her adviser and lab mates. While M herself was relieved and grateful to know that there was a name that she could have for the ways she was feeling, several of her lab mates, instead of acknowledging that relief, had nodded sympathetically, mentioning how "horrible" this must be and hoping she "recovered" soon. M's adviser had ignored this disclosure altogether, turning the larger conversation back to the question of lab outcomes and publication. I share M's narrative here as one example that underscores the sanist undercurrents (Price 2011; Dolmage 2017) that often cause Mad graduate students to feel uncomfortable with disclosing our identities, much less with taking pride in our Madness.

"I don't need help," M spat when relaying this incident to me. We have since then had numerous conversations about the ways in which Madness has always rearranged the spatiotemporal logics of our lives such that we no longer inhabit normative desires to make our lives work the way the university thinks they're "supposed to." M's summary of the incident in her lab—"I'm not sure we can say we are mad and be taken seriously as Mad people"—points to the ways in which Mad graduate students' own voices about our experiences are considered less worth taking seriously than biomedical discourses about a cure.

When these experiences of receiving university "care" are read against some of the key principles of disability justice (such as those offered by Leah-Lakshmi Piepzna-Samarasinha in *Care Work: Dreaming Disability Justice* [2018]), it is evident that the university's responses through individualized accommodations attempt to schedule and manage Madness at predictable times that are convenient primarily for the university, when Madness would otherwise be most apparently "disruptive" to examinations or other course deadlines. This concerted drive to manage and ultimately "fix" Mad persons' bodyminds does not make room for the experiences of those of us whose deviance has been apparent since long before the start of graduate school. Accommodations can—and do—erase some of the ways Madness feels in the body, sometimes in the form of week-long bouts of exhaustion after a flashback, rendering these ways immaterial because they are not immediately in need of management. When I first began graduate school, I struggled with how accommodations were often described to me as an adjustment that the university was making on my behalf, for my bodymind, when in practice these accommodations often felt more limiting than inclusive. As I attempted to find the words for my own discomfort with the university's attempt to manage my meandering bodymind, I increasingly turned to online communities for the memes.

On several occasions, my Mad peers and I have wondered, only half-jokingly: What of those of us who are alright with our Madness, who do not want it cured or relentlessly managed? From the safety of our computers, we have also wondered if our Mad graduate communities would ever have seemed feasible on campus—Would we have met and grown to know each other as Mad (junior scholar) kin? "Not a chance in hell," F noted, "because I feel like we're never even told that there are other Mad students. All kinds of Madness are often described along a spectrum of negative thoughts or anxiety or worse, stress, and we never wind up meeting people who actually live with Madness." Everyone else agreed—the university's attempts to "fix" us often made us ashamed of ourselves, wondering if there was something so deeply "flawed" about us that we had never noticed before.

"You can bet there won't ever be something like what we have with each other—the university cannot care for us like we can care for each other," C said later. "Yes," F chimed in, "because when you go to request an accommodation, most times you're told it's just you, you're special, and no one else needs this stuff, you know? Then I started to wonder if I was just doing even worse at grad school than I had imagined—how could I be the only one that needed accommodations for my poor mental health?" Our affirmation that we might never have found each other "in real life" further emphasizes how university programming around mental health is often centered around remedying the presumed deficits in the individual bodymind rather than around acknowledging that these identities are also a source of pride and the basis for forming Mad communities. Against this backdrop, finding Mad kin online has been both an active space of resistance and a source of deeply joyous community.

Memes and Mad Kinship

Memes form the basis for this chapter and for the Mad communities I have found in academia. Among graduate students, memes are often presented as humorous responses to deeply serious underlying issues within the academy. They do the work of acknowledging the brokenness of a system that has no capacity to care for us in the ways that we would need it to, while also allowing us to imagine an "otherwise"—a way to talk about the heaviness of graduate school without focusing on the heaviness alone. Although I had lurked in graduate student meme groups for quite a while, I began to look at them more closely only when C, a Mad friend from preschool who was now beginning graduate school, had asked casually if I might have any advice for how they could navigate what sounded like a deeply terrifying journey. I did not, I confessed—my graduate school cohort never talked about Madness, and the only thing I could think of doing was to laugh off abrasive and deeply uncomfortable interactions with the university through memes in graduate student groups.

Shortly after I had added C to these groups and complained about the absence of Mad community, C texted me one evening, excitedly: "Wow, it looks like lots of people in graduate school are also Mad! Thank goodness." Having only thought through Madness in graduate school thus far as it related to disclosure and institutional accommodations, I was a little surprised—Where was C noticing Mad graduate students? "Look at the memes people share, and at how many people find these memes relatable—we're not alone," C pointed out. C's understanding of Mad belonging (and, soon enough, mine too) was expansive: while I had searched for Mad community in graduate school in the form of other students who might want to talk about their embodied experiences and administrative responses to them, C's commentary on memes as ways of signaling Mad belonging allowed me to think beyond—or away from—Madness as only the diagnosis and management of it.

I include here two brief examples from the many thousands of graduate school mental health memes that I have encountered. These memes have appeared in several different locations across the internet, including in groups and meme repositories, and are thematically similar to others that I have encountered within private Facebook groups. The first meme, which I call "Surviving Grad School," depicts a cartoon of a red-haired person (originally a screenshot of Fry from the TV show *Futurama*) thinking hard, their eyes barely open. The text accompanying their thoughts reads, "Not sure if actually depressed, or just in grad school." The second meme, which I call "Grad School Broke My Spirit," has also circulated in several locations. In it, a person holds a book and is about to begin jumping into the air. The text next to them reads, "Grad school is easy. It's like riding a bike. Except the bike is on fire and you're on fire and everything is on fire and you're in hell."

As I started to engage more closely with memes, liking and commenting on them, I noticed that they served as a way for graduate students to talk about our experiences of graduate school without diminishing the seriousness of our concerns; rather, memes first recognized structural issues and then offered the chance to build communities that were based in loving humor. Among the groups that I had started to become more active in, these memes shared common characteristics: there was an unequivocal sense of understanding that sharing our embodied experiences, even if through various characters that were not ourselves, was a difficult and fraught thing to do for the ways in which it signified (in)formal disclosure. Comments on memes were largely affirming, serving as reminders that the original poster was not alone in feeling this way, regardless of the location of their graduate school and their program of study.

These online communities have emerged as spaces for collective care and access in which "access needs aren't shameful [and where] we all have various capacities which function differently within different environments" (Berne 2018, 28). Care within these meme groups looks different than disclosure within academia because it often involves commenting on posts to respond to and affirm the validity of the original poster's ways of being in the world and sometimes consists of tagging friends in the comments of memes posted. In my experience, these comments have also moved into text conversations and turned into friendships, each on their own timeline. Memes are both a means of communication and further entry points to longer, more textured conversations about being Mad in the academy that are no longer contained only within the comments section. These online conversations that I describe here are easy entry points into life-giving Mad friendships in ways that in-person conversations often might not be because they provide us with as much anonymity as we like; online platforms make it less fraught and more comforting to be out as a Mad person (Kafai 2021).

Shayda Kafai's explanation of the Mad border body dismantles the boundaries that the university constructs between Madness and sanity, arguing instead that "individuals can exist simultaneously in states of sanity and madness" (2013, par. 25). In one group conversation about navigating Madness in academia, F pointed out: "It isn't like we're not saying we're mad, though—there's nothing to hide. They're just assuming that all of us are normal, that there can't really be mad students they don't notice." In response, R, another early-career academic, asked, "Where are we saying it, though? We certainly aren't going to tell our advisers." F pushed back, "But we are telling each other and telling the world—these memes don't hide my psychotic breaks." Our conversations continue to center around the constant navigation of Madness and disclosure in academia. Our fear is not without reason; we remind each other again and again—our Mad border bodies are often assumed to be otherwise, and the university is often not the safest space for many of us. Even in the absence of formal diagnoses, even when we're told over and over that we're just "imagining things," we remind ourselves that self-diagnoses are valid. All disclosure is work, we tell each other, and, most importantly, all forms of disclosure are valid, even through memes. "Memes," R pointed out, "are kind of like a way to invite other Mad folx in, to tell them we're mad. We're being deliberate. We're saying we're mad, and none of these words are jokes. You think we're joking, but you'd get it if you wanted to."

These friendships thrived (and still do), developing quickly and continuing to be an anchor amid our everyday in-person and now virtual academic experiences. More than a dozen different threads connected the conversations in my inbox, sometimes spilling over into each other when one of us would express a need—"I'm having a hard time focusing on my writing because I'm so anxious about the news"—and others would find a way to bring worlds together to provide care around this need, which in this instance was through the scheduling of a time when a few of us could write together virtually. Our online spaces are somewhat different than other university groups with similar purposes because they are devoid of the sense of shame that the university associates with Madness. As one Mad friend, K, noted, "I could not possibly say that psychosis was the reason I was unable to show up to my daily writing group—but here, I know y'all are going to ask me questions about what I need to be cared for without the empty reassurances that I'll be able to get well soon." K's response points to the difference between our many forms of community care, which asks what a Mad person needs when they request care, and university "care," which emphasizes quick healing and recovery, as if Madness were a temporary state. F responded, "We're not ashamed of ourselves, but they're ashamed of us. My program director can never say I took a leave of absence for mental health reasons. He just says I had things going on and I had to take care of them."

Mad Care and Survival

Within these online Mad communities, we talk a lot about survival, gently. Even on our roughest, most frustrating days, we remind each other that we have survived a sanist, carceral system and that we have done this work of surviving by showing up as we are within the academy. When we note how hard it is to be as we are in academic spaces, our kinship also makes room for us to talk about what it is within these spaces that makes it so hard. Here, I think of P, a friend institutionalized thrice in the first three years of her graduate program. Upon her return home, she noted that she had been instructed to "keep busy after discharge" in order to prevent panic attacks. What did being asked to keep busy mean, she wondered, and how did this institutionally imposed busyness shape narratives of self and worth? "It's almost like they were asking me to keep busy to keep me away from myself, to go through the motions of being normal," she pointed out.

"How would they know if you were not keeping busy?" I wondered, almost naively. "They're watching, don't worry," P joked, "and they're checking in with me every day, asking me what I am doing to keep myself busy—all the time, where and how can I prove that I have been trying to fix myself?" The university's provision of care to those of us who are certified as Mad often depends on an extensive network of surveillance that does not leave room for Mad bodyminds to participate in and shape our own care. As P noted later, "I could tell them that I don't want to be busy like this, all the time—that it isn't good for me when I'm trying to heal. I'd be much better off being less busy, but I feel like saying that busyness isn't working will make them think I'm much Madder than I already am." So many times we talk about why university care does not work—how it is offered within a carceral network that conflates surveillance with healing, leaving little room for us to recognize our bodyminds for their wholeness (Sins Invalid 2016; Piepzna-Samarasinha 2018). The carceral nature of university care for "mental health" is not unlike several other forms of carceral care (see Piepzna-Samarasinha 2018 for examples), thereby limiting the utility of the care provided and deterring graduate students from wanting to access it.

Our own forms of Mad community care differ tremendously from university surveillance. In a group conversation one day, K asked, "You won't call the cops on me, right? Even if I tell you something and I'm not sure how to say it?" No, we reassured her, we wouldn't. We're not the university, we half-joked, don't worry. "You know, though, that if I told anyone on campus I was struggling, panic attacks with the world swirling around me, hear tracing, not sure how to pace myself through the night—they'd panic and call the cops. This isn't far-fetched," K pointed out. No, we jumped in, agreeing—we hadn't meant to joke this away; it isn't far-fetched. K continued: "Because this one time I told another girl in the dorm how I was feeling, and she went and told on me to a faculty member, and they freaked out—there were four cops knocking on my door that night. I said I was OK, but they didn't believe me—but I can feel like I could say I wasn't OK on here, and it would still be OK, right?" Yes, we promised, it would be OK, whatever OK might mean for each of us separately and for all of us together.

Conclusion

I have shared several conversations in this chapter both with permission and with the heaviness of knowing that if academia were on the whole a different space, especially for students of color and international students, many other Mad graduate students would be thinking about and writing this chapter with me. Instead, as we collectively talked about how we might safely navigate disclosure, several events have further shaped our shifting senses of safety: the pandemic, restrictions on the movement of international students to the United States, and an academic job market that has been both precarious and punitive across geographic locations and fields of study. In an early online conversation, a friend, S, offered: "Being Mad is a deeply powerful way of knowing. . . . I'm often treated as a miracle in my program for being able to succeed despite my psychotic fits, but it is Madness that allows me to care more deeply about what I want to know." It is to acknowledge the power of Madness in academia and the particular role that Mad kinship plays in imbibing our everyday moments as graduate students with this power that I have written this chapter. I hold this kinship alongside what Shayda Kafai describes as "fear in the telling and owning of madness" (2013, par. 1), knowing that the borders of Madness, the particulars of diagnosis, disclosure, and cure, shape and are shaped by our belonging to queerness and to our communities.

What might an alternative academia look like for Mad graduate students? As I continue to think of the remarkability of this transnational, transdisciplinary community of fellow Mad graduate students, it remains evident that Mad resilience looks like several different things—words typed and erased, memes shared, check-in direct messages, very long video calls that never have to touch on why we're making them if we'd rather not. The emergence of this unlikely space has made room for us to work through undoing our own internalized ableism and sanism. When several of us first thought of submitting a proposal for a chapter in this volume, among other things, we noted our excitement but wrestled with the difficulties of navigating disclosure given our previous difficult experiences. "Let's submit this proposal together," F suggested, "and then never list it on our CVs?" P offered instead: "What if we choose to write about something else? I'll never be able to navigate telling my adviser that I chose to write about Madness instead of leaf tissue variations, and she will never count this toward a publication." In response, R said, "We could just come out and say how we met and navigate this whole disclosure thing upfront." M pushed back: "We can't really say where we met because I don't know if I'll want this published or on record, but I wish there were more worlds like this one—maybe one day in academia?"

Works Cited

Berne, Patty. 2018. "10 Principles of Disability Justice." In Leah Lakshmi Piepzna-Samarasinha, *Care Work: Dreaming Disability Justice*, 26–29. Vancouver: Arsenal Pulp Press.

Dolmage, Jay Timothy. 2017. *Academic Ableism: Disability and Higher Education*. Ann Arbor: Univ. of Michigan Press.

Kafai, Shayda. 2013. "The Mad Border Body: A Political In-Betweeness." *Disability Studies Quarterly* 33, no. 1. At https://dsq-sds.org/article/view/3438/3199.

———. 2021. "The Politics of Mad Femme Disclosure." *Journal of Lesbian Studies* 25, no. 3. At https://doi.org/10.1080/10894160.2020.1778851.

Kafer, Alison. 2013. *Feminist, Queer, Crip*. Bloomington: Indiana Univ. Press.

Piepzna-Samarasinha, Leah Lakshmi. 2018. *Care Work: Dreaming Disability Justice*. Vancouver: Arsenal Pulp Press.

Price, Margaret. 2011. *Mad at School: Rhetorics of Mental Disability and Academic Life*. Ann Arbor: Univ. of Michigan Press.

———. 2015. "The Bodymind Problem and the Possibilities of Pain." *Hypatia* 30, no. 1: 268–84. At https://doi.org/10.1111/hypa.12127.

Samuels, Ellen. 2017. "Passing, Coming Out, and Other Magical Acts." In *Negotiating Disability: Disclosure and Higher Education*, edited by Stephanie L. Kerschbaum, Laura T. Eisenman, and James M. Jones, 15–23. Ann Arbor: Univ. of Michigan Press.

Schalk, Sami. 2018. *Bodyminds Reimagined: (Dis)ability, Race, and Gender in Black Women's Speculative Fiction*. Durham, NC: Duke Univ. Press.

Sins Invalid. 2016. *Skin, Tooth, and Bone: The Basis of Movement Is Our People: A Disability Justice Primer*. San Francisco: Sins Invalid.

20

On Mad Advantage, Redux

Covering, Passing, Negotiating (in) Higher Education

Diane R. Wiener

> *Content notes*: suicide, trauma, forced institutionalization,
> hate crimes, police brutality, gun violence

Decades ago, in a community space set up to engage, center, and honor Mad folx, the feminist writer, artist, activist, and educator Kate Millett (September 14, 1934–September 6, 2017) asked me during a private conversation if I had ever "been on the inside." She was asking if I had ever been psychiatrically incarcerated—if I knew what it was like to be "locked up." I responded that I had not been "inside" in that way. I felt out of place at that moment, which she clearly sensed. I wondered to myself if I was an outsider in an insiders' landscape and perhaps did not belong where I thought I had been welcomed. She noticed my facial expression, then paused and continued, telling me that I had work to do "as a spy," meaning that I had a role to play in trying to change systems from within. She knew that I was at the time a full-time social worker. Kate faced me directly and asserted that just because I had not been locked up did not mean I was not Mad or didn't have the right to call myself that. I felt emboldened by her words, compassion, and understanding. I eventually internalized her wisdom, taking it to heart. That moment helped to solidify, for me, what networks of Mad solidarity "looked" and felt like—and could do and mean.

Reflecting on this foundational interaction that occurred all those years ago, I think today about what being a "spy" means to me in the present, being out as "Mad" in higher education and altogether. I have discussed with my students and colleagues the ways in which they might embrace a "spy" identity, too, to strategically influence from "within" contexts that tend to be sanist, mentalist, and ableist. I join others in thinking about how doing this work can be accomplished without putting Mad folx in harm's way because risks to Mad folx of course vary greatly based on one's position, role, intersecting identities, and so many other factors. In this chapter, I discuss my own experiences of uncovering as a solidarity strategy in university settings. I am mindful that others might employ uncovering strategies similarly or differently (from the ways that I have)—if they can use these approaches at all—based on the varying and often changing risks that Mad people face with respect to consequences, including danger and harm, in large part because of our different and complex identities in the context of power.

Between 2005 and 2022, I served as a tenure-track professor, a student affairs administrator (the founding director of a Disability Cultural Center), and a research professor. For me as a teacher, colleague, liaison, adviser, supervisor, mentor, writer, and researcher, activism remains at the heart of my academic dreaming and waking.[1] Folx in higher education have sometimes sought me out to discuss how to combat oppression and what they might do to become more welcoming. My position as a "crazy" or Mad professor remains marginalizing, yet this identity can be perceived simultaneously as an advantage of interest.[2] Some people have wanted to converse with me because doing so has supported their wish to nuance their understandings of myriad bodyminds—by moving away from "us" and "them" dichotomies so often shored up by prevalent ableism,

---

1. As Leah Lakshmi Piepzna-Samarasinha asserts, "We know that one of our biggest gifts is the Mad, sick, disabled, Deaf dreams we are always dreaming and have always been dreaming, way beyond what we are allowed to dream. Not in the inspiration-porn way that's the only way many abled people can imagine that disabled-people dream of 'not letting disability stop us!'" (2020, 253).

2. Since this chapter was first written, I have returned to full-time social work practice. No longer a full-time professor, I retain an affiliation within higher education as an editor, writer, mentor, educator, and consultant.

mentalism, and sanism in the US academy and mainstream society.[3] On several occasions, I have been invited by student leaders to speak out publicly on mental health, suicidality, depression, anxiety, and Mad Pride. I am especially honored and grateful to have been presented with such opportunities.

I own the privilege that accompanies my ability to access these decisions and make these choices. My history and current circumstances can consequently make my goal of solidarity with Mad folx who do not know me at times difficult to achieve. I must earn others' trust. Mad solidarity can at times be a slippery thing or a nonlinear pathway. This is the set of contexts that informs how I continue to take up Kate Millett's call to action, her encouraging me to think of myself as a "spy." These circumstances ebb and flow, connecting with and influencing my un/covering choices. As I am affected necessarily and gratefully by community-building solidarity work, I hope to affect others meaningfully as well.

Navigating My Mad Identities

In the *Huffington Post* in May 2016, I published the essay "On Mad Advantage: A Letter to 'the Normals' (and to the Rest of Us)," in which I began to unravel experiences of stigma and to trace my journey toward self-disclosure, self-acceptance, and pride without idealization vis-à-vis my identities as intermittently emotionally disabled and intermittently Mad. Within academia, including and particularly in my previous role as a research professor, I think about and live daily with questions about how I negotiate my positionalities with my identities. Once one is labeled as "mad," and even at times when one takes up a capital *M* Mad identity, there is a loss of social capital in the world of normals. In some cases, if

---

3. Heartfelt thanks to Margaret Price for *bodyminds*, a term as well as a conceptual framework now widely used in disability studies and elsewhere. Our bodies and minds are not separate—on the contrary. For more on this term, see Price's book *Mad at School* (2011). In addition, my understanding of what I now know to be "academic ableism" would not be possible without Jay Timothy Dolmage's book *Academic Ableism: Disability and Higher Education* (2017).

one passes, this loss can also happen within the world of fellow Mad folx and in the broader world. In the case of the former, especially—that of the normals—once labeled one cannot be taken seriously as alinear, for alinearity is understood oftentimes as "symptomatic."

Within the academy and beyond, I have resisted an overdetermined narrative that my persnickety approaches—while (yes) needing to be toned down so as not to become "workaholism" or self-righteousness—are connected primarily to surviving my father's suicide and other family members' significant physical and mental health "issues" or as predominantly "symptomatic" of my own mental health "challenges." In my estimation, such reductions exemplify ableism, sanism, and mentalism in that they invalidate specificity and ignore complexity.

Madness as an experience and a political and social position/identity influences my teaching, research, and service in the interdisciplinary field of disability studies and how I am perceived and treated inside and outside of the academy. Although I am far more "centered" and "stable" than I was in my younger years, I will not withdraw from claiming a Mad identity because I know daily that being "crazy" is as variable as it is suspect and complex.

I now think of myself as Neurodivergent and Neuroqueer.[4] As part of these identities, when I describe something as "tangential," I mean that my communicating and thinking are not "typically" occurring from point A to point B in a sequence understood by many as linear. Alinearity underscores the idea that linear sequencing is not everyone's mode—by possibility, tendency, or preference (for me, all three). However, I can usually switch between these approaches—linearity and alinearity—and often joke that I "pass" as linear as an accommodation to and for other people. The switching between covering and uncovering my tangential patterns and alinear orientations further complicates the false binary between Mad and not Mad.

During many meetings and conversations at noncrip conferences and elsewhere—although most dare not say so overtly or articulate it, otherwise—I often feel as if I am either "too mad" or "only mad," but I can also

---

4. My understanding of being neuroqueer is indebted to Nick Walker's "Neuroqueer: An Introduction" ([2015] 2021).

be rendered or understood as "not mad enough." These unexpressed sentiments occur in the context of my Mad difference: one is (I am) not taken seriously if one is (I am) "too mad," and one is (I am) not taken seriously if—once known as Mad—most everything is reduced to "the reason (for x, y, z) being Madness."

Since I have not been "on the inside," never having been locked up, I am more privileged already than would be the case if I had been institutionalized—or were at greater risk of institutionalization than is presently the case. Although less often than when I was younger, I am still told regularly within professional and personal circles that I "need to try" x, y, z pharmaceuticals, that my "condition runs in the family," that "this isn't my fault," and so on. These messages are replete with arguably well-meaning advice about how I might—or should (?)—aim to pass and cover. Moreover, my kinship with other Mad scholars is sometimes complicated by my privilege. Although I do not seek to pass or cover, I could do so, as I have often been told, "with effort"—or so that I am "read" or understood differently by some "normals" as well as by some Mad brethren.

If I am "only mad" or reduced to a Mad identity as overarching, the rest of who I am is erased. If I am "only mad" when I am also somehow at times "not mad enough," I may be taking up a mantle that risks appropriation. How do I advocate for my experiences not to be denied, while refusing the alienation of those who are far more endangered by their identities and biographies than I have been?

There are expectations that become fuzzy or even occluded, rendered just under the surface, as well as delivered explicitly, conveyed during the meetings and the conversations, via email and phone exchanges, and so on, noting that I must be a poet "because" of my Mad experiences—as if depression, anxiety, dissociation, and trauma do not at times destroy and instead solely advance ideas and make creativity possible. The idealization of Madness and the renunciation of Madness are twinned in these narratives. Double pattern creation, double pattern erasure, and twinned expectation impossibilities are not the only themes in "the academy," indeed, but they are important points to emphasize.

While I am keenly aware that some may perceive my refusal to relinquish a Mad identity as a form of appropriation (as mentioned earlier),

I likewise believe that this ruminative concern of mine runs the risk of spiraling into debilitating anxiety—unironically a part of the very Madness that I continue to negotiate and claim. I think often about how these at times confusing experiences and reflections not only emblematize my personal commitments and values but also underscore far more macro-level and systemic implications.

My gender nonconformity and gender queerness do not compromise my safety in the egregious, life-denying, and life-threatening ways that happen so frequently to trans Black folx, Indigenous folx, and people of color as well as to trans white folx, in particular those who also identify as Mad. The expectations and language associated with being or being perceived as "too mad" or "not mad enough" (or both—sometimes at once) are potentially harmful to community building. It can be tricky as well as tough to be a "spy" when negotiating the slippery slope between too much and not enough. Simultaneously, the presence of certain forms of privilege can intersect with opportunities for protecting and supporting fellow Mad folx, advocating for new policies, and so on.

Along these lines, I employ my identities as opportunities to protect, support, and be in solidarity with Mad brethren whose positionalities are far more compromised and challenged than my own owing to unfair power dynamics, inequitable care, and differential access. I take these opportunities seriously while checking in consistently with peers as well as mentees to be sure that I am sharing and taking up space fairly and that I am communicating without condescension. After all, "protection" and "support" have long associations with Mad folx being patronized or undermined, and I obviously have zero interest in being complicit with such dynamics or practices, intentionally or unintentionally.

An existential question remains: How might I and others avoid capitulating to worrying about a stereotype when some parts of these reductionistic descriptions might (sometimes) also be true?[5] If or when Mad folx's

---

5. What gets labeled as workaholism and hypervigilance are two of many familiar techniques adopted by disenfranchised and oppressed people in the face of stereotype threat. Claude M. Steele and Joshua Aronson define stereotype threat as "being at risk of confirming, as self-characteristic, a negative stereotype of one's group" (1995, 797). Intriguingly,

behaviors and "choices" are labeled as workaholism and hypervigilance, the specter, perception, and treatment (*sic*) are quite different and much riskier for us than for normals. Knowing this difference and communicating openly about it on an everyday basis are purposeful facets of Mad solidarity—my mindful kinship with other Mad folx. For me, the stereotypes of unreliability, flightiness, and inconsistency as well as the fear of being perceived as "being" these "things" or displaying these "characteristics" are avoided or forestalled in some cases by my "overcompensation."

However, I cannot "just be tangential" (without consequences); normals often understand my (and others') so-called alinearity as a sign of presumed "irregularity," "imbalance," or being "out of sorts." I do not describe my (or others') variances solely as creative or unique, either, for doing so would demonstrate a kind of complicity with the romanticization of mental illness or emotional difference as necessarily "closer" to experiences of creativity and vivacity. Doing so minimizes the truisms that accompany despair and what is deemed by psychiatry's majority practitioners—and by certain lay folx in mainstream society—as "psychotic," "manic," "hypomanic," and so on (Wiener 2016).

In the next section, I discuss the distinctions and overlaps between covering and passing, how my work on the margins has influenced my attitude toward Madness and Mad Pride, and how these experiences have affected my engagement with students and colleagues.

"Choosing" (Un)Covering

Higher education has simultaneously enriched and troubled my reflections on my status or role as a Mad, nontenured professor and the ways that I must navigate each decision regarding covering and passing as compared with claiming and enacting my Mad identity by uncovering.

In *Covering: The Hidden Assault on Our Civil Rights* (2006), Kenji Yoshino invokes Erving Goffman to argue that individual and collective covering is distinct from passing. Yoshino notes: "Goffman distinguishes

---

disability is addressed relatively little in Claude Steele's later work, the often-cited book *Whistling Vivaldi: How Stereotypes Affect Us and What We Can Do* ([2010] 2011).

passing from covering by noting that passing pertains to the *visibility* of a particular trait, while covering pertains to its *obtrusiveness*. He relates how Franklin Roosevelt always stationed himself behind a table before his advisors came in for meetings. Roosevelt was not passing, since everyone knew he used a wheelchair. He was covering, downplaying his disability so people would focus on his more conventionally presidential qualities" (18). In Yoshino's roles as advocate, ally, and accomplice, his framework—as offered via his reading and invocations of Goffman and others—is instructive and applicable. Un/covering is, for Yoshino, largely a matter of physicality, yet "mental" differences—including emotional ones—are still present in his formulation and prove highly useful for my own understanding of what it means to be a Mad scholar with both hidden ("invisible") disabilities and their hypervisible claiming.[6] Put differently, because Yoshino's descriptions of covering and the implications of uncovering extend to mental and emotional formulations, his work has the potential to be very useful to Mad scholars.

Although I have been very assertive in my work, aiming neither to pass nor to cover, there are nearly always consequences and attendant risks. Moreover, without either minimizing or denying my own experiences of marginalization, I am fully aware that any consequences I have endured or attendant risks I have negotiated would be far more serious if I did not hold the identities that I do, as discussed earlier. Not passing and not covering—or mostly doing neither whenever feasible—are part of my history and current life as much as they are aspects and reflections of my advocacy on campuses as a nontenured person across my career trajectory in higher education.

When I think of my commitment to—and relationship with—Mad solidarity and my desire to be a part of Mad community, my decisions or

---

6. Some autistic and other folx use the term *masking*, which has strong connections with the assertions I forward in this chapter. As an example, the novelist Helen Hoang's *New York Times* article "Coming Out with Autism" (2020) begins by discussing the fraught word *crazy* and its relevance to—and utility in—her coming out as autistic to her mother. As Hoang notes, masking is "the process whereby autistic people (usually women) hide or mask their autistic traits to better fit in with society" (2020, par. 6).

On Mad Advantage, Redux   339

tendencies neither to pass nor to cover are informed not only by my privilege but also by the importance of my owning and naming that privilege consistently. Uncovering is far more complicated than merely a refusal of assimilation within the ubiquity of unequal power dynamics and various oppressions, the presence of which I have aimed to underscore throughout this discussion. My respect for, awareness of, and actions toward disrupting inequity influence my choices. These approaches and actions exist in tandem with my own concurrent marginalization and privilege, necessarily complicating the possibilities and meanings of my choices—and what *choice* means in the first place.

Being an academic means negotiating behaviors and so-called choices that are often necessary, yet being a Mad academic, especially one that refuses to "pass" or "cover," means risking that these "choices" will be interpreted as pathological forms of workaholism and hypervigilance. Some colleagues and others have explained my stalwart work ethic—simultaneously appreciated and understood by others (as well as by myself) as "overdoing it"—as hypervigilance borne largely out of trauma and as informed, if not caused in part, by my depression and anxiety.

While workaholism and hypervigilance tend to be championed within the academy, it is also the case that their harmful effects are not supposed to be apparent. The approval and even celebration of hypervigilance and workaholism within higher education have great costs that are not experienced equally by all who come to suffer from the consequences of this orientation and its expectations' ableism, mentalism, and sanism. Simultaneously, Mad folx refusing to be pathologized for setting boundaries with respect to these harmful expectations may be met by allegations that individual "problems" are to be blamed rather than a status quo within a system that endangers both Mad and not Mad people's bodyminds and wellness—understood in mainstream parlance as our physical and emotional health. And, again, not everyone experiences these dangerous expectations in the same ways or equally, especially with respect to the multiplicity of intersecting oppressions, differences in roles and identities, and so on.

I uncover by quipping during conversations, meetings, and conferences and when I am teaching that (as noted earlier) I pass as linear as an accommodation to and for other people. I uncover by narrating myriad, multilevel (and "subordinate") clauses in my communication—at times to my own detriment because of how my "style" has the potential to frustrate rather than support others, regardless of my intentions (to be inclusive and nuanced).

My "choice" not to cover—a "choice" informed by the privileged position of being able to make such a choice in the first place—builds solidarity (or has the promise to do so), I hope, with fellow Mad folx, crips, and other disabled people inside and beyond the academy.

I have worked in solidarity with many disabled peers, allies, and accomplices to address academic ableism, mentalism, and sanism in their myriad structural manifestations (spatial elements, curricular design, pedagogical approaches, linguistic choices, meeting and event setup, etc.).

When I uncover—as tangential, despairing, anxious, not experiencing normative reality, overwhelmed, and even at times a hot mess—I believe I am making pragmatic decisions that are simultaneously risky, borne out of my privilege, and modeling of what I consider to be a kind of fierce vulnerability.

Paths to Solidarity

Mental illness has at times been imagined as a rather different kind of "gift" than other kinds of disability ingenuity, even in crip cultural spaces. As I discussed in my article "On Mad Advantage" in the *Huffington Post*, for me, "the idea of madness as a plurality underscores a range of thinking and feeling. These explicit as well as hidden variances in cognition and affect are expressions of diversity and uniqueness; they have the potential to contribute to experiences of Mad cultural pride and the furthering of variegated 'crip' identities" (Wiener 2016, par. 12). As with my communication during meetings, with colleagues via email, and so on, teaching holds the promise for me to be a "spy" in a vital environment within higher education—the classroom (in-person and virtual)—and with the constituents who matter most to me in academic spaces, the students. Teaching presents me with yet another set of ways and opportunities to strategically uncover.

My uncovering influences my approach to course design, digital platform setup, syllabus construction, classroom interaction, assignment evaluation—really everything connected to my pedagogy. For several years, I taught an undergraduate honors course called "(Dis)abling Comic Books," which grew in part out of "'Cripping' the Comic Con," the disability and comics symposium created by Rachael Zubal-Ruggieri and yours truly at Syracuse University. "(Dis)abling Comic Books" contained extensive content on graphic memoirs, including a final, written assignment that expected students to select a printed graphic memoir or webcomic and comment on several, interrelated prompts on disability representations, ethics, accessibility, axes of difference and intersectionality, relevance to disability communities, and so on.

The students knew from early on in the course that I identify as Mad, as crip, and as disabled—and as an array of other identities (some marginalized, some privileged). Universal Design for Learning and design justice were built into every course element. Put differently, the course was cripped—through and through. The syllabus included my candid commentary about accessibility, learning variance, and a commitment to going beyond formalized definitions of impairment and disability in order to create a welcoming learning environment that did not center one kind of intelligence over others.

The course expectations, assignments, and activities were structured with a decidedly Mad and crip approach, decentering the normative at all times. Students were also taught about captioning, image descriptions, alt-text, descriptive audio, and a variety of accessibility approaches and components using a cross-disabilities perspective. One of my goals was to create a deliberate, consistent learning space of Mad and crip solidarity.

Among other questions, the course "asked" students to think about how disabilities are represented in comics and their adaptations, and in connected genres; how disabled creators, artists, and authors are—and (often) are not but should be—included in this world; and how to make comics and their adaptations accessible. Mad solidarity, affect, and emotional diversity were central course components—topically and by design.

At the beginning of the semester, I presented an anonymous accessibility survey. Students could update this anonymous survey anytime they wished. They did not have to be affiliated with a disability-services provider officially or formally to complete the survey, which included ongoing and emergent access requests, trigger and content-warning requests, and related questions. The anonymous accessibility survey accompanied the not anonymous student questionnaire that I asked each student to complete at the beginning of the semester. The information sheet included questions on how the students learn best, what they hope to get out of and put into the class, and whether they have any concerns or needs I should be made aware of (by them). From the outset, I hoped the students received the message that I invited them to uncover if they wished. However much I seek and sought to flatten hierarchies, though, I am aware that power dynamics, axes of difference, and many other variables influence and contribute to what and how much students can and will share about themselves (even anonymously).

It is my hope that these activities modeled for students the ways in which they might choose to "speak truth to power" and the degree to which they can do so safely, depending on their own positionalities and other factors. Disrupting hierarchies, critiquing stigmatization, and seeking to suspend, at least temporarily, aspects of power that cannot be dismantled entirely contribute, I hope, to Mad and crip solidarity in the classroom and beyond.

I wondered at the time if what the *Mad Scholars* volume editors once called my "defiant vulnerability" in the context of terror, rage, death, inequity, brutality, and uncertainty (particularly in the wake of COVID-19, rampant police brutality, rising hate crimes—including racist, anti-Semitic, and Islamophobic violence—climate emergencies, and ever-present school shootings) helped the students in the spring 2020 and spring 2021 versions of "(Dis)abling Comic Books" feel more empowered than might otherwise have been the case. It seemed that the students knew that they could "speak truth to power" about their own vulnerabilities and uncertainties, perhaps at least in part because I had modeled this practice for them and had done so consistently and without condescension. More importantly and in any case, the students certainly modeled this practice for and to each other as well as for and to me. This is a gift that can come from uncovering, from working in community to grow and steward a liberatory, Mad solidarity.

The interactions that the students and I had about Madness and Mad Pride—before and during the pandemic as well as during local and global Black Lives Matter protests—exemplified the potential, nonidealized power adhering to, and risks underpinning, Mad pedagogy. If I had not told the students that I was Mad identified, that my father had killed himself, that mental illness and trauma were foundational to my family history, I do not think they would have addressed or shifted in their own passing and covering in quite the same way. Although I do not know any of that for certain, I do know that my experience of shifting away from psychic repression in my students' presence—for their sake and my own— was informed by our conversations, our historical contexts, our different identities, and their and my own learning. I am forever grateful to my students for weathering personal, societal, and pandemic storms to (en)counter stigma.

Over the course of the past decade or so in my teaching as well as in my professional life, my uncovering has been greater than the amount of uncovering I did prior to that time. There is anecdotal evidence as well as direct, anonymous, and nonanonymous feedback from my students regarding how these "choices" of mine with respect to uncovering in teaching and elsewhere have been impactful in their learning and in our co-creating of Mad and crip spaces of solidarity.

One of the assigned texts that particularly intrigued the spring 2020 semester's students was the final chapter in Elizabeth J. Donaldson's edited volume *Literatures of Madness: Disability Studies and Mental Health* (2019). Jessica Gross's contribution "It Doesn't Add Up: Mental Illness in Paul Hornschemeier's *Mother, Come Home*" is an unabashed discussion of mental health complexities, including what Gross calls a "traumascape" in graphic memoir and comics—obviously with Hornschemeier's text as the topical fulcrum. Gross's chapter in Donaldson's text was assigned as required reading in my class, although I knew it was "heavy" and would require content warnings, which I provided.

Many of my students were affected strongly by Gross's chapter as well as by other work on mental illness, Madness, and emotional variance as depicted in the graphic memoirs and myriad fictionalized texts that we addressed throughout the semester. By the course's conclusion, many of the students shifted in—or in some cases ceased—their own passing and covering with respect to emotional variance. I believe I did, too. It would be "easy" to claim that the 2020 global health pandemic's urgency was a contributing factor in these transformations. Although I agree with that perspective, I also conjecture that there were other reasons why the students and I shifted away from psychic repression, thereby countering sanism, mentalism, and ableism.

We dared to talk about despair and emotional nuances via our required asynchronous, online course discussions as well as during the optional synchronous meetings that I hosted virtually every class time, when we would have been meeting in person had we not been living in a world within which the majority of instruction became necessarily and fully digital. Students also talked with me one to one about these matters, further cultivating a Mad and crip space of solidarity.

In these respects and so many others, the students and I found emergent ways to co-create community. Aided by our uncovering(s), we negotiated the nuances of accessibility during a deeply troubling time. The students told me that the class felt connecting, that it undermined and even in some respects combated alienation. As always, I was and remain a learner as well as a teacher. My students showed each other and taught me that there are many ways to be bold, to be subtle, and to share expertise, innovation, and creativity. The conversations we had and the experiences we shaped together will continue to flourish. This chapter is dedicated with my gratitude to my Mad and crip students and their not Mad, not crip peers.

Works Cited

Dolmage, Jay Timothy. 2017. *Academic Ableism: Disability and Higher Education*. Ann Arbor: Univ. of Michigan Press.

Gross, Jessica. 2018. "It Doesn't Add Up: Mental Illness in Paul Hornschemeier's *Mother, Come Home*." In *Literatures of Madness: Disability Studies and Mental Health*, edited by Elizabeth J. Donaldson, 215–33. New York: Palgrave Macmillan.

Hoang, Helen. 2020. "Coming Out with Autism." *New York Times*, July 13. At https://www.nytimes.com/2020/07/13/us/disability-reveal.html.

Piepzna-Samarasinha, Leah Lakshmi. 2020. "Still Dreaming Wild Disability Justice Dreams at the End of the World." In *Disability Visibility: First-Person Stories from the Twenty-First Century*, edited by Alice Wong, 250–61. New York: Vintage.

Price, Margaret. 2011. *Mad at School: Rhetorics of Mental Disability and Academic Life*. Ann Arbor: Univ. of Michigan Press.

Steele, Claude M. [2010] 2011. *Whistling Vivaldi: How Stereotypes Affect Us and What We Can Do*. Reprint. New York: Norton.

Steele, Claude M., and Joshua Aronson. 1995. "Stereotype Threat and the Intellectual Test Performance of African Americans." *Journal of Personality and Social Psychology* 69, no. 5: 797–811. At https://doi.org/10.1037//0022-3514.69.5.797.

Walker, Nick. [2015] 2021. "Neuroqueer: An Introduction." *Neuroqueer: The Writings of Dr. Nick Walker* (blog), rev. and exp., Summer. At https://neuroqueer.com/neuroqueer-an-introduction.

Wiener, Diane R. 2016. "On Mad Advantage: A Letter to 'the Normals' (and to the Rest of Us)." *Huffington Post*, May 25. At https://www.huffpost.com/entry/on-mad-advantage-a-letter_b_10071806.

Yoshino, Kenji. 2006. *Covering: The Hidden Assault on Our Civil Rights*. New York: Random House.

21

Landing without Falling

The Fucking Blue Dots

Holly Pearson

Content note: self-harm

Let's start off with this question: What is the difference between standards and expectations? Standards are about a level of quality, whereas expectations are the belief that something will occur/take place. Still fuzzy? That is OK. Let's shift gears—online dating. I know, I know. Just go with it. What are the parallels between online dating and academia? If you have not experienced online dating, it is this bizarre process where you willingly meet strangers with an agenda—one night of pleasure, a relationship, companionship, and so on. We often go in looking for one thing and then find something completely different. Why? This has to do with standards and expectations.

Dating by Lion, a social media platform, has amazing videos about relationships and dating. One of his videos uses a red-and-blue dots analogy. He asks the audience to take a moment and notice all the red dots in the room, and then he asks them to tell him how many blue dots are in the room. "Wait, what? You asked me to pay attention to the red dots!" That was exactly his point. We often think we know what we want, so we get tunnel vision—which results in our missing out on all the other possibilities. The red dots/blue dots analogy is a beautiful representation of the difference between standards and expectations and is meant to help people on the dating market. You start off with your list of wants—often based on previous relationship experiences and/or trauma—and the list is often too narrow. Does this person meet my criteria (e.g., wants kids, thin, no beard, healthy, taller than I am, etc.)? Nope? NEXT! Letting go of expectations—what we assume will happen, the imaginary person we expect—is when we can begin to focus inward and gain greater awareness of who we are as a person: our values, beliefs, and strengths. It is only here where we can build a foundation for everything else that is being stacked on top. This does not mean letting go of standards! Standards are our backbone! Instead, the point is—to remember the blue dots. To have a strong foundation and clarity of those standards, we need to have a clear sense of self because it is from here that we can see our true self constantly changing and learn how to value ourselves as people. If we cannot see ourselves, we cannot value ourselves. We too often have an idea of who we are, but that identity or person is based on expectations.

For instance, because of my Asian appearance, people always expected me to be well versed in Asian culture, language, geography, and so on. I had no fucking clue. I grew up in Alaska, and I was adopted into a white family. But because of people's expectations of me, I ended up doing a two-year crash course in college on how to be Asian. I not only built my knowledge of Asian language, culture, and geography but also adapted my style of talking, mannerisms, and appearance to align with people's expectations of what being Asian meant. As a result, my sense of self became disconnected and fragmentized. I ultimately lost myself. I spiraled into a deep abyss for a period until I was able to crawl my ass out of that hole. I wish I could say I found myself after that experience— insert laughing emoticon. That did not take place until a decade later.

During those ten years, I was functional, but I was a weeping willow: bending and swaying to expectations. It was not until I developed my "fuck it" mindset, when I started shifting away from those expectations and focusing on standards, that I started to look at academia with new eyes. Please note that when I use the word *academia*, I am not talking about a particular person or institution. I am talking about academia as a whole. Everything that we do as academics and the culture we participate in: that is what I am referring to.

What We Are Looking for Cannot Be Found in Academia

Commence ripping off the Band-Aid. We cannot find our sense of happiness within others. It must first come from within us. And academia cannot teach, model, instill what we are looking for. There is a plague of unhappiness in academia, and it unfortunately affects multiply marginalized folks disproportionately. But this chapter does not focus on my thoughts on higher education writ large. Instead, I want to shift the conversation to ourselves—(re)centering the lived trauma and pain of multiply marginalized folks. BUT please do not make the mistake of defining our existence based on trauma and pain alone. We are beautiful complex beings who deserve and have every right not to be boxed into a single damn checklist. What if, instead of expelling so much energy and rage at academia, we reframe this process? What if we shift to the blue dots?

Academia will never be what we want it to be. It was built on values that are not in alignment with humanity, respect, love, and interdependence. It is dysfunctional; it has built itself on hyperproductivity, privilege, power, and status. It can teach us only how to bullshit, to exhaust, and to disrespect ourselves. But can we fully blame academia alone? Academia is a product of its own fountain of expectations. It has never had the opportunity to learn other ways. If a person grows up never eating or making a peanut butter and jelly sandwich, then how can we get mad at the person when they cannot give us a PBJ when we want one? The damn sandwich was never part of their reality. Academia sucks all the energy out of folks who occupy the landscape. It encourages autopilot and discourages creativity. As a result, many of us expel so much more energy than necessary trying to understand what the fuck is going on while trying to stay afloat with all the shit that we are trying to juggle. It really is a sand trap. We constantly feel as if we are sinking, but we are too distracted, too exhausted, too pissed off while running the hamster-wheel race. And ultimately: academia is what it is.

For me, this realization was a long time coming. I spent the past decade as contingent faculty. I went into my PhD program with the expectation that I would graduate into a tenure-track (TT) job. I did everything according to the game—research, teaching, and service—from day one until I graduated. I applied and ended up with no job after I graduated. Second year out of PhD school, I landed a one-year contract at a state university. I reapplied every year, which created a ball of anxiety not only about having an income but also about health insurance, where I was going to live, whether I should go into a relationship or wait—nearly every aspect of my day-to-day life. A trickling feeling of maybe this is never what I wanted in the first place eventually emerged. Throughout the PhD program, the unspoken expectation is you want a TT position. Every single opportunity is built around achieving this status. I remember asking early on: But what if I don't want to go into academia? I would be told over and over: "Of course you want a TT job." There was no "but."

Remember that word—*expectations*? A-ha moment, right? But when that realization started kicking in, I was very resistant to the idea. I felt a wide range of feelings—guilt at how I was supposed to want a TT position; rage over how shitty the system was; sadness as I saw so many of my colleagues struggling and not happy in academia; traumatized as I tried hard to not lose my shit over the things that I was so desperately trying to control. Over the years, I grew more frustrated and angrier. Not just my position in/toward academia but all aspects of my life fell apart—relationships, parents, self-fulfillment, and so on. Amid the chaos, I was desperately trying to cling on to everything as a form of control. Trying to predict the future, trying to control the outcome wore me out physically and mentally.

Do not get me wrong. I loved the students. I loved my dear colleagues, who had my back and still have it now. I loved parts of my scholarship. But the instability, the lack of control, and the lack of fulfillment were too exhausting. When COVID hit, all my energy went into getting the students through each day, every week, every semester. I excelled when many did not. I received positive feedback from students and colleagues. My work and time and energy were acknowledged in the form of a distinguished faculty award. But during my last year of teaching, I was so burnt out that I could not give a fuck anymore. It took every ounce of myself to get up and go to class, to check on the students and see what they needed. I was honest with them that I was exhausted, and I was struggling. I made it very clear to them that I was trying my best to focus on one step at a time. But I knew, deep down inside, I was done. I could not bear the idea of doing this any longer. My dear colleagues knew as well, which is why they advocated for me to receive the award. But when it came around, it was already too late. My dear students knew as well, and they made me tear up as they reached out and checked in and sent me funny memes amid all the anxiety, trauma, and violence they were struggling to unpack as well.

Before we continue, I wish to make it clear that I do not regret my time in academia. I still get pissed about what happened, but I do not regret it. Being a contingent faculty member has made me stronger. Even with all the breakdowns and fear and stress, everything that I have achieved and accomplished in the past decade has led me and prepared me for the position I am in now. As I see it now, academia was a detour that unexpectedly taught me a great deal about standards and expectations. For that, I will always be forever grateful.

It's OK to Let Go . . . Seriously, Give Yourself Permission

I run a lot—not only as in getting up at 5:00 a.m., pulling on my shoes, blasting my KPOP music but also as in running from aspects of myself. Running means working myself to death through side gigs, cramming my schedule full with workouts and social time as a coping mechanism so I do not have to process emotions or thoughts that I do not want to deal with.

My body shut down the last half of April 2022. After a few months of sixteen-hour days and four-hour-sleep nights, my body just shut down. For two weeks, I could barely function. All I could do was sleep and lie around in a daze. Making food was tedious. Showering zapped all my energy. I could not stand to look at a screen. Normally, my brain is swirling with so many different ideas and connections, but during this time I could barely handle one thought at a time. It was bewildering to have my brain on silent mode. As a result, the dam broke loose, and all the damn emotions bubbled forward. Thoughts emerged that I had been stuffing away like dirty laundry into the drawers to make the place seem presentable when an unexpected guest shows up.

One of the thoughts that really stung was that I truly struggle with allowing myself to be happy, to recognize that I deserve and I have the right to be happy. To be able to speak my mind; to be able to breathe. When I receive recognition, I often deflect it to someone else or make jokes or hide and avoid everyone. How the hell did I get to this point where I cannot even embrace the joy in being appreciated?

But why am I even asking that question? I already know the answer.

I cannot be happy because I genuinely do not believe I deserve it. I cannot be happy because something bad will happen. I cannot be happy because someone will leave. I cannot be happy because—

The past few years have been painful—in a good way. I have been finding my chosen communities and families. Learning how to lean on others and let them lean on me. Finding my laughter that comes from deep within and not for the sake of someone else's ego. Entering into a space with a gentle "fuck you" mentality of confidence. Calling out/on/in people even when I am shaking on the inside. Realizing that I want to see this story to the end.

Growing up, I never expected to see the end of this story. Yes, you read that correctly. But at some point in the past few years, I decided no—I actually do want to see how this story plays out. I was done being a shadow.

I was fine. I was good. A forced smile on my face as my spirit screamed, "No, I am not fucking fine! I'm pissed!" I was struggling to extract the jagged glass pieces wedged into my body, heart, psyche, and spirit, shards embedding themselves deeper over time. At times, they sting like a paper cut. They are still there. Not quite forgotten. Triggering psychic disequilibrium. Yet the irony is that it is a thousand times more painful trying to pull them out one inch at a time.

This is not a happy-ever-after story. No heteronormative Prince Charming to come save the day. The physical scars are still visible on my forearm. Psychic and emotional scars are still very much present and alive. I did not expect this level of pain/trauma. I knew I had been affected, but I did not realize the full extent. However, richness was there as well. Richness in being surrounded by people who have my back and fight with me, for me, who love me for me even when I say the most random shit, when I am pissed, when I am depressed. I still am not used to this. I am still struggling to embrace this richness. The richness in who I have become up to this point and coming back to who I am. This past decade has been a steep learning curve—in putting aside the bullshit and the toxicity, I have learned not only about myself but also about the skills and knowledge that have prepared me for the next step in my journey and given me a clearer vision of what I want to achieve. That step is the same one I have seen in front of me since I was a kid—making the world a little better every day not just for everyone else, not anymore, but also for myself. My fucking joy matters, too.

Ironically, what drove this realization home were TikTok videos about love and dating—a random, unexpected discovery that provided clarity in ways that I did not anticipate (remember the blue dots). In one of his amazing videos about self-care, Ivan Nicholo made clear that there are times when you love something so much but also know you need to leave it. The situation is toxic. Too often we are taught to suck it up, to push through, to persevere. When do we draw the line? When do we get to invest in ourselves? When I look at my godkid and his sibling, that lesson always hits home. I cannot keep self-sacrificing like this because this is not what I wish for them to do. I do not want them to kill any part of themselves. That's what it comes down to. You do not deserve to be put or forced into a situation where you are sacrificing yourself.

What I thought I wanted did not actually pan out. Instead, I was looking for something else. As I was in academia my last semester, I came to realize the parallels between my job and my romantic life. I was in a relationship—putting all my energy into finding a partner, finding a TT job. But then I realized that the person/institution never felt the same way about me; it was clear that our priorities were not in alignment at all. In the end, effort is what matters. Endless TikTok videos consistently return to this point—effort—whether it is a text saying good morning or someone stopping by to see you even if it is for only a few minutes, to remember your favorite drink, to send you pictures of things that remind them of you. If there is no effort, there is no relationship.

Academia does not have the ability to teach you this. Academia is not going to teach us how to enjoy our life. To value ourselves as human beings. If a relationship is not reciprocal, then there is no relationship. It will not be fulfilling. Instead, it will be cheating life, and we all know—more than ever now—that life is precious. We have only limited time—and even less time for ourselves. With online dating, I learned this lesson quickly.

The question remains: Why did I not do this with academia? I tolerated so much in academia, shit that I normally would have not tolerated from another person. I had to let it go. I had to break up with academia and move on even though I love academia with all my heart. It was not working out. I could not breathe. It was time to leave.

To make it clear—this was not easy at all. It was far from fucking easy. When I finally left, the exit was three years in the making, held up by relapsed denial and hopefulness that things would change. And I still felt a tremendous amount of guilt. Guilt in knowing that I had crawled my way into achieving a PhD. Guilt in knowing I was one of the few there who represented multiply marginalized folks. Guilt in feeling as if I were throwing away an opportunity.

In one of the last few conversations I had with my grandfather, I told him that I wanted to follow in his footsteps and become a surgeon. He calmly looked at me and asked: "Do you want to be happy?" I looked at him with a confused expression. "Well, yeah. . . ." "Then don't become a surgeon," he said. At that time, I did not understand why he would say that. Now I get it. And I will encourage my godkid and his sibling to do the same—to follow what makes them happy and fulfilled. Not to chase false illusions of expectations or external sources of satisfaction and worth that were never designed to give them the support they need. To know themselves, deep down within—where their confidence, resilience, joy, and values lie—and to trust that knowledge over any external source.

Academia does not know how to love itself in healthy ways. Academia does not know how to build healthy relationships. But that is where it is at. Is it our right to expect it to change on its own when it does not know how to? No, especially if we do not know how to prioritize ourselves and our own well-being. So much energy is being expelled in the hope that something will change when academia does not know how to do so. We put too much weight on external factors for our own happiness.

Manifestation of FUCK IT

I focused and built my entire life on the goal of getting a TT position. I did everything in accordance with the game—publish, teach, present, and so on. If you do not believe me, I do not fucking care. My CV shows it. I *expected* a TT job when I finished, for academia to have those jobs—an expectation that resulted in a blind spot. The data do not lie: the number of people who get TT jobs is shrinking. And I am tired of wasting energy being mad at academia in the expectation that it will change. It is at this point that we can allow standards to guide or gently nudge us, which will prompt us to take the power back.

My motto now is "fuck it." It is a motto I developed in the past few years and strengthened during my yoga teacher training. Every time I am in the face of hypocrisy bullshit, I just mentally chant, "Fuck it fuck it fuck it." I spent a chunk of the past decade trying so hard to control the outcomes based on the expectations I had and the expectations that others had. I grew tired of the inconsistency—I got tired of the bullshit. Now I assert boundaries. I hold to standards—I do not rely on expectations.

What still pisses me off is that we spend so much time trying to find home, to find solidarity, to carve out spaces within these toxic environments. In striving toward a TT, I gave up relationships; I stayed in a toxic relationship; I moved away from home; I gave up the possibility of ever building a home due to the instability of whether I would have a job next year. It was in nonacademic spaces—among friends and colleagues, in activism and in yoga—that I came to realize that finding myself, loving myself, cannot be scripted, as much of academia tries to script it. Things just do not work that way. As in the dating TikTok videos, yoga was a blue dot. Something completely unexpected.

What are you seeking? What is that one thing that is important to you? Being open and present is one of the most powerful things we can do. Yoga has taught me the value of being present. Whether it is about our body, our tension, our breath . . . or being open to possibilities. To be in the moment. To be in the present.

I never once aspired to be a yoga teacher. I dabbled in yoga over the years but never pursued it seriously until very recently. Yoga was one of those things that was always there—ready to be picked up whenever I was ready for it. I needed that space to retreat to, to ground myself again. I had no idea what to expect, and for once I was OK with that. I had no idea what I would do with this, but I trusted it all would unfold as I was ready to receive and process and feel. Once I did this, just enjoy yoga for what

Landing without Falling 355

it is, and did not have expectations to be something or to do something with yoga, I learned skills, messages, affirmation, and values that I was subconsciously seeking.

One of the strongest implied messages I received as a child was to be grateful for the second chance. I am sure the person who instilled this in me had no ill intentions. But that is not what is important. The takeaway message was, "You got a second chance. A life in America. Do not fuck it up. If you do, you can be sent back to Korea." Having adopted parents does not guarantee a nice life. It is always the same story: "You are lucky to be here." We also receive this message in graduate school, especially when we see one of us be the "first" of whatever: the first Black professor in this department, the first Asian woman to receive this award, the first to—blah blah blah. Massive kudos to the person who achieves the accomplishment. But for the rest of us, this is not a positive message—at least as I see it. It is a reminder to pull yourself up by the bootstraps and push your way through at the expense of yourself. Do so at the cost of your comrades, colleagues, and friends. And be grateful for whatever comes your way, even though you are paid differently, have to work a hundred times harder to be recognized, and often have to take on greater burdens. Well: fuck it. And academia: fuck you. For telling me I should be grateful for something completely out of my control. For the gentle yet toxic reminder that I should be building a life based on your expectations and not my standards. Fuck that shit. I am done playing a game where I have no say and the rules are constantly changing.

Through yoga, I learned tools for how to fight back, how to carve out spaces, how to dream and be creative, how to develop my own voice or stance. This is how I am going to change the world. To make things different. The most unexpected occurrences are some of the most awesome that we experience and encounter. We do not plan them. We cannot plan them. But the joy of being surprised is one of the best things we can have as human beings. Blue dots.

Too often we have a very narrow sense of what joy looks, feels, sounds, and smells like. To leave academia was a bizarre feeling. I never expected I would leave. When I closed my office, I cried so much. I rarely ever cry: some bullshit doctor had told me to stop being so emotional, or I would get sick. And it is true that whenever I experience high amounts of emotions (depression/happiness), I get vertigo and tinnitus. As a result, I was tightly wound so I would not be overly emotional. But now I have a hard time dealing with my emotions. I tuck them away and ignore them as long as I can, until my body comes back screaming at me for ignoring them and not slowing down. So in my office I broke down crying. I am not talking about a few tears: I am talking about full-on sobbing. I sobbed out all of my rage, disappointment, love, and guilt. Disappointment in how what I thought was going to happen never came about. Yet I also cried in relief—relief that for the first time in a decade I would finally have a sustainable job. I was finally leaving a toxic living situation. I finally bought my dream car. I finally was open to falling in love once again after a long time of cocooning myself in recovering from previous toxic relationships. Things were finally shifting, moving.

Letting go of our expectations allows us to see the blue dots, to see beyond to the possibilities that are out there, gently nudging us each day to live life in accordance with our values and to value ourselves as a gorgeous complex human being. To value ourselves at times involves letting go. That is not losing or proof that we are lesser than or a cowardly act. Instead, letting go is sometimes a means to move toward what we truly want deep down inside. We have the right to be viewed and treated as human. But this starts with treating ourselves as human beings—being gentle with ourselves when we are exhausted, allowing ourselves to feel joy, allowing ourselves to curse rather than constantly wearing the stoic academic persona. Giving ourselves permission to leave. We have every right to grow as people—to learn, to change, to evolve. If we do not do it for ourselves, how can we expect to model this approach to life for those around us—our mentees, our children, our students? We cannot cheat ourselves and then turn around and expect others not to do the same. The cycle is only going to be perpetuated unless we stop it. Consider what blue dots are present in your life.

22

Orienting toward Togetherness

A Mad Phenomenology

Shayda Kafai

I feel, therefore I can be free.
—Audre Lorde, "Poetry Is Not a Luxury" (1985)

What lies beyond our grasp remains unnamed.
—Robin Wall Kimmerer, *Braiding Sweetgrass* (2013)

> *Content note*: settler colonialism

I felt disembodied yesterday. Time as sensation expanded past the twenty-four hours we are told exist in a day. The living room was not the living room. Colors retreated into monotone. Although I was moving slowly, I was sweating and fatigued.

One word for this experience is *dissociation*, but that description does not feel right, does not align; what I felt was *distant* from myself. *Distant* is a more accurate designation, a more authentic naming; however, it, too, lacks, leaks, falters. Feeling distant from myself connotes a searching, a desire for orientation.

I was able to burrow, to shelter into these somatic experiences, after beginning the ecologist and Indigenous writer Robin Wall Kimmerer's new book *Braiding Sweetgrass* (2013). In her descriptions of her kindred and tender relationship with wild strawberries, she gave me the language to name what I could not access. She writes, "It was the wild strawberries, beneath dewy leaves on an almost-summer morning, who gave me my sense of the world, my place in it" (22). Yesterday I was not "in the world"; I was only an observer.

Today, I raked leaves with my uncle. Since his stroke, he has what the medical-industrial complex calls "aphasia," a naming that limits, that hangs inadequate. After witnessing him, I know aphasia to be more complex than an inability to express speech. My uncle has his own grammar, his own diction. There are fricatives and sounds that are connected to his expressions, his hands; he has become an embodied language. This morning my uncle stood outside and gestured toward the maple tree in the backyard, toward its pile of leaves; I followed. He began raking, while I slowly shoveled the leaves.

It was a strange day, a strange time. It was January and 72 degrees Fahrenheit in Southern California. The maple's leaves had just turned scarlet and yellow. Its body told us about climate chaos and the distressed beauty of it all. As we worked, the heat landed heavy on my back, and I was surprised at how the sun built on my neck and arms. My growing succulent tattoo sleeve saw sun for the first time, and I cannot express quite how quickly and fully the heat returned me to my body. I was invited into this reflective place because of my uncle's pacing: his jolting limbs, their slowness, and his intentional footing, the embodiment of gathering in relation to the tree. It was a combination of this meditative outdoor ritual and the texture of the weather that allowed me to relocate myself. How quickly we become distanced from ourselves; how quickly, still, we return.

We, the Mad many, are often mood travelers. I shift, for example, from moments of presence and rootedness toward wreckage and disorientation. This way of "being-in-the-world" (Toombs 1988, 202) is also always located in-between. I am a "Mad border body" (Kafai 2012), someone unbounded by the fictional and unstable categories of sanity and insanity. My Mad border body exists in the world in a slippery way, in a neither-this-nor-that way. The container of a day does not necessarily relegate my shifts, which come and go, only to return again. It is an unexpected feat, this Mad magic. During these moments of variation, my bodymind needs to remember that I am limbs and organs, that I have weight. Today I walk in the yard by the winter vegetables that are trying to grow despite the temperature. I walk barefoot to remember that I am tangible. I walk barefoot to be made familiar to myself once again.

It is a Mad practice to invite bodymind tangibility, to invite tethering. From this place, this Mad political rooting, we orient ourselves from our bodyminds outward. We have, as disability phenomenologists name it, robustly dynamic ways of "being-in-the-world" (Toombs 1988, 202). Our bodyminds are not just components of who we are. Informed by traditional phenomenological traditions, in particular that of Maurice Merleau-Ponty (1962), S. Kay Toombs defines phenomenology as more than an act of embodiment: "I am embodied not in the sense that I *have* a body—as I have an automobile, a house, or a pet—but in the sense that I *exist* or *live* my body" (1995, 10, emphasis in original). Rather, Toombs names embodiment as "the basic scheme of orientation, the center of one's system of coordinates" (1995, 10). To understand my Mad bodymind as that which I *exist* in, as my "vehicle for seeing" (Toombs 1995, 10), I engage with phenomenology as a framework. It becomes a way to understand how our lived experiences affect how we journey in this world, what Corinne Lajoie and Emily R. Douglas name "body-world-reciprocity" in their introduction to the *Journal of Critical Phenomenology* special issue "Critically Sick: New Phenomenologies of Illness, Madness, and Disability" (2020, 2). I call forward the scholars who have written about disabled phenomenology (Murphy 1987; Toombs 1995; Paterson and Hughes 1999; Abrams 2020; Diedrich 2021; Padilla 2003) and apply Mad tools to extend and employ this unique framing, a materialization of dreams and thoughtfeelings.[1] What might a Mad phenomenology offer? *Feel* like? What portals could it orient us toward?[2]

---

1. "Thoughtfeeling" is a concept created by the Queer Futures Collective, a way of acknowledging that our thoughts and feelings inform each other. Rather than distinct responses, thoughtfeelings are interwoven and reciprocal (see Schlauderaff 2019).

2. Traditional phenomenological traditions were established by Maurice Merleau-Ponty (1962), Martin Heidegger (1962), and Edmund Husserl (1983). However, because these frameworks did not consider disabled embodiment, Mad phenomenology relies

Sara Ahmed explores the need for orientation in her book *Queer Phenomenology* (2006). She writes, "To queer phenomenology is to offer a different 'slant' to the concept of orientation itself" (4). As queer folks, as gender-nonconforming and transgender folks, we find ourselves by diverging from cis-heteronormativity. We skew. We slant. We imagine other ways of loving ourselves and one another. Who we occupy space with, who we orient toward, is informed by how we maneuver our bodyminds in cis-heteropatriarchal systems not made for us. This queering is our refusal. It is resistance as a generous love practice. It is ceremony.

Throughout *Braiding Sweetgrass* (2013), Kimmerer aligns orientation with ceremony. There are moments of pause and reflection when, for example, she writes about her family's tradition of pouring an offering of coffee onto the ground with gratitude and thanksgiving when they were camping in the Adirondacks: "I know that in the long-ago times our people raised their thanks in morning songs, in prayer, and the offering of sacred tobacco. But at that time in our family history, we didn't have sacred tobacco and we didn't know the songs—they'd been taken away from my grandfather at the doors of the boarding school" (35). In this meditation of memory, Kimmerer names ceremony as being in kinship with nature, as a practice of collective memory making. Ceremony is that which lives despite colonization: "What else can you offer the earth, which has everything? What else can you give but something of yourself? A homemade ceremony, a ceremony that makes a home" (38).

When we orient back toward ourselves, we engage in tender ceremony. Orienting in this way allows us to make homes in our bodyminds even when all the institutions tell us we are expendable, unworthy, and invaluable. This intervention is what Ahmed names the "slant," the deviation that invites us to contemplate a new way of existing and being in the world.[3] In the slant, we are invited to "feel at home" in our bodyminds

---

on more contemporary frameworks of phenomenology that are informed by critical disability studies.

3. The process and experience of disorientation is not something that only Mad or neurodivergent folks experience. As Mad folks, we are more often forced into an

once again (Ahmed 2006, 7). We, the Mad, express so much in our everyday ceremony, our practice of homecoming; it is ceremony to wake up, feed ourselves, take our medicine and tinctures, soak our bodies in water. We send each other memes, femme love notes, money for food. We remind one another that some days simply waking only to sleep again is enough. These are the moments of our living, our Mad orientations.

Another thought: maybe Madness *is* the slant, the intentional disorientation of and misalignment with sanism, with neurotypicals, with normativity. There are so many of us who occupy and thrive in the slant. The Mad slant stretches time and helps us create digital kinship networks. Our Madness journeys us toward the simultaneous, rebellious joys of in-between living, all the change making that our refusing, deliberate Mad selves call for.

My Madness and its persistence have taught me that I am sustained by my community of fellow disabled, Mad, chronically ill, queer femmes of color and that I do not require fixing. None of us does. And yet, despite this understanding, my bodymind requires orientation, requires a root structure, desires growth and connectivity. Some days, orientation expresses as a need for sun sitting and soaking, a need to be submerged in water, a need to rub my hands along the rosemary bush in the backyard. Other days are guided by the intention to *do*: to write, to do yoga, to garden. These intention days become containers for the unexpected, the doom scrolling, the napping, the time I did not know I needed for processing. As an educator, I bring these needs with me into the classroom. I name this seeking and this intentional practice "Mad phenomenology."

In addressing disability and phenomenology, Lajoie and Douglas write, "Illness, madness, and disability transform how we orient ourselves in everyday lifeworlds. . . . A phenomenological approach turns our attention toward the many orientations and disorientations that these experiences prompt, the moments of doubt, loss, joy, grief, pain, solidarity, and

---

awareness, a realization, that we must move and live differently if we are to thrive despite sanism and neurotypicality.

clarity that make up ill, Mad, and disabled lives" (2020, 2–3). Although we are told that classrooms are neutral spaces, that we are meant to leave our bodyminds behind before arriving to our seats (whether tangible or digital), we as disabled, Mad, and chronically ill educators carry these multitudes, these orientations, and these disorientations with us upon entry. We begin to navigate the day's lesson plan while our thoughts rapid race. We answer student questions while simultaneously moving through rising anxiety. We dissociate on campus during the long walk or roll between classes. We do all of this knowing that, normatively, academia does not welcome our Mad phenomenologies into the classroom. We do this knowing that while these ways of behaving are not intrinsically Mad practices, academia compels our awareness of and focus on its ableism and sanism.

As Mad and neurodiverse bodyminds in academia, we are aware of how the institution forces us to adjust ourselves further and further away from our authentic selves, from our most genuine needs. Neurotypical oppression steers us away from our tethers, our points of orientation. In this way, academia and all its mandates "impress[]" themselves on our skin and on our bodyminds (Probyn 1996, 5; Ahmed 2004, 9). Imprint. Influence. Impact. I am beginning to understand Mad phenomenology as a practice of reciprocal impressions. When Ahmed describes the role of impressions in phenomenology, she writes, "As I have suggested, phenomenology reminds us that spaces are not exterior to bodies; instead, spaces are like a second skin that unfolds in the folds of the body" (2006, 9). I think here of all of the ways in which we border-live, the many ways in which we exist out of bounds. I think of all of ways we as Mad, neurodiverse, queer folks of color have been taught by an ableist, sanist, white-supremacist, cis-heteropatriarchal, and capitalist world to press on, to render our capacity and needs irrelevant. We are sternly told to fit and avoid the slant.

When I prepared to teach my first university class at twenty-three years old, I tailored myself. I understood the words *instructor, professor,* and *educator* to exist in proximity to whiteness. As an Iranian American Mad queer femme, I oriented myself accordingly: I interpreted professionalism as wearing dark colors and slacks. I rarely joked or smiled in class, and I never discussed care or my bodymind needs. My pedagogy

Orienting toward Togetherness   363

manifested normative rigor with all of its ableist, sanist, racist, and classist underpinnings.

My "embodied reality" (Ahmed 2006, 112) of educator in those early years was oriented around whiteness; it was also deeply inauthentic. I think this is why glitter is such a powerful part of my Mad phenomenological practices, femmeness, and identity now as an assistant professor. Glitter is unapologetically messy. In fact, glitter is diligent in its messiness. It resists the lessons of perfection that have been impressed upon me, the lessons of quietness and smallness, of togetherness and absorption. These are the origin lessons of a first-generation immigrant, the lessons of an impressionable, Mad, queer Iranian girl whose family bought and parked a white Dodge Caravan in the driveway to fit into their white suburban neighborhood. Glitter refuses the folding, and it expands and lingers in a way that my Madness does. Both are unrelenting, disappearing only to be found again.

Our students, too, engage in this exhaustive act; they, too, carry impressions from the performativity of togetherness, the performativity of fitting in. Sometimes my students come to student hours and begin by sharing how lost they feel. Sometimes they begin by telling me how often they have started to reach out and ask for help, only to retreat again; they are caught in the constructed cycle of independence, in the fear of being perceived as "weak."[4] Here, I also think of the external impressions of academia my students have shared. When a Black student tells me that his professor won't honor his accommodations from the Disability Resource Center because he doesn't look "disabled enough," and when a queer and chronically ill student asks—after deep personal struggle—for an

---

4. The myth of independence and its reliance on ableism and sanism has been explored and untangled by critical disability studies scholars and disability justice activists. See *Why I Burned My Book and Other Writings on Disability* (Longmore 2003); "Disability: Representation, Disclosure, Access, and Interdependence" (Brueggemann and Kerschbaum 2015); and "Toward a Full-Inclusion Feminism: A Feminist Deployment of Disability Analysis" (Rohrer 2005). For a disability justice definition of interdependence, see *Skin, Tooth, and Bone: The Basis of Our Movement Is Our People* (Sins Invalid 2019).

extension in another class but does not receive one because their faculty believes that the assignment deadline is "fair," I witness tangible, body-mind impressions of inequity. Fair according to *whose* framework of time? What must the normative rubric of disability *look* like? What does a trustworthy student *look* like? I witness how academia's sanism and ableism intersect with its anti-Blackness and racism;[5] I witness how oppression is folded onto our bodyminds. As someone who was also taught that body-mind needs have no place in the classroom, I understand my students' surprise and uncertainty when we discuss slowness, disability, Madness, and care in the classroom. For so many of us, our perception of a learning space is always-already neurotypical, is always-already capitalist, racist, and cis-heteropatriarchal. Fellow Mad educators and I carry the traumas of getting sick in grad school. Some of us step away, only to never return.

Informed by disability justice and my initial framing of the Mad border body (Kafai 2012), Mad phenomenology is always-already intersectional. On its own, phenomenology as a tool, particularly for Ahmed, invites us to acknowledge how the tangibility of racialization affects space and orientation (2006, 112). In our presence as bodyminds of color within the university, our navigation of racialized microaggressions and white supremacy leave us "disoriented" (Ahmed 2006, 111) from ourselves and from one another, from an inherent sense of belonging. So we scatter, and we are impressed upon.

Mad phenomenology instead invites us to name our Madness, to embrace its imperfect and slippery meaning making. As a name, "Mad phenomenology" has purpose. It enables us to see that there is a mechanics, a rhythm, to our Mad making, that Madness is our way of being-*in*-the-world. My ritual of naming Madness and now of naming a Mad phenomenology takes me far away from the immigrant narratives associated with being a "good" American citizen. I revolt. I push. I realize that binaries fail us, just as the seasons do during climate chaos, just as the new mounds of maple leaves do when the wind arrives.

---

5. For more, see *Black Madness :: Mad Blackness* (Pickens 2019), *How to Go Mad without Losing Your Mind: Madness and Black Radical Creativity* (Bruce 2021), and *The Protest Psychosis: How Schizophrenia Became a Black Disease* (Metzl 2010).

Orienting toward Togetherness   365

Mad phenomenology invites us to bring our whole selves into the classroom. It frames Madness as origin point, as that through which we learn and teach. My disability justice politics are braided with this practice. Created out of need by disabled, queer-of-color activists in 2005, the movement-building framework's sixth principle of sustainability offers an accessible example of the transformative classroom space Mad phenomenology invites.[6] Disability justice defines sustainability this way: "We learn to pace ourselves, individually and collectively, to be sustained long-term. We value the teachings of our bodies and experiences and use them as a critical guide and reference point to help us move away from urgency and into a deep, slow, transformative, unstoppable wave of justice and liberation" (Sins Invalid 2019, 24–25). The practice of sustainability is based in phenomenology; it begins from our bodyminds outward. Informed from this place, I share with my students that our classrooms can be liberatory places, that our bodyminds deserve to guide the process of learning and unlearning.[7] I ask them to name their bodymind needs during class: What's our capacity today? What are we carrying into the classroom? When will we need a break? How long should our break be? Many admit that this centering of self, this consideration that sustainability deserves voice, is a new, uncomfortable practice.

It is important for me to share with my learners that I stopped taking fifteen units a semester after my first year in community college, that I was often hospitalized as an undergraduate, that I often needed extensions. In thinking through sustainability's invitation that "we pace ourselves,"[8] Mad

---

6. The concept of "disability justice" was created by Patty Berne, Mia Mingus, and Stacey Milburn. They were soon followed by Leroy F. Moore Jr. and the disabled trans activists Eli Clare and Sebastian Margaret.

7. There is a history of education scholars informed in particular by critical race theory and feminism who explore liberation and liberatory practices in the classroom. See *Pedagogy of the Oppressed* (Freire 1970), *Teaching to Transgress* (hooks 1994), and *The Art of Critical Pedagogy* (Duncan-Andrade and Morrell 2008).

8. Sustainability is a radical, transformative act. It does not align with the capitalist and ableist suggestion that we continue to overwork ourselves while simply extending deadlines. Sustainability from a disability justice perspective honors the need for our bodyminds to set the pace without shame or guilt.

phenomenology empowers me to reorient my relationship to the classroom and share strategies of neurodiverse, Mad thriving.[9] It is vital for my students to know that extensions and incompletes are powerful forms of access, that assignment due dates should be conversations, and that we all can collectively set the pace of the day. If this list seems impossible, unrealistic, or not "rigorous," I ask that you inquire: What perceptions of academia and rigor inform your answer? How do your bodymind experiences in academia orient you? What narratives are you tethered to?

Mad phenomenology has everything to do with Mad orientations of time and with slowness. I write this piece—I write every piece—in Mad time, in its slow iterative cycles.[10] Here, writing and processing are luscious *and* grating. When I think back to the maple tree in the backyard, I am reminded of the slow speed at which the tree buds; I think of the precise need for balance in temperature, water, soil quality, and nutrients. I think of how growth becomes a process of waiting. Writing becomes, too, a series of fits and starts that place me on a repetitive loop: self-doubt meets joy meets the desire to quit meets exhale. Yesterday was a day of intentions and processing; I did not write. Today, I move sentences and reconsider word choice. I remember that writing these personal reflections is an essential component of theory making itself, of self as theory, of "theory near the flesh."[11]

When I travel too far from myself, I stop and follow my uncle again. We pull patio chairs into the sun to sit, and soon we sleep. This is also Mad phenomenology, the somatic realization that sleep can be a remedy

9. See *Mad at School* (Price 2011) and "Critical Disability Studies and Mad Studies: Enabling New Pedagogies in Practice" (Castrodale 2017).

10. Crip time has been explored as a place of flexibility, slowness, and grief (Kuppers 2014; Samuels 2017; Kafer 2021), but Mad time has yet to be explored with the same expansiveness. Although Mad time certainly has parallels with crip time, perhaps one of the most pronounced distinctions that neurodiversity invites is the persistent fluidity of Mad time, the pockets of what Pau Abustan (2022) calls "swirly time."

11. In *Living a Feminist Life* (2017), Sara Ahmed writes, "Theory can do more the closer it gets to the skin" (10). I understand this to mean that theory rooted in embodied/enminded experience is transformational, that the stories of the bodymind are political.

to the scatter-pull of Madness. The work and art making of the Black activist, writer, and dreamer Tricia Hersey informs my sleep practice. Having founded the Nap Ministry in 2013 and the "Rest Is Resistance" framework in 2016, Hersey writes, "My rest as a Black woman in America suffering from generational exhaustion and racial trauma always was a political refusal and social justice uprising within my body. . . . Rest pushes back and disrupts a system that views human bodies as a tool for production and labor. It is a counter narrative. We know that we are not machines. We are divine" (2022, para. 1). Sleep is a place of forgiveness and permission. In sleep, in rest, I dream. I am memory. I am porous narrative. I am cumulative histories, movement from a time when my Madness was unnamed and internalized as shameful. In sleep, I forgive the stories I have internalized, the imposter experience, the immigrant mandate of constant work. I give myself permission to write my own bodymind story without using the words *remorse* or *guilt*. In displacing normative embodiment/enmindment, Mad phenomenology opens portals of possibility. It invites us, invites you—dear Reader—to skew and slant the potential of the classroom. Mad phenomenology invites us to dream transformative dreams.

As I write this, the spring semester has neared its halfway point. My students and I discuss our bodymind exhaustion, and we search for an orienting ceremony, something that will root us again amid everything that is disorienting us: "I have been struggling with my mental health"; "I know I shouldn't feel guilty, but . . ."; "I haven't been able to catch my breath"; "I don't know how to advocate for myself."[12] I wonder how many times my students pressed delete before sending these emails to me. I think back to all the times I, too, retreated into academia's small panic spaces. Perhaps this is how we reorient: in community, in togetherness, in tender leanings as plants do toward the sun, as the surf does toward the moon. Engaged with a phenomenological practice that holds space for all our bodyminds, we name and craft our tethers, together.

12. These quotes are from my students, voices of exhaustion and great vulnerability shared in emails.

The sun arrives in angles, casting shadows on my feet. My eyes are drawn to what is happening in the shade while I maneuver my body to catch the sun. I think of this as the feeling of being-*in*-the-world, and it occurs to me how so much of this embodied, enminded practice helps me name my needs. I reflect on my orientation, I move sustainably from my bodymind outward, and I know that if we could orient ourselves from this place, if we could negotiate the impressions of an inequitable university from *this* place, then we could begin to understand our neurodiversity, our Madness, as practice and threshold. What parts of your neurodivergence tether you, orient you? What, dear one, do you draw yourself toward?

Works Cited

Abrams, Thomas. 2020. "Disability at the Limits of Phenomenology." *Journal of Critical Phenomenology* 3, no. 2: 15–18. At https://doi.org/10.5399/PJCP.v3i2.2.

Abustan, Pau. 2022. Personal communication to the author, Feb. 13.

Ahmed, Sara. 2004. *The Cultural Politics of Emotion.* Edinburgh: Edinburgh Univ. Press.

———. 2006. *Queer Phenomenology: Orientations, Objects, Others.* Durham, NC: Duke Univ. Press.

———. 2017. *Living a Feminist Life.* Durham, NC: Duke Univ. Press.

Bruce, La Marr Jurelle. 2021. *How to Go Mad without Losing Your Mind: Madness and Black Radical Creativity.* Durham, NC: Duke Univ. Press.

Brueggemann, Brenda Jo, and Stephanie Kerschbaum. 2015. "Disability: Representation, Disclosure, Access, and Interdependence." In *How to Build a Life in the Humanities: Meditations on the Academic Work–Life Balance,* edited by Greg Colón Semenza and Garrett A. Sullivan Jr., 183–92. New York: Palgrave MacMillian.

Castrodale, Mark Anthony. 2017. "Critical Disability Studies and Mad Studies: Enabling New Pedagogies in Practice." *Canadian Journal for the Study of Adult Education* 27, no. 1: 49–66. At https://cjsae.library.dal.ca/index.php/cjsae/article/view/5357.

Diedrich, Lisa. 2021. "Illness (In)Action: CFS and #TimeForUnrest." *Literature and Medicine* 39, no. 1: 8–14. At https://doi.org/10.1353/lm.2021.0001.

Duncan-Andrade, Jeffrey M., and Ernest Morrell. 2008. *The Art of Critical Pedagogy: Possibilities for Moving from Theory to Practice in the Classroom.* New York: Peter Lang.

Freire, Paulo. 1970. *Pedagogy of the Oppressed.* Translated by Myra Bergman Ramos. New York: Seabury Press.

Heidegger, Martin. 1962. *Being and Time.* Translated by John Macquarrie and Edward Robinson. New York: Harper & Row.

Hersey, Tricia. 2022. "Rest Is Anything That Connects Your Minds and Body." Nap Ministry (website), Feb. 21. At https://thenapministry.wordpress.com/.

hooks, bell. 1994. *Teaching to Transgress: Education as the Practice of Freedom.* New York: Routledge.

Husserl, Edmond. 1983. *Ideas Pertaining to a Pure Phenomenology and to a Phenomenological Philosophy.* Translated by F. Kersten. The Hague, Netherlands: Martinus Nijhoff.

Kafai, Shayda. 2012. "The Mad Border Body: A Political In-Betweeness." *Disability Studies Quarterly* 33, no. 1. At https://doi.org/10.18061/dsq.v33i1.3438.

Kafer, Alison. 2021. "After Crip, Crip Afters." *South Atlantic Quarterly* 120, no. 2: 415–34. At https://doi.org/10.1215/00382876-8916158.

Kimmerer, Robin Wall. 2013. *Braiding Sweetgrass: Indigenous Wisdom, Scientific Knowledge and the Teachings of Plants.* London: Penguin.

Kuppers, Petra. 2014. "Crip Time." *Tikkun* 29, no. 4: 29–30. At https://doi.org /10.1215/08879982-2810062.

Lajoie, Corinne, and Emily R. Douglas. 2020. "A Crip Queer Dialogue on Sickness (Editors' Introduction)." In "Critically Sick: New Phenomenologies of Illness, Madness, and Disability," edited by Corinne Lajoie and Emily R. Douglas. Special issue, *Journal of Critical Phenomenology* 3, no. 2: 1–14. At https://doi.org/10.5399/PJCP.v3i2.1.

Longmore, Paul K. 2003. *Why I Burned My Book and Other Writings on Disability.* Philadelphia: Temple Univ. Press.

Lorde, Audre. 1985. "Poetry Is Not a Luxury." In *The Broadview Anthology of Expository Prose,* edited by Laura Buzzard, Don LePan, Nora Ruddock, and Alexandria Stuart, 217–20. Guelph, Ontario: Broadview Press.

Merleau-Ponty, Maurice. 1962. *Phenomenology of Perception.* Translated by Colin Smith. London: Routledge.

Metzl, Jonathan. 2010. *The Protest Psychosis: How Schizophrenia Became a Black Disease.* Boston: Beacon Press.

Murphy, Robert F. 1987. *Body Silent: The Different World of the Disabled*. New York: Norton.

Padilla, René. 2003. "Clara: A Phenomenology of Disability." *American Occupational Therapy Association* 57, no. 4: 412–23. At https://doi.org/10.5014/ajot.57.4.413.

Paterson, Kevin, and Bill Hughes. 1999. "Disability Studies and Phenomenology: The Carnal Politics of Everyday Life." *Disability & Society* 14, no. 5: 597–610. At https://doi.org/10.1080/09687599925966.

Pickens, Therí Alyce. 2019. *Black Madness :: Mad Blackness*. Durham, NC: Duke Univ. Press.

Price, Margaret. 2011. *Mad at School: Rhetorics of Mental Disability and Academic Life*. Ann Arbor: Univ. of Michigan Press.

Probyn, Elspeth. 1996. *Outside Belongings*. New York: Routledge.

Rohrer, Judy. 2005. "Toward a Full-Inclusion Feminism: A Feminist Deployment of Disability Analysis." *Feminist Studies* 31, no. 1: 34–63. At https://www.jstor.org/stable/20459006.

Samuels, Ellen. 2017. "Six Ways of Looking at Crip Time." *Disability Studies Quarterly* 37, no. 3. At https://doi.org/10.18061/dsq.v37i3.5824.

Schlauderaff, Sav. 2019. "Re-learning My Bodymindspirit through Trauma Studies." Sav Schlauderaff (website), Oct. 27. At https://savschlauderaff.wixsite.com/website/post/re-learning-my-bodymindspirit-through-trauma-studies.

Sins Invalid. 2019. *Skin, Tooth, and Bone: The Basis of Movement Is Our People*. 2nd ed. San Francisco: Sins Invalid.

Toombs, S. Kay. 1988. "Illness and the Paradigm of Lived Body." *Theoretical Medicine* 9, no. 2: 201–26. At https://doi.org/10.1007/BF00489413.

———. 1995. "The Lived Experience of Disability." *Human Studies* 18, no. 1: 9–23. At https://doi.org/10.1007/BF01322837.

Glossary

*Contributor
Biographies*

Index

Glossary

ableism: The systemic structures that frame disabled bodyminds as deviant, less than, and "bad" compared to nondisabled bodyminds (Davis 2014; Dolmage 2017). Disability justice activists and critical disability studies scholars of color have also amplified that ableism as a system of oppression replicates and is upheld by, for example, white supremacy, colonialism, capitalism, and cis-heteropatriarchy (Berne 2015; Miles, Nishida, and Forber-Pratt 2017; Lewis 2020). Ableism also places value on "ability" based on normative ideas rooted in productivity; these principles are reinforced within academia in particular (Dolmage 2017).

autigender: A communally crafted term that identifies autism as being a central and complicated part of a person's gender identity. There are many differing definitions of *autigender* as a self-defined, community-rooted term. TikTok, Twitter, and Instagram have served as crowdsourcing spaces where autistic community members have shared and discussed definitions of this burgeoning term.

crip: A shortened identity term that reclaims the derogatory slur *cripple*. Disabled activists have reappropriated it as a term of empowerment. In disability studies in the 1990s in particular, *crip* shifted from being used as a political disability identity to also being a verb, similar to the trajectory of the word *queer* (Sandahl 2003; Kafer 2013). Beyond being a lens, crip as a theory has also been placed "in relation" to queer identity formation and practices (McRuer 2006).

demi-rhetoricity: A term that resists allistic assumptions that distance rhetoricity and credibility from autistic identity. Rather than removing the agency and autonomy of autistic writers, demi-rhetoricity invites transformation; it "holds potential as a reclamatory strategy" (Yergeau 2017, 33).

disability studies: An interdisciplinary field of study that explores disability through multiple lenses, including the social, historical, cultural, and political. It

374   Glossary

affirms disability as a valued identity that resists the dominant framings of normativity and nondisability (Swain and French 2000). Critical disability studies soon emerged to acknowledge new critiques around the binary limitations of the social versus medical models, the British versus American frameworks of disability studies, and the notion of disability versus impairment (Shuttleworth and Meekosha 2017). This growth has resulted in new areas of focus, including feminist disability studies and disability and critical race theory (DisCrit). Most recently, the activist and movement-building framework of disability justice is informing the field and inviting crucial conversations around transformative and structural change.

health/medical humanities: A transdisciplinary field that unites the social sciences, humanities, and health professionals. Although there is no decisive definition of this field, the Health Humanities Consortium offers the description that health humanities as a transdisciplinary practice centers "deep textual reading, and slow critical thinking to examine the human condition, the patient's experience, the healer's experience, and to . . . provide renewal for the health care professional" (2021).

Mad studies: A discipline that was informed by and grew from antipsychiatry, survivor advocacy, and Mad Pride activisms, particularly in Canada. In this work, Mad studies presses against the medical models that for so long have pathologized and hierarchized neurodiversity. It is important to stress that activists continue to debate the use of the terms *Mad* and *Madness* specifically because of their lack of uniform meaning (Beresford, Nettle, and Perring 2009; Beresford et al. 2016). As a discipline, Mad studies honors the "experiences, history, culture, political organising, narratives, [and] writings" of the Mad community (L. Costa, qtd. in McWade, Milton, and Beresford 2015, 305).

medical-industrial complex: A framing that goes beyond the medical industry to examine structural notions of science, medicine, health, access, and safety. From a disability justice perspective, activists such as Mia Mingus (2015) identify the medical-industrial complex as an organism that is informed by eugenics, capitalism, colonization, and the prison-industrial complex. As a system, the medical-industrial complex replicates power, profit, exploitation, and trauma.

misogynoir: A term coined by Moya Bailey (2021) to describe the unique intersection of anti-Blackness and misogyny that Black women experience. Her definition specifically explores this intersection in visual and digital spaces, examining in particular modalities of resistance by Black women.

neurodiverse, neurodiversity movement: A movement and area of study that views "all embodied diversity . . . [as] accepted as a facet of human nature" (McWade, Milton, and Beresford 2015, 306). Its central goal is to resist neuronormativity's pathologizing narratives, in particular those based in the biomedical models of disability and impairment.

neuroqueer: A term rooted in the work of activists, online blogging communities, and activists. It serves as a "crip project of disidentification" (Egner 2018, 123). Informed by intersectionality, *neuroqueer* is used both as an identity term and as a verb by communities that identify as neurodivergent and queer in terms of gender and/or sexuality.

sanism: The "systemic subjugation of people who have received mental health diagnosis or treatment" (Burstow et al. 2013, 339). Sanism can be expressed in the form of microaggressions, stigmas, blatant discrimination, structural oppressions such as white supremacy, colonialism, capitalism, and cis-heteropatriarchy.

Works Cited

Bailey, Moya. 2021. *Misogynoir Transformed.* New York: New York Univ. Press.

Beresford, Peter, Mary Nettle, and Rebecca Perring. 2009. "Towards a Social Model of Madness and Distress?: Exploring What Service Users Say." Joseph Rowntree Foundation, Nov. 22. At https://www.jrf.org.uk/towards-a-social-model-of-madness-and-distress-exploring-what-service-users-say.

Beresford, Peter, Rebecca Perring, Mary Nettle, and Jan Wallcraft. 2016. *From Mental Illness to a Social Model of Madness and Distress? Exploring What Service Users Say.* London: Shaping Lives and National Survivor User Network. At https://shapingourlives.org.uk/wp-content/uploads/2021/08/FROM-MENTAL-ILLNESS-PDF-2.pdf.

Berne, Patty. 2015. "Disability Justice—a Working Draft by Patty Berne." Sins Invalid, June 9. At https://www.sinsinvalid.org/blog/disability-justice-a-working-draft-by-patty-berne.

Burstow, Bonnie, Andrea Daley, Megan Davies, Shaindl Diamond, Lilith "Chava" Finkler, Rachel Gorman, Ji-Eun Lee, et al. 2013. "Glossary of Terms." In *Mad Matters: A Critical Reader in Canadian Mad Studies,* edited by Brenda A. LeFrançois, Robert Menzies, and Geoffrey Reaume, 334–40. Toronto: Canadian Scholars' Press.

Davis, Lennard J. 2014. *Enforcing Normalcy: Disability, Deafness, and the Body*. London: Verso.

Dolmage, Jay Timothy. 2017. *Academic Ableism: Disability and Higher Education*. Ann Arbor: Univ. of Michigan Press.

Egner, Justine E. 2018. "'The Disability Rights Community Was Never Mine': Neuroqueer Disidentification." *Gender & Society* 33, no. 1: 123–47. At https://doi.org/10.1177/0891243211880328.

Health Humanities Consortium. 2021. "HHC Toolkit: Defining Health Humanities." At https://healthhumanitiesconsortium.com/hhc-toolkit/definitions/.

Kafer, Alison. 2013. *Feminist, Queer, Crip*. Bloomington: Indiana Univ. Press.

Lewis, Talila "TL." 2020. "Ableism 2020: An Updated Definition." *Tu[r]ning into Self* (blog), Jan. 25. At https://www.talilalewis.com/blog/ableism-2020-an-updated-definition.

McRuer, Robert. 2006. *Crip Theory: Cultural Signs of Queerness and Disability*. New York: New York Univ. Press.

McWade, Brigit, Damian Milton, and Peter Beresford. 2015. "Mad Studies and Neurodiversity: A Dialogue." *Disability & Society* 30, no. 2: 305–9. At https://doi.org/10.1080/09687599.2014.1000512.

Miles, Angel L., Akemi Nishida, and Anjali J. Forber-Pratt. 2017. "An Open Letter to White Disability Studies and Ableist Institutions of Higher Education." *Disability Studies Quarterly* 37, no. 3. At https://dsq-sds.org/index.php/dsq/article/view/5997/4686.

Mingus, Mia. 2015. "Medical Industrial Complex Visual." *Leaving Evidence* (blog), Feb. 6. At https://leavingevidence.wordpress.com/2015/02/06/medical-industrial-complex-visual/.

Sandahl, Carrie. 2003. "Queering the Crip or Cripping the Queer? Intersections of Queer and Crip Identities in Solo Autobiographical Performance." *GLQ: A Journal of Lesbian and Gay Studies* 9, no. 1: 25–56. At https://doi.org/10.1215/10642684-9-1-2-25.

Shuttleworth, Russell, and Helen Meekosha. 2017. "Accommodating Critical Disability Studies in Bioarchaeology." In *Bioarchaeology of Impairment and Disability: Theoretical, Ethnohistorical, and Methodological Perspectives*, edited by Jennifer F. Byrnes and Jennifer L. Muller, 19–38. New York: Springer.

Swain, John, and Sally French. 2000. "Towards an Affirmation Model of Disability." *Disability & Society* 15, no. 4: 569–82. At https://doi.org/10.1080/09687590050058189.

Yergeau, Remi M. 2017. *Authoring Autism: On Rhetoric and Neurological Queerness*. Durham, NC: Duke Univ. Press.

Contributor Biographies

Melanie Jones has published on Mad studies, international medical humanities, trauma studies, and horror studies. She shuttles between her Mad, queer community in New York City, where she has taught with the Bard Prison Initiative, and her home in rural Washington State, where she lives with husband, Colin, and dog, Finnegan. Melanie's upcoming book traces the impact of the trauma model of mental illness on Mad expression and community. She received a PhD in comparative literature from UCLA in 2021.

Shayda Kafai is assistant professor of gender and sexuality studies at California State Polytechnic University, Pomona. As a queer, disabled, Mad, Iranian American femme, she commits to practicing the many ways we can reclaim our bodyminds from systems of oppression. To support this work as an educator-scholar, Shayda applies disability justice and collective-care practices in the spaces she cultivates. Her scholarly writing focuses on intersectional body politics, particularly on how bodies are constructed and how they hold the capacity for rebellion. She is the author of *Crip Kinship: The Disability Justice and Art Activism of Sins Invalid* (2021). She lives in Southern California with her wife, Amy.

Sav Schlauderaff is a queer, trans, disabled scholar who earned their PhD in gender and women's studies from the University of Arizona. Their current research in critical disability studies focuses on online biohacking communities and the analysis of illness/wellness narratives as well as on the construction of "health" within these spaces. A sometime-artist, sometime-academic, they blend their academic training in genetics, molecular biology, disability studies, and gender studies with narrative, poetry, and new media. Their MA thesis at San Diego State University, "Rejecting the Desire for 'Health': Centering Crip Bodyminds in Genetic Testing" (2018), researched the effects of the Health + Ancestry Direct-to-Consumer genetic-testing kits from 23andMe on disabled,

380 Contributor Biographies

crip, and chronically ill bodyminds. You can find Sav's published work in *Fat Studies, Feminist Formations, Lateral,* and the *Disability Studies Quarterly* community blog.

Shawna Guenther, PhD, analyzes how early modern vernacular medical writers represented women's bodies, in particular women's breasts, breast milk, and breastfeeding practices. Her recent publications include "Threatening Maternity: Early Modern English Medical Texts and the Querrelles des Femmes," in *Interdisciplinary Humanities* (2021); "Food for Survival: The Importance of Food in English Renaissance Health," in *The Routledge Companion to Literature and Food,* edited by Lorna Piatti-Farnell and Donna Lee Brien (2018); and "Negative Capability in Space: The Romantic Bowieverse," in *David Bowie and Romanticism,* edited by James Rovira (2022). She presented the paper "Uncertainty in Early Modern English Vernacular Medical Discourses about Lactation" at the Swiss Association of University Teachers of English conference in May 2023. Under the pseudonym "Jane Arsenault," she has published creative nonfiction in several journals, including the *Waggle* and the *Pomona Valley Review.*

Rebecca-Eli M. Long is a disabled scholar, activist, and artist whose work disrupts ableist structural violence. An avid knitter, Rebecca-Eli uses creative forms of knowledge making to advance social change. They are a PhD candidate in anthropology and gerontology at Purdue University, where they strive to make autistic futures—individual and collective—more possible.

Jess L. Wilcox Cowing researches nineteenth- and twentieth-century literary studies, feminist disability studies, and settler colonialism. They earned a PhD in American studies from William and Mary in 2020. Jess served as the American Studies Association's Critical Disability Studies Caucus cochair from 2017 to 2021 and recently served as a visiting assistant professor in women, gender, and sexuality studies at Goucher College. Their work is published in the *Journal of Feminist Scholarship* and *Disability Studies Quarterly.* They grew up on Wabanaki homelands and live and work on Piscataway-Conoy, Nacotchtank, and Susquehannock homelands.

Sydney F. Lewis is a lecturer in the Harriet Tubman Department of Women, Gender, and Sexuality Studies at the University of Maryland, College Park. She received her doctorate in the English Department at the University of

Washington. Her dissertation combined Black feminist theory, cultural studies, and queer theory with critical readings of African American cultural productions to consider how Black women can and have configured their nonheteronormative sexualities outside of the language given to us by white-dominated LGBTQ scholarship. Sydney's work and teaching strive to blur the boundaries among the academy, art, and advocacy. Her areas of interest include gender performance and performativity, Black feminist theory and culture, and intersectional Black liberation. Her published works explore Black femme subjectivity, literature, and performance.

Leah Lakshmi Piepzna-Samarsinha is a nonbinary, femme, autistic, disabled writer, space creator, and disability and transformative justice movement worker of Burgher and Tamil Sri Lankan, Irish and Galician/Roma ascent. They are the author or coeditor of ten books, including *The Future Is Disabled: Prophecies, Love Notes and Mourning Songs* (2022), *Beyond Survival: Strategies and Stories from the Transformative Justice Movement* (2020, coedited with Ejeris Dixon), *Tonguebreaker* (2019), *Care Work: Dreaming Disability Justice* (2018), *Bodymap* (2015), *Dirty River: A Queer Femme of Color Dreaming Her Way Home* (2015), and *The Revolution Starts at Home: Confronting Intimate Violence within Activist Communities* (2011, coedited with Ching-In Chen and Jai Dulani). They are a Lambda Award winner, a five-time Publishing Triangle finalist, and the winner of Lambda's 2020 Jean Cordova Award "honoring a lifetime of work documenting the complexities of queer of color/disabled/femme experience." A Disability Futures Fellow since 2009, they have been a lead performer with the disability justice performance collective Sins Invalid. Raised in Rust Belt central Massachusetts, they have called Toronto, Oakland, South Seattle, and the diasporic disabled dream space home.

Caché Owens is a mixed-media storyteller, educator, and community organizer who lives and works on the ancestral lands of the Wabanaki, Abenaki, and Pennacook peoples (southern Maine). They are a Black, fat, disabled, queer, and nonbinary former teen mother, and their personal art practice (writing and visual art) explores themes of resilience, body autonomy, grief, play, softness, motherhood, and embodiment through the lenses of identity, radical imagination, and anticapitalism. Caché holds bachelor's degrees in public administration, nonprofit management, and environmental planning from the University of Wisconsin–Green Bay as well as a master's in community development and a PhD

382 Contributor Biographies

in urban and regional analysis from the University of North Carolina–Charlotte. Their research has historically focused on topics related to regional models of community organizing, educational equity, disability justice, and fat liberation. They have worked as a program manager, communications professional, strategic leader, educator, and facilitator for more than ten years.

Sarah Cavar is a PhD candidate in cultural studies at the University of California–Davis, traversing the nexuses of transMad and queercrip ways of writing, thinking, and (un)knowing in/around digital publics. Their works across genre and form can be found or are forthcoming in *Lateral, Electric Lit, Disability Studies Quarterly*, the *Journal of Literary and Cultural Disability Studies, Nat. Brut*, the *Review of Disability Studies*, and elsewhere. Sarah is also the author of a novel, *Failure to Comply* (2024), and five chapbooks.

Rua Williams is an autistic, Mad, disabled, queer scholar of critical disability studies, science and technology studies, and human-centered computing. They have been an assistant professor in the User Experience Design Program at Purdue University since 2020 and are a Just Tech Fellow with the Social Science Research Council (2022–24). Their research interests focus on the interaction among technology, society, and disability, in particular disabled ontology as a context for design rather than a site for intervention. Their publications include "Cyborg Perspectives on Computing Research Reform" in *CHI '19* (2019), "Prefigurative Politics and Passionate Witnessing" in *ASSETS '19* (2019), "Metaeugenics and Metaresistance: From Manufacturing the Includable Body to Walking Away from the Broom Closet" in the *Canadian Journal of Children's Rights* (2019), "Oh No, Not Another Trolley: On the Need for a Co-liberative Consciousness in CS Pedagogy" in *IEEE Tech & Society* (2021), "All Robots Are Disabled" in *Robophilosophy* (2022), and "Only the Old and Sick Will Die: Reproducing Eugenic Visuality in COVID-19 Data Visualization" in *ISTAS '22* (2022).

Kelan L. Koning lives and breathes student support and considers herself truly blessed to have engaged in this heart work on the California State University–Northridge campus for nearly twenty-five years in roles in the Educational Opportunity Program, the Chicano/a Studies Program, and the English Department. For the past six years, she has also had the opportunity to deepen and share her learning and knowledge as a professional-development coordinator with 3CSN and Unite-LA, focused on supporting colleges in the California

Contributor Biographies 383

community college system in their goal of increasing student success. Her work is currently focused on creating stronger classroom and campus communities and destigmatizing mental health diversity and neurodiversity. She has presented widely across California on supporting students through community building, metacognition, reading apprenticeship, trauma-informed pedagogy and social emotional learning, and identity work. Kelan's poetry has been published in the *Northridge Review* and *Chapparal*. In her down time, she immerses herself in art and travel. She enjoys a peaceful and creative life with her brilliant husband, Rogelio, mother, Judy, and furbabies, Arya and Charlie, in the Los Angeles suburbs.

Liz Miller, PhD, is senior lecturer in rhetoric and disability studies at Ohio State University. Her newest publication is a coauthored piece titled "Our Cartographic Selves: Neurodivergent and Disabled Embodied Writing during the Pandemic" (with Millie Hizer, Elena Kalodner-Martin, and Dennis Etzel Jr.), published in the *Journal of Multimodal Rhetorics* in 2022. Liz's current work seeks to account for kinship networks developed among graduate students as they rhetorically navigate oppressive institutions alongside each other.

Samuel Z. Shelton is a nonbinary, queer, crip violence-prevention strategist at Iowa State University. Sam's educational background is in women, gender, and sexuality studies, with focuses in critical disability and trauma studies as well as social justice pedagogies. Their research interests include violence/trauma; resistance and social movements; and feminist, queer, and other critical pedagogies.

Pau Abustan is assistant professor of women's, gender, and sexuality studies at Cal State–Los Angeles. Their research centers queer, critical race, feminist, disability justice world making in youth-centered learning, animated storytelling, and activisms. They cofacilitated intersectional coalitional activisms in Southern California (Tongva/Chumash lands) and cofounded a youth learning program and a 2STQBIPOC-led organization in eastern Washington (Niimiipuu lands). Dr. Abustan is working on their first book reflecting on their experiences as a queer Pilipinx cripnographer who witnessed youth and youth-educator-led disability justice world making at an elementary school. They are alumni of the University of California–Santa Barbara, California State University–Northridge, and Washington State University. They taught at Western Washington University, Highline College, University of Washington, and Washington State University.

384 Contributor Biographies

They are a faculty mentor for the University of California–Davis Bulosan Center for Critical Filipinx Studies and Mentoring Hall of Fame with the National Disability Mentoring Coalition.

A-M McManaman received their PhD in English (critical studies) at the University of Illinois–Chicago. Their work explores Madness as a formal technology of the novel and argues that the novel does Mad work. When they are not exploring the intersection of disability, queer, and Mad studies, they are dreaming of Mad worlds and (dis)embodied Mad futures.

Jesse Rice-Evans is a disabled technologist. She works as the OpenLab manager at the City University of New York School of Professional Studies and is a doctoral candidate in rhetoric at the CUNY Graduate Center.

Andréa Stella is an autistic mother of two star beings and a lifelong New Yorker. She was pushed out of academia and works as a user-experience researcher.

Sarah Smith is a queer, Mad, disabled, psychiatric survivor with a PhD in gender studies from Queen's University in Kingston, Ontario. They are currently a research associate with the Centre for Sexual and Gender Minority Health Research in the Dalla Lana School of Public Health at the University of Toronto. Their work sits at the intersection of gender studies, Mad studies, disability studies, and public health, with a keen focus on self-injury and student mental health.

Grace Wedlake is a PhD candidate in the School of Kinesiology and Health Studies at Queen's University in Kingston, Ontario. Their doctoral work traces the experiences of LGBTQ+ individuals living in Canada who have left the non-affirming Protestant Church.

Sarah Arvey Tov is a disabled educator-scholar-activist focused on the intersections of race and disability and on curricula that center disability identity, community, and culture. She collaboratively designs higher-education coursework, teacher-education programming, and K–12 curricula grounded in disability justice, and she is especially excited to be in a community with disabled artists and activists of the One out of Five: Disability History and Pride Project. She loves spending time with her zubby, friends, family, and sweet puppy, Abri, and biking in the beautiful Northwest!

Contributor Biographies   385

Kim Fernandes is a researcher, writer, activist, and educator interested in how the body meets and moves through the world. They are also a joint doctoral candidate in anthropology and education at the University of Pennsylvania, where they work on the intersections of disability, data, and technology outside of Global North contexts.

Diane R. Wiener, LMSW, PhD, is a Mad, crip, neuroqueer activist-educator and social worker. Between 2011 and 2018, she served as the founding director of Syracuse University's Disability Cultural Center. From 2019 to 2022, she was a research professor and the associate director of Interdisciplinary Programs and Outreach at the Burton Blatt Institute in the Syracuse University College of Law. A widely published academic author, cultural critic, poet, and creative nonfiction writer, she is also the editor in chief of *Wordgathering: A Journal of Disability Poetry and Literature*, housed at Syracuse University. Diane is proud and honored to be part of the Mad Pride, disability justice, and mental health liberation movements.

Holly Pearson received her PhD in education from Chapman University, specializing in critical spatial studies, disability studies, and social justice and critical pedagogy. After almost a decade as a contingent assistant professor, Holly transitioned to a nonacademic position to work closely with multiply marginalized communities.

Index

Aaliyahbreaux, 170, 173
Abel, Emily K., 167, 173
ableism, 14, 31, 156, 166, 294, 362–63
Abrams, Jasmine A., 93, 98
Abrams, Thomas, 359, 368
academia, 32, 47, 72, 151, 352
access intimacy, 72, 214, 246
accommodation, 34, 47, 68, 113, 210
accompliceship, 131
Adichie, Chimamanda Ngozi, 158, 161
adjunct, 7, 96, 121, 274, 277
Ahmad, Farah, 36, 40
Ahmed, Sara, 24, 66, 67, 71, 72
Aho, Tanja, 1, 102, 254
allistic, 102, 124
Amsler, Sarah, 150, 152
anti-blackness, 38, 153, 271, 280, 364
anxiety, 4, 13, 50, 225, 335
attention-deficit/hyperactivity disorder
 (ADD/ADHD), 33, 85
autism, 110, 129, 164, 166–67

Bailey, Moya, 79, 91
Baril, Alexandre, 165, 168
Bascom, Julia, 111, 164–66
Ben-Moshe, Liat, 1, 23, 102, 225, 254
Beresford, Paul, 8–9, 11, 22–23
Berne, Patty, 38, 97, 244, 246, 286, 325
Big Door Brigade, 38

biocapitalism, 212–13
biomedical model of disability, 9, 23,
 132, 321
bipolar disorder, 10, 33
bisexuality, 132, 313
Blackness, 23, 49, 243, 364
bodymind, 35, 83, 149, 210, 260
Brown, Nicole, 2, 148
Brueggemann, Brenda Jo, 1, 191, 211,
 363
burnout, 22, 76–79, 93

cancer, 112, 123
capitalism, 82, 91, 119, 127, 159, 310
care, 31, 67, 158, 215, 278; work, 84, 184,
 214–15
Castrodale, Mark Anthony, 9, 101, 191,
 366
chronic illness, 21, 30–31, 38, 79, 81
cis-heteropatriarchy, 95, 193, 360
Cite Black Women Collective, 172
Clare, Eli, 23, 30, 38, 278, 365
class, 111, 114, 269, 272; working, 108,
 117–18, 276
collective care, 96, 160, 206, 290
colonialism, 14, 29, 31, 70, 134, 226, 236,
 294, 305, 310, 357
community, 40, 69, 158, 164, 246
complaint, 65, 67, 71, 91

Index

compulsory able-bodiness, 5, 11, 213
compulsory able-mindedness, 223–24, 226, 320
counseling, 33, 84, 68
COVID-19, 75, 122, 171, 197, 210
crip, 13, 77, 243, 341; time, 79–81, 152, 244; cripistemologies, 172, 184
critical disability studies, 191, 246, 360, 363, 366
critical race theory, 15, 304, 365, 374
cure, 30, 52, 133

decolonial, 70, 178, 294
demi-rhetoricity, 175, 177, 186
depression, 4, 13, 37, 47, 77, 132
deviance, 134, 139, 171, 199, 322
diagnosis, 39, 128, 170, 218, 255, 258
diasporic, 120, 239
disability, 37, 66, 133, 149, 211; justice, 9, 82, 92, 97, 309–10, 322; studies, 7–8, 37, 191, 222
disabled, 26, 31, 39, 48, 92; *see also* Trans Disabled (TD)
disclosure, 35, 39–40, 320, 324, 326
discourse, 6, 127, 226–27
disordered, 7, 9, 50, 66, 178
Dolmage, Jay, 37, 152, 211, 278

embodied, 175, 183, 204, 213
enminded, 21, 166, 366
epistemic injustice, 102, 165, 172
equity, 62, 210, 230
Erevelles, Nirmala, 176, 181, 244, 269

fat, 147, 221
feminism, 227, 331, 336

feminist, 266, 277, 331; Black, 95, 122–23, 266, 274, 304; disability, 76–77, 79, 82, 222
femme, 108, 265, 267, 361
Fireweed Collective, 38, 297, 312
first-generation, 108, 117, 154, 200

Garland-Thomson, Rosemarie, 5, 67
gaslighting, 91, 94–95, 265, 272
gender, 13, 69, 84, 126, 150
gender identity, 166, 169; autigender, 166; cisgender 13, 155; neogender, 168–70, nonbinary, 84, 108, 150
Gilbert, Sandra, 45, 197
Gumbs, Alexis Pauline, 117–18, 123
gun violence, 7, 126, 197, 221, 331

Hamraie, Aimi, 82, 184
Harvard Medical School, 33
health, 24, 29–30, 38; mental health, 5, 31, 77, 97, 226
Hersey, Tricia, 22, 82, 367
heterosexism, 14, 94
higher education, 6, 14, 72, 225, 320, 332
hooks, bell, 157, 191, 199, 266, 365
hypomania, 311, 314

Icarus Project, The, 225, 297, 312
identity, 3, 76, 122, 136, 166, 246
indigenous, 12, 70, 97, 111, 187, 237
interdependence, 96–97, 244, 265, 280, 289, 312
interdisciplinary, 47, 127, 153, 224, 334
interethnography, 168–70, 172
intersectionality, 205, 247–48, 267, 305, 364

Index 389

job security, 2, 274
Jones, Melanie, 46, 315
joy, 157, 217, 313–14, 321, 352
justice, 70, 84, 230, 26, 365; healing,
  38, 312; prison, 115–120; social, 31,
  82, 225, 296, 367; transformative, 38,
  237, 246

Kafai, Shayda, 246, 254, 320, 329
Kafer, Alison, 80, 152, 224, 320
Kerschbaum, Stephanie L., 24, 35, 363
Kim, Jina B., 83, 243
Kuppers, Petra, 21, 222, 366

Lajoie, Corinne, 359, 361
LeFrançois, Brenda A., 128, 192, 217,
  255
Levins, Aurora Morales, 117, 232, 246,
  248
Lewis, Talia TL, 31, 83, 92, 110, 269
liberation, 97, 224–25, 232, 309
Linton, Simi, 9, 23, 101
literature, 55, 103, 127, 140, 257
Longmore, Paul K., 23, 363
Lorde, Audre, 118, 228–29, 278

Mad, 4, 49, 66, 76, 114, 128, 147;
  border body, 254–55, 320, 326,
  358; community, 10, 304–5, 314,
  324, 328; histories, 310–12; identity,
  223, 246, 307, 309, 334–35, 337;
  kinship, 230–32, 287, 289, 292,
  320, 329; pedagogy, 191–93, 198,
  202, 205, 209; pride, 8, 302, 312;
  studies, 24, 102, 133, 217–18, 224,
  254–55, 296

madness, 22, 31, 60, 134, 156, 183, 223,
  254
madwoman, the, 45, 197, 261
mania, 46, 310
McRuer, Robert, 8, 101, 165, 172, 184
medical humanities, 7, 128, 139
medical industrial complex, 226
medical model of disability, 9, 61, 77,
  222, 231, 255; see also biomedical model; see also social model of
  disability
mental illness, 30, 46, 156, 222, 304,
  337
microaggressions, 12, 90, 364
Milbern, Stacey Park, 38, 176, 187–88
Mingus, Mia, 72, 113, 226, 231, 246
misogynoir, 80, 91
Mitchell, David T., 3, 22, 134, 136, 139
motherhood, 147, 150, 156

Nap Ministry, The, 82–83, 367
neoliberal, 226, 246, 289; model, 4–5;
  university, 71, 94, 152, 290, 320
neurodivergence, 76, 92, 204, 247, 273
neuroqueer, 2, 8, 13, 223, 334
neurotypical, 102, 110, 272, 309, 361
nondisabled, 80, 94, 212, 293, 305
normate, 5, 9
normativity, 222, 374; neuronormativity,
  224

oppression, 83, 93, 154, 213, 231, 241,
  266, 311; Mad, 225, 230

pathology, 9, 22, 37, 133, 137, 170, 222,
  254

390   Index

patriarchy, 108, 157, 159, 161, 191, 292, 310

pedagogy, 146, 199, 236, 242, 259, 278

phenomenology, 359–60, 364

philosophy, 127, 140

Pickens, Theri Alyce, 47, 130, 154, 176, 178, 304

Piepzna-Samarsinha, Leah Lakshmi, 6, 176, 187, 214, 270, 314

Pilipinx, 236, 238–39, 241

police brutality, 14, 87, 221, 289, 291, 331, 342

postmodernism, 10, 135, 140

Price, Margaret, 5, 35, 78, 211, 228, 271

pride, 77, 221, 323, 333

psychoanalysis, 134, 139

psychosis, 10, 23, 50, 166, 326, 364

Queen's University, 289–92

queer, 79, 132, 240, 310; studies, 261, 275; theory, 15, 132

race, 240, 261

racism, 38, 91, 271, 294, 305

rape, 93, 112, 122

Reaume, Geoffrey, 24, 137, 217

rhetoric, 102, 136, 175, 211

Rodas, Julia M., 176–78, 181, 185

Samuels, Ellen, 22, 48, 80, 320

sanism, 2, 47, 72, 155, 292, 306; academic, 2, 7, 60

Schalk, Sami, 83, 222, 320

schizophrenia, 36, 101, 134, 176, 186, 291–92, 364

self-harm, 4, 13–14, 50, 147, 271, 296

settler-colonialism, 14, 226, 239, 310

sex 132, 227; sexism, 94, 96, 299; sexuality, 13, 89, 93, 126–27, 132, 222, 239–40, 243, 310;

Sins Invalid, 224, 246, 285, 309, 328

Snyder, Sharon L., 22, 134, 136, 139, 223

social media, 87, 166, 346

social model of disability, 9, 133, 149, 157

speech, 10–11, 175–76, 182, 192, 202, 269, 358

spoons, 21, 121, 123

stereotypes, 14, 151, 336; threat, 356

stigma, 33, 39, 132, 307, 313, 333

subjectivity, 103, 137, 154, 167, 199, 222, 381

suicide, 32, 289, 296, 314; suicidal ideation, 4, 35, 61, 64, 297

surveillance, 30, 68, 71, 172, 268, 327–28

teaching, 76, 119, 129, 158, 181, 199, 222, 265

Toombs, S. Kay, 286, 359

Trans Disabled (TD), 164–68

transdisciplinary methodologies, 127, 329

transgender (trans), 5, 13, 170, 191, 237–39, 242, 244, 360

trauma, 37, 96, 165, 225, 310, 336, 348; studies, 139, 379–80; survivor, 84, 215

triggers, 9, 37, 50, 91, 203, 306, 342, 351

undergraduate, 58, 66, 72, 277, 341, 365

violence, 69, 93, 118, 136, 171, 178, 229, 292

Wendell, Susan, 5, 22, 31
white privilege, 266, 294
white supremacy, 14, 270, 305, 311
whiteness, 226, 271, 305
Wolframe, PhebeAnn, 6, 8, 35, 47, 139

World Health Organization (WHO), 29, 46, 78

Yergeau, M. Remi, 175–77, 186, 211, 278

www.ingramcontent.com/pod-product-compliance
Lightning Source LLC
LaVergne TN
LVHW041627060925
820435LV00016B/113